THE PLAY WAY

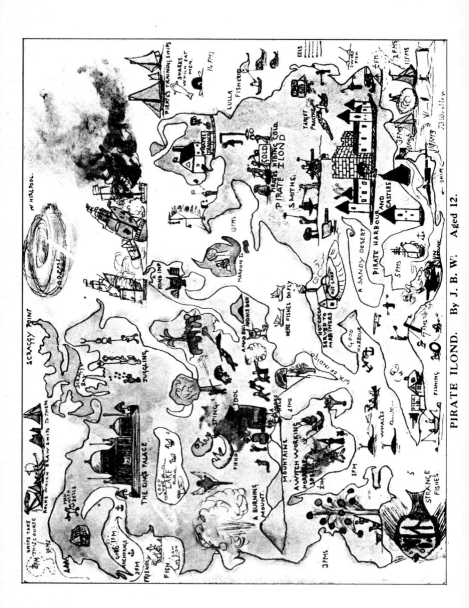

PIRATE ILOND. By J. B. W. Aged 12.

THE PLAY WAY

AN ESSAY IN EDUCATIONAL METHOD

BY

H. CALDWELL COOK, M.A. Oxon.

PLAYBOYS OF THE EIGHTEENTH CENTURY
[*After Corbould*]

LONDON
WILLIAM HEINEMANN

First Edition September 1917
Second   ,,   February 1919

London : William Heinemann, 1917.

Reprinted 1966 by Cedric Chivers Ltd., Portway, Bath,
to whom the copyright has been transferred, at the request of
the London & Home Counties Branch of the Library Association.
ECM - reprinted in Belgium by Jos. Adam

TO

DR. W. H. D. ROUSE

HEAD MASTER OF THE PERSE SCHOOL
CAMBRIDGE

PREFACE TO THE SECOND EDITION

THE satisfaction felt in returning to schools and scholars after more than three years in a somewhat uncongenial employment has not in any sense altered my desire to help in effecting a lively reform in these quiet and studious places. I feel the classroom stuffier than ever, the autocracy of the pedant more unbearable, the process of spoon-feeding more repugnant ; and have received, on the other hand, a full confirmation of the doctrine of self-responsibility and the driving-power of *interest*. The methods of instruction even in the army have developed noticeably in the direction of the Play Way, and the old bullying style of the barrack square is giving place to common-sense training based on the pupils' interest, and using as a medium games and the acting of what is to be learnt.

Now that the social revolution spoken of above is in every man's mouth as "Reconstruction," let us see to it that the fight for liberty (for the peoples have found this outstanding principle through all complexities) is not rendered tragically unavailing by our incapacity rightly to interpret the freedom won. And just as in affairs of State it will be found that we must temporarily readjust our old life to the new conditions before undertaking this wholesale "Reconstruction," so let us realize in the schools that before we can attain to a complete all-round scheme of natural education in self-governing communities we must undergo a transition stage of "partial liberation from the classroom." To demonstrate how this may be undertaken is the purpose and scope of this book.

H. CALDWELL COOK

LONDON, *January* 1919

PREFACE

THIS book sets forth some ideas and practical suggestions on educational method which it is hoped may prove helpful to those teachers who have not shut their minds against proposals for reform. The whole conception of the Play Way is the outcome of original thought and fancy. But if most of the practices recommended, and all the ideas upon which that practice is founded, can be traced to known influences and matched in the past history of education, then so much the better for the Play Way. For we must keep in touch with tradition. The only originality claimed is a fresh realization of the oldest truths,

Though not unmindful of the great influence which the present war must exert upon education, I have intentionally abstained from attempting to draw any conclusions from the current upheaval, partly because what is here written was conceived before the war broke out, but chiefly because it is as yet too early to speak confidently of the results for education which it will bring. Many thoughtful people claim to discern a conflict of principle in this war and they are much to be envied their belief. The issue is very complex, but it is certain at any rate that the war, with all the sacrifice it involves and all the nobility it has awakened, is being considered by those who rule our rulers as a commercial transaction on a consummate scale. It is the biggest business deal on record. All the ideal aspects of this world commotion, the liberation, the choice of rule and the renewal of spiritual activity in the life of the peoples will still remain to be undertaken by idealists and workers after the military operations have ceased. A social revolution of some kind will be necessary in England after the declaration of peace on the Continent ; for, even supposing some fair principle

PREFACE

established by force of arms, it has still to be wrought into a living practice by right education and good government. For many of us the greater war is yet to come. In any case we are still only at the very beginning of the changes which this generation will see. The reader will understand, therefore, why I have not allowed any thoughts upon the meaning of the present unrest to complicate these few simple chapters on schoolmastery.

It was originally intended to include three further chapters, on Prose and Verse Composition respectively, and a sketch of the organization of an ideal Play School. But the manuscript proved too long for one volume and so these chapters have been removed. The reader, however, who is desirous of studying the method as applied to Prose and Verse Composition is referred to •the Perse Playbooks.* The Utopian scheme of a Play School Commonwealth which we hope to see founded before long in England as a model for all English Schools must remain to be pictured in another book.

Finally I must ask the reader's indulgence for the discursive and disordered state in which the argument of this book is presented. For the past four years I have been intending to write the book of the Play Way, but have always been deterred by the magnitude of the task. And now, for fear lest the book should never be written at all, I have been compelled to make the best of my case in a great hurry. What should have been the careful work of years is here offered with an apology as the work of a few overbusy months, eventually brought to a conclusion somewhere in France. If the reader will bear this in mind I will undertake to requite him hereafter with the fuller and more reasoned discourse which will be possible in a more quiet time.

H. CALDWELL COOK

CAMBRIDGE, *November* 1915

* Perse Playbooks, Nos 1–5. (W. Heffer and Sons, Cambridge.)

NOTE

THE most part of a series of articles contributed to the *New Age* in 1914 have been incorporated in this book by permission of the Editor. Certain passages from the introductions to the Perse Playbooks have also been included. A few paragraphs from an article contributed to *Poetry and Drama* have also been used with the Editor's permission. The photographs of Playtown were taken by a professional photographer, one or two pictures of the boys by Mr. H. L. Watkinson, and the rest by the Author. I am also indebted to the kindness of Mr. Watkinson for the plan of Playtown, and to Mr. R. B. Appleton and to Mr D S Paterson for much assistance in the reading of manuscript and proofs.

*We laugh at his foolish sports, but his game is our earnest ;
and his drums, rattles, and hobby-horses but the emblems and
mockings of man's business.*

JOHN EARLE, " Microcosmography "

*In their education, therefore, the care must be the greater had
of their beginnings, to know, examine, and weigh their
natures ; which, though they be proner in some children
to some disciplines, yet are they naturally prompt to taste all
by degress, and with change. For change is a kind of
refreshing in studies, and infuseth knowledge by way of
recreation. Thence the school itself is called a play or
game, and all letters are so best taught to scholars.*

BEN JONSON, " Discoveries "

CONTENTS

LIST OF ILLUSTRATIONS

LIST OF ILLUSTRATIONS

CHAPTER I

GENERAL PRINCIPLES OF THE PLAY WAY

Quickly would I make my path even,
And by mere playing go to heaven.
                    HENRY VAUGHAN

THE natural means of study in youth is play, as any one may .
see for himself by watching any child or young animal when it
is left alone. A natural education is by practice, by doing
things, and not by instruction, the hearing how, as you may see
in the flight of a young bird. And telling can only be the
servant of trying, not its substitute. Certainly preliminary
advice and warning might save us from many a sore trial, but we
rarely profit by any experience other than our own. The burnt
child dreads the fire, but the child that has only been warned
is still to be burnt. Therefore wild oats are more approved by
men of the world than moral lectures. But instead of leaving a
child to gain wisdom by painful as well as pleasant experience,
it is well to let him try as much as he can for himself under
guidance. It would not be wise to send a child innocent into
the big world ; and talking is of poor avail. But it is possible
to hold rehearsals, to try our strength in a make-believe big
world. And that is Play.

The main concern in a child's life is that manifold business
understood clearly by him, and dimly by his elders, as Play. He
wakes up in bed even before the dawn, and plots out a fairyland
of play-doings for the day until he is allowed to get up. Then
while the fires are still crackling on the wood you can hear him
pattering about the landing or singing on the stairs. Dressing
is a nuisance because it requires his presence in one place for
some twenty minutes ; toys must come to table ; food itself must
furnish a game. Porridge is an island in a sea of milk, and he

would be rather more interested than shocked to find a chicken in every egg. School, above the kindergarten, is a nuisance because there is no play, So he lives on throughout the daylight hours, playing many parts, as pirate, or king-in-a-crown, or beast of prey ; in the tree tops, or underground, or sailing merrily on the salt sea, until that little nightly tragedy of bedtime.

After dark, nurse, however amiable, comes as a fury with abhorrèd shears. As an onlooker at the drama I always regard her coming as the prelude to an affecting finish. She is the executioner whose summons must be obeyed. Have you not admired the fortitude with which the little hero—though there are cowards, we know—goes on his round of farewell to the waking world ? Have you not observed that he always carries an air of detachment, salutes even his mother as though he were thinking of something else ; and how he looks back from the door ? However, one shall find upstairs certain friends who can float in a bath ; and after all

> My bed is like a little boat ;
>   Nurse helps me in when I embark.
> She girds me in my sailor's coat,
>   And starts me in the dark.

And so to dream.

It must have occurred to every one that since a child's life under his own direction is conducted all in play, whatever else we want to interest him in should be carried on in that medium, or at the very least connected with play as closely as possible.

Why should there stretch such an abyss between the nursery and the classroom ? Ah, yes, they tell us, but life is not going to be all a game. They must learn the *serious* side of things. By the life of the world ! What could be more serious than child's-play ? I know of nothing so whole-hearted, so thorough, so natural, so free from stain, so earnest, as the spontaneous playing of a child. Take a child in the nursery and consider him beside these grave adults at their concerns. Compare a game of toy soldiers with the conduct of a campaign. The difference is in degree and not in kind. Consider whether the little maid in the day nursery is less engrossed in the care of her doll than the other maid in the night nursery is in the care of the baby. Do you play more fair at politics than we do at ninepins ? And has any man as much care for the rules of the game in commerce, and as much respect for his opponents, as he has in cricket ? In the one it is a question of what he can make, in the other all is subject to fair play. I tell you that sincere endeavour and honesty of purpose can only be relied on under conditions that favour their continuance ! Whether he be paid well or not, so long as a man's heart is in his work it is well with him and well for the work. Beyond that we cannot go. The force of extraneous need, or compulsion of any kind, however necessary it be, blunts honesty, dulls the zeal of whole-hearted endeavour ; and if it come in much strength will spoil all. The child is the true amateur, he does a thing for the love of it. Among all workers he is the player, and alone is fit to stand beside the genuine artist, the self-sacrificing physician, and the inspired poet or seer. His hearty interest is a powerful engine which will carry a heavy load eventually to its appointed destination. What though you claim to know where that may be, and to know also of a shorter route ? Is it not better to follow the engine that pulls the train, rather than drag it back, even though its route be round-about ? It may be that the way will prove more level and the countryside more beautiful. A child following his natural bent will play. His whole power is in play. Beware of trying to make rivers run up hills instead of flowing round them.

To me it seems obvious where the trouble lies : the teacher works, whether consciously or unconsciously, on his own lines, and not in and for his children. The teacher may have a beauti-ful system, a course of work schemed, graded, and ordered in admirable shape, and thoroughly approved by his or her chief, and by his Majesty's inspector to boot. But what if the child's mind does not work orderly ?—which happens to be the case. What will his Majesty do then, poor thing ? What if a growing mind scorns systematic progress (which also is true), and leaps back and forth over the field of study, now shining with the brilliance of a light full focused, now showing as black as the back of a lighthouse lantern ? Let us have outline schemes by all means, but leave the details to the hour in which it shall be told us what we shall do. Let us remember that without interest there is no learning, and since the child's interest is all in) play it is necessary, whatever the matter in hand, that the method be a play-method. Otherwise there will be no guests at the table, and the feast will lie stale in our hands.

*　　　　*　　　　*　　　　*　　　　*

Much of what I have to say is obvious, but that is unavoidable, for the most well-accepted principles are generally ignored in practice. The conduct of most people is founded on the principles they most condemn.

I have said that when you consider a child you will find, as Stevenson says, that "he intent, is all on his play-business bent": and, therefore, whatever you want a child to do heartily must be contrived and conducted as play. It may seem a strange thing to suggest that the boys and girls of the upper school should have as much play as the infants in the kindergarten, but this is what I do propose. Boys and girls nowadays have their play gradually thinned out until little is left to them as adults but a round of golf or a game of cards. When work and play are separated, the one becomes mere drudgery, the other mere pastime. Neither is then of any value in life. It is the core of my faith that the only work worth doing is really play; for by play I mean the doing anything with one's heart in it.

The Play Way is a means, but I cannot say what the end may be, except more play. In like manner the whole purpose of life for me, being no philosopher, is simply living. What I have now to say sounds very puerile, but I have no doubt the same could be found subtly said in many learned books. We must let ourselves live fully, by doing thoroughly those things we have a natural desire to do; the sole restrictions being that we so order the course of our life as not to impair those energies by which we live, nor hinder other men so long as they also seem to be living well. Right and wrong in the play of life are not different from the right and wrong of the playing-field. We must obey the clear rules; and what is more, have a sense of fair play, and, in chief, play with all our hearts in the game.

Is this foundation of the Play Way so simple as to need no statement? Look in our nurseries, look in our schools, look in our fields, factories, and workshops. Which of us has the chance to do thoroughly that which he has the desire to do?

4

But the right of every man to live a human life is daily becoming something more than a sentimental platitude. And when, long hence, every man shall find work to his hand that is noble to do, and leisure also to rest from his labours, there will be few found subtle enough to say where the work ends and the leisure begins. Work that is done with joy at heart, and leisure that is not wasted, merge into one as Play.

But my especial concern is with the schools. Can any one say that life in school is so ordered as not to impair those energies by which the children live ? If the children were moved by natural desire to do as we now make them do in school, then there would be no need of this same compulsion. Of the children's view of the work we give them is it not still true to say, "Love goes toward love as schoolboys from their books " ? And as for their view of the play we plan, who has not heard of that crowning indignity, compulsory games ? "Some boys, are by nature slack," says the public-school man, "and have to be brought up to scratch." "By nature they are the children of evil," said the teacher of old time, "conceived in wickedness and born in sin." "Many of us are born blind," say I. "Let us have the Play Way."

The advice in " Hamlet " that " the purpose of playing, both at the first and now, was and is, to hold, as 'twere, the mirror up to nature," is said of actors. But Shakespeare also said :

> All the world's a stage,
> And all the men and women merely players.

So the words in " Hamlet " come fitly as a text ; the more so since child's-play, being less artificial, is a nearer parallel to life than is stage-play.

However dense a maze of difficulty may arise in the application of it, the one principle of human conduct is clear enough. A man's aim in life is to carry out the promptings of his instinct, to do as he was born to do, to be natural. It is possible to go wrong of course, because man has a faculty of free will, as any one may learn in the third book of " Paradise Lost." The sole directions towards right are the example of the external world, and the promptings of the human heart by which we live. The urging of nature is subject to the control of reason, but reason is not the compelling force. Thoughts and deeds can only be held by reason as right or wrong, wise or unwise, fair or foul, in so far as they further or retard the one end of life, which is to live in accord with our nature, giving scope to every faculty, exercise to every power (for good, we might add, but that vice is only virtue misdirected, power ill-used).

The function of reason is to maintain a just equipoise. Take the analogy of the body. Food is necessary, but if a man eat too much his body is made unfit to live well : the same if he eat too little. And so with sleep, exercise, and the other functions of the body ; all of which are pleasurable in order that man may be persuaded to live and be healthy. A natural function is instinctively pleasant so that it may not fall into disuse : and the one end of life is to take these pleasures indicated by nature as a means to life. But " with this special observance, that you o'erstep not the modesty of nature."

Health of body or mind is a matter of balance, it is the level. But health is a positive thing, not merely the negation of sickness and disease. To be fit should be our first endeavour. But fitness implies fitness for something. Health itself is only the beginning of things, the floor cleared for dancing. But how few of us go in for large spaces in our dealing. How many are content with compromise, with a modicum of comfort, with freedom from pain. Having cleared a little space we are happy to sit down in it. Having borne a little burden we look for sleep ; and there is neither room nor time for play.

A healthy body tingles with an intense power of joy, is triumphant in his great hold upon life, looks in the face of heaven, and is himself a god. The body that is full of health knows neither labour nor loafing, but only play. It seems there is nothing he cannot do with ease and delight. The red of his cheek is not hectic, there is no exertion in his vigour, and his calm is without strain. His very walking is full of unthought grace, for he does nothing unlovely. But I find that I have described the Playboy.

Just as this positive feeling of bodily well-being comes only with the fitness of every nerve and muscle, so there is a fullness of life that can come to the spirit of man only in the free play of all his natural desires.

GENERAL PRINCIPLES

There are necessary functions of the body without whose operation it dies; and some which, though not so essential to existence, are essential to well-being. Nearly every man or woman you know lives only on those functions which are essential to existence, and ignores those essential to well-being. Few men starve their bodies, but most men starve their souls. It is clearly as sinful to take too little of a good thing as to take too much. But of this the narrow-minded, stay-at-home type of mind will never be persuaded.

Home-keeping youth have ever homely wits.

The present-day puritan has that negative habit of mind which condemns all forms of excess but excess of restraint; though all may see that the nonconformist conscience stands for a very debauch of denial.

What a talk there is nowadays, too, of saving time. It were easy to say that time is to be spent, not saved; only one knows that, do what we may, time will go by us. The sole concern of such as are wise is to take the full yield of every harvest, not to sow acres that shall never be reaped. Not he who covers the most ground, but he who has most delight in his journey, is the better traveller. Hard labour now in the hope of a longer rest later on is a delusion that any child may discover. When my brothers and I, as little boys, grew tired in walking we used to run on ahead of the nurse to rest on the next seat or milestone. But she came upon us unpleasantly soon, and we were still panting. To-day cannot be set aside to be spent next year. This sacrifice of a present joy in the hope of obtaining a greater in the future is immoral only because it is so hopelessly futile; it is selling one's soul with no prospect of anything better to buy. He who saves up all the meals of a week for one great feed on Saturday finds himself with no stomach for the banquet.

The application to our schools is this: Education nowadays is study or, at best, theoretical training. That is, the learning how things have been done or, at best, how to do them. Study, simple of itself, is a means only; and training, as training, has always some distant end or other. When the joy is not yet felt the value is still to seek. But whenever we have joy in what we are doing it is then the doing that is of first importance. Of course, in doing we are doing something, so we must not look upon the Play Way simply as a notion of adding interest to undertakings. In going we are going somewhere, so the whole of my suggestion is not merely that we go gaily. For the Play Way is not a bunch of contrivances for making scholarly pursuits pleasurable, but the active philosophy of making pleasurable pursuits valuable. But the claim here put forward is not for the destination, but chiefly for the journey. Any means that becomes in this way an end in itself I call the Play Way. Play is the one means that is an end in itself, for " that we would do, we should do when we would." It is of no use to seek further for a definition of Play. Play is one of the fundamentals of life, capable of anything but a further explanation. The refinements of the learned may lay bare the simple, but they can never solve it.

*   *   *   *   *   *

Why this everlasting slavery to books ? We are frightened of initiative, and cling to what we fancy is established. But it is only established because we cling to it. It is not knowledge we store in books, it is ourselves we bury ; for we do not use our book as an encouragement, a test, or a diversion ; we make it the very prop and mainstay of our lives. And yet those very books that make their mark, the ones we admire, are those which break new ground, and not the ones that glean behind a long-ingathered harvest. And still we are fearful of stepping out ourselves without handbooks, guide-books, textbooks. Many a man will not write even a course of lectures without consulting as many volumes as he can reach, giving as much to search and research as he does to his own thinking. And the poor child's life in school is all books. We adults, for all our whole-hearted belief in printed wisdom, would not tolerate day after day the literary confinement we put upon these little disbelievers. But each generation in its turn so orders the affair of its successor that revolt rather than recognition becomes more and more the sign of manhood. The grown youth no longer dons the *toga virilis*, he throws off his jacket to fight against the rule of his elders,

Can we not rid ourselves of the tyranny of print even for a little while ? To subordinate books to a more active conduct of life, whether in the region of original thought or in the busy traffic of men and things is to put no slur upon the mighty book-men that have been. The best of them used or made books, and did not let them use or make him. And where are your historians, from the makers of earliest epic down to the latest biographer, apart from the life they witness ? For the fabric of their chronicle is wrought of the deeds of men, so that however noble the record they make, or the prophecy either, life itself, and not its recital, is still the stuff of their say. Moreover there are many who feel that the more intense is the glow of romance, and the more ideal the portraiture, only by so much the more near comes that showing forth to the real figure of life, quick and working. But because doing comes before saying, or, coming after, is greater nevertheless, I do not deny the poet the highest place in the hierarchy of men of power ; but I put him first as a maker, a creator, which supposes things still to be, and not as a recorder, a mere repository of a gleaming past,

The world goes on, and the life of each individual with it, not in telling what has been done, nor in saying what yet remains to do, but in the present doing of present deeds. Let the reader squirm if he will because I labour the obvious ; I will writhe, too, because for all our knowledge we do not act on it ; power runs to waste, and the water overflows the wheel it will not turn. A moment's thought, a pause to recall old faded realizations, will tell you at once what is lacking. It is the will to do. We do not feel what we know ; that is, we have not the will to translate power into deeds.

Interest must be the starting-point in all we do, or we shall not do well. The best expression of one's thought is the use of the right words in their fullest sense, the unfolding of the latent philosophy in words. I can make no clearer exposition of my thesis than may be found in the true reading of the terms here in use. Interest is " what matters," the one thing needful. You may call it " interessence," if you will ; that is, the being at the very heart of the matter. Once there you have only to do as interest bids. The operation of interest is Play. To do anything with interest, to get at the heart of the matter and live there active—that is Play. You need not ask how we are to come by this interest, for it is the heart's desire we are born with. There is no truth but the old truth : interest is only what your hand finds to do, and play is but doing it with your might.

Consider what pedagogy is doing for the child. This elfish little being with itching fingers and restless feet, full of curiosity and a desire to investigate ; this quaint embodiment of wonder, this ache of instinctive longing, is taught to read before he can word his questions intelligibly, is given information on subjects which have no interest for him, while yet his real wants remain unsatisfied ; is set to pore upon the thrice-diluted opinions of others rather than allowed to try anything for himself. He is bound over to letters in defiance of the spirit, and of the play-call of nature which alone speaks with authority and not as the scribes.

For fear of a possible misunderstanding I must here most definitely dissociate the Play Way and myself from any who decry study and belittle the value of books. We yield to none in our love of and faithfulness to literature. Our complaint is against that pedantic *misuse* of books which represents · the greater part of what is called education at the present time.

Why this everlasting slavery to books ? The defenders of the old regime protest that there is much virtue in your book. Certainly it is the storehouse of wisdom, and treasures up the achievement of old time. But to what end ? Is there not virtue also in your boy ? I say the boy shall master the book ; but not if he is bound a slave to it. Where is the boy to find the real experience of his life if not in his own doing and thinking ? You give him moulds for his brick-making, and overseers, and models and straw. But you give him no clay.

I sometimes feel that the best models for school-books are those manuals of conjuring wherein nothing is intelligible until you set to work upon the apparatus ; or dance-books full of impossible jargon which must be translated into action before it can have meaning and delight ; or cookery-books which satisfy neither hunger nor curiosity until the pudding is made— the proof of which is always in the eating.

For one boy who has gained any knowledge at school through the experience of his own senses, five hundred—nay, five thousand—have been deluded with the shadow of knowledge cast in the form of some one else's opinion. That one lad is generally " a lazy good-for-nothing scoundrel." Another time

10

I should like to take up the discussion of the scholar's mental
content. How much of the learning he possesses is of any value
at all as his own ; and how far does he merely exist in handing
on the conclusions of other men as he has taken them over
entire ? I fear that many a famous scholar is no better than a
shopful of ready-made goods.

The sad condition of our schools is mainly owing to the
teachers' unthinking compliance with a rotten tradition. The
defence of those who *have* given thought to the matter of book-
learning amounts to no more than this : " The individual child
cannot try over again for himself all the experience of the ages,
and therefore he must study the record of the past." But this
study, to have any value, must persuade the child to live over
again, briefly in his imagination, the ages gone by ; and my
simple contention is that the child be allowed to express his
imaginings in the manner that most appeals to him, the way that
is most natural. This will be the Play Way, with the high
thoughts and noble endeavour of that super-reality which is
make-believe.

It comes in the end to this : Why should we stop a game now
going on in order to dictate the rules of another which we do not
intend shall ever be played ? Why call in Robin Hood and the
Redskins and the Pirate Captain from the playground to read of
Luther, or even of Cœur de Lion ?

" But we have pretty pictures in our books."

" Ah, yes, so we have. And here is a man wielding a sword
just like the one you made me leave in the lobby. Please may I
go and fetch it ? "

" No, you may not."

" But, please sir——"

" Get on with your work."

Old habits of mind are not easily broken. You are convinced,
are you not, that school is a place of learning to which a boy
must come in order that he may learn ? But it is not so in
truth. The boy is first. Again, you have told your pupils very
often—have you not ?—" You must remember that you come
here to work." Quite apart from the mean way in which the
whole question is thus settled without reference to the wishes
of the one most concerned, this point of view is entirely wrong.

THE PLAY WAY

What the Greeks called σχολή, and the Romans *ludus*, can only be expressed in English by the word *play*.

Once you realize that the teacher only exists for the learner, once you believe that the soul of any other being entrusted to your care is greater than the furniture of your own mind, once this belief in you reaches the level of a *faith*, then, believe me, the mountain of your learning and self-sufficiency is easily removed and brought to the feet of the prophet.

*   *   *   *   *

In religion, in philosophy, in poetry, in politics, in all the affairs of men that go far enough to require a guide, there is every now and then a revolution. The flow of human thought is subject to deep-reaching disturbance from time to time. Numerous causes co-operate to produce a periodical troubling of the waters, a welter in which the principles of all human concern are involved. At such a time faiths are transformed, new ideals set up, and the hope of millions set in another direction. Fused in the heat of active change, institutions lose their character, and creeds, doctrines, and opinions are all melted and remodelled. Nothing passes scatheless through the fire, and the world, as man has made it, is created anew.

If this spirit of revolution could be summed up in a phrase it would be found always to represent a clearing away of encrusted dogma, a breaking from bondage grown irksome, an upsetting of the tables of authority, and a restatement of direction and aim. But, to the great joy of all true believers, the new ideals are only revivals of the old, stripped of base accretion ; the new heaven and the new earth are those of the old creation, only cleansed by the flood. Your true revolutionary is only a conservative endowed with insight.

The seer brings his vision to the market-place, and urges the people to destroy their city and rebuild it. They do so, but live on in these new homes, adding from time to time a coat of paint or a crust of stucco, and still calling them new until reawakened by the coming of another seer.

Though it would be unwise to prophesy any definite changes which the war will bring about in education, yet it is possible for us to recognize even now its cathartic action, and to feel that

12

a spiritual freshening is abroad. It is certain that many educational fads and quackeries have already been killed by this war. It is perhaps not quite so clear what positive gain education will have made. I believe the gain will show itself in a more practical and common-sense view of the whole problem. There will be less musty scholarship, less doing of things simply because they always have been done, less of the dogmatic pedagogue with his cut-and-dried doctrines and systems, less spoon-feeding of ready-made opinions. There will be more life, more reality, more conformity with present-day needs, more recognition of the pupil's point of view. We shall come nearer to making our school a place for the life-training of boys and girls, instead of a place where unworldly men and unimaginative women give instruction in set subjects. We might even attain a school of which it would be true to say, ".Here we learn," instead of, " Here they teach."

The spiritual freshening will soon show itself in schools in the reform of method. The boys (I cannot safely include girls in any statement I make, for I have had no experience in teaching them)—the boys, then, being looked at individually instead of being overlooked collectively, will at once gain in freedom. For we must not suppose that a teacher will recognize the existence of John's or Harry's personality only to crush it. In the very first use the boys make of their comparative freedom you will have indications of what was lacking in your method. And the more eagerly they show their desire to do or not to do this or that, the more clearly you will see what is needed. I do not suggest that the boys should be allowed to wreck the classroom as a demonstration of their distaste for sitting still in their desks ; nor that they should be permitted to make a bonfire of French and Latin grammars as a protest against the difficulties of formal language-study. But I do say that the teacher who makes the best use of every opportunity that arises for letting the boys move about the room in ordered play will soon be convinced that boys *can* learn without always sitting still. And it is a case already proved to the general satisfaction of the intelligent that languages are more readily as well as more pleasantly learnt when the study of formal grammar is subordinated to real practice of

13

the language in speaking. The boys will unconsciously make clear to you many things about the teaching of boys so soon as you give them the opportunity.

It will perhaps be said that it does not need a colossal war in Europe, the armed conflict of a dozen nations, to show us how to teach boys. But, in the first place, nothing could more plainly show the need of a better education in all countries than a tragedy of this magnitude. And further, I maintain that only some such universal troubling of the waters as we see in this present cataclysm is powerful enough in this era to break the old habits of thought, to clear away the obscuring mists of prejudice, self-sufficiency, and hypocrisy, and to let in the fresh air of common sense, along with the sunshine of new interest, to the minds of men. The schoolmaster, certainly no less than other men, has need of this fresh air and sunshine.

But then, if incrustation is a natural process, and therefore unavoidable, and if periodical outbreak is in consequence equally necessary, must not the world submit to these costly regenerating cures from age to age. What is the solution ?

The solution, as it seems to me at least, is this. We must keep us alive through all our living days, and not give way to security or the indulgence of lethargy. The longer we keep pent up those energies which should be daily brought into play, the greater will be the explosion when they must come out. And, on the other hand, the more dross we suffer to accumulate the greater must be our effort to get rid of it when at last it becomes stifling and insufferable. As the process of metabolism by which our bodies live is a continuous process of change and readjustment, and not a periodic renewal, in which waste matter is normally eliminated in proportion as living tissue is created ; so must our mental and spiritual life go on by performing equally its two-sided function of creation and destruction, of going forward and of leaving behind.

So far as in us lies we must neither allow our own minds nor compel those of others to accumulate more than is assimilable. On the one side there is storing up, on the other side there is using up ; and beyond a certain limit both of these are harmful. To take a little more than is needful, whether for the body in the way of food and rest, or for the mind in the way of learning or contemplation, makes for luxury. To admit more still above this unfixed margin of luxury * makes the body or the mind sick and in need of cure by change and exercise. The same truth holds in the case of too much exercise and use, with too little nourishment and recuperative rest. The body or the mind will then again fall out of health and be in need of cure by rest and recreation.

Those who make the body politic their study will find like conclusions to hold good also of statecraft.

We must, then, for health and well-being, preserve a balance in the conduct of our lives. Health, power of decision, sanity, justice, goodness, all these things are his who stands, thinks, lives *at poise*. The right ordering of this balance or poise must be a daily, even an hourly concern, in fact an ever-present cure. For if we permit ourselves to run to excess in this or that direction, subject only to a periodic self-examination, a deferred audit, we shall soon again find ourselves mantling and stagnating like the later nineteenth century, and then exploding like 1914.

The Play Way is an endeavour to achieve right conduct in a true blend of the functioning of all man's powers. If it is true to say that we must not act without thinking, why is it not equally true to say that we must not think without acting ?

If all men had kept alive in them the faculty of poetry, that divine unrest, they would never be satisfied with make-shift settlement, but would be for ever striving, ever making. But the exciting influence is always short-lived. The need of constant change and renewal as the indispensable condition,

---

* It is, of course, impossible to say exactly when we are making a boy swallow too much learning. But the mean in all things is never possible to be determined with exactitude ; it is but a man's judgment between extremes. I believe that a perfect education should aim at giving a boy a many-sided active life in school, teaching him at the same time how to acquire the knowledge needed for each occupation, and how to apply it. Thus he would not be equipped with a store of learning enough to last him a lifetime, but would rather be taught how to learn in order to do, and how to do in order to learn. To call such a training a " general education " would be a just description. The " general education " of the age now passing has been a banquet of instruction without any practice in the use of the learning so obtained.

not alone of growth, but of life itself, is not realized by the common gathering of men. It is the daily inspiration that is lacking ; the spirit that can be tuned afresh by every new appeal of beauty. There is no strength from without, nor inward reservoir of power upon which we may draw in the hour of hurry or doubt. The manna of to-day will not be sweet to-morrow, for the love of our reliance must be new every morning.

To supply this hourly stimulus is the chief function of poetry ; but of poetry active, not embalmed in printed books. Poetry keeps alive the spiritual significance which informs all ceremonial observance, and reinforces that strength and hope which differentiate work from drudgery. Poetry deals with real life, but it must deal with the aim and intention of life, its aspirations and outreachings. It should have but a very small place as a chronicle of everyday occurrence, with its tale of vain endeavour, or as a criticism of passing custom, with its fads and eccentricities. That is more the province of *Punch* and other satirists. Poetry must concern itself with those ideas and appearances which either inform or typify human enterprise at its highest. " Poetry is the breath and finer spirit of all knowledge ; it is the impassioned expression which is in the countenance of all Science."

The class of poetry to set before boys is that—whether ancient, mediæval, or modern—which is full of the spirit which is stirring at the present day. Also the boys must themselves come forth as poets. Thus and thus only can the poetry they read have anything more than an æsthetic appeal. I am confident that a good teacher, given fair conditions, could lead his pupils to regard poetry as the inspiration of their daily life. And this is Play in its finest form, namely, the ideal in action and reality. Poetry, the work of a maker, must itself be creative ; must not stop short at impression, but originate expression ; must not be magniloquent only, but magnificent as well. " Poetry is the first and last of all knowledge—it is as immortal as the heart of man."

Play, as I mean it, goes far deeper than study ; it passes beyond reasoning, and lighting up the chambers of the imagination, quickens the body of thought, and proves all things in action. The study of books, however thorough, may yet remain but superficial, in the sense that there may be no feeling of reality behind it. " No impression without expression " is a hoary maxim, but even to-day learning is often *knowing* without much care for *feeling*, and mostly none at all for *doing*. Learning may remain detached, as a garment, unidentified with self. But by Play I mean the *doing* anything one *knows* with one's heart in it. The final appreciation in life and in study is to put oneself into the thing studied and to live there *active*. And that is Playing. Thus the source of all art is imitation in the fullest sense, not copy, but identification. We know that in appreciating a poem one is a poet oneself. But why? Because the piece only lives by being played over and over again for ever, by players who have the true feeling for it at heart. But in order to earn the high title of Play, the appreciation must be not only felt, but expressed.

> And this hath now his heart
> And unto this he frames his song.
>
> .   .   .   .   .
>
> As if his whole vocation
> Were endless imitation.

By definition Play includes the practice of all the arts. And so I am brought to face a paradox, which is none of my making, " Work, then, is Play," says a disputant, smiling. Elaborately we reason it out that if Play is the doing anything with one's heart in it, a man's life-work is Play, and all lesser works are only to be justified by their contributing, in greater or less degree, to this greatest work—which must be Play. Yes, I subscribe to this.

There is a belief most prevalent among hard-headed business men that while they are really doing good work an artist is only playing at it. That is what so annoys the bourgeois, and it helps to account for the attitude of scornful tolerance with which the artist is generally regarded by philistines. The man thinks he is working, and yet he is quite openly and shamelessly enjoying himself! It isn't at all right in their opinion that any one should " have it both ways."

Those unwritten scriptures which guide the souls of rigid puritans to their damnation distinguish very markedly between work and pleasure The dullest and most soul-killing work is rich in virtue, and will have its reward, if not here, then hereafter. But even the tamest of pleasures is very risky and savours not a little of wickedness. If one could really get at the inside of the puritan conscience, I doubt not this surprising discovery : That he does not admit that a diversion may be a recreation. For him no diversion is quite innocent. And those little pleasures he allows himself a secular concert, a picnic on the river, anything in fine more daring than a walk in the park—all these are as it were a yielding to human frailty lest one be thought arrogant ; a propitiatory offering to the archtempter lest he haunt us in the hours of toil. A puritan feels much self-gratification in toiling up a hill, and is rather ashamed of coasting down the other side. He looks, possibly a little in envy and certainly much in awe, upon that other daring fellow who is cheerfully undertaking the climb with nothing better in view than the immediate reward of achievement. The puritan is of opinion that every race should be an obstacle race ; and is convinced that he who goes the primrose way is destined for the everlasting bonfire.

There is more of the puritan in your average schoolmaster than is generally recognized, and though of course he does not frown upon play in its due place out of school, he finds it very hard to see how play and study can be carried on at one and the same time. To him it seems that taking joy in the enjoyable part precludes industrious application to the more laborious part. As though work and play, pleasure and learning, a measure of natural freedom and a natural measure of restraint were mutually exclusive terms.

It is a principle of the Play Way that the finest conceptions of the mind are not lessened in value, but enhanced, by being put to use, brought into play. This form of play is not in any sense a diversion. It is an active expression of what one feels, and might almost be called an observance of some spiritual rite. And it is another principle of the Play Way that the use of certain forms of expression, forms of play, and traditional observances can themselves help us to appreciate the spirit which made them. Let us examine this more fully.

Religious faith is a spiritual passion of which art in all

its forms may be the expression. A religion which could embody itself in stated form on a tract or in a creed would be worth nothing to art. The deepest things do not easily admit of definite statement ; they need the power of imagination to body them forth. But tracts and addresses are merely exhortations to men that they should give their thoughts to religion ; and hymns and prayers, and rites and ceremonies, and impassioned sermons are the various efforts to articulate something of the spirit which is felt by the devotee. It is always assumed that the spirit must first be perceived before we can worship it. But my purpose here is to show that help may come from the other side. If the spiritual feeling which should initiate devotional exercise be weak or apparently lacking, it may be, and often is, stimulated and even created by the trustful observance of the rites and ceremonies and of traditional and conventional forms in which the spirit has been known to reside.

Not necessarily all art, but the best art is the expression of faith in some ideal. Faith is an emotional experience to which a man's life may bear witness and which his death may ratify, but which art alone can express. But art does not express the spirit it serves by preaching to the reason to obey, but by stimulating the imagination to create for itself. I can neither make clear to myself what I believe, nor teach another what he shall believe. All I can hope to do by my art is to get others to bring their imaginative powers into play, to make them gods of their own. For, as my tutor used to say, " Art teaches, not by a definitely didactic force, but by an indefinite spiritualizing."

Mr. Edmund Holmes, in his educational essay " What Is and What Might Be," makes, if I remember rightly, a severe criticism of obedience to authority as a guiding principle in life as contrasted with reliance upon one's own ideal conception. The word " religion " is closely connected with the word " rely," and religious faith is always said to give an ever-present sense of being guided, a sense of having some touchstone by which to distinguish the good from the bad (when it is not a matter of taste !), a sense of being supported in pursuit of the one and delivered from the temptation of the other. *What* we are to believe in, what faith we are to hold, is of course the one subject of the deepest speculation, and consequently far beyond my powers. But though each several man must interpret for himself the highest experiences of his spiritual life, yet there is possible a community of reverence and a community of worship ; and in the end it is only communal worship which gives a reality to private belief.

So that, though I do not make the absurd claim of preaching a definite faith, of dispensing religion in tabloid form, yet I do think that any man may preach worship ; that is, a recognition of the things of value and the value of things, and a living in accord with this recognition. Worship is the *active* recognition of worthiness. The commonplace that worship is not merely the acknowledgment of good, but the practice of it, enables me to make my point clear. It is that this statement is equally true, and in my opinion far more true, when read the other way on : *Only through the practice of anything can come a full acknowledgment of its worth.* This, being such a definite statement, implies a host of qualifications, but I must be allowed to hold them in suspension for a while.

Accordingly, if it be asked : "How shall we revive a feeling for art values in the minds of the people ? " I suggest in reply : Open up again the practice of the arts, and the stream of tradition will flow again through your handiwork, and give it life.

> Lift up your heads, O ye gates ;
> Yea, lift them up, ye everlasting doors :
> And the King of glory shall come in.
> Who is this King of glory ?
> The Lord of hosts,
> He is the King of glory.

When I wish to help little boys to see the might and beauty of poetry, I do not discourse upon poetics. As a playmaster I know it is more practical to start the whole miracle with the one word "Make." You must fall straight away upon the actual work, and you will find out what you are doing as you go along. More and more you feel what you ought to do, and now and then, if you are lucky, you manage to do it. And all the time, of course, you have a sympathy and understanding with the art-doings of others, whether those others be the past-masters of your craft or merely your fellow-prentices.

20

GENERAL PRINCIPLES

To do a thing first in the hope of finding out later on how, and eventually why, may appear at first a queer suggestion, as though one should deliberately put the cart before the horse. But, short of visions and divine revelations, how else, I may ask, are we to acquire an impulse to work and a skill in working? Of course it is not denied that a great artist often starts with an idea which he gradually works out into some expressive form. But, even in his case, consider the manifold additions that accrue to him as he goes along, the miraculous gifts latent in the nature of tool and material, the fullness of inspiration that comes only in the hour of doing. I may instance, in passing, the conventions of the Elizabethan theatre, which served as it were the office of a mould to shape many of the most wonderful achievements of Shakespeare. Or call them paths down which he ran and rivers he had to bridge. If good plays are to be made, they must be wrought on an existing stage convention, and wrought fit, not written out of a man's head. It is the same with other arts, they must cease to be airy nothing, and get them a local habitation.

So long as we sit still and ask why some one doesn't get up and do something, nothing will happen; but so soon as we rise and fall to, then it will all be happening as before. The gods help those that help themselves. If the Devil finds work for idle hands, which I doubt not, it is equally certain that God Himself directs the busy. What right has any one to speak of faith who does not admit that there is some higher aid to be hoped for than lies in his own poor efforts? The wise artist is like a young mother trimming a cradle, and sewing tiny garments against the happening of a creative wonder. Build you a fair nest overnight and you may wake to find a bird in it.

It is my expectation, then, that the beliefs and traditions, which now seem all so dead, will be restored among us when we observe again the forms and ceremonies in which they reside. Do we await the visitation of a god? None but a visitation of wrath seems possible to-day.* Let us build a fane, and therein, over the consecrated altar, shall the unknown god be declared. The sun shines all over the earth, but no flowers grow on the cinder-heap, which is kept arid by the daily piling up of ashes.

* This was originally written in the spring of 1914.

THE PLAY WAY

Where in these days shall the spirit find an abiding-place, and
where shall he set up his rest ? While temple there is none,

> Nor altar heap'd with flowers ;
> Nor virgin-choir to make delicious moan
> Upon the midnight hours ;
> No voice, no lute, no pipe, no incense sweet
> From chain-swung censer teeming ;
> No shrine, no grove, no oracle, no heat
> Of pale-mouth'd prophet dreaming.

CHAPTER II

GENERAL METHOD OF THE PLAY WAY

And, in after years,
When these wild ecstasies shall be matured
Into a sober pleasure ; when thy mind
Shall be a mansion for all lovely forms,
Thy memory be as a dwelling-place
For all sweet sounds and harmonies ; oh ! then,
If solitude, or fear, or pain, or grief,
Should be thy portion, with what healing thoughts
Of tender joy wilt thou remember me,
And these my exhortations !

WORDSWORTH

THE subject of this chapter is such a wide one that the various matters to be dealt with can best be discussed under a few positive maxims.

The method of study is quite as important as the matter studied.

The classroom should to a very large extent be considered the boys' place, and not a sanctum nor a penitentiary.   Vittorino da Feltre, that playmaster among Renaissance educators, called his school at Mantua " La Casa Giocosa," or the House of Delight, and decorated it accordingly, so that the children might be brought up in beautiful surroundings.   But teachers of to-day have to work under authorities so blind to the finer influences of education as to provide only the barest accommodation.   But our methods of teaching the children need not be bleak and gloomy to match the surroundings.

The mind is its own place, and in itself
Can make a Heaven of Hell, a Hell of Heaven.

The creative fancy of Littleman in play can " make a sunshine

23

in a shady place," and under due encouragement he will not only make this dungeon bright, but will triumph over many another obstacle which would seem to the teacher to make real play impossible. If the classroom is really regarded as the boys' room, if the boys' point of view is given fair consideration in all that takes place in that room, then many play-methods will come into being of their own accord. Certainly the teacher must initiate many play-ways, but there can be no doubt that the boys if they are given leave will initiate many play-ways of their own.

A teacher's chief thought all the while he is in the classroom should be for the boys. If he is not present simply for the sake of the boys what is he doing in the classroom at all ? Is he practising there for a slave-driver, or cramming the poor wretches for an examination ; or is he simply earning a living while he fits himself for another profession ?

It is not denied that many teachers do give careful thought to presenting the subject-matter of their teaching in an interesting way. But few, if any, have realized for themselves (or will be ready to admit now that it is suggested) that with young boys *the method of study is quite as important as the matter studied.*

It is upon a recognition of this principle that most of the classroom practice in play is based. Consider what that statement implies. The teacher instead of being mainly, if not exclusively, interested in putting some particular subject-matter before the class, and seeing that they swallow that and attend to nothing else, will be quite ready to find emerging out of the subject he introduces some method of study which will develop a life of its own. It may even leave his original subject-matter far behind. It will occur time and again that what was at first undertaken only as a method of dealing with certain subject-matter will become itself the main concern.

Can such a thing be justified ? Let us take an illustration.

In the kindergarten and the elementary school play-methods are quite familiar. The simplest illustration, then, can be drawn from the teaching of very young pupils.

There are lessons for which the children bring daffodils to school. The lesson begins perhaps with questions and answers connected with a simple study of the daffodil (nature study). Then Wordsworth's " Daffodils " is read and discussed (poetry). In many cases teachers have songs about flowers for the children to learn (singing). And however many lessons all this may have taken it is certain that, before they have finished their study of the daffodils, the children will make pictures of them (drawing and brush-work). And there is no teacher of little children who would not, if she had the means, bring out of those few simple words

> And then my heart with pleasure fills
> And dances with the daffodils

all the joy of spring which the poet put into them, by teaching the children to perform a " Dance of the Daffodils." Series of lessons such as this, comprising a play-activity of several kinds, are an everyday occurrence in elementary schools. The fact that the verses used in such lessons are too often the merest rubbish, and the music and dancing, when included at all, of the worst possible type—sentimental wishy-washy stuff— is a great pity, but it does not in any way affect my illustration. The subject-matter of such a lesson as this might be described as " The Daffodil," It probably is thus simply entered in the syllabus of work done. But it is obvious that the whole value of the lessons lies in what the children have done in reading, singing, painting, and dancing, and in the way all this activity is bound up with the beauty of flowers, the joy of spring-time, the feeling for music, and the glad experience of rhythmical movement. Here then are many of the finest experiences of life centred round the alleged study of one flower. The value has come, not from the subject, but from the method of treating it.

Could not something of the same method be carried out in secondary schools ? Why should we give up all that is active and real and alive in method so soon as the subject with which we are concerned becomes of serious moment ? Why should children be considered adult so soon as they leave the kinder-garten ? The play-method is not asking for every school subject to be treated as though it were a parlour game. But it is asking that school studies should be brought more into relation with the activities of daily life. Some teachers speak and behave as though a man actively engaged were always just amusing himself, or otherwise wasting time which he might be devoting to study !

Others imagine that while active movement may be desirable and easily possible in connexion with such things as the acting and making of plays, it is in no way an essential part of more formal subjects such as mathematics, science, or language study. It is often thought that an active play-method in connexion with such studies can only be introduced as a means of diversion or for the lightening of the burden of abstract study. That in itself were surely reason enough for including a measure of play in all our teaching. But it happens that play as treated in this book includes always two meanings, one, the sheer enjoyable activity. of a game, and the other, that active side, that bringing into play of what one knows, which in real life is always as large a part of any undertaking as is the learning side. That is a modest statement, for in real life we gain proficiency far more through practice than we do through instruction or theoretical study.

What active measures of play, then, can be suggested in the study of the more formal subjects ? At this point I can only offer a few tentative and rather humorous suggestions which would have to be shaped into practical use by the specialist teachers of such subjects ; for one cannot give detailed proposals for the teaching of subjects of which one knows nothing. But I am convinced that the general method of the Play Way is in accord with the nature of boys, and that it can be adapted by any original teacher to suit his special circumstances.

Small boys learn geometry nowadays instead of Euclid ; and this, I understand, has the advantage of giving them a few little operations to perform carefully with instruments. This exercise requires some dexterity and neat fingering to ensure absolute accuracy. But we should go further than this in the use of implements and handiwork in connexion with mathematical study. Milton says, " At the same time might be taught them the rules of Arithmetic, and soon after the Elements of Geometry, even playing, as the old manner was." Several mathematicians have assured me that many parts of their subject could be taught actively in connexion with handicrafts, such as carpentry. Working to scale from a plan suggests itself at once. Accuracy and clean work are essential to a carpenter. That necessary precision of a joiner, who by measurement makes things *fit*, is surely a mathematical quality. There is assuredly much scope for active handwork and the making of things in connexion with *elementary* mathematics.

In addition to plays there are many other sides of English teaching which have flourished in our classroom in an atmosphere of games and "goings on." If such an essentially literary thing as a poem can be turned into a game, if a good prose style can be honestly shown as the outcome of a course of noisy play, what an opportunity there must be for the teachers of mathematics, elementary science, and handicraft to come near to the boys' real interests. For most boys are fascinated by technical and mechanical things. They love engines and motors and dynamos and explosives and aeroplanes and photography. If their intense love of these gins is not made use of in connexion with the school subjects most nearly concerned, then those teachers are surely neglecting a most powerful aid to their work. Even such a commonplace toy as a boy's kite offers scope for much in the way of practical lessons. If an ingenious master of geometry should give a course of lessons, as a result of which twenty-five boys had made twenty-five kites, I think those toys would not be the sole result. And what a sight it would be when they all trooped out on the first windy day to fly them on the hills !

More than once I have sat in a classroom and looked on at a fascinating lesson, in which one determined the width of a given river, not by direct measurement, but by doing learned things with convenient and obliging trees by means of angles, and many strange signs and tokens. Possibly the position of the sun was brought in also, but of this I am not sure. I was always consumed with a desire to ask two questions. First, *why* one should want to know the width of the river ? and secondly, what one would do if the tree were not there, or happened to be in the wrong position ? I have spent many days boating or swimming, or lounging by the river-side, but never yet saw any one attempting these calculations on a real river. But perhaps it is done.

When a mathematical master comes to that point in his teaching where the width of a river is to be determined, why should he not hold a class by the river-side, with a few patrols of senior scouts ? Under the direction of the scoutmaster and the woodwork master the boys might then build a bridge. Even the Latin master might turn up, and contribute not a little by improving the luncheon interval with a few quotations from the text of Cæsar !

But, jesting apart, much might be done with formal studies, even in the classroom, to link them up with the *doing* of something, if masters would but give their minds to it. Not only handicrafts are required, but some active *application* of the thing learnt such as is here described in connexion with English studies. If some thought were given to use and skill in all school subjects, as well as to knowledge and appraisal, education would soon become more truly a training for life than any one can claim it to be at present. Let us not forget how much of life-practice it was possible to plan for the tiny children in the simple study of a daffodil.

Direct instruction is only a small part of what can take place in the classroom.

The habit of spoon-feeding has become a second nature to most of us, so that we are now unable to realize that in our teaching we are all the while giving first consideration to what is after all merely a partial treatment of some subject. We give scarcely any *positive* consideration to the boys. All is conceived in relation to the sacred Subject. This will be vigorously denied by teachers. But let us take an illustration which will remove the scales of habit from our eyes.

Suppose yourself to enter a classroom full of boys, with no intention of administering a dose of any subject whatever. The boys would sit and wait, and you would sit and look at them without the remotest notion of what to do with them for forty-five minutes. Without a dose of some subject to ad-

28

minister you would be powerless. The period would probably be frittered away in desultory conversation.

How much worse is the position when illness or something else prevents the master from taking his lesson. If the boys are left unattended they do absolutely nothing of any educational kind. If some one comes to set them to work it is always desk-work, exercises done from the book; that is to say, self-spoon-feeding from a store of preserves.

One of the best experiences of practical method which could be planned for training college students would be to take a classroom full of boys—any group of boys more or less of an age—and require the student to take charge of them for an hour, under a promise not to " take the lesson " himself, not to teach any recognized subject, and as far as possible to avoid giving any instruction at all.

" But what is the poor man to do ? " you ask. That of course is the first question which would occur to the student, " What do you want me to do with them ? " My reply would be, " Anything you or they can think of, for this first period ; and after that you won't need to ask."

It is some such position as this which he who wishes to understand the Play Way methods should start from. Not that the Play Way implies in any sense the negation of a subject to be taught. Far from it. But the daily dose of a subject is not the only thing that makes a lesson. And this device of trying to get through a whole period without a " subject " might be the quickest way of discovering for oneself all the possibilities there are of " things to do " other than direct instruction.

It would be an excellent plan if a free period could be assigned once a week, or once a fortnight, to every form in every school ; the boys being left to decide for themselves, either individually or collectively, what should be done with the time. At first they would merely read books or talk idly. Soon they would begin to band together in concerted play. A few hints or some play organization by the master could then set afoot all kinds of activities which, as time went on, would gradually become more purposeful, more serious. And in the end this " free " period, in the hands of a tactful master, could, with the enthusiastic consent of the boys, be filled with some " goings on " which would be quite as valuable from the point of view of learning as any of his direct instruction lessons.

The matter has been approached from this aspect, not because there is any practical advantage to an understanding teacher in starting from sheer undirected play, and working gradually up to learning, but in order to make it quite clear (i) that direct instruction is only a small part of what can take place in the classroom, and (ii) that the play-methods suggested throughout this book are not a relaxation or a diversion from real study, but only an active way of learning.

It may be thought that the wretched student turned into a classroom full of boys with apparently nothing to do would be lucky to come out with his reason unimpaired at the end of the hour. But boys always " try it on " with a new teacher, and there is no reason why the student should be any better off if he were trying to instruct the class than if he were willing to let them have their own way for this first period. Boys accustomed to the usual system of classroom instruction will certainly make a great noise during their first lesson with *any* new teacher, and will continue to " rag " him until he has gained command over them. But for how long do you fancy the class would continue to be noisy if the student informed them that they could do as they pleased for all he would say ? Of course if he tried sarcasm his chances of gaining their goodwill would be considerably reduced. Boys accustomed to classroom instruction all their days would, I fear, be unable to suggest any occupation for that hour, and the student would have to " put them up to something," at least to give them a start. Thus he would fail in the letter of his promise. But at all events he would have had a good initiation into the possibilities of practical method. But with boys accustomed to undertake some part of their classroom studies in active play there would be no such difficulty. The new teacher only need have the wisdom to leave everything to the boys at first, and then gradually make his influence felt in their counsels. If he bounced in and began ordering them about, these boys would forget all their self-government, all their habits of unconscious discipline, and would turn round and " rag " the new-comer as unmercifully as did the boys who had had no such training. In return he would have to assert his authority by every means in his power, and it might then be months before any system of self-government could exist under him.

Boys accustomed to learn in active play are not only able but anxious to continue their work, whether the master is actually directing or not ; and will take a pride in looking after themselves even in his absence. No one denies that the master is a necessary part of the scheme. He is of course the very centre of it, or, better still, he is the circumference, the *primum mobile*. And no one denies, either, that it is an important part of a master's duty to give the boys direct instruction. But his work with the boys should not be merely a succession of daily lectures and " obstinate questionings," but rather an influence continuously operative, though not constantly asserted.

Self-government is not a matter of discipline only, but a condition which makes it possible for the boys to learn by themselves in actual lessons.

Every teacher knows that boys can conduct certain revision lessons on their own account. And in many small ways boys are already permitted to learn without help, to correct themselves from a book, or even to " hear " one another. But the self-teaching system is capable of much extension.

If active play-methods have been running for some time under the master's guidance, the method will have become familiar to the boys, so that they can not only repeat what has already been done, but carry on into the study of new matter. If a certain class has worked through " The Merchant of Venice " on the play-method, there is no reason at all why the same boys could not go through the first reading of " Julius Cæsar " or " Macbeth " without a master being present at any one of the lessons. This is possible because the first reading merely consists in acting the play straight through under the direction of a mister,* without any unnecessary

* See p. 67.

interruptions.* The master would of course go over the ground with them a second time to deal with scores of interesting and important points. And a third and even a fourth reading would still leave much to be studied. But any class which did not contain too large a proportion of stupids could carry through that first reading quite alone, and obtain great benefit from it. While this was going on the master, in another room, could give special tuition to one or two boys at a time.

This actual experiment has not been tried, but there are obvious advantages in the plan. For instance :

1. The boys would be doing as Dr. Johnson recommended in the study of Shakespeare, i.e. First of all to read the play straight through from beginning to end for the sake of sheer enjoyment in the story, passing over all difficulties, and completely ignoring all that the critics have said.

2. They would get first of all their own view of the play, uncomplicated by any possible influence from the master.

3. They would be learning to study for themselves.

4. They would be learning the advantages of working amicably together in pursuit of the same end, without the possibility of recourse to a higher authority, who would settle disputes by crushing one side of an argument or the other.

5. They would be sure to make the study an enjoyable one (because there would be no occasion to make it anything else) and would thus discover for themselves the *pleasant side of learning*.

* Of course there will be many mistakes. I remember a very amusing misconception of a mister who was directing the production of " Macbeth " while I was present. In Act i, Scene 7, there is a very important stage-direction : " Hautboys. Torches. Enter a Sewer, and divers Servants with Dishes and Service over the stage. Then enter Macbeth." I told the boys that this was important because the procession of servants going in with dishes is all we are shown of the banquet which occupies Duncan and the rest while Macbeth and Lady Macbeth speak together outside. The mister seemed to have more players than were necessary, so I asked him, " Who are these two boys ? " " Those, sir," replied the mister confidently, " are the *Ho-boys*."

6. They would also discover that *play with something of substance in it* was more satisfying than aimless amusement, and thus lay the foundations of an intelligent use of leisure hours which might well last them a life-time.

In another chapter instances are given of a junior class which (in the presence of the master) conducted its own oral composition lessons for a whole year in the form of original lectures ; and of a group of Belgian boys who, though new to the play-methods and previously most unruly, not only conducted one chance lesson in the absence of the master, but actually petitioned to run that lesson in private for themselves as a regular thing. The petition was granted.

Such instances as these, which could be multiplied, are given prominence here because teachers who put faith in methods of self-government are still too apt to look upon a boy's own charge of his learning as something unusual, a chance experiment which even if not very successful they find entertaining, much as one does the tricks and antics of a performing dog. Dr. Johnson, when making a similar comparison, said : " It is not well done, but you are surprised to see it done at all " Teachers must not look upon self-teaching as a kind of side-show. They must not be surprised to see it ; and they must allow enough practice at it to ensure its being well done. If the play-methods are in any way to mark an advance upon the old repressive methods, it must be in their absolutely *natural* character. The boy under the old system has no chance to be himself. We must make sure that any new system does not involve an equally artificial behaviour, but that the boys are free to be boys, frank and genuine in the pleasure they take in their work, and not deceiving either themselves or the teacher when they behave well and work well without compulsion.

The educational advantages to be obtained from including this self-teaching as a regular part of the school course require but little demonstration for those who are not prejudiced. The interest of the boys can be counted upon with greater certainty if they are working in their own way, and under their own responsibility, than if they were always under the instruction of a teacher. And when instruction time comes they will give a truer and more active attention—first, because their respect for the teacher is not based upon fear of punishment, but upon a sure knowledge that he is trusting them, and that he has even a greater belief in them than they have in themselves; and, secondly, because they have a *use* for the content of that instruction. Boys about to act a Shakespeare play under their own mister will listen closely to the master's preliminary instruction lesson about the conditions of play-production in the classroom. This lesson would not of course consist of warnings against misbehaviour, but would embrace much teaching in the craft of the stage, and of Elizabethan conventions concerning costume, scenery, lighting, business, properties, and " shows." And after the first reading there would be literally *hundreds* of questions asked, and an intelligent audience ready to give good heed to the answers, and able to understand them.

The *active* form in which the boys' own lessons are generally conducted gives them an understanding of the relationship between learning and doing, between study and practice.

Of course it is possible for one boy to instruct the rest, instead of the whole class taking active part. Some interesting examples of this have been seen, notably a series of three lessons given by a boy of thirteen to the fourth form when the master was absent through illness. They were Latin lessons, and throughout each whole period of forty-five minutes scarce a score of English words were uttered in the room. The lad was only just tall enough to be seen over the mountain of huge tomes such as classical masters pile upon their desks. And it was a delight not easily to be forgotten to see his alert and merry face bobbing up and down behind the leather-backs, and to observe how, the more difficulties he had to negotiate, the more he enjoyed himself. Every now and then he would turn aside with a learned air but doubtful, as who should say, " M-yes, but I wonder if you would find it in Cicero ? " and forthwith consult a tremendous dictionary which was almost more than he could lift. He had been called out unexpectedly to take the lesson, and so there was more need to consult Lewis and Short than he could have wished. In the evening he excused

34

himself from a dress rehearsal of his own play, which he was stage-managing, on the ground that to-morrow's Latin lesson must be very thoroughly prepared. He also asked me if schoolmasters ever had to prepare their lessons ; and I replied that of course they had to look over the matter, unless they already had it at their finger-tips.

But as a general rule it is best, in those lessons where the master himself is not teaching, for instruction to be suspended, and for as many boys as possible to engage in operations. For though one boy may not often be able to *teach* the rest very much, a number of them playing together can *learn* very well by themselves.

Particular methods of self-teaching in connexion with oral composition, playmaking, and other subjects are given in full in other chapters. But a system of testing " Repetition " and other memory work may be described here.

The hearing of " Repetition " is a great nuisance. ·Either a few selected boys only are tested, in which case many others feel, though of course unjustifiably, that their labour of the night before was wasted ; or the whole class is heard in turn, and the best part of a period is thus frittered away. In either case there is no real opportunity for teaching anything in the way of delivery or expression, because the lines are only just known, and the boy's main attention is therefore given to recalling them. And for the whole class to write out the set passage means either encouraging careless writing and neglect of punctuation, or, alternatively, a punctilious attention to these things, which takes the mind off the appreciation of the poetry, which was presumably to have been the valuable part of the exercise.

Repetition can very well be heard in partnership.* The boys sit in pairs and each hears the other, and marks him according to some scheme agreed upon. At first our playboys organized a competition between Rights and Lefts. The

---

* A special study of Partnership in classroom teaching has been made by Mr. Norman MacMunn, and the method worked out in connexion with the teaching of French and other subjects. Partnership has obvious limitations, and can never become the principal method in the classroom ; nevertheless it can be put to very good use.

marks of all those sitting on the right hand of a pair were added together, and compared with the total of all those sitting on the left of a pair. For a few weeks they used to watch for the totals with interest. But one day some thoughtful boy in the third form pointed out that, as there was no combination of effort among the members of a side, they could share no common glory. At that the adding of totals was abandoned amid laughter.

The boys fall upon the hearing of repetition of Shakespeare passages as soon as they enter the classroom, and they waste no time over it, in order that the acting may begin as soon as possible. While the hearing is in full swing the noise is considerable, but it is one of the most gratifying experiences of their goodwill and discipline to hear this great babble of voices, which gradually thins out until but one voice is left. The latest reciter generally makes a brave show, because he knows every one can hear him. Then he also ceases. In the silence the mister rises with his list and calls only the first name of the roll. Each boy in turn cries out his marks. Precious time is not wasted in calling out all the names.

Twenty or thirty lines can thus be tested from the whole class in a few minutes. It is not pretended that this is anything but a test of repetition. Expression and delivery must be dealt with separately. Also, the affair is not always put through so neatly as I have described it. But the boys should in this, and in all other matters, be encouraged to aim at a *perfection of discipline*. A piece of business of this kind, if thoroughly well done, has a beauty of its own.

If boys are to be taught by means of play the master must have a genuine interest in the play.

All boys are alike in some respects, but no two boys are alike in all respects. The duty of the master is to be for ever making opportunities for boys of every type of character to express themselves, and so bring about the natural perfection of their several abilities. He must so order his method that the group of boys under his guidance may act as a corporate body, influenced by communal ideas ; and at the same time

36

he must see that scope is given to the development of individual personality. There is many a *must* in educational practice, but the most urgent of them all is the *must* which nature has implanted in the character of the boy.

Although the members of a class are seldom enough treated as individuals, it is even more rare to find a class treated as a conscious group. The boys are either addressed collectively, or they are set to do each his version of the same task separately. It is an excellent plan to treat the class, whenever possible, as a body of workers collaborating. Will not the habit of thought thus induced fit them better for their after life in the world ? Or is it our object to train them all either to be typical imitators, characterless units of a mob, or to follow the occupation of being " in business on their own " ? As the combined movements of several dancers are knit up into a figure of the dance, or the several soundings of the string and wind instruments together compose the concerted orchestra, so may the common labours of the playboys together bring about what no one of them could compass alone. Combined effort and corporate discipline are familiar on the playing-field. Such things have come naturally into being there because the business in hand is action. Combined effort and corporate discipline will never be possible in the classroom until the master relinquishes the sole command, and until the boys are permitted to undertake some parts of their course of learning in an active form.

A master must of course understand boys. But it is not enough for him to understand boys in a general way. He must know the particular boys now under his guidance, and, so far as in him lies, regard everything from their point of view. In order to be on friendly terms with his boys it is not enough for a master to mix with them in a condescending manner. He must join in their interests in school and out of school, honestly and heartily, not with any idea of amusing the boys, but because he is of like passions with them. Some teachers are afraid that the boys may not respect them if they do not maintain an artificial dignity. Is it such a frail thing, then, the respect they inspire in their boys ? Will the boys in their hearts think any less of a master who confesses himself human ? On the playing-field, where both boys and master behave in a perfectly natural way, they can play together without any loss of dignity to either side. The sternest of schoolmasters can in a Rugger game butt into the very scrum with his boys. Why should he not be on equally good terms with them at all times, and frankly enjoy with them the play of the classroom as he does the play of the games-field?

If at any time you aim at giving boys play solely because *they* like it, surely your very presence will be apt to dull their enjoyment. The play that celebrates a relaxation of authority cannot be enjoyed under the eye of authority. Therefore there is a type of play (out of school) in which a master has no place. There will always be play of sheer exuberance, " letting off steam," the expression of animal spirits. In this form of play mischief has no small .part, and half the fun consists in doing what one ought not to do and taking the risk. For there will always be the play of the mice when the cat's away— be the cat never so sympathetic.

Full opportunity should be given for this natural free activity of children. But the play suggested as a classroom method is of a different kind. It is play with a purpose. But be careful that you do not leave all the play to the boys, and find yourself sole keeper of the purpose. Just as the boys must appreciate the purpose, so must the master appreciate the play.

Though it is not necessary for the master to take an *active* part in play, yet he cannot be a playmaster unless he appreciate Littleman's point of view. It is evident that unless the master can help in the planning of games he will be unable to turn those games to good account in the direction of learning. In other words, it is useless for him to stand aside and consider Littleman's idea of play merely as a relaxation from the master's idea of work.

In the play that goes on in the classroom while the master is present he must have as keen an interest as the boys themselves. Only in such a case can they feel that his part is genuine, and not fear that he is " getting at them." Littleman will undoubtedly feel this if the master appears in any sense to be pandering to his childish tastes. For the ambition to be manly stirs early in him—long before there is any need for him to put away childish things, or any wisdom in encouraging him to do so. With ever so little untimely encouragement the man-instinct, which is his future strength, will overbear the child-instinct, which is his present glory.

If the games-master played cricket only to amuse the boys, and not because he liked the game, the boys would discover it at once, and forthwith despise both cricket and the games-master. It is the same with the play of the classroom so far as real interest is concerned, for the master though he rarely takes an active share in classroom play must be in it heart and soul. Littleman of course knows that the presence of the master has a distinct influence upon the character of the play—he would be a poor master who hadn't—but any possible dissatisfaction felt at the presence of a grown-up playfellow is easily counterbalanced by the pride of having a grown-up fellow to play with. So much will be clear to any one who really knew how to play when he was a child, or who has ever joined in the play of children since he has grown up. But in the classroom of the present day you may add this consideration : The boys recognize all the time that you are the master, with authority to say, " These revels now are ended ; " yea, at a word to abolish the great globe of self-government itself ; to require again the dead labour of common drudgery, and even to inflict punishment for misdemeanours occasioned or imagined by the state of your own nerves.

It is indeed a pity that this spectre of Orbilius still looms in the background, that there is in the mind of Littleman a fear, however dormant it may be, that if he is not careful the goblins will get him. Any day, for all he knows, the prince may turn back into an ogre, and the volcano erupt and break up the fairyland. It is, I say, a great pity, but that fact remains, and it perhaps helps to explain why Littleman is so ready to be taught in play, so willing to keep the rules, so anxious still to dream.

It is the blend of pleasure and duty, of freedom and direction, that makes the boy so prolific in those *works of play*, rising even to true lyrics and tragic drama,* which in ordinary life the nursery does not demand and the classroom will not allow.

* For lyrics see Perse Playbooks, Nos. 2 and 5 ; for tragic drama, No. 3.

THE PLAY WAY

As an adult you cannot hope to be a fully qualified *player* among children in the nursery, and by the same token you need not exercise the powers of a fully authorized *master* among children in the classroom. But if you are to qualify in any positive sense as a *teacher* of Littleman you must combine the qualities of both player and master. So I call you a playmaster.

One knows of course that there are genial uncles who would not for the world interfere with nursery fun for the sake of bringing in some sense of reality, some matter of substance ; uncles home from the Front, for instance, who would stand by and applaud Littleman's spirited assault upon an opposing trench, even though in his dash and daring he ignored the enemy's wire defences. One knows also that there are teachers who would not for a fellowship permit Littleman to stir from his desk ; teachers hot from college who would pester Littleman with every device of notes, diagram, paraphrase, résumé, synopsis, and examination, without a thought of that boyish interest in playing the thing, trying some active form of it, seeing how it works, which makes the study for him so much more worth the undertaking. But the playmaster must be a true blend of the genial uncle and the exacting academic teacher. There are some characteristics of masters which, though they do little harm among senior pupils, really render a man unfit to teach little boys. Such are the haughty demeanour of the man whose standard for all work is nothing short of perfection, and who will have no mercy upon mistakes of any kind ; the absent-mindedness of the man whose thoughts are fixed all the time upon his subject, and who pays little regard to his pupils ; and the insensitiveness of the man who does not properly understand small boys and their feelings, and who is half the time at cross-purposes with them on this account. I fancy that this last type of failing is more common than we think, and that quite half the worries and troubles of the junior classroom arise out of a misunderstanding between boy and master owing to the master's lack of a nice perception, want of tact.

We are confident that the Play Way system could be administered in such a way as to suit all boys, but we have never been so sanguine as to believe that it could suit all masters ;

for many masters have already formed habits and opinions which it is beyond our power to influence. These teachers, however, do not concern us here, for they would never consent to join forces with us.

One of the first qualities of a playmaster is tact.

In view of the immaturity of his charges a playmaster must be a fellow of infinite tact. There is no occasion to be mawkish and over-tender with boys. They are hardy little rascals in many ways. And, in any case, one of the functions of school is to make them ready for the buffets of the world. But the boys themselves may be trusted to do enough buffeting of one another. The master can well leave " ragging," ridicule, and the whole process of " rounding off the corners " of an individual boy to that boy's peers. The master will be doing better educational service in acting as a pilot to steer each little individuality on its voyage. The waves are often trying for the little craft.

A playmaster must be easy of approach and always regarded by the boys as a person naturally helpful. Thus they will not be afraid to ask questions, however childish they may seem, and will have no dread of making silly mistakes. One should never laugh at a childish misconception, nor even smile indulgently, however the fault may tickle one's sense of the ridiculous. For although among boys there are many sturdy ones who do not feel a joke at the expense of their lack of knowledge, yet many of those who venture to suggest an answer rather than to ask a blunt question are the sensitive ones. And unfeeling ridicule, however gentle it may appear to you, often hurts them more than a blow. Who has not heard some blundering unsympathetic fool laugh aloud when a small person approaches him with a quiet question ? " Just listen to this," he announces to the crowd grinning in anticipation : " here's a fellow who wants to know . . ." And then he gives a cruel parody of the timid question. The crowd being expected to laugh, laughs ; for crowds like to signalize their advantage over some helpless victim. The poor shy boy thus held up to ridicule smiles feebly, though he is often nearer the verge of tears than any one knows. That boy may never ask another question of that man.

This care for a possible sensitiveness must be constantly exercised, even in the mildest instances of error. When a boy, for instance, reads such a word as *Antipodes* as three syllables—as any one naturally would do on meeting it for the first time—some jolly teachers laugh. It is such an amusing " howler." But after such an experience a boy may for months after be reluctant to read aloud. Such a feeling in the boy is not a softness to be knocked out of him. It is a sensitiveness in his nature of which due care must be taken. In our regard for sense we must not lose sensibility.

I give this rather obvious question some importance because I know from personal experience how real a trouble it is to a boy—and not by any means a small boy only—not to have at hand some one whom he may question on the most trifling matters without fear of being made to look a fool. For after all we must learn the very simplest things from some one.

Can the reader remember his anxiety as a boy when he first went out to a dinner-party ? Can he still feel in the pit of his stomach the nervousness he felt when he had to glance furtively round to find out how a certain dish should be negotiated ? Or was my reader one of those brazen creatures who would have turned to the hostess and said in a loud voice, " What rum food you have here ! "

Few adults seem to realize the discomfort and often actual misery they occasion boys by taking for granted that they are at ease anywhere and everywhere. Dinners were bad enough ; but a boy's first experience of a large club, or of hotel life, or of taking a long journey alone, have generally been occasions of perspiring anxiety unless there was a tactful elder at hand to initiate him.

Grown-up people quite frequently cause one another annoyance for want of a little tact in mentioning some necessary information. People often invite one to a homely dinner without any warning to " come as you are." The unfortunate man who goes in full dress and finds the company in flannels is as wretched as the man who turns up in a lounge suit at a fulldress function. And who has not been asked on sitting down to dinner, " Now what will you drink ? " A most tactless question, which prompts the almost irresistible reply, " What have you got ? "

Once a young fellow *knows* how to eat asparagus, how to make use of the hall-porter, how much to tip a waiter, how to sleep on a train, how to pass the custom-house, and all other such things, he will be perfectly at ease in those things for ever after. But the process of discovery is often needlessly discomforting.

The reader, as I say, may have been a hardy devil-may-care in these and similar matters. But we are not all so gifted. When I was a boy I sacrificed pleasures many and many a time, and stayed away from gatherings of various kinds, not from a feeling of lasting shyness, but for fear of the opening stages, for lack of knowing the ropes. Actual instances of the simple things I feared, and the shifts I made to avoid them, would convince the reader at once of the good sense of this appeal. But I dare not give any actual instances, for fear you should laugh at me !

The way to spare young people all such distress is in the first place to be easy of approach, always to greet a timid question as though it were the most natural inquiry ; and in the second place to make a point of telling them exactly what to do whenever you think they may need the information.

Some one may ask if this recommendation is not against the spirit of our educational principle, namely, that boys must not be pampered and spoon-fed, but allowed to gain experience for themselves. But a moment's thought will show that it is not so. These little tactful aids are a recognition of the small yet disconcerting difficulties any boy will meet so soon as he leaves the nursery. In giving him information about these small matters of social life you are really giving the boy the rudiments of self-reliance. Without some launching he might well fear to venture the least thing, and remain shut up within himself.

Schoolmasters whose acquaintance with boys is limited to the classroom, where they are merely inactive students of some book-matter, may wonder what relevancy to education the foregoing paragraphs can claim. But those who know boys

best out of school will agree that such things are intimately
bound up with the growth of a boy's experience. Parents
who are in the confidence of their sons will bear me out in
this.

The need of instruction in these obvious matters of daily
life is rather the concern of parents than of schoolmasters.
But I have taken these very plain instances to point a moral.

When will schoolmasters realize that, because of their
iniquitous preoccupation with their "subjects," more than
nine-tenths of the growth of a boy's experience is going on
without any influence from them ? When will they realize that
a boy is somehow, or anyhow, adjusting himself with life quite
apart from all their school-teaching ? Because of their lack
of sympathy and contact with a boy's real interests he is all the
time out of their reach. Let any schoolmaster honestly consider which boys he is influencing, and he will find them to
be those whose interests he shares, those in whose confidence
he is, and these will not necessarily be the boys who are any
good in his "subject." And the intimacy upon which this
influence of his rests is for the most part an out-of-school
companionship or understanding. A master's educational
influence often has very little to do with the subject-matter
of his teaching, and sometimes none whatever.

In any case, most boys learn so little of these precious
school "subjects," even under the most efficient instructor,
that it is time teachers were shamed into more effective action
of some kind. I would ask all teachers to remember that by
widening a boy's boundaries you extend his reach.

How full of meaning is our maxim that " Direct instruction
is but a small part of all that can take place in the classroom."
Even if the master refuses to consider anything but that *the
boys must learn the lesson*, how much else will nevertheless
be taking place in their minds, which neither he nor any other
can stop, and of which he might just as well decide to make
use. What silent processes of growth quite unconnected with
the classroom or the mathematical master are quietly and
steadily going on in that bullet head of Johnny Jenkins while
he is learning quadratic equations. And among all the multitude
of images and thoughts which pass through the mind of young

Dick in the course of a day, of what relative importance is it to him that verbs in the ablative are always feminine ?

Scientific investigators may proceed with the study of psycho-physiological pedagogy until all that is plain has been made obscure, and even now those learned men are probably saying the same things as we are in their own way. The truth remains, however we arrive at it and however we state it, that every boy requires special treatment. A method that is wrought in keeping with this realization can only be administered by a teacher who is on intimate terms with the boys, and in touch with their individual needs. To be thus in the confidence of boys requires the constant exercise of tact. The measure of a teacher's sympathy is the measure of his influence, and the measure of his influence is the measure of his responsibility.

The basis of educational method must be a regard for the pupil's interests.

Some wag has defined genius as an infinite capacity for making other people take pains. This is essentially the genius of the playmaster. The boy *takes* pains because his interests have been considered first. When the subject of study is given first consideration the boy finds the pains thrust upon him, often not unaccompanied by penalties.

Most teachers put the subject first in their estimation, and give the boy second place. As a result of this, compulsion has to be the basis of method. Teachers will say that we exaggerate in this statement. But would the boys come to school at all if they had any opportunity to stay away ? How many of them would come back to your classes if it were open to them to do anything else ? Compulsion *is* the basis.

If you put the boy first and subordinate all subjects to his needs and abilities, then you may find that, while *he* comes gladly to school and demands all kinds of learning, it is the *subject* which will then be under compulsion—all kinds of learning needed by this little fellow, all kinds of masters required, subjects and teachers collected by order from all sides for the service of the real educational force—interest. This conscription of subjects in the interest of the boy is a promising line of thought. The reader may find it tempting enough to pursue it for himself.

But when we claim that the Play Way takes the *interest* of the boy as a starting-point, some teachers affect to believe that by interest we mean mere amusement. This criticism arises either out of intentional misrepresentation, or a limited intelligence on the part of the critic. For it has been stated plainly and often that interest, in our use of the term, is that which you have nearest at heart, that which has your very being in hold. Our Play is the play of interest in this sense, and not the play of entertainment.

What is the master to do, then, if he is neither to force a subject of study upon a boy from outside, nor yet to tempt him from outside with the sweet baits of pleasure ? My answer is this :

He is to go straight to the interest which the boy has at heart. There he will find guidance for all the rest of his duty. That is the secret of playmastery.

If the teacher is thus in complete and thorough sympathy with his pupils, under his encouragement and guidance the boys will find in what he gives them to do the satisfaction of their instincts, the exercise of their inherent powers, and the true expression of their natural desires. Boys thus rightly treated are keen to learn and to do and to be ever active-minded. When boys are lazy and stubborn the fault is only half their fault. There is something amiss between them and the teacher which must be set right.

If every teacher cannot be expected to have such an understanding of his boys as all this implies, then every school should have at least one playmaster. But surely we can all approximate to this true sympathy for the boys' point of view. One sometimes hears it said, " Ah yes, how true all that is, if only teachers could do it." Does this mean that our school system must for evermore be based upon this iniquitous spoon-feeding, because teachers as a body are unfit to do anything else ? Let us not be so modest.

GENERAL METHOD

Under a natural system of education there can be no absolute standard of discipline. Right behaviour is a relative condition to be determined by its appropriateness to the occasion.

A playmaster should give his pupils all the space and freedom they can possibly make good use of. If the right comes worthily from his hands it will not be abused. There need be no fear that, once a meadow is thrown open, nothing but leap-frog and horse-play will follow. That is the fear of those who are accustomed to see the coarse outburst of spirits fermented by unnatural restraint. The healthy body is moderate.

The practice of self-government of all kinds should be encouraged, both in the individual that he may learn responsibility for his own actions and form for himself a body of right habits, and in the community that they may build up a system of good order based on mutual understanding. Every boy should grow early accustomed to command without a trace of domineering and to obey without a taint of servility.

If a boy asks " Why ? " after the order " You must," he may not be questioning authority, but seeking a reasoned adjustment with it. In any case the retort, " Because I say so," is enough to anger any ·one into rebellion. Prompt obedience should certainly be exacted ; but the reason for the giving of an order should always be understood. If teachers would honestly bear this in mind they would soon observe how many orders they give out of the habit of their unquestioned authority for which no reasonable defence can be found. Such are the perpetual injunctions to " Sit still." Why ? To sit still for a protracted period is not only quite a feat for Littleman, but it is usually quite unnecessary.

That " sit-stillery " is a useful accomplishment is not denied. But it is not nearly of such general utility as teachers imagine. *Learning how to move* is of immeasurably greater importance than *learning to sit still*. In all natural life, for one moment of apparent stillness there are millions of active movements. A child who is left to profit by experience will soon learn when to be still, when to move, and even *how* to move, in due accordance with the need of the occupation he is engaged upon.

THE PLAY WAY

The narrow outlook to which most teachers have restricted themselves has limited the word " discipline " in its school sense to that particular form of restraint which means the inhibition of active movement. But there is an appropriate discipline for every aspect of life, mental and bodily.

The question is too wide for present discussion, and in any case the classroom imposes obvious limitations. But, in passing, teachers may be recommended to make less fuss over " sit-stillery," to allow natural movement, and, in allowing it, to pay some attention to the fitness, aptness, and beauty of movement—in a word, to rhythm.

In all effective action the amount of muscular force exerted is more than would be necessary for the mere execution of the action, but this strong force has to be controlled and guided by a complementary muscular restraint equally strong. Over-restraint will render action ineffective as easily as will lack of restraint. One hears so much on this unnatural system of boys being told to restrain themselves. But, if you will believe me, under natural conditions they quite as often need encouragement to let themselves go.

Teachers often sigh after some sense of corporate responsibility among a group of boys. It is the easiest thing in the world to set afoot if you go the right way about it. Boys can readily understand and effectively carry out a corporate discipline. But the master and the boys cannot both rule at one and the same moment. If the master rules continuously, then he must not look for any sense of responsibility in the boys —for he grants them no responsibility.

Even a little boy can appreciate for himself the meaning of individual mental discipline, self-control.

The following instances will probably surprise the reader who has had no experience of boys other than that of so many honey-pots to be stored with the sweets of learning :

Form IIa (average age under 12½) used to have Stick-wagging (that is, the group-recital of poems in play) in the second morning period, and Speeches in the fourth period, for it had seemed advisable to put at the end of the morning a lesson in which all the boys but one were resting, and listening to an interesting lecture. But fatigue, from which all little boys suffer after two or three hours of lessons, soon made itself felt in the Speeches. The speakers had not the requisite grip of their subject-matter. They were not fresh. Their delivery showed hesitation ; and the *er* and *hum-and-ha*, common to adult lecturers, which the Littlemen were so proud to have abolished, came in again. The frequency of the hammer-rap * became unbearable.

" What *is* the matter ? " I protested.

" He keeps saying *er*," replied the hammer-boy.

" But as a rule he does not hesitate."

" No, sir, but we always used to have Speeches in the second period. It's much harder to speak well at the end of the morning I found it so myself just now." Observe that correction and criticism were in the right hands, for the hammer-boy knew from experience the precise conditions of the speaker he was correcting. Yet for all his knowledge of the difficulties he would not abate a rap of his requirement.

" What is your opinion ? " I asked the lecturer.

" I don't feel I'm speaking very well," he replied, " but then, you see, the class is not attending properly, and that makes a difference."

The obvious reply would have been that it was the speaker's business to hold their attention. But that would have been a shallow observation—one of those unthinking retorts so cleverly used by teachers. The truth of course was that the fatigue of the speaker and the fatigue of the class reacted upon one another. When a master addressing the class under like conditions finds the same difficulty, would it not be more fair and honest dealing for him to say, " I know you are tired. Perhaps I am not claiming your attention so firmly as I might, because, I suppose, I am tired too. But let us all make an effort to do ourselves justice in the last lap."

There is a jolly chorus to a folk singing-game which ends,

> I'll do all that ever I can
> To push the business on.

And if schoolmasters were not obsessed with the indefensible notion that method in teaching is a kind of trade secret, they

* A rap of a little hammer is used for current criticism.

might take Littleman openly into their confidence and share with him the inspiration of those lines. Instead, they visit their wrath upon the unfortunate boys, whether the fault be in the time-table, or in the weather, or in the enforced dullness of the subject, or merely in the state of their own health. I do not of course claim immunity from this condemnation for myself. We are all in the same box, and that box is the classroom.

The Littlemen and their master agreed to change the lessons about, to hold Speeches in the second period and to put Stick-wagging in the last. Stick-wagging is our active play-method of reciting poems in chorus. Many of the poems have developed into games, and with some of them are associated toys such as cats, birds, and ships. Many voice inflexions and modulations are heard in the chorus recital, sticks are waved, the little ship sails in a dish of water, the cat pounces upon the bird, and the boys make expressive gestures of all kinds. There is need for the master or the boy-conductor to keep the reciters all together in expressive rhythm, just as an orchestra is controlled by the conductor. Each boy also must exercise individual self-control in order to take his due part—and neither more nor less than his due part—in the chorus-recital. If well done, this method of rendering poems is in itself an effective and beautiful art form.

Well, when we put Stick-wagging as the last lesson of the morning the recital gained tremendously in life and gusto, but the boys exaggerated their expressive effects. The bangs and drum-taps and shouts which were part of the poems were overdone, and the "Hark, hark, Bow-wow," and "Cock-a-diddle-dow" of the Ariel song were rendered with such vigour as to spoil all sense of art in the recital. Also the raps of the hammer-boy interrupted every opening bar. "Start together," he insisted. No one who saw those lessons could deny that we all enjoyed every minute of the time, and that we did some exceedingly good work. But from a director's or teacher's point of view there was an uncomfortable looseness about the whole business. There was not enough conscious discipline for art. The thing wanted pulling together.

Once after a particularly energetic rendering of "Hunting" *

* See Perse Playbooks, No. 3.

GENERAL METHOD

I observed, " You boys were too tired to make good speeches at the end of a morning and yet you seem always to have more vigour than is required for the play-songs. How is it," I asked, " that you Littlemen make more noise, and seem to be more full of energy when you are tired ? "

The question was too much for most of the small people. But presently a quiet boy of eleven, who never, I think, can have made a noise in his life, said, " Isn't it because the more tired you are the less you can control yourself, and so you keep letting yourself go ? " I agreed that it was so.

When freedom and ease are necessary for the forwarding of the business in hand, then freedom and ease must of course be permitted by the playmaster. During many lessons the playboys have been allowed to " unsit," that is, to attend in any comfortable attitude. Many sit on the desks or the windowsills and dangle their legs. Others stand about the room in easy postures. The only criticism made is of ungainly positions, or of those prejudicial to health. A Littleman sitting in comfort, or standing at ease and giving all his attention to a speech or a play which is going on, is often an unconsciously beautiful figure. It is some such easy standing posture as this which I should choose for a statue of Littleman. And of the same boy sitting in the stocks with his arms folded, I would make a cartoon to the perpetual shame of the repressionist spoon-feeder.

It has been said that boys have sometimes actually to be persuaded to let themselves go. This of course is mainly seen in connexion with acting and the other forms of play which are full of movement. But the reader will not by this time be likely to imagine that the play-method sets order, quietness, and systematic discipline at naught. On the contrary, play-methods in the classroom demand a far more rigorous attention to systematic order and true discipline than do the dead conditions of pedant rule. But in connexion with what business soever, you cannot get so real a discipline by coercion as you can by relying on the goodwill of the company and their recognition of what is required for the matter in hand.

There must be in your playmaster a spice of the drill-sergeant.

He must be exacting of precision. But there is not so much need of severity as there is of stimulus and encouragement. Enthusiasm will do more than bullying, and a quiet insistence is more forcible than shouting. The boys can be brought to take a pride in their corporate discipline. They can be made to feel that there is a distinct joy and beauty in precision of movement and in absolute trim, just as there is in rhythmical motion, or dancing in time.

In Greek education—but let us not for shame pursue that line. The glory that was Greece is represented in the schools of to-day as an ancient language to be studied, nothing more.

A play-method is designed to make leisure valuable and labour light. Sincerity of purpose will dignify the merest hobby, and interest will lighten the severity of deep study. Wrongly applied, a play-method can as easily spoil a good game by requiring too much care as it can render a serious undertaking of no account by admitting too much wantonness.

When order, silence, and discipline are required then the playboys know how to observe the strictest order, the dead silence, and a discipline that is really a living and *potential* thing. Have you really considered that discipline is not an absolute necessity, but a relative one—a potential condition ? There is no strain about this silence and calm. The master whose class gives him the perfect discipline of a ready trust finds the boys responsive to his touch, not struggling against his rule, nor sunken into sulks, but quietly alert and ready, " awaiting but the signal to begin." Among teachers, only a playmaster in thorough accord with his boys can know what it means to have one's finger on the pulse of life.

These maxims of the Play Way, and discourses in explication of them, might be continued indefinitely. But it should not be necessary to go on. Those who have not been stimulated by what has already been said to work out particulars of method for themselves would not be persuaded or convinced by anything more in the way of argument or exposition which might be written here. For a player, like a poet, must he born before he can be made. For the born player there is no doubt of the main question. It is answered in his very being. And as for those who are not players, well, we wish them good luck in their arduous ways. It is of no avail to quarrel and get angry with one another over these things. If you are born a cat and I am born a dog, then I shall no more be able to persuade you to be canine than you will find it possible to convert me to felinity.

If a disputant offer criticism, and cavil at details, he may help you to amend ; but if he deny the principle upon which your whole action is based, the principle you were born to believe, then his criticism is not positive in any sense for you, but negative entirely, and you must let such words go by you as the idle wind which you respect not, for they are a very denial of the faith to which you owe adherence.

The minds of men are not at bottom subject to mere whim, but are moved constantly, though most often without their knowledge, in pursuit of one aim. It is predisposition, the inherent cast of mind, that in the long run gives us to agree or disagree with any given thesis. That is why a man convinced against his will is of the same opinion still. We are *born to believe* this or that (unless we are born without brain enough to believe positively and intelligently in anything). Against this predisposition or settled habit of mind logic is of no avail. No appeal, however reasonable, wins through the ear when the mind is shut, for man is a creature not guided by reason but by prejudice—" is either a little Liberal or else a little Conservative."

To be thus in earnest, then, as we are in the views expressed in this book—to have one's feet thus planted on a rock of certainty—does not come of having accepted a doctrine after logical consideration, but it comes of innate belief ; for the springs of human action lie not in the reasoned intention of the individual, but in the intuition of man's mind, in the gathered energy of inherited tendency and communicated desire. And so this expression of an educational ideal will ultimately appeal only to those who already feel an answer to it within themselves.

CHAPTER III

SELF-GOVERNMENT

The baby figure of the giant mass
Of things to come at large.
" Troilus and Cressida "

THE subject of self-government is here treated in two parts. The first part deals with discipline and the charge of affairs in the hands of boys. The second discusses an aspect of teaching rarely considered in connexion with self-government, and too often neglected altogether—namely, the individual boy's government of himself, and his responsibility for his own learning. The question of self-government in discipline is treated from a purely practical point of view, and a few experiments are described. But the wider aspects of the subject are dealt with in connexion with individual responsibility.

We need not spend much time in arguing the case in favour of giving self-government to boys in school. The subject has been discussed in theory often enough. It is one of the cardinal tenets in most proposed reforms of educational method. So we may presume that if teachers have not by now adopted some form of self-government with their boys, it is either because they are not convinced of its value or because they are still waiting to be shown how to set about it.

Those teachers who are not convinced that self-government is a natural and necessary part of school administration need not detain us now. But those of us who do believe in the principle must put it into practice from now onwards, consistently and whole-heartedly, so that the new tradition of freedom may soon get a firm hold upon our schools, and remain rooted there. The method of teaching which consists of spoon-feeding under repression—overriding the natural habits and desires of boys

54

so that they may be crammed with instruction in certain subjects—is already discredited. Few defend the old system now. The most you will hear from the old-fashioned pedant is a querulous complaint that he is not a pedant. And the harshest of disciplinarians now feels it necessary to justify his severity. The spirit of freedom is strong enough to make every one profess adherence to it.

But, as we all know, spoon-feeding and repression go on as before, and the classroom system upon which all schools are run, is still based upon these twin demons of futility.

The practice of education reforms itself very slowly, partly because all men find it easier to continue in bad ways than to amend them according to their better lights, and partly because the schoolmaster in particular has so little outside pressure to keep him up to the scratch. The only thing required of most schoolmasters is that they should dodder on in the same old way.

Apart from a few foundations recognized as progressive or experimental, school as we know it to-day is a gigantic humbug. Reformers for the most part have been afraid to fall upon this ancient fraud itself, and have gone aside to found little modern schools of their own or merely to become a voice in the wilderness. But those who earnestly desire to see an immediate reform of school method would be well advised to stay in their present schools, and begin the reform from inside. This will, of course, mean for the present the restriction of all their ideas to fit the limitation of the classroom. Periods of forty minutes in a room full of desks with twenty-five boys (and in elementary schools often double that number) do not offer any great scope for any one whose ideas of education embrace wider activities than reading, writing, and figuring. But much can be done under such limitations ; and it is in the hope of their being of some service as hints that the following experimental devices have been described.

When a teacher is set down to conduct lessons in a certain subject at stated times he cannot of course give the boys much freedom of choice. If the school time-table says " Arithmetic," then arithmetic it must be, and any teacher whose ideas of self-government should go so far as to allow the boys to do anything else in that period would be failing in his duty to the school. But when your subject is a wide one, such as " English " for example, it should be possible to include many various activities. If the authorities who are responsible for the scheme of work insist on drawing up a rigid syllabus for you, stating that one period shall be given to dictation, one to reading aloud, one to parsing, one to learning verses by heart and so on, then I admit you are done for. There is nothing for it but to abandon your ideas or abandon the school. But in many schools to-day a responsible subject-teacher is given a reasonably free hand within the periods devoted to that subject, and can apportion the time among the different phases of his work to suit his own intentions.

But with only three or four periods a week in which to teach all that goes by the name of English, where are you to find time for the practice of self-government ? Our plan was to set up some kind of governing system, and then let it run concurrently with the subject-study. The master need not always be teaching, the boys can conduct many lessons themselves. Then there is the round of daily routine duties, and these also can be entrusted to the boys. Finally, there is the maintenance of discipline—for discipline in an active community does not run itself, it has to be maintained—and this also can safely be left in the hands of the boys. Let us, then, take these opportunities for self-govenment, and consider them from a practical point of view.

One of the first essentials of self-government is the election of a body of officials. Some portion of the school-time may at first be set aside for this government business, but once it is firmly set afoot the boys may be willing to transact these affairs in their own time. As a beginning it is well to ask the company to suggest posts to which they will presently elect officials. A chief is necessary, and him we call the Prime Monitor. Sometimes he chooses his own cabinet, and sometimes the whole committee is elected by the citizens. One monitor will be responsible for the homework, another will take charge of the acting of a play, a third will see that the classroom is kept tidy, and so on. The cabinet makes rules and regulations for the conduct of debates, settles the responsibilities of monitors and the duties of the citizens, and may (if you decide so) even impose penalties for misdemeanours. The power vested in the cabinet has varied from time to time, but one of the most interesting experiments was when the boys of the third form had complete control, not only of discipline, but of all their schoolwork in English. " The Junior Republic of Form IIIb " (average age about thirteen) held sway for two whole terms, much to the joy of the playboys, and entirely to my own satisfaction. The House at first divided on the question of Prose and Verse. The books to be studied during the term had already been chosen by myself. There was a book of ballads, and an anthology of poems, and, for prose, a collection of essays. When the Verse party were in power they conducted lessons only in verse subjects. When they were thrown out we had only prose for a time. In reality the boys had a fairly equal interest in all the books, but they had to divide on something as a beginning, until actual practice of self-government should reveal a more genuine and less artificial difference of opinion. And, as a matter of fact, though prose or verse were in equal favour for reading, many of the boys had a decided preference for making ballads and poems as homework instead of writing prose compositions. The debates held on the relative merits of prose and verse were naturally rather feeble. But the real interest centred in matters of administration. The Verse government would be defeated by the opposition, not because the majority of the class felt an urgent desire to study prose, but because under a vote of censure they had been found guilty of slackness in certain duties, and were consequently held to have forfeited the confidence of the community. One government went out because its Homework Monitor had failed to set the homework one night. He protested that every one knew what he would have set, and therefore every one ought to have learnt it. But certain members of the opposition boldly asserted that they had done no homework simply because no homework had been set. So the leader of the opposition was able to score a telling point, and he made it very plain to the Prime Monitor that under his administration the class was not doing all it should do, and was not even given a chance of doing its duty. So the vote of censure was passed and the opposition formed a government.

57

THE PLAY WAY

The boys were really anxious to show that they could work properly without any need of compulsion. Every one enjoyed the game of debates and voting. But once when a certain section nominated the stupidest boy in the form for some office, just for the fun of the thing, the prominent leaders on both sides were very angry. They said precisely what any master would have said—namely, that fun was all very well, and they hoped the debates would continue to be conducted with good humour. But if any one thought he could turn the whole thing into a " rag " by setting up " Aunt Sally candidates " then he would soon find himself mistaken. " It is no good doing the thing at all," they said, " if you can't do it properly."

The case as put by another speaker against tomfoolery was that, if the practice of self-government degenerated into a " rag," Mr. Cook would abolish the Republic, and they would all return to ordinary lessons. Which was true, I suppose, for school conditions would have required that action on my part. Yet I am convinced that even without any fear of a higher authority stepping in with a threat of abolition, public opinion among a group of boys would ensure an earnest respect for order. The majority would be in favour of seriousness and would keep the " raggers " in hand. The experience of other teachers who have had fuller opportunities for putting this to the test bears out my opinion. But this seriousness of purpose can only be expected on one condition : *there must be something to be serious about.*

In those little communities which are entirely run on self-government lines, such as the Junior Republics in the United States and The Little Commonwealth down in Dorset, the driving-power which makes the citizens conduct their affairs seriously is real social necessity ; for what is not done by the citizens for themselves in the way of rule is not done at all. They must earn their own living, and therefore cannot be idle ; they must safeguard their possessions and their peace, and therefore must uphold the law and punish wrongdoers. I am one of those who believe that all schools should be run as far as possible on such a genuine system of self-government. But while we are confined to the classroom, and our main efforts are devoted to the study of some subject imposed, it is obvious that we are not living under natural conditions governed by necessity, and so we must find some other central force, some other driving-power. There must be some artificiality here, for there is no getting away from the fact that it is not a *necessity* for a boy to learn, for instance, a play of Shakespeare. What then shall we devise of equal power to claim the boys' serious interest, to gain their goodwill and enlist their whole-hearted co-operation ?

The answer is, Play. The subjects to be learnt must be presented in an interesting way, and then the boys will have a natural desire to do the work. They will work well under free conditions partly out of sheer enjoyment and partly for fear of losing these rights.

As regards discipline during lessons, I know that many a teacher's time and temper are wasted away because of his endeavour to enforce an unnatural discipline, when it should be obvious that the only discipline worth having is a natural one got by *interest and habit*. The play-method not only does require order and attention, but for its efficient working demands that higher discipline which is habitual and has become so by the operation of interest. To subject the will to perform subordinate duties mechanically, leaving the thinking part a free agent, is one of the conditions that make possible the intellectual life of man. If every small act of daily life demands attention every time, if self-control is always to be conscious, men could never rise above the level of machines. The discipline maintained by a ruling fear or by the immediate imposition of an outward authority (" your eye on the class ") is but a *rigor mortis*; the free, self-government kind of discipline is simply a necessary condition of Play. It is the rule of the game, and a sense of fair-play. If you have it not you are merely drilling your class.

That is how you enlist their co-operation in the classroom. It is, I hope, unnecessary to insist that the freedom postulated is freedom from hampering conditions, not freedom from doing the work. Yet some people have spoken to me in criticism of the Play Way as though it meant abandoning work for play, and letting the dear boys amuse themeslves instead of bothering their little heads with learning ! *

* Of course it is on these lines that the Play Way will always be criticized. We have answered the criticism time and again in these pages.

THE PLAY WAY

The Junior Republic of Form IIIb, then, settled down to do good work and to maintain good discipline. I once went away to Oxford for a day without making arrangements for any one to take their lessons. One master looked in, but they begged him not to stay. As they grew in practice they found their real differences very few, and gradually ceased to make opposition for the mere sake of it. They got over party politics as a puppy gets over distemper, for the simple reason that the whole body was working to achieve a healthy system.

It is important to state at this point that although the " politics " side of this self-government experiment interested the boys at first it gradually fell out of favour. The speeches, elections, and parliamentary business generally had very little practical educational value at any time. I never expected them to have much. The value expected of this self-government scheme lay in the school work done by the boys under their own officers, and in the hearty spirit of freedom which informed that work ; and not in the election of the officers or the passing of votes of censure. The boys after a time felt this themselves, and in every class with which I tried a system of self-government the same thing happened. The boys felt unconsciously that all this political business was an artificiality, and after one term or so politics generally fell through.

I will confess now that I was often disheartened at such happenings, though at the time I would not confess as much even to myself, for very fear of killing belief. It seemed to me that even in the stupid old classroom self-government ought to be possible, so I made it a point of honour to set afoot some form of self-government in every class that came into my hands. In the end I saw that this faith was justified. But before showing how, I will relate the story of a most disheartening experience :

The form was a certain IIa, average age about twelve and a half, and the best form I ever had. Other masters agreed at the time that the school had never had such a group of boys. More than half of them were distinctly able, the kind of boy who is found in twos and threes at the top of most classes. All but a few were very willing to try their best, and, whether clever or stupid, they were all good fellows. They had been in charge of their own affairs for a whole year, but under various play-schemes (such as a band of knights), and not on the parliamentary system. For a term or so the parliamentary system ran its course, governments rose and fell, Prime Monitors and their cabinets, " dressed in a little brief authority," held sway for a time and then were defeated. But in the end there was a motion put forward and supported by a powerful body of opinion, not for the defeat of one government or another, but actually for the abolition of self-government itself. You may imagine with what feelings I heard that motion stated. It was the most hotly contested fight we ever had in the school. It was certainly true that the cabinet in power was very weak, but that was not a sufficient reason for doing away with cabinets altogether. There was one boy in the class who had made a perfect Prime Monitor, though as it happened he was the youngest of them all. In his time of power he had been most efficient, and had insisted upon his colleagues carrying out all their duties properly. Moreover he could control the class with a word. The party now in power, finding a strong move-ment afoot for the abolition of self-government, invited this boy to come and lead them. The Prime Monitor (himself a boy very good at all his work, but no leader) pointed out rather pathetically that his own failure need not bring about the downfall of self-govement itself. And there and then he resigned, and nominated Sir Pelinore as his successor. But Sir Pelinore refused to stand. He kept his own counsel, and never declared either for the abolition of self-government or for its continuance. But the fact was plain, that if Sir Pelinore declined to take command, the whole fabric would topple down in ruin. The No-government party became clamorous, and in despair the other side, who still had a shaky majority, set up a totally untried fellow, who, though not remarkable for ability, was big. His adherents spoke brave words about a strong right arm, and implied that here was a Dictator. But at the hour of dismissal, when the class should have remained sitting still until homework and other business had been trans-acted and they had the Prime Monitor's leave to go, one member of the No-government party rose from his place coolly (though pale with anger and excitement) and strolled out. The wretched dictator told him peremptorily to sit down. But his rule was ignored, and so another anti-government member made to walk out. Then this Prime Monitor, vaunted by his adherents for strength of arm, stepped between this second defiant and the door. And I sat watching, and wondered if government would descend to a trial of brute force. But he of the strong arm was weak to command, and the second defiant walked out. Others followed him. Fortunately no one appealed to me. But it had been clearly established long ago by Sir Pelinore that a boy's rule which rested on the master's authority and could be enforced at his command was no self-government at all. So I was a mere onlooker. Having seen enough I also walked out, remarking to the dejected Prime Monitor that he had better take some measures for the morrow, before dismissing his adherents and what remained of the class.

The Prime Monitor who had lately resigned had a long and excited tale to tell his mother; and from her I had it afterwards. He maintained that the one thing needed was a strong Prime Monitor, who had the confidence of the class and could manage his cabinet and keep them efficient. So he laid all the blame for the cataclysm upon Sir Pelinore, who had refused to come from his retirement and step into the breach.

Meanwhile great excitement prevailed at the School House, for it happened that three or four of the malcontents were boarders there. The wretched dictator, he of the strong arm, was also a member of the School House; and before the evening was out the agitators had converted him to their point of view and made him promise to resign! A day now intervened on which no government business was held; but both sides prepared eagerly for the coming struggle. The No-government party in the School House chose green as their colour. They had a two-handled banner made, with a design on it, showing the Prime Monitor's mace being severed by a sword-blow. I was told afterwards that the School House had heard little else but self-government talk throughout the week-end; and one boy, usually very quiet and retiring, had stated repeatedly and with great emphasis, " Self-government must be abolished. Down with the Prime Monitor! Mr. Cook shall rule over us."

SELF-GOVERNMENT

The debate when it came was exciting, and before the end speeches gave way to violence. The leader of the No-government party began an oration, while two supporters held his green banner overhead. But he dared his opponents too far, and when he grew eloquent about the sword-blow that should shatter the Prime Monitor's mace, the Government party rushed the platform. A fight ensued in which the banner was destroyed; and the supporters used the sticks of it upon their assailants. When order had been restored the motion was put to the House, " That Self-government shall be abolished." By a crowning jest of fate, many of the malcontent Littlemen voted *No*, thinking in their excitement that they were voting against self-government. So the No-government party, although they had by now an overwhelming majority, were defeated. But the next division-day saw the downfall of self-government. So the boys thought, at all events.

Too much importance must not be made of such incidents as this, but some interesting comments arise from it. The first is that teachers who really give their boys freedom of speech and action, and do not only make a pretence of it, must be prepared to look on and see differences of opinion carried to such extremes as this. If you interfere at any point and say, " I can't have this," then you are abolishing self-government in those four words. If the boys are to worry through on their own account, and in the end achieve some good working system, the teacher must give them time, and be patient while they work out their experiments.

My second comment is this: The boys for all their excitement were not abolishing self-government at all, but merely the political or parliamentary aspect of it. The cry, " Mr. Cook shall rule over us," simply meant that, as Sir Reginald had said, the one thing needed was a strong Prime Monitor. The boys were tired of nagging, tired of votes of censure and an almost weekly change of government. But under my rule the boy-officials carried out their appointed tasks as before. The only change was that I was not called a Prime Monitor, and that I called my cabinet a committee !

But while such fights as this were going on, and before I saw how little they really touched the principle of self-government among boys, I used to feel very disheartened. Let us then consider divisions and votes of censure and such machinery abolished, and see what it is that the boy-officials really do in the way of self-government. The following is an account written a year or two ago of our experiments with the lowest forms : *

The most well-ordered classes are those in which a body of boy officials has control. There are so many details of organization in the rule of a corporate body that the form-master who would run his class systematically must either spend half his time in matters of routine, to the neglect of his teaching, or omit some details of the necessary administration. In the lowest forms where *everything* has to be systematized and done by rule, we hand over a large proportion of classroom administration to the boys. The youngest playboys need the strictest rule, but the strictest rule itself can be administered by the youngest playboys. In the first form you may have a single monitor and a number of attendant spirits. His assistants are responsible each in his degree for the tidiness of desks, the readiness of books, the opening of windows, and the boys' part of the scavenging. The monitor himself plays many parts. He pricks the late-comers and the absentees, and collects their excuses ; he harasses the staff for the weekly reports, marshals his men at need, and acts deputy in the master's absence. He announces the homework in the evening and collects it the next morning. All these duties are his even when the master is present ; and it is he who waits until the class is quiet before dismissing them. A form-monitor is appointed for his fitness, and is not always at the top of his class. It has proved a good plan to put in authority aged persons who otherwise might be in danger of doing little or nothing.

In IIb (average age under twelve) it chanced appropriately in connexion with our reading of " Le Morte Darthur " that certain boys should be knighted for single deeds of prowess or for general renown. Thus it happened that a certain six came to be known as *The Knightly Guard*. There was the Knight Captain, who held supreme sway, while the rest divided among them

* See Perse Playbooks, No. 4, p. 21.

the control of the homework and the desks, and those other cares with which a Knight could be charged. In this form the officers have a fuller responsibility. A Knight of the Guard holds a daily *wapenshaw* to assure himself that all have fit and ready their equipment of pens, ink, and paper ; and the Knight Captain marshals his men orderly from one room to another. The Knight Captain has his troubles of discipline just as any teacher has. But there is always perfect goodwill on both sides. Let us emphasize this point.

At the end of the school day the class is restless. Perhaps after prayers the inefficiency of the Knight in charge of the homework delays dismissal. Several squires make protest, others volunteer information. The master simply waits. Add to this chatter the hum and bustle of other traffic, such as the collection of exercises and the packing of satchels, aggravated now and then by the intrusive voice of some Casca crying " Peace, ho ! " and you will understand that " disorder " is the only word to describe the condition of this perfectly well-meaning class. Now the Knight Captain has a badge of office, a mace made by one of the Knights, consisting of a gold handle of wood about a foot long attached to a blue wooden ball about the size of a man's fist. With this the Knight Captain knocks once on the table, and silence immediately follows. I say that on the tap of the mace *all* traffic and bustle is suddenly suspended. flitting functionaries slip into their seats, and there is dead silence. Then at an intimation from the Knight Captain, " Homework " confesses that he cannot remember " the Maths," and some one is called upon to make good the deficiency. The homework is then properly announced ; and perhaps another official gives warning that certain cards are to be brought without fail on the morrow. Maybe the Knight Captain, in giving out his various notices, requests that certain boys remain to confer with the master about some work. Then he taps again. All sit breathlessly quiet while the Knight Captain solemnly holds aloft a pin, and then drops it. Every one hears the resounding fall of the pin. Then follows a final tap of the mace, and off they run. Such was the daily ceremony of dismissal in this Form.

In saying there is goodwill on both sides I mean that

intentional noise or " ragging " is unknown between them. Thoughtless and undisciplined some small boys will be, but to " rag " the Knight Captain has never entered any one's head. On one evening in the week I did not appear at dismissal. By report I gathered that there had been some good healthy noise in the transaction of affairs. Busybodies and sticklers for accuracy delayed the class, and then " every man said his advice and the noise was great in the Court.' But all members agreed that things were getting better every week. My dictum would be that the noise they make is the noise they are learning not to make. A visitor who was present one evening told me : " There was a fair shindy, but they got all the business done and were not dismissed until there was absolute silence. But I should like to see any one try that game with our boys. They would be off in a great racket without waiting for the homework or any blessed pindrop ! "

Which set of boys has been *spoilt* ? Those given the freedom and self-government of Play, or those others who are taught that work and play are incompatible, so that they look upon school as a necessary evil ? There are head masters, and even assistant masters, who are saying : " No play for me ; but strict obedience and hard work. The boys shall do what *I* wish. Give them their heads indeed ! Life's not a game, sir, or a joke, if that's what you mean with your ' Play.' The great fault of this age is to be casual, to take things easily. But I'll knock the slackness out of these loafers. I'll make 'em sit up." * When I hear this I think that life is indeed a very good joke, and most laughable.

Although the boys when left to worry things out for themselves soon find the party game artificial and unsatisfying, they never tire of taking charge of real affairs. There are a hundred details of class administration which one is able with perfect confidence to leave in their hands. One relies on the assurance that a little thing is often better done by some one who considers it no small matter, but one of the weighty responsibilities of office. And the official duties are not always trivial by any means. The librarian's office, for instance, is

* This, I fear, sounds very coarse ; but the words are those of a head master of a secondary school as quoted to me by one of his assistants.

no sinecure, for books are constantly being borrowed from the shelves, and he alone is responsible for their return. It may take him a week to trace a borrowed volume that has gone from hand to hand unregistered. The official who is responsible for the collection of written exercises has also an important task. Even on the old cut-and-dried homework system, where the same exercise was set overnight for the whole class, and collected on the morrow, it was not always easy to get all the exercises delivered punctually. And homework with us generally consists of half a dozen different types of work on the same day, such as prose studies, ballads, chap-books, and ilonds. Some of these take several nights to complete, and need not be presented every morning. Such things as this complicate the duties of the official.

The word " official " did not please us long, and none of the words in common use, such as " monitor," " prefect," " captain," " director," " manager," seemed to us fitly to describe the boy-official-in-charge-of-the-lesson. So I introduced the word *Mister*. The word is a coinage, but it is coined of sterling metal. The word " mistery " still exists (though now confounded with " mystery " and written with a "y "), and means a craft or occupation. The dictionary will show you that " mistery " is parallel with " ministry " ; so our new word " mister " is coined as a parallel to " minister," and means " the fellow in charge of the craftsman-players." " Mister " is not pronounced like " Mr." but as though it were written " mistère " and pronounced with a thoroughly English accent.

The teacher who has permitted self-government in his classes, on whatever system, must be careful not to interfere when interference is not necessary. Force of habit may cause the teacher on entering the room to say to the homework mister, " Collect the homework, Jack."

" Yes, sir," says Jack, and begins to do so. But he possibly remarks, " I intended to collect them after the lesson." That means that Master Jack is a little hurt, look you, and justifiably so.

Even while conducting a lesson myself, asking a series of questions or expounding some matter to the class, I have found it feasible to leave the responsibility for order and quietness in the hands of the chief monitor. You may think that the boys could hardly be disorderly while a master with any disciplinary power at all is actually addressing them. But the Play Way methods are nearly always stimulating. Questions are asked in such a way that (theoretically) every one is anxious to answer at once. A matter is expounded in such a way that, even while the master is speaking, half the class is bursting with questions, and the other half bursting to tell the master what he apparently doesn't know or has chanced to overlook. There is a liveliness about such lessons, an effervescence, which is most heartening. It is possible, of course, for the master at the same time to keep the class as lively as this and to keep them in hand. In reality he has them in hand all the time. But there are good reasons in poetry and in composition lessons why he should confine himself to stimulating the boys, and leave the mister to keep them within bounds.

One of my friends affirms that such a live condition of the class would kill him in a week. During the lessons when he himself is teaching he will not allow one boy to fidget with a pen or to finger his ink-pot. He says it gets on his nerves. So while he roams about the room, waves a pointer, or does as he will with his hands, the boys must sit still and forget they have hands at all. Of course it is just a matter of what the teacher sets himself to do. If you demand *dead silence*, a little clicking noise may easily drive you frantic; but it is wiser always to be prepared for just a little more noise than the class is likely to make. Thus, so far from having to crush the signs of interest and energy, you are always expecting them.

But of course no gratuitous noise need be allowed, and no show of spirit countenanced, that is not clearly directed to the advancement of the work in hand. The mister can look after this while the master teaches.

Again, if it should be necessary for the master to speak when a lesson is running itself, or when the class is dispersing after a lesson, he could of course cry " Silence." But it is equally effective and more in keeping with the self-government principle for him to turn to the mister and say, " Get me a silence." Then the mister taps with his mace, and the class is attentive.

These suggestions will appear not only ridiculous but shocking to many teachers, but they are only addressed to those who have already instituted some form of self-government in their classes.

Sometimes when teaching a self-governing class of which I was not the form-master, I have put both the mister and all his men on their mettle, and instantly obtained model behaviour simply by observing, " The discipline of this class seems to be rather weak."

If, owing to shortness of time or for any other reason, a teacher is disinclined to allow the institution of a cabinet, or any body of officials, he should nevertheless have at least one mister at all times. This mister should be elected by the class, but if one boy, and one boy only, seems fitted for the office the teacher may deem it wise to appoint him. The advantages of having a mister are many. He represents not only all that was represented by a " form monitor " in our day, but a great deal more. He will perform for the master all the duties which a company sergeant-major performs for an officer. A good mister is one's right hand man, and can be a very busy little person. I once had the same boy as my mister for a whole year. The committees in charge of various lessons, such as Speeches, Shakespeare Acting, Chorus Recital of Poems, and the rest, changed from time to time, though this boy held a prominent place in most of them. And when the class for a time ceased to bother about electing committees he remained as my ever-ready assistant. He was a very quiet boy, and did not enjoy the position for the sake of any opportunity it might afford for officiousness or showing off. On the contrary, he was too retiring altogether, and could not be persuaded ever to act a part in any play or even to make a speech during lecture-lessons. Perhaps some measures should have been taken to make him come into the open, since so much of the class-work was active and oral. But he was by no means idle during these lessons, nor did he lose the value of whatever was being done, for the *administration* of the whole affair was always in his hands. It was he who found the speakers, or did the stage-management.

And when these little boys performed a play in the school theatre it was the mister who saw that the clothes were put away in the right places after each of the many rehearsals. It was the mister who helped them to dress, handed each his properties as he required them, and ran all the business behind the curtain and in the tiring-house, without a master's assistance. Only he who has had to act as manager, producer, dresser, and general nurse to some twelve or fifteen boy-players of twelve years old can appreciate the magnitude of this feat for a boy. But this boy would never appear in public. His was really an extreme case, and it was obvious that the little good he would get from acting a part now and then, or making a few isolated speeches under urgent entreaty, or even under pressure, would be more than counterbalanced by the acute distress he would feel all the time. For it was plain that such reluctance to appear publicly would never wear off even if he should be compelled to appear every day. After all, he certainly knew what he *could* do, and he gave the community a more thorough service than any other boy I have known. It is important to state, too, that as he found more and more scope in the charge of affairs his other work in English showed a distinct improvement, and though he was not a boy adapted for school studies at all, teachers of other subjects, including French, Arithmetic, and Nature Study, made special mention of a noticeable change at this time.

In his capacity as mister there were many occasions on which he should have made announcements, but these he either persuaded another official to give out, or he pinned a notice on the screen, or simply asked the master to tell the class so-and-so. For a whole year this mister was in charge of the discipline of the class, and his position was never challenged nor his authority openly questioned. Only on two occasions did he report a difficulty, and in each case his judgment was found right. Once was when he had made a boy scavenger for leaving waste-paper about. The boy made no objection, but as his scavenging was not satisfactory the mister kept him at it for a second week. To this the boy objected, but it was not he but the mister who came to me for an opinion. Then the three of us in conclave came to the momentous decision that a scavenger must scavenge. The second occasion was also a matter of untidiness. The mister always pinned up a list of the names of those whose desks had to be made tidy before the same hour of the next day. Once he added to this the names of two whose satchels were bulging with an accumulation of old papers, and so stuffed that nothing could ever be found in them when wanted. The culprits in this case protested that their satchels were their own concern. But when the mister had pointed out that the state of their satchels occasioned trouble for them and for him and for the master, owing to the temporary loss of homework and other necessary papers, they had to admit the justice of his case.

This mister fulfilled many clerkly duties. For a year he kept the chronicles of the lectures and recorded the title of every lecture, the speaker's name, and the marks. This book has been of inestimable service for purposes of reference and reminder in the writing of one of these chapters. He not only collected weekly reports from the masters (some of whom were busy outside the school and difficult to catch), but copied all these reports on to the cards ready for the form-master's signature. Many an administrative duty which in the rush of busy days a form-master (surely to the detriment of his boys) cannot but neglect, or at least postpone, was thus punctually and efficiently carried out.

Business connected with a little school theatre often detained me in another building after school lessons were over. But the mister could always be relied upon to see that homework in all subjects had been set, and to conduct an orderly dismissal. Dismissal by the mister can become so much the order of the day that the boys, when the master is there, do not regard him as being present for that purpose ; in fact, so long as the master remains in the classroom after school one boy after another will have some little matter to discuss with him, or some piece of work he is engaged upon to present for approval. All those countless questions which only children can think of will fill the air, until the master takes flight, and then the mister calls order for dismissal.

This mister held himself responsible for the good name of his class at all times, and delighted to relate accounts of their doings in other lessons. Once the whole company got into trouble with a master, and were all put down for detention. The mister of his own accord reported the whole matter as it had fallen out, and concluded, " And then, sir, Mr. —— said he would put us all in detention."

" Well, what of it ? " I asked, judging that I was expected to see Mr. —— and persuade him to let them off.

" Nothing sir," replied the mister, " only I thought you'd like to know how it happened."

INDIVIDUAL RESPONSIBILITY IN LEARNING

The sense of responsibility for one's own actions, pride in self-control and loyalty to one's group are a great stimulus to well-doing. If self-government were established in schools, not experimentally here and there, but as a *tradition* of method, a boy would no more dream of fooling during lessons than he would think of fooling while his side was fielding in a cricket match.

If this seem an exaggeration, that is because the master's attitude has still to be considered. I mean the master regarded as subject-teacher. If he persists in spoon-feeding, then what has just been said in praise of self-government will not hold good, because spoon-feeding and complete self-government in a classroom cannot exist at the same time.

Why not ?

Because complete self-govenment must include for the boy the control of his learning as well as the control of his discipline. That is a very important view of the scope of self-government, and one to which too little attention has been paid.

Suppose for the sake of clearness we divide a boy's school activity into two parts, behaviour and learning. Now most teachers in considering self-government think of it only in relation to discipline. Those who have tried it find that the boys *behave* much better when given responsibility for their own behaviour. Very well then, why not bring in self-government for the other side of school activity, and test whether or

72

not the boys will *learn* much better when given responsibility for their own learning ?

But how can this be done ?

The question of how to persuade a boy to feel responsibility for his own learning, and to realize that nothing can be taught him which he does not cause himself to learn, is perhaps the most difficult problem which a teacher has to face. I have had the privilege of discussing the problem very thoroughly with two or three thoughtful teachers. All agreed that spoon-feeding was bad. But they said one often had to fall back upon it when the boys did not pursue learning of their own accord. That form of teaching (or learning) is best, we agreed, in which a boy sees a mark and aims at it. The function of the teacher is to stimulate the boy to fix his eye on a mark, to encourage him to pursue it, and to help and correct him when necessary. But all this activity on the part of the teacher presumes a previous *activity in learning* on the part of the boy.

This activity on the part of the boy is what I mean by self-government in learning—responsibility for his own studies. And the problem is, " How can the teacher set in motion this *activity in learning* ? " *

Well, I have my solution. I cannot answer for teachers of a different class of subject ; and perhaps for the teaching of Latin, French, Mathematics, and Science my suggestions will be of no avail. But for the study of literature in the mother tongue, and for the *making* of literature in the mother tongue, in plays, poems, and prose, the suggestion which I am about to put forward has proved satisfactory over a period of four years. And further, the principle, so far as can be seen, holds good in the practice of other arts such as acting, speaking, dancing, and also in handicraft.

The driving-power must be interest. One can be interested in the means or in the end, but the means is only right if it leads to the end. Therefore, you say, we must first decide what is the end, and then work towards it. True, but what do we mean by the end ? An immediate end or an ultimate end ? Immediate ends must satisfy, for we shall never find

* The word " activity " in this connexion must not be confused with the physical activity of the methods described throughout this book.

the ultimate end. If there is any ultimate end to our pursuit it is so far off that none of us can see it. That elimination leaves us with ends near and ends remote, but no ultimate end, and therefore we are always on the way.

But as the means is only right in so far as it leads to an end, we must postulate an end of some kind, in order to determine our course of action. And this is where teachers fail their pupils. They give them no end to work towards, no mark upon which they may fix their eyes.

Suppose a boy asks, " Why must I do this exercise ? " The reply is, " Because it will help you to learn the language." A shrewd boy sees that this is no answer, because he can always ask, " Why must I learn the language ? " And after five minutes of such questions he would have pushed the wisest philosopher to the last refuge of casuistry. Such questions the schoolmaster in self-defence cuts short with, " Because I tell you to," or " Because you must, and there's an end of it." Thus compulsion is the end, and instead of some mark before him upon which he may fix his eye, the boy gets only a peremptory push from behind.

But what is the alternative ? What is there to save us from this nightmare of an ever-receding objective ?

My answer is that we must give our attention to what is usually called the means, and make that our end. Thus we get something definite to do at once : what lies nearest. We put ourselves heart and soul into pursuing this immediate " end," which of course is no end at all, but just one of those milestones marking the stages of the eternal way.

A discussion of the ethical side of this question would be engaging, but the reader expects definite and practical proposals. So I will endeavour to be quite explicit.

If a boy is to be responsible for his own learning he must have an interest in it. I have already shown how much is included in this term " interest." A boy must have his heart set upon what he is doing. Some things are interesting in themselves, others are not. Those that are not interesting must be associated with the things nearest at hand which *are* interesting.

Interest, whether immediate or remote (but not too remote),

is what the teacher must depend upon to set in motion and to keep in motion that *activity of learning*, the creation and fostering of which was our problem.

For the practical purposes of school the immediate interest is what you must chiefly rely upon, more especially with young boys. But tasks not immediately interesting in themselves will be undertaken readily and accomplished thoroughly if they contribute directly to something not too far off which *is* of interest.

Take an example : a boy may not find it interesting to learn lines of blank verse by heart, and so long as he cannot see that any end or purpose is served by learning them he will not be active in his learning, will not be doing the work because his heart is in it, but because the master has the power to make him. The fact that his general culture is served by the performance of this work leaves him cold. The end is too distant, and so the work becomes not a pleasure but a task.

But now suppose that same boy to be learning blank verse lines in order to take his part in the performance of a play. Now the uninteresting work contributes directly to something near at hand which *is* of interest. Instead of twenty or thirty lines poorly studied and delivered, without life, you will find him readily learning even two or three hundred lines. And being now active in his learning the boy is anxious to be taught still further, and willingly studies to master the extra tuition in the way of expression, delivery, action and so on which his teacher gives him.

Similarly, a boy may find it a bore to write well, but if you ask him to practise until his handwriting is neat enough for him to copy some of his work (or even some one else's work) into an album in which you take a pride he will do his best at once.

Drill may be dull, and smartness at a detention drill can only be obtained by the harshest discipline of a drill sergeant. Fear is the motive. But if you are practising scouts for a display, or cadets for a section competition or for an inspection, you get them to take a pride in their smartness and efficiency —so much so that the good fellows rejoice in a strict and exacting sergeant, and are very unhappy if they are drilled by some weak or inefficient commander. Interest now is the motive. Those who think there can be little room for self-government in such a thing as drill simply do not understand what self-government means.

Notice that the interesting end for which a dull task is willingly undertaken is not always greater than the task. The means is generally of more value than these false ends. For, as I have said, these so-called ends are only encouraging mile-stones marking stages on the eternal way, and it is the going that really matters. A boy may be persuaded to do the really valuable work he disliked for the mere sake of some compara-tively trivial thing he is interested in. The drill, for example, is the thing of real importance, and the display or the inspection is nothing but a tape a hundred yards down the course for him to run to. When the boy's interest is not stimulated in some way he has to be pushed, and you never yet saw any one run at top speed with some one pushing! Carrots ahead are better than a stick behind, for a goal is always better than a goad.

Teachers are ready to admit all this, but they seem unable to find carrots or bits of tape. They do certainly give marks and prizes, but that the use of these as an *incentive* is either ineffective or harmful needs no demonstration here. But until teachers look at things from the Littleman point of view they will never be able to lead Littleman.

Further to illustrate the contention that interest in even a trivial " end " will cause a boy to do really valuable work which he could not otherwise be brought to take an interest in, let me give an extreme example : The writing of poems and ballads seems to me a good thing for a boy's study of language and literature. A boy may fancy he cannot make poems, or is not interested enough to try. You can of course set him to make ballads as a task. But the work is all but useless to the boy unless he takes an interest, and is active in his own learning. Well, many a Littleman who saw no fun in writing poems did see the fun in making a chap-book of his own, a gaudy little book tied with bright ribbons and bearing a fine title on the cover. But there has to be something inside the chap-book. So many a boy who cared little for poems for their own sake has put his whole heart into making them, and making them good enough to pass chap-book standard. Strange, is it not ? But if that is Littleman's way it is the teacher's business to take count of it.

But not only will a boy sometimes do good work for an apparently trivial end : the other aspect of the case is also true. That is to say, boys who are not interested to achieve some end can be encouraged to achieve it if the means thereto be made interesting. This does not mean that schoolwork shall all be made easy and pleasant. Keenness takes necessary labour in its stride. Once the boys' interest is aroused they will cheerfully overcome that modicum of drudgery which is an indispensable part of all undertakings.

Take an example of this other aspect—a study, which does not in itself interest the boy, mastered because he has been interested in the stages which led up to it. I consider a knowledge of stage-craft essential, not only for the practice of play-making, but also for a due appreciation of Elizabethan dramatic literature. Young inexperienced boys would find this study very dull, for by stage-craft in this connexion I do not mean mere matters of entrances, exits, scene-divisions, and scenic or lighting effects ; but rather a critical study of the dramatist's art and workmanship. When I gave a course of lectures on this subject to senior boys, we read plays and some of the best dramatic criticism, and one or two of them entered into the spirit of the study. But eight out of ten, although this was a chosen group out of the sixth form, were as bored as possible. and though the matters under discussion were interesting in all sorts of ways, they would not become active in their own learning.

This failure to learn on their part was probably due to the fact that I was spoon-feeding, doling out facts, and then doling out conclusions drawn from those facts, and leaving these boys no responsibility in the study, no self-government in the process of learning. For they were not idle or stupid boys, and therefore the fault was most likely in the method of teaching.

The same study was then undertaken with junior boys in the third form, and even in the second, but on the Play Way. The magnitude of the undertaking never appalled them, for " The study of dramatic art and workmanship " was never mentioned. Long prosy discourses did not bore them, because discourses were not delivered until the boys had obtained enough interest in and knowledge of the subject not to find them prosy. And then they delivered the discourses themselves !

We simply took a play of Shakespeare and acted it. We soon found that certain things had to be done, and that their doing was directed by the dramatist. The boys were interested in acting the play, and soon became interested in observing many things essentially connected with the acting of the play. They were fascinated when many examples showed how the " scenery " was given as part and parcel of the play, and was meant to be carried in the mind's eye. When it was further shown, not in lectures, but always in a passing reference while play was going on, that Shakespeare also gives most of the necessary stage directions in the lines, the boys were delighted, because as they said, Here were they acting a play, and the play itself told them what to do. Then it does not need any great persuasion to get a boy who is acting a certain part to study the character he represents. And by such natural processes, always mingling the practice with the instruction, and drawing rules out of examples instead of hunting for examples to illustrate rules, the interest was maintained through all the upward stages.*

In the end these boys had a considerable acquaintance with stage-craft and dramatic workmanship. Several third-form boys gave lectures on the subject in connexion with Henry IV. The lecture of one boy (aged 12½) lasted through four school periods because the others raised so many points for discussion and questions with which he had to deal.

* Although these active methods are here instanced as ways of engaging the interest of the boys their attractiveness is not by any means the sole reason for using them. We act the plays we study, not only because it is entertaining to do so, but because plays are made to be acted. The making of broadsides and chap-books also was introduced (and many another handicraft proposed), not only for the fun of the thing. All this was really a tiny part of an ideal scheme for connecting the arts and the crafts, of bringing lore to life and life to lore. But the classroom system made any adequate realization of this dream impossible. We must wait for a Play School Commonwealth.

Does any one imagine that third-form boys could find enough interest in this subject of dramatic craftsmanship unless their interest had been catered for step by step from the start ?

In connexion with plays the need for acting is obvious, but in other connexions people have often thought there was an unnecessary amount of play in our classroom. Visitors have indulgently observed, " Of course your aim is to represent the extreme as a demonstration of the Play Way." Toys and a miscellaneous assortment of apparatus, much jumping about, some dressing up, and often quite a din—all this as a method of teaching literature and composition has often moved my friends to jocular comment. There seemed to be more of the gamesome element than was really inherent in the subject under study ! Quite so. But the boy is more important than the subject, and I fancy there was rarely more of the Play Way than was suited to the nature of the active self-learning, self-teaching student, Littleman.

Such, then, is my solution of the problem, " How is the teacher to set in motion *an activity in learning* on the part of the boy ? " As has been said already, the method was only devised in and for the practice of what can best be described as " the arts." But it may be that some of those masters of arts engaged in teaching languages, mathematics, history, and science would find their younger pupils more active in learning if the masters and the boys between them could devise methods of study which were at once as interesting as the finest game and as valuable as the deepest study—in short, Play-ways.

CHAPTER IV

LITTLEMAN LECTURES

> He first begins to perceive himself, to see or taste, making little reflections upon his actions of sense, and can discourse of flies and dogs, shells and play, horses and liberty : but when he is strong enough to enter in arts and little institutions, he is at first entertained with trifles and impertinent things, not because he needs them, but because his understanding is no bigger, and little images of things are laid before him, like a cock-boat to a whale, only to play withal.—JEREMY TAYLOR.

THERE is a school-lesson which is able to hold children from other play and old men from the chimney-corner   The game may be played anywhere and by any number of persons, and no apparatus is required.   All the work is done by the boys, and the master may if he likes take no active part at all.   Yet every moment of the time is filled with something of value to all.

Briefly the scheme is but this : The boys come out one at a time and speak to the class for a few minutes on subjects of their own choosing.   The lectures may be either prepared or extempore.   One member of the class acts as chairman and announces the speaker, another goes about to discover who is ready to speak next and upon what subject, and a third official at the close of each lecture ascertains the marks.   The marks are apportioned by the boys of the class, voting with a show of hands.

This scheme, like most of our methods, originated in a chance discovery, which was afterwards adapted in various small ways to suit current requirement.

In the summer term of 1914 I was much interested in oral composition.   We had just published a book of prose studies,* and the boys were reading these in class, and trying to equal them.   The published work of their fellows in

* Perse Playbooks, No. 4.

"The Gods" dictating their Lines after inventing the "Rag" Scene
in Baldr's Death (Act II, Scene 2)

the class above had an immediate interest for the Littlemen. And, for my part, I was so full of enthusiasm for the pages we were reading as to overlook for the moment the method which had produced them. We were, in fact, working on entirely wrong lines, for those prose studies had not come of reading prose and admiring it, and trying to equal it in imitation. They had come of new practice. So the books were put away, and the boys were called upon to deliver extempore prose studies orally. But the boys, come hot from the study of literary models, naturally kept their attention fixed upon the *style* of what they were saying.

The result was horrible. Boys would go up to the platform one after another and either spout forth turgid orations, insincere and meaningless, or they would build up with much pausing and going back for self-correction the most laboured of narratives and the most highly-coloured descriptions. We heard too much of *evening* and of *sunset* ; the " gentle breeze " became terribly familiar. People ceased to go naturally from place to place, they either " wound their way slowly down the hill," or " wended." One came to anticipate with a nervous fidget such phrases as " The silence was only broken by . . . ," or " Now all is bustle and confusion," or, as a peroration. " Until at last the something somethinged and all was still."

I soon saw what was amiss. Our interest in the finished work of others had led us to believe that we could take up the work as it stood, and carry on. The boys were working on the assumption that the use of this effect or that turn of phrase would make good prose. As a result they were simply cultivating *cliché* and empty journalese. Although I had just written an emphatic exposition of the play-methods which had brought about these very models, I had actually been encouraging the boys to start from the wrong end of the stick.

This mistake has been described here as a warning to other teachers, who may on such an occasion be equally thoughtless. It is perilously easy to fall away in practice from our own good theories. A teacher of English literature and composition must often be tempted to say to his class, " Let us use this writer as a model," or " Let us take a hint from this essay, or that." But we must never forget that the first essential of good writing is the having something to say. Many teachers with a fine piece of literature before them in class are content to point out the merit of the work rather than to insist that it was only brought about by this measure of toil, by that kind of discipline, and above all by that eagerness which presses forward to make rather than halts at each step to remark progress.

So we recollected ourselves, and returned to the Play Way. There had been no lack of interest in the work, but it was obvious that we had to get back to the position of having something to say. So, one summer morning, when the class-room was very stuffy, the boys were let out into the play-ground—to talk. I suggested stump-speeches, street-corner tub-thumping, believing that a period or two of sheer " rag " would clear away the cobwebs of the artificial effort at " style," and persuade the boys to find their own means of expression. You will see what came of it.

We trooped out into the yard. A chair was brought, and one boy at once stood on it and began to shout against Woman Suffrage. I encouraged the crowd to cry disagreement, or to murmur approval, and to heckle the speaker with searching questions. A defender of the cause followed, and soon the crowd began to show some interest. There were now not only cries, but counter-cries. Next came a crude attack upon Home Rule (the reader will recollect that such matters occupied men's minds in 1914). By this time the class was so loud in the expression of its opinion that I had to reassure several earnest prefects : for prefects no less than masters are apt to confuse noise with disorder.

But mark what happened. While there was actually an opportunity for making a real big noise during school-time, while the master was actually urging the crowd of listeners to shout for or against the speaker's views, and expecting to see a surging crowd of Littlemen making belief of difference for the sake of turmoil—the third speaker mounted the chair and observed that, although he was unable to speak forcibly upon subjects which would cause commotion, yet he was anxious, if they would allow him, to describe certain methods of fishing.

Fishing ! Could anything be imagined more in contrast to the tumult I had been trying to stir up ? But of this offer the

Littleman crowd expressed genuine approval. They cried "Hear hear," and prepared themselves to listen in silence. Now, the very same lecture might have been given under the regime we had just abandoned, for the Littlemen had been quite free to say whatever they liked. So a thoughtless person might easily say that my attempted excursion into Hyde Park oratory was a piece of gratuitous tomfoolery.

Superficially regarded, this shifting from the classroom to the playground, and the incitement to noise and disorder may indeed seem pointless But if you will consider the matter you will agree that it was mainly owing to the uprooting, this breaking away, and the starting of new groups of association in the mind, that the boys were able to rid themselves of the classroom obsession with its tyranny of the book, and to be free of that too heavy burden of models.

When you put less faith in mere instruction and give more regard to the boys' point of view you must take such things as this into consideration. Play Way notions may often look absurd at first sight, but there are more things in boys and the way of treating them than are dreamt of in your pedagogy.

The lecture on *Fishing* began. While it was going on I retired from my place in the crowd.

The speaker divided his subject well, first enumerating the various ways of fishing, and then dealing briefly with each in turn. It was clear that on some points, he could easily have spoken more fully than he did. The class awarded him full marks. The next lecture was on *How to milk a Cow*. It was a short and practical description by a country train-boy, who told us that he spoke from everyday experience. His unsmiling description of some common errors, and the resulting mishaps, caused great amusement. The lecturer seemed surprised that we laughed at the cow plunging her foot into the pail, or lurching so as to upset pail, milkman and all. He was thinking doubtless of the spilt milk and the clumsy milker. But we laughed the more at his earnest manner, and enjoyed it all very much. But he repeated himself once or twice, so the class gave him only seven marks out of a possible ten.

None of the boys remarked on the abandonment of our original plan. They were interested to hear what the lecturers had to say, and had no wish to make a noise. On the other side of the playground railings runs the main street of the town, Yet the attention of the class was not noticeably distracted. I had grouped them so as to *face* the passing traffic, and so every boy without turning round could see that there was nothing to see. The speaker stood on his chair facing his audience, and when any lecturer allowed the noise of the passing vehicles to drown his speech, we simply set him, not nearer his audience, but farther off, and thus persuaded him to make better use of his voice.

On the day when the oral composition lesson came round again the boys were unanimously in favour of going to the playground. They did not pause to think that we could give our lectures with less effort indoors. The interesting lesson was now associated with the playground ; and I really believe that if we had been kept in by rain the Littlemen would have had to think twice before realizing that the lesson was not necessarily ruined.

One of the boys of this form (IIb, average age about 11) came to ask if he might be mister. This meant that he would take complete charge of the proceedings, see that lectures were forthcoming, announce each speaker and his subject, give due opportunity for criticism, see that the marks were apportioned by a vote of the class, and be responsible for the general order of the gathering. Since the petitioner was one of the less able boys in the form, an old-stager, I was very glad to grant his request. Within five minutes the mister had benches set out, a deputy appointed to call for the marking, a lecturer on the chair ready to begin, and the whole class sitting attentive before him. This class, be it said in passing, had never been subject to a mister before. And this new mister was not in any sense aided by my presence. Indeed I was not present at the start. While the first lecture was going on the mister canvassed the circle, and took promise of speeches to follow.

At the close of a lecture the marker stands up and takes the marks in this way. He counts, not very slowly, from one to ten, and the boys raise their hands as he reaches the number they judge fit.

Delays may at first be occasioned by the company's falling

A Littleman lecturing Out of Doors

[See p. 84

A Littleman lecturing Indoors

[See p. 111

into conversation between lectures. This is not a harmful practice, but a perfectly natural one, and should not be ruthlessly suppressed. The boys and I have found it very congenial to chat in pairs and groups about the last speaker and his subject. To break out into a buzz of talk after a period of silent attention —is it not common to audiences the world over ? Why then should this be prohibited in eager boys, O pedagogue ? But we are only permitted a few moments of chatter, for the marker knows his business, and steps out almost at once to take the marks.

There may also be a slight initial difficulty with the voting. Most people are unwilling to rely entirely upon their own judgment, if there is any chance of gauging first the opinion of others. At first during the counting you will see many of the Littlemen looking round to see how the others are voting before raising their hands. But if the boys are warned of this tendency (Littlemen are much interested in Play-ways, and quite frankly discuss ways of learning things), and if they are asked to be ready with their several decisions before the counting begins, they will at once take a pride in their individual judgment. Hands will be thrown up most decisively on seven or eight or ten, as the case may be, and the business put through with dispatch. An experienced marker can count from one to ten and announce the decision in less than a quarter of a minute. That is because he does not actually count the hands held up for each number he calls, but relies, as it were, on the " show." He gets his eye in. The mister then announces the next speaker : " The Chicken will now give a lecture on Architecture." The interval between speeches, for conversation, marking, and announcement has been at most a minute.

At the close of that second lecture-lesson the mister on his own initiative handed me a report-sheet which is now before me. It is dated July 7, 1914, and there are two columns, headed respectively " Speeches " and " Marks " Titles of seven lectures are given (the Littlemen still call them " speeches " from that first tub-thumping experiment), and the marks are chronicled. Then follow eight names bracketed, with the note : " Were going to speak, but there was no time." Then five more names bracketed, with the comment : " Did not offer to speak." At the bottom of the page appear the names of the mister and the marker. Here, then, were twenty-two boys of whom only five were unwilling to take an active part. Truly we had invented a type of lesson which interested the boys. Three of the laggard five were only temporarily indisposed, for they lectured a few days later, as my record shows. These were the subjects chosen by the speakers in that first real lecture-lesson :

> Flying a Kite.
> On the Use of a Handkerchief.
> How to do your Hair.
> Learning to swim.
> Saturn and his Rings.
> Motor-Buses.
> The Rule of the Road.

The lecture *On the Use of a Handkerchief* was interesting because at first sight it appears that there is nothing seemly to say. But the speaker dealt with his subject in the manner of a Book of Courtesy, giving directions of what to do, and warnings against things to be avoided. He made a point of the unobtrusive nature of the operation, counselled his hearers not to indulge in any preliminary wavings, and gave a graphic description of what happens in the urgency of a sneeze, when the handkerchief has to be snatched hurriedly out of a pocketful of accumulated boy-stuff. He raised merry laughter by his catalogue of the miscellanea which most of his hearers had at that moment in their pockets—string, pencils, papers, stamps, knife, whistle, and Littleman alone knows what. Another point which delighted the listeners was the serious warning against " that loud trumpeting sound," though the lecturer, with conspicuous restraint as it seemed to me, refrained from any illustration.

The choice of *How to do your Hair* as a subject also surprised me, for to all outward seeming Littleman does not as a rule " do " his hair at all. But the speaker was a boarder, and had doubtless observed the scrupulous care with which some of the senior boys in the House attended to their toilet. I well remember a clique of youths, when I was about sixteen, who spent nearly an hour on Sunday, between breakfast and morning Chapel, in " doing their hair." There was much talk of " partings," much care to have them clean and straight. And it was essential for smartness to part your hair in the middle rather than at the side.   I always affected to take my hair as a matter of course ; but I bestowed much thought upon selecting among some half-dozen ties, and very nice was I about the adjustment of a tie-pin I had.   But recollections of one's own schooldays must not intrude here.   Perhaps the life of the adolescent boys in our public schools will yet find its H. G. Wells.   But that will be a very different story from the story of Littleman.

Saturn and his Rings was a very good lecture. As an ordinary ignorant schoolmaster I could not on that morning have said two words about Saturn and his Rings, so I listened attentively to this boy of eleven while he told us what he had seen for himself through his astronomical telescope, and what he had read in books.

In common with most other people I have attended popular lectures on many scientific subjects, and I can say that a good Littleman lecturer, speaking very plainly and without tiresome repetitions and unnecessary explanations, will give an attentive listener more information in ten minutes than the usual adult lecturer will in half an hour.   Littleman is not discursive, he says a thing once and leaves it.   Very much, of course, depends upon one's audience.   Littleman is not conscious of any need to talk down to his hearers.   In any case his hearers are boys of like passions with himself.   One thing which makes for a good straightforward style, full of matter, is the need to be brief. The boys listen to every word the lecturer says, and if the interest should lapse or if the speaker should wander into unnecessary wordiness the class at once shows impatience.   " Hurry up," they say ; and show their anxiety to get on to the next speaker.   No one could desire closer attention from a class than is shown during these lectures.

Two American visitors who happened to be present during this experimental period were surprised to see the boys themselves apportioning the marks, and asked if they were capable of judgment.   I said they were as fit to judge in this matter as their master ; more fit perhaps, because they knew more about the subjects chosen, and had themselves tried making such speeches.   At this moment a very good lecture on *The Rule of the Road,* explaining why traffic has to keep to the left, came to an end. The class voted the speaker only four marks.'

" That isn't fair, surely," whispered the visitor.

" How do you know ? " I replied. " There must be a reason.' So I made a little speech, pointing out that in my judgment the lecture was quite as good as others which had been voted twice as many marks. One of the boys in reply pointed out that all they had just heard had been told them in class by one of the masters a few days before. That was the reason. But he paid the speaker a compliment on his style and delivery. Then the clock struck, and so ended the first whole period of Littleman lectures.

When the boys were gone one of the American visitors expressed surprise at the fluency of the speakers, and the width of their vocabulary. " How long," she asked, " has it taken to bring them to such a high standard ? " I told her that this was only the second " lesson " in free lecturing, and that none of these lectures had been specially prepared.

" But how is it possible ? " she insisted. My answer was that in this matter the boys were not being taught at all. They were simply being allowed to speak naturally and easily on subjects which interested them. Any boy can speak fluently if he knows what he wants to say. And as for the erudition shown by some of the speakers, and their familiarity with technical and scientific terms, that also is common among small boys on subjects which interest them. It is only school-teachers who find small boys ill-informed.

But the visitor was charmed above all by the entire absence of self-consciousness. There was no shyness, no faltering ; every one spoke as one speaks to one's friends. That, I agreed, was the most delightful part of this work ; and I was trying to make clear that Littleman is frank and happy and unselfconscious simply because he is not yet adolescent, when this good lady burst in with, " Yes, it's wonderful, but what I don't see is *how you teach them to be natural* ! " Then I saw that I had before me *the* absolute thing in American teachers ; so I simply said, " I don't," and fled after the boys.

After that day, throughout the whole school year, " Speeches " has been the most popular lesson in Forms

IIa and IIb. Improvements in the method of procedure made their appearance one by one. Before long some sage fellow complained that the class was giving the best marks for the most enjoyable speeches, without giving due attention to the style. He suggested that the marks be taken twice, once for "Interest" and once for "Style." This excellent suggestion was at once adopted.

A master who introduced speeches with another class suggested marking also for deportment, because while some boys stood upright and faced the class, others were slovenly in their attitude. This deportment column he proposed to call "Stance.' We experts in IIa approved of the intention. Perhaps the more so because we had observed that masters often addressed the class with their hands in their pockets, a habit of which Littleman had long since cured himself. But we did not add the "Stance" column to our mark-table because we decided that the deportment of a speaker was either satisfactory or unsatisfactory, and could not be appraised in degrees of one to ten.

After two and a half terms had passed it occurred to one of the boys that there should be a column to represent the master's opinion. Certainly some adjustment is necessary in cases here and there, if you intend religiously to copy all these marks into a mark-book, and then periodically to add up the rows and rows of figures, and delude yourself that the result signifies anything. Marks are always given for these speeches, and recorded in the book where all the titles are chronicled. But I never add them together. A numerical mark is quite a useful means of indicating your opinion of a single speech or a piece of prose or even a poem, and so we have always given marks both for oral and for written work, but it is years since I gave up adding these tokens together ! An *order* based on marks in such a subject as English is so unrepresentative, so meaningless, that it might as well be abolished.

A valuable part of the procedure which soon made its appearance was "Criticism." The mister calls for this after the speech and before marks are taken. The coming of criticism did away with the general conversation which had previously filled the intervals. Some of the criticism has been very good, and all of it interesting. Criticism rarely exceeds two sentences in length.

THE PLAY WAY

Anything may be said as criticism, a flat contradiction in a matter of fact,* a correction of some inference drawn or an amplification of some important point treated too briefly. Mannerisms of style, such as the too frequent use of one word or a constant repetition of the same form of sentence, are soon picked out. " Stance " is also dealt with by the critics.

Single speeches were occasionally criticized for lack of interest, or the marking was sufficient to show the feeling of the class. But on one occasion an excellent lecture in several chapters on Architecture was abandoned out of deference to their wishes. The boy had given a chapter each on :

> Greek Architecture.
> Roman Architecture.
> Byzantine Architecture.
> Norman Architecture.

They were excellent lectures and well prepared. The speaker used the troublesome architectural terms correctly and with ease, and his sketches were always clear. Visitors found these lectures very interesting, but some of the Littlemen were bored. No complaints were made during criticism, perhaps because of the master's evident approval. But out of school some of them suggested to the lecturer that he should give it up. So he did. And for his next lecture he brought in a puff-ball as big as his head and gave a most popular object-lesson ! I easily persuaded him not to drop his architectural studies by asking him to write for me " Littleman's Book of Architecture." Thus criticism does make citizens of us all.

But praise is expected as well as blame. Praise is so much more difficult that it may be recommended as an adjunct for set use by those teachers who feel that free lecturing by itself is too much of a game and not sufficiently a task. It is evident that even a few words in appreciation of a lecture just given must be a studied piece of work, and cannot come trippingly on the tongue unless it is merely a bunch of conventional phrases.

Among boys " taught to be natural " criticism in the form of praise is of course rare. One boy, Sir Bevis, himself all but

* There was once a three-cornered discussion about electricity and magnetism which lasted some time and was quite unintelligible to me.

unsurpassed as a lecturer, and a double-tenner nearly every day, made a series of efforts to encourage weaker boys when after long silence they had been persuaded by the mister to make their appearance. But his appreciation generally took this form :

" Sir, I am sure the class has enjoyed the lecture on *Cranes* which Jim has just given. It is a good thing he has wakened from his long sleep, and I hope we shall soon hear him again." Sir Bevis was much in love with his metaphor of hibernation, and used it three or four times in a fortnight. But very soon Sir Bevis was squashed by his peers and bidden to "take a long sleep." It is very difficult to praise well.

In addition to the criticism which comes after a lecture there is current correction by the hammer. One boy in the class holds a small mallet and raps with it smartly on his desk whenever he wishes to pull up the speaker for some error.

What follows here is not a digression from the subject of Littleman lectures, but a brief account of some errors which are corrected by the hammer-boy in current criticism while the lecture is going on. Much of the boys' knowledge of the English language is thus at once learnt and made sure in practice. As they go gaily along they pick up facts of vocabulary and forms of construction, which as a rule—if they are taught at all—are taught in dull lessons by themselves. These facts are in any case not *learnt* in such dull lessons for in the absence of any free practice in speaking during school-time it is impossible for boys to bring this knowledge into play and so make it their own.

The two words *nice* and *lot*, which are the only words I absolutely forbid (save in their special meanings), do not require the hammer. They have become so unutterable that if they *should* slip out in an unguarded moment the whole class jumps and cries " Oo ! " and the speaker hurriedly corrects himself. The hammer-boy raps whenever he misses a word and says, " Louder, please," or simply, " Can't hear." He knocks also for bad grammar, mispronunciation, or any obscurity. In fact it is his business to knock whenever the speaker makes a fault. If he fails to knock some one else cries correction, and the hammer is his. If any reader should fancy that the need of hammer-correction is confined to small boys in school let him attend as carefully as a Littleman to the next adult lecturer or preacher he sits under, and count the number of hammer-raps he might have given if he had had the chance.

In the matter of vocabulary women are great offenders. It is rare to find a woman who troubles herself at all about any relation between the words she uses and their meanings. I have heard a woman use the word *nice* over sixty times in an hour. The word was used to cover about forty meanings such as " warm," " cold," " pretty," " interesting," " useful "; it was also used as an intensive, as in a " nice hot bath," a " nice big bun "; and also to express irony, as in " Here's a nice state of affairs ! " or " A nice mess you've made of it." But *nice* is perhaps chiefly used to express inarticulate approval. Where a baby would gurgle, a cat purr, or a dog wag his tail, a woman says " *Nice*." This use expresses a vague satisfaction upon which the intelligence has not been brought to bear. " How nice ! " " Nice and cosy," " Nice man."

This is at present the most misused word in our language, but many more are being rendered almost meaningless by the habit of overstatement so common to-day. Thus " perfectly," " absolutely," " simply," " hopelessly," " vast " (" a vast deal " is current journalese for " much "), " fine," " splendid," " wretched," " heaps," " tons," " ages." And in fact most of the strongest and most expressive words are becoming daily weaker and less expressive.

Teachers' lessons are not the best corrective of this tendency. The trouble does not arise from lack of knowledge, but from careless, unthinking speech ; and so, after the evil has once been pointed out, it is best corrected while the speaker is actually speaking. The hammer-rap is effective because it gives correction on the spot, and easily prevents the formation of bad habits which later on would be almost too hard to break.

Littleman lecturers are fluent speakers, and do not as a rule indulge in *hum* and *ha*. But the slightest hesitation is ruthlessly shown up by the hammer-boy. A lecturer may say, " This is called the —er—gauge." Rap, goes the hammer. " No *er* ! " says the boy. I have heard this correction many times, although I had not noticed the *er*. Here again you have Littleman as a more exacting critic than his master.

Adult public speakers might gain some benefit from an occasional practice at home, subject to the hammer-correction of their children ! Suggestions of this kind are apt to shock such self-satisfied people as preachers and public speakers. I have tried the suggestion upon one or two. They snort through their noses, and walk up and down uneasily, and talk about " making the boys into abominable self-satisfied little prigs." The abominable self-satisfied big prig, look you, will not have his preserves invaded. Children have been so long suppressed that we had really come to believe that adults were the only ones who could teach, and children the only ones who required teaching.

It is repression which makes for priggishness, smugness, and hypocrisy. A boy treated naturally remains natural and frank and open, and corrects his master just as freely as he corrects his fellows, and not with any malicious glee.

Certain common errors, such as a split infinitive or the beginning a sentence in one construction, and finishing it in another (very common to all speakers), can be pointed out once by the master. The hammer then drives the point home by insisting upon immediate correction whenever the fault occurs. Another familiar mistake is our old friend, " Being a wet day I wore a mackintosh." You may find instances of this error every day in the newspapers, for instance, " Arriving at the station no one was there to meet me."

These mistakes the Littlemen soon learn by practice to avoid ; but there is one error which no amount of correction in school has stamped out. That is the use of " lay " for " lie." When a speaker says " There he laid for an hour," we ask him, " Eggs or bricks ? " And I have expounded many times on the blackboard the distinction between " lie, lay, lain," and " lay, laid, laid." But I now believe the confusion has taken root in the language, and that in another twenty years or so teachers will be accepting even " Lay down " (in the imperative) as inevitable.

But the hammer is heard more often in correction of pronunciation than anything else. To retard as far as possible the deterioration of spoken English I have suggested that *the vowels in unaccented syllables should be pronounced*. At present these vowels are all becoming degraded into a uniform *er* sound. Among us there is a formal speech and an " informle " speech. During lectures the formal is the only one allowed, and

the hammer-boy insists upon " away " instead of " erway,"
" question " instead of " quesch'n," " possible " instead of
" posserble," " general " instead of " gen'rle," and so on.

The subject of pronunciation is, of course, a wide one and full
of technicality. But this particular proposal for reform, namely,
that we should *pronounce the vowels in unaccented syllables* can
be set before boys of twelve without any lengthy or technical
exposition. In fact I set the whole business afoot among the
Littlemen in five minutes, simply by pronouncing a few words in
the formal way as examples. For instance, the following pairs
of words do not rhyme :

table	label
fowl	vowel
boil	royal
garden	pardon
letter	debtor

Try the following also in formal pronunciation : " Seven,"
" message," " pavilion," " absurd," " courage," " interval."

The boys see at once what is suggested, and the practice begins
immediately. At the end of the first lesson—not a lesson on
pronunciation, of course, but a period of Speeches—many will
be proficient in the formal style. You may think it absurd when
you first hear this formal speech. You may be offended at the
pedantry of it. But no one unprejudiced will deny that it is
more beautiful than the jabber and grunt of the everyday slip-
shod pronunciation. It is comfortable to listen to also, because
you hear every syllable clearly instead of having to guess at the
half of every second word. Many visitors have said, " How
clearly the boys speak, you can hear every syllable distinctly.
But they pronounce some of the words rather queerly, don't
they ? " " Yes," I say, " but remember that you only hear
them so clearly *because* they pronounce unconventionally. This
morning you have *heard* syllables carefully pronounced, which
are generally slurred, slipped, or swallowed—left, in fact, to your
imagination. The very fact that those syllables are pronounced
gives an unfamiliar sound to the speech."

Readers may test the sound of this proposed formal speech by
reading a page aloud and pronouncing the vowels in unaccented

syllables. Most people will of course shy at such words as *choc-o-late, en-gage-ment, period, e-lev-en, par-tic-u-lar-ly*, but the use of some formal speech such as this is the only practical means to save us from that process of deterioration which will soon find us saying—if indeed we do not already say—choklit, 'lem, 'tikly.

This proposal that we should endeavour to make our spoken English more clear and more varied by pronouncing the vowels in unaccented syllables has been warmly opposed by several professors of phonetics. But so far as one can judge by their works these phoneticians are chiefly, if not solely, interested in *recording the existing sounds* of spoken English. Recording speech is one work, and an effort to improve the standard of speech is quite another work, and much vain controversy will be avoided in the near future among students of the language if that simple fact is borne in mind. If it is thought advisable to set up soon some official standard pronunciation of English, Englishmen will be wise not to entrust this work entirely to phoneticians. Many of the well-known phoneticians in England to-day* are, or have been, associated with the reform of spelling. And the pronunciation given by them in the books and pamphlets printed in their new spelling should be a warning to all men of taste. I, for one, shall never countenance the slovenly forms of London middle-class pronunciation as standard English speech.

If, then, the pronunciation of English is ever to be more clear and more pleasing to listen to than it is to-day, people other than these satisfied phoneticians must insist on taking a hand. The council of reformers must be truly representative of educated English opinion. Dr. Bridges, the poet laureate, is an eager advocate of the betterment of English, as distinct from the mere stereotyping of present speech as it is. But the point of view represented by him in his book " English Pronunciation " and in the formal speech practice suggested here is deserving of more active support than it can boast at present.

Corrections in grammar and pronunciation, then, are made in passing, in obedience to the rap of the hammer. The interruptions are not so frequent as you would suppose. Though of course some speakers need more correction than others and some

* Among others, Professors Daniel Jones, Noel Armfield, and Walter Rippmann.

hammer-boys are more exacting than others. At the start the mister gives the hammer to one boy, and he relinquishes it as soon as he misses a fault. The hammer often goes through the hands of six or seven boys during one period.

If an error occurs with which the boys entirely fail to deal, the master may at his discretion either interpolate a correction or postpone the matter for more general treatment at a better opportunity.

In the course of the year's experiment a few conventions have grown into our practice and procedure. Some of these are interesting. Many boys found it impossible to compress all they had to say on one subject into the space of a single lecture. Lectures vary in length from five minutes to about fifteen. Some boys are known to have skill in moulding their lectures so that they round off naturally in ten minutes. These the mister leaves alone. Others are known to lose thought of time, and to these the mister makes a sign when they should stop. Boys soon chose large subjects such as *Railways*, *Aeroplanes*, *Dickens* ; and these lectures were given in a series of chapters, or fits. We always call them fits.

A lecture on *Astronomy* was given in six fits, (i) Saturn and his Rings, (ii) Mars, (iii) Venus, (iv) Asteroids, (v) Jupiter and his Moons, (vi) Nebulæ. The boy (aged 11) used no notes, and the speeches showed no trace of labour. He was, in point of fact, just telling us straightforwardly what he knew about the planets. Yet a verbatim record of his lectures would have made an excellent little handbook of astronomy for boys. The same speaker followed with five fits on *Aeroplanes*. We had by this time returned to the classroom (for it was now the Christmas term), and the blackboard was available for diagrams. Another speaker, also aged eleven and a half at this time, lectured on *Modern Fighting Ships* in no fewer than twelve fits. He not only showed a thorough acquaintance with all types of fighting ships and their armament, but proved himself really eloquent. From that time until the end of the year he has been recognized both by boys and masters as our principal lecturer. There is never time for more than six speakers, but whoever else might speak the boys insisted on hearing John W. in every lecture-period. I find in the chronicles that he has spoken on :

LITTLEMAN LECTURES

The Mechanism of a Zeppelin.
Japan.
The Royal Marines.
Contraband.
Turbines.
Explosives.
Military Tactics.
The Battle of Copenhagen.

And on many other subjects. And in every case he is recorded as having received full marks for interest and full marks for style. The fact that most of these subjects are technical, and none of them the kind of subject likely to be suggested by a teacher to a boy of *eleven*, is most significant. And if any reader fears that a good " literary " style is not likely to be developed by speeches on such subjects, I can only tell him that his fears are groundless. Those who have heard these lectures agree that one could not desire a readier or more finished lecturer.

Some taste of his quality will be found in the written lectures given in this book : *The Condition of Affairs in Germany* and *Methods of Defending a Ship from Torpedoes and Mines*. Fortunately it occurred to him at the end of the year to write on *How to make a Speech or Lecture*. The work is also included here. The last-mentioned essay was completed at one sitting in school hours during one of those breaking-up days when regular work is over, and the boys do more or less what they please. Some of the other boys were tidying their desks, some were playing Nine Men's Morris, and the room was full of a most admired disorder. But the writer, so far from being disturbed, was making as much noise as any one in the intervals of his writing.

At one moment he walked up and down the room waving his arms and making a most unaccountable din.

" Steady," I protested, "'that surely isn't necessary."

" Yes, it is, sir," he replied, " some one behind was talking too loud about a secret, and I had to drown his voice."

The secret concerned a presentation they were making to myself. It is a wise practice not to be angry at apparent breaches of discipline without inquiry !

This form IIa was an average form, yet it included six speakers who might lecture with credit even to an adult audience. At the other end were some six poor speakers who preferred to remain silent if they could. The remaining ten or twelve were sound and reliable, willing to speak frequently, and always interesting ; but they were not so well informed as the first group.

It has several times happened that a silent member, who has been thought " weak," has tried his voice one day in criticism or questions, discovered to his surprise that speaking is easy (for a Littleman), and turned out within a few weeks to be one of the best lecturers.

There are not only long lectures which are divided into fits, and lectures which just fill ten minutes or so, but also speeches made up of disconnected observations on a variety of subjects. This kind of speech is called a *Mixed Grill*. If any teacher wishes for a graduated scale of effort culminating in the twelve-fit lecture, here it is : (i) Short question, (ii) Longer question, (iii) Criticism, (iv) Mixed Grill, (v) Single-fit lecture, (vi) Several-fit lecture. But we have found no need of systematic teaching in this matter.

The Mixed Grill serves many purposes. It is a useful safety-valve for the talkative fellow. After his interruptions and proffered remarks have been quashed, his criticism cut short by the mister, and his reiterated questions ruled out of order, he finds he can bear it no longer. So he puts in for a Mixed Grill. He gets the ear of the house, and then " lets them have it "—says his say right out. It is a useful stand-by, also, for the silent member when the mister importunes him for a speech. He has no speech, cannot think of anything perhaps, so he puts in for a Mixed Grill and fills five minutes or so with general remarks, congratulations, reminders, suggestions, or what-not. The Mixed Grill also gives the master an opportunity for saying a few words without seeming to hold up the proceedings. In the space of five minutes one can give the orders for the day, make announcements, point out faults, bestow praise and even set the homework and distribute corrected papers. The only drawback to the master's making a speech or his use of the Mixed Grill is that it invites comparison between his fluency and that of the Littlemen ! This may seem an affectation to some reader, but I can assure him from experience that it is *not* easy for an adult to speak as plainly and fluently as a Littleman. There is the hammer of Damocles too—and " No *er* ! "

It is probable that this scheme of lecture-lessons could be carried right up the school as the boys grew older. But it is certainly advisable to *start* it with boys who are still Littlemen.* If they had a weekly lecture-lesson from the age of ten up to the age of sixteen, the self-consciousness which comes and spoils all about the age of thirteen or fourteen might be rendered less troublesome by the force of *habits of self-expression*. I mean that shyness, awkwardness, and the self-consciousness which often makes adolescent boys unintentionally rude and unsympathetic —these shades of the prison-house might close in less harshly upon a boy who " still is nature's priest," and the shadow fall almost imperceptibly upon one who looked ever about him upon the " vision splendid."

But to *start* lecture-lessons with adolescents (and most public-school masters are chiefly concerned with adolescents) would be quite a different thing. Isolated speeches might be good, as in debating societies, but there would be little of the corporate spirit in the work. Criticism would not be so frank, brief, and to the point. In a word, the spontaneity of Littleman would not be the informing spirit.

But I had an encouraging experience in this respect with Belgian boys. There were nearly forty Belgians in the school, but the group I speak of numbered about twelve, and their ages ranged from eleven and a half to seventeen. They had been in England about three months. They were being taught English proper by other teachers ; and their periods with me were to be devoted, not necessarily to any subject, but to what one of my friends calls " Cookery." . We began by trying to act " Thorr's Hammer."† First a scene was read and explanations given, and then it was acted on the stage with full complement of dress and properties. They enjoyed the acting of course, but understood only the bare plot. The reading was unintelligible both to readers and listeners, for blank verse at its simplest involves many uncommon words. Before long I found that the course would be nine-tenths explanatory teaching and one-tenth

* A Littleman is any boy under thirteen.
† Perse Playbooks, No. 1.

acting ; a proportion which caused me to abandon the play after a first rough reading, for I hold only that teaching effective in which there is at least as much of practice as there is of instruction.

It appeared that these boys knew hardly enough English to put one sentence together, but I decided to introduce them to Speeches. Some of the Belgians had attended lecture-lessons in IIa, so they knew the usual form of procedure. In the absence of a subject I suggested to one boy to narrate the story of Freyr's Wooing,* which they had seen played a day or two before. This was done, but the amusing underplot concerning Beggvir and the blessed pig was omitted. The relation of this underplot made the second " Speech'" By the time the third speaker was due the game was well afoot, for the mister announced. " Constant will now tell us the story of Black Beauty, Fit 1." The fourth speaker told a fairy tale. And with the fifth we made a start in lectures. He lectured on " The Pig." The title of the sixth was " Cambridge." And that brought the period to an end. It appeared after all that these boys could speak English after a fashion. Each spoke continuously for more than five minutes.

One of the first conventions to arise among a company of boy-speakers seems to be a conventional way of beginning and ending a speech. The English boys generally open with " Sir, I have come up here this morning to tell you about so-and-so," and they plunge right into the matter forthwith. They close with, " That is all I have to say " ; or " That is all I will tell you in this fit about so-and-so." The Belgians soon found a little conventional phrase of their own which nearly all of them used. It always made me laugh. They laughed also, but they kept the phrase. " Sir, I will make a speech about so-and-so. I think it shall be very interesting for you." At the close it came again. " That is the end of my little speech. I think it has been very interesting for you."

The chronicles record titles of nearly a hundred and fifty speeches by this group of Belgians alone. Some of them are stories and fairy tales from all sources, including Grimm, " Robin Hood," the " Arabian Nights," and " Robinson Crusoe." One of the eldest boys undertook to tell the story of Monte Cristo. He

* Perse Playbooks, No. 3.

MIXED GRILL ILOND. By T. W. L. Aged 13.

went steadily on day after day, until the chronicler lost count of the fits, and the mister simply announced, " Monte Cristo, next fit." He must have reached fit twenty when the school year ended and left him in mid-career. His younger brother, aged twelve, gave an account of their journey from Belgium, and an expert lecture, on " How to grow Chrysanthemums," from his own very thorough experience. He also gave us " The Tale of a Cherry-Tree."

This was a delightful true history of a cherry-tree which grew in the garden of the English house they now occupied. The old gardener—" He is a very silly old man with a white beard "— asked the boys' father to buy the cherry-tree in the garden. The father said he had no use for the tree, but would buy it on condition that the silly old gardener sat in the tree to keep off the birds. Then the old man went to the boys' mother, and our lecturer acted as interpreter. The mother said that cherries were only cherries for her when they appeared upon a plate. So in the end the three boys bought the cherry-tree from the old man for four shillings. Jean hung a bell in the tree and connected it by a string to his bedroom window. When he wakened in the morning he pulled the string, " and all the birds fly away and eat no more the cherries." The boys sold the fruit to their mother on a plate, at so much a pound ; and, at the last I heard, were on a fair way to regaining their initial outlay in addition to getting their share of the cherries. That, briefly told is the story of the cherry-tree. " I think it has been very interesting for you."

Many of the lectures given by the Belgians were on the usual Littleman subjects, Submarines, Torpedoes, Birds, Flowers, Insects, Architecture. But they made an interesting development of the Mixed Grill. Several boys described tricks with paper and string, or asked conundrums, or tasked us with problems concerning donkeys, fox, geese, lengths of rope, railway-sidings, and the crossing of rivers. More than one lecture-lesson with the Belgians was given over entirely to these parlour tricks and problems. My only stipulation was that the demonstrator should, after the manner of a professional conjuror, *talk all the time.*

But the Mixed Grill in the hands of one boy, H——, became quite an art form. He stood up with a diffident, semi-cynical

air and made a series of observations, so obviously disconnected
and unrelated that the amusement of the class, beginning with
a smile, culminated in roars of laughter. And still the wonder
grew how long he could go on thinking of fresh topics for his
detached observations. It was a most amusing and finished
variety entertainment. The class soon learnt to call eagerly for
" H—— in a Mixed Grill." I will attempt to recall something of
his style. But the quaint effect of his accent and his diffident
air must be left to your imagination.

"Sir, I will give a speech. I think it shall be very interesting
for you. No, it is a Mixed Grill. M—— is telling very well
his Monte Cristo. I think he will finish it some day. Perhaps.
The flowers in this room will soon be dead. I think J—— will
bring us some more. It is very good to have flowers. Yes.
The swimming races was very good. I did not race. I am no
good to swim. L—— is in long trousers to-day. His legs looks
very silly. I think long trousers is no good for him. The people
of Cambridge speaks very bad. They speak in the nose like this.
[Here a good imitation of the Kimebridge accent.] Yesterday
I went to take tea with my friends. Yes. It was a good tea.
Plenty of jam and cakes. Soon I will go again. Yes. English
gardens have no flowers. In Belgium we say of garden without
flower, ' English garden.' Mr. Cook is laughing. I don't
know why he is laughing. Albert is a silly ass, he has broken
my penholder. IIIb acts very well Shakespeare. I like to see
Sir Toby and to hear sing the other chap. I don't know what
he is call, but he sing very well ' O Mistress Mine ' . . ." And
so on *ad libitum*.

The serious-minded will find this ridiculous ; but it is at least
as useful as the usual " exercise " composed of disconnected
sentences. The errors do not, of course, go uncorrected. The
hammer in the hands of another Belgian boy is always ready to
pull up the speaker. There is also another piece of apparatus,
used only by the Belgians. It is a massive wooden thing in the
form of a letter H which is dropped with a great noise whenever
a speaker misses an aspirate. This is called the Belgian H.
But I made no pretence of correcting every single mistake, or
the very idea of free practice in speaking would have been destroyed. The hammer kept them up to the mark in simple

grammatical points, and from time to time I corrected and explained general errors, or mistakes which showed a misunderstanding, such as a confusion in sound between " afraid " and " frightened." For the rest they were simply learning to speak English by speaking it. Whatever happens it is essential that the speaking shall go on. Whether with English boys or Belgians the lectures are the thing of main importance in learning the use of oral English, and if you hold fast to this all the lesser things such as points of correct grammar and right use in vocabulary shall be added unto you.

This is perhaps not so obvious to all as one could wish, for many textbooks on composition still set out to teach first of all the rules, and only bring in actual sentences as examples to illustrate these rules ! Many a class of boys, who, if the teacher only realized it, could be freely lecturing in admirable English periods, have to undergo a laborious study of sentence-making, in which, after much exposition, an exercise is set which consists of sticking together jig-saw scraps of phrases. In this he is most skilful who can best conceal the joins. Chapters in some manuals of composition discuss at length the various figures of speech, and the boys marvel to encounter, and struggle to distinguish, Metaphor and Simile, Allegory and Hyperbole, and even—if you can believe it—Antonomasia and Paranomasia. In a book called " English Composition " I have even found paragraphs on Epanaphora, Epistrophe, Litotes or Meiosis, Prolepsis, Epanorthosis, and Aposiopesis. I do not pretend to remember what all these terrific words mean, but I have copied them faithfully from a modern textbook of composition now in front of me. That sounds more like a catalogue of diseases than anything to do with this our mother tongue. These are, indeed, some symptoms of the disease of pedantry—a malady most incident to teachers.

It is false to claim that these cumbrous phraseological monstrosities of rhetoric are needed even for the special study of literature. Present-day teachers can do no better service to English letters than by encouraging the clear, straightforward saying of what one has to say. Simplicity and brevity do not perhaps exhaust the desirable qualities of style, but they come first. And clear style can only be poisoned by the use of those tricks, graces, paddings, and affectations which are the most noticeable result of successfully working through primers of composition.

Consider, moreover, whether the usual school custom of setting subjects to speak or write upon is not a deliberate fostering of the artificial and the insincere. Even if it is not so, it is at least an unnecessary limitation. Boys will find quite enough to talk about without any officious nursing. The following list of subjects is taken direct from the Littleman chronicles. They are not selected, but represent *forty speeches given on seven consecutive lecture-days.* I give them (except for the grouping of fits) in the order of the chronicles for the purpose of illustrating their variety. Only the first two subjects were suggested, and even those I submitted to the class and not to individuals.

  1. Eating in the Olden Times.
  2. The Willow Pattern.
  3. Maxim Guns.
  4. Nebulæ.
 5–9. Aeroplanes (in five fits).
 10. Air-trains.
 11. Ways of Fishing.
 12. Police Traps.
 13. Work in Nature Study.
 14. Turbines.
 15. Foreign Stamps.
 16. Making an Ilond.
17, 18. Meccano (in two fits).
 19. Preparations of the Germans.
 20. The Classroom Toy-shelf.
 21. Chapbooks.
 22. Military Tactics.
 23. Spring Guns.
 24. Musical Instruments.
 25. How to start a Long Poem.
 26. The Tidiness of the Form-room.
 27. The Largest Crane.
 28. On the Kaiser's Brain.
29, 30. Self-Government (in two fits).

LITTLEMAN LECTURES

31. Explosives.
32. Early Arms.

The remaining eight of the forty speeches chronicled for these seven days are long criticisms, " winding-up speeches," or Mixed Grills.

How to start a Long Poem was advice from the author of the only long Littleman poem, at the time when he was engaged upon *My Christmas Week at Little Pinewood End.**

The four lectures *Ways of Fishing, Spring Guns, Musical Instruments*, and *Early Arms* are all by one boy. His chief delight is in strange gins and quaint contrivances. His ways of fishing were not the usual ones of net or rod and line. Nothing so commonplace would suit him. The essential point of the schemes he described was that one didn't fish in person at all, but set afloat upon the water some ingenious contrivance of planks and string and balancing things. A baited line dangled in the water, and was attached above to a bell or to the trigger of a pistol. " You then lie down and slack it, or you go about your work near-by, until suddenly you hear the bell ring, or the pistol go off *bang*. Then you take a boat and row out——"

This kind of fishing cannot have been indulged in either for the pleasure of the exercise or for profitable return. It must have been devised out of sheer joy in the working of home-made gins. One of our best illustrators brought to school one day a picture he had painted of a quiet meadowland by the river. On the bank a person was lying in a deck-chair while some contrivance floated upon the water. The picture was called " One of Johnny's Gins." His spring guns and his musical instruments were of a like character, ingenious and unorthodox. He could not have invented them all, but there is no doubt that he eagerly collected them from boys' papers, a junior encyclopædia, and the records of savage tribes—those " natives " so dear to the hearts of boys.

The *Early Arms*, again, were all implements of death with something peculiarly and grotesquely effective about them. He drew them on the blackboard, and described with satisfaction the curve, or the twist, or some other diabolical characteristic

* Perse Playbooks, No. 5.

which made these daggers, spear-heads, or bayonets so delight-
fully horrible.

This boy started very modestly, but presently became one
of the three or four best speakers. At first he was very nervous,
and on this account spoke too rapidly. But because of his
wonderful speed the class always called for him if it happened
that only a minute and a half remained before the clock struck !
Not one minute could be wasted.

" Finish up, mister," I would say, " there remains but a
minute and a half."

" Johnny ! " the class would cry, " Johnny can easily do one
in the time." And Johnny always did. I wonder which of my
readers would care to answer such a call.

In spite of this rapid nervous delivery there was never any
fumbling. If he saw a blank ahead where a wanted word was
missing, he went round it. Periphrasis, look you, come into
use, not from study, but from a practical discovery of the need
of it. And with all his hurry he was rarely pulled up for careless
pronunciation. On the contrary, he was correct to a fault. So
much so that he always pronounced *the* and *a* as *the* and *a*, which
is not in accordance even with our formal speech. This and
other overcareful peculiarities caused me to suspend the hammer-
rap altogether during his speeches. The faults of nervous delivery wore off in a little while, and though the rapidity remains,
the correctness remains too, both tempered by much practice.
And it is, as you may well believe, a pleasure to hear a lecture
full of matter delivered briskly and in a clear and almost fault-
less pronunciation.*

If my readers could have been present last term they would
have found it difficult to say whether they enjoyed most
the swift description, aptly illustrated, of Johnny's innumerable
Gins, or the fuller and more measured eloquence of John W. on
the subject of Ships or Military Matters or Foreign Affairs—his
speech never hurried, never dragging, but rounding off smoothly
through period after period until, without any sign of conscious
peroration, one foresaw the inevitable close ; or the thoroughly
practical and equally humorous technicalities of Sir Bevis, or the

* A lecture on *Gins* and two fits on *Model Aeroplanes* by the speaker
referred to will be found at the end of this chapter.

purely simple narrative of Mac, telling straightly what he knew of *Two Birds.**

Sir Bevis lectured always in a number of fits. His subjects were Astronomy, Aeroplanes, and Railways. He spoke upon any topic with equal ease, but one chiefly remembers these three —and his criticisms. His astronomy has already been mentioned. The lectures on aeroplanes, though I can claim no expert knowledge, were certainly most thorough. Every passing detail was made clear by diagrams on the blackboard, every technical term used was explained, and the whole subject divided among the fits with a masterly regard for " plan," " scheme," or whatever we teachers call it when we cut up a subject for purposes of outline.

" That is all I have to say about gliders. In the next fit I will tell you of the experiences of the brothers Wright when they first applied engines to their craft."

It is important to record that Sir Bevis (aged eleven and a half) did not by any means exhaust the material he had available for each fit. He it was who instituted " Questions," in addition to " Criticism." It was his custom to end a fit with these words : " I will not tell you any more in this fit, in order to allow time for questions." The class always had questions to ask—as Sir Bevis expected—and the master also rose to the occasion. For whether or not one's interests ran among aeroplanes, Sir Bevis could always stimulate one to a question or two. Boys would come up to the rostrum one after another, and, with finger on the diagrams, ask for further information. In the end this lecturer found it necessary to give half his time to exposition and the other half to " Any questions ? " In fact the Littleman teacher on the rostrum and the Littleman class in front of him seemed to be so absorbed in one another and in their study of the subject that the official teacher found himself for the time being ignored. But this often happens on the Play Way. This boy's lecture on Railways was not nearly finished when term came to an end. He gave fits on " The Inside of the Engine," " The Wheels," " The Coaches," " The Track," " Signals," and so on. One of his

---

* I do not here exaggerate a single particular, and those who heard the Speeches will bear me out. I have most carefully stated exactly what was to be heard.

minor written lectures is given at the end of this chapter. Out of school Sir Bevis is above all things a Pirate Captain. I have in my possession a big book of his in fifteen chapters called " Littleman Pirates." It was written last winter, and records the pirate play of him and the band he led since June 1910. In 1910 he was only seven.

Mac always lectured on *Two Birds*. He told us of the birds and their habits, described all he saw when he went bird-nesting, and handed round eggs for our inspection. But it was never explained on what principle, if any, he associated the two birds of each lecture. One day it would be " The Starling and the Blackbird," another day " The Thrush and the Wren." It was not because what he had to say of one bird would not fill the time. Because however short or however long his speech might be it was always on *Two Birds*.* Possibly this was an inkling of the comparative method of study. His delivery is simplicity itself, and his pronunciation of English is the most beautiful I have ever heard. It was pointed out to me by an observer that this speaker was also nervous. But one would scarcely have guessed it. The only trace of shyness was in his screwing up a little piece of paper in his fingers. This boy, like the others I have mentioned, was eleven years old, but very childish, and in his manner and appearance might have passed as a year or two younger. I mention this because, according to my experience, it appears that the younger a boy is the better he speaks.

The advice I would offer to the teacher in the matter of the boys' delivery is " Let well alone." There are of course scores of things one *could* tell them, but they are not necessary. I cannot remember having told these boys anything at all about delivery. The obvious danger is that so soon as you mention delivery, or give any directions, you set the boys thinking of how they are speaking instead of giving their entire attention to what they are saying. This seems to me obvious, but I am afraid the warning is needful ; for if there is one thing teachers *will* do, in and out of season, it is—teach. Just as teachers think more of their subjects than of the boys, just as they prefer grammar and figures of speech and the study of sentence-structure to the

---

* In Fit 2 of the written lecture given on p. 122 there are three birds, but that is exceptional.

free making of original prose and verse, so I fear will those who adopt Littleman Lectures soon fall into the habit of directing and correcting delivery, interfering with a boy's own plan of his fits, and in the end even going so far as to set the subjects of the lectures. Then when things go wrong, as they certainly will if Littleman's interest is set aside and his creative power of play harnessed to pull a load of formal rubbish, the teacher instead of loosening the bearing-rein will tighten it ! Littleman will work less well in proportion as his point of view and the needs of his nature,

> Delight and liberty, the simple creed
> Of childhood, whether busy or at rest,

receive less consideration. The learned taskmaster remarking this deterioration, will not think of blaming himself but will blame the boys, and will rule more and more strictly, and *teach* harder and harder. The upshot of this senseless procedure will be " As you were," and repression and compulsion will soon again be the order of the day.

The delivery of one or two Littlemen after a time was marred by signs of striving after effect. I showed a mild disapproval and thought to discourage these precocious arts by laughing at them. The class took it up and there was a ready ridicule for conscious effects. As a teacher I ought to have been satisfied with this success. Is it not so ? But I was not satisfied, I was frightened. I saw that the hearers were not so much expressing a genuine disapproval as they were following my lead. The power of suggestion in the hands of a master who has the good-will of his boys is simply tremendous. One has to be careful how one uses such an influence. Encouragement to a boy to do his best is the one right use. Self-gratulation and scorn of weaker (or merely different) boys could as easily be encouraged by suggestion. Therein lies the responsibility. Any one who has influence must realize that though it is his duty to exert it, his plain duty quite as often is *not* to exert it.

Blackboard illustrations to the lectures are of two kinds, diagrams and pictures. The diagrams are necessary for a lecture on *Periscopes*, for instance, or *Architecture*. These the lecturer draws for himself as he requires them. But he must not be allowed to pause and turn his back to the class while he sketches on the board. He must take the diagrams in his stride, as it were, without interrupting his description. That is one advantage of their use. Another is that the diagram not only helps, but compels the lecturer to be explicit. For he can scarcely be vague and superficial in his account if he is making a diagram of the mechanism as he describes it. The disadvantage of diagrams is that they explain many points which it would have been better for the boy to describe in words. It is therefore useful to recommend to a technical lecturer from time to time that he forgo the aid of diagrams for a fit or two.

Apart from diagrams the pictures in illustration of a lecture are generally drawn by other boys. During a speech on *Spies* or *Lion Hunting*, or during the narration of a story the mister allows two or three of the class to come out and draw on the board in coloured chalks. What they hear they draw; and if they misrepresent the speaker or let their imagination carry them away they generally hear of it during " Criticism."

It was stated in the beginning that no apparatus is required. But though it is not strictly necessary there is nothing to be gained by forbidding it. The lecturer on birds likes to show the eggs he is describing; and when a speaker tells how to make simple toys he is expected to give something in the way of demonstration. Object-lessons given by the boys are much more interesting for the class than those given by the teacher, and quite as full of matter. Once, after several boys had lectured on conjuring tricks and magic coins and so on, we proposed to set aside a whole lecture period for demonstration purposes. The idea was to get a table and put on it some bottles, corks, glasses, pins, coins, sheets of paper, and so on, and then invite speakers to come forward who could make a performance out of these materials. Examinations fell due and interfered with the project, but " I think it should have been very interesting for us."

For the last two terms or so we have had two permanent platform properties without which the boys now feel that lectures are not really lectures. One is a little round-topped table, like a garden sundial column. The speaker stands beside this. The other is a brass bell with a figure of Shakespeare for the handle, and it stands on the table. The mister opens the proceedings by tinging the bell, and he always does so before announcing any speaker. Such trifling details as this have their part in giving character to the proceedings. The hammer, the bell, and the black table; the lecturer standing in the middle of the platform with the mister sitting on one side and the marksman on the other—that and the strict rule of our procedure make up a kind of ceremonial which adds a dignity. And it takes out of our minds unpleasant associations of lessons in which the master, in solitary state upon the platform, faces his class in the stocks, and takes complete control.

In the foregoing account many small and apparently trivial things have come in for notice. Toys, parlour problems, and amateur conjuring tricks have found a mention, and even blackboard scribbling has received official sanction. Most noticeable of all perhaps, to teachers, the small boy's passion for general information and his " love of hearing himself talk " have been taken seriously. Valuable school time has been sacrificed to sheer boys' talk, without so much as a pretence at teaching.

Externally regarded the Play Way certainly appears to consist largely of a busy preoccupation with trifles of all kinds, We cannot recite little poems without our sticks to beat time ; and when we chant

> Rolling, rolling, rolling
> O'er the deep blue sea,

the little cork boat floating in the dish of water seems to claim as much attention as the ship which is the subject of the poem. A boy acting a king must have a crown, even if it be only a paper one. Mister makes a fuss if his bell is missing, and would rather wait while it is fetched than go on without it. This, as every child-lover knows, is characteristic of Littleman the world over. He must have it *right*. Similarly no speaker, whether master visitor, or boy, may omit the conventional opening, " Sir." * He will be " hauled " before he has said ten words. These are all trifles, but every facet of a tiny gem may envision the whole width

---

* Other masters, and visitors too, have on occasion been found bold enough to deliver a speech, or to take a share in debate.

of sky. Toys and games and conventional properties are small
things ; but grammatical rules learnt by heart, and copy-books,
and writing on one side of the paper only, are small things too,
and not so entertaining. I had rather make a mountain out of
a molehill than be the mountain in labour that brought forth a
mouse. Coleridge might have said,

> He playeth best who loveth best
> All things both great and small.

The criminal error of the spoon-feeding pedant is that in his vain-
dealing he ignores the great things and elevates the small to
their place.

For all the care which teachers spend to give importance to
such things as correctness in grammar, accuracy in mathematical
calculations, and precision in scientific experiments, can it be
claimed that the boys feel at all strongly the necessity for this
care and accuracy ? Does it worry the average boy if his nouns
are in the wrong case, or his verbs in the wrong mood ? We all
know it does not worry him ; that is our grief. Yet who will
deny that the same boys can be most punctilious about their
rights, and about the observance of the most minute school
customs ? Who has not seen a hot dispute arise over the breaking of the smallest rule in cricket or football ? Who has not
marked the strength of feeling a small boy exhibits against any
bad form or false play even in the least particular ? Why this
strange difference between in-school and out-of-school ? Don't
ask the boys, ask the teachers. But the teachers cannot tell you
—or rather they won't. It is a matter of *interest*.

Once in asking a question about aeroplanes I called a tractor
a propeller. I was pulled up at once by the boy-lecturer. It is
no use trying it on and saying, "Oh, well, it's all the same." How
would you feel if your pupil regarded indicative and subjunctive
with the same levity ? An illustrator once put one mast too
many on a ship he was drawing. The lecturer happened to look
round and see it. He took the duster and the chalk and put the
matter right before proceeding. The description of engine
wheels by numbers such as 2-4-0, or 0-6-0 is part of a mystery I
have not mastered, but in spite of this I am sure no boy has ever

112

been allowed to describe them wrongly or even to draw them wrongly, in my classroom !

Some one may ask me why the small boy's insistence upon accuracy in story-telling and in lectures and his demands for obedience to rules in games cannot be turned to good use upon his spelling, arithmetic, and so on. My good sir, it can be. It should be. It has been. That is one of the chief claims in this book. If a boy's heart is set upon anything he will see that he gets it right. If his heart is not set on it, the insistence is left to the master, whose heart *is* set on it. It seems clear enough. The Play Way is not a proposal for the relaxing of rules and discipline but a demonstration of the only way in which rules can be naturally enforced, and discipline made to live of its own accord. And that is by the operation of interest. But in education, as in life, the game must not be brought in only to make the rules palatable ! The play's the thing, and only the boy's real interest in it can make it worth the playing.

From the first there has never been any doubt that the boys were interested in Speeches. If for any reason a Speech-period was turned to other uses, it had to be given back somewhere else. On the other hand, the Belgians succeeded in borrowing periods for Speeches which they never paid back. They had a lesson with me in the afternoons of Monday and Friday. For the corresponding Wednesday lesson I was off duty, and they were supposed to be working by themselves in hall. One Friday there were references to recent speeches of which I had no recollection. Also I seemed to have lost touch with Monte Cristo ; and the other lecturers were a fit in advance of what was expected. Inquiry showed that they had held a lecture-lesson by themselves on the Wednesday. They said, " You were absent, sir, and so we make the lesson ourselves only." I pointed out that according to the time-table they should have been in hall. The mister for the day being then asked to give an account of Wednesday's proceedings described a normal lecture-lesson. The chronicles showed also that the usual number of speeches had been made. On the whole, it was quite clear that the stolen lesson had been the counterpart of any lecture-lesson at which I had been present. This was their first introduction to the possibilities of self-government,

and these Belgians were at this time the most unruly members
of the school.

Of course the boys, once they had left the hall and got into
a room alone, especially since that room was in a separate building, might have done as they pleased. And that is what they
did ; for Speeches and good order pleased them better than idle
chat and tomfoolery. The Belgian Littlemen found it difficult
to believe that the time-table was correct. The same mistake
occurred the following week ! In the end they were allowed the
Wednesday period for Speeches, and I saw to it that they " made
the lesson themselves only."

The active interest taken in Speeches by another boy was
remarkable. He was from New Caledonia, and had spent many
years in France, and only a few months in England. It was
nor surprising that he took small interest in the Shakespeare
lessons, nor that he should in consequence have come to be
looked upon as a slacker. He was one day present at a Belgian
lecture-lesson. The following day he brought a list of subjects
upon which lectures might be made. It includes the following :

Monuments of the World.
Rare Animals.
How different Things are made (e.g. Paper, Glass, etc.).
Ways of Defence through Centuries.
Ways of Transport through Centuries.
Ways of Hunting in Wild Countries.
Comparison of Wars in the Past with the Present One.

He also introduced among the Belgians two other topics upon
which many Speeches were made. One was *How I made my Boat.*
Any playboy who has spent a holiday near a pond must have
made a boat, and ventured out in it. We heard tell of many
escapades as interesting as could be found in boys' books. There
were as many speakers on this subject as we had time for. Otherwise I should like to have told of the boats my brothers and I
had made. In especial I remember a home-made punt in which
we sailed on a shallow salt lagoon somewhere at the other side
of the world. We had a stiff cowhide for a sail, and we went out
to shoot black-necked swans and flamingoes. The boat, of

course, leaked—home-made boats are poor fun if they don't leak—and we baled it out with the carpenter's hat. As we couldn't speak his language, nor he ours, this resource perhaps brought home to him as much as anything the flaws in his handiwork. While we were cruising about and trying not to sink, the men on the shore, some of whom had never seen a boat or a fish in their lives, killed and skinned a sheep, then built a fire and roasted it, basting the meat with salt water from the lagoon. And that brings me to the second inviting topic which this boy suggested. He began with *How they cook Fish in New Caledonia*. Another Belgian boy followed with *How the Indians in North America cook a Pig*. A third described *How I cook Potatoes on the Seashore in Belgium*. A fourth told us *How a Boy Scout cooks Meat Out-of-doors*. And this topic also lasted until the end of its period.

The boy I speak of lectured well on every occasion. He gave us in several fits his journey from Australia, describing Bombay, Port Said, Stromboli, Messina, and other sights and places vividly, and without the tedious reflections of a travelbook. His triumph came when he lectured one day for a whole period on New Caledonia to the most part of three forms and their masters and several visitors, an audience of fifty. He dealt with the geography of the island, its mountains, rivers, towns, and the coral reef surrounding it ; he described the natives and their customs, their boats, and the pearl-fisheries. Animal life came in also, from the octopus to the birds ; and the coco-nut and date-palms were but the beginnings of an account of the fruits. Nickel-mines were to have been fully described also, but there was no more time. I have never heard a lecture so full of matter.

Not many boys have travelled so far and seen so much of life in other parts of the world. But there is no doubt that in any class of twenty-five boys you will find at least one who is as stimulating as this fellow. Boys are full of information, and always ready to come out with it under encouraging conditions.

When one class has found the joy of Speeches the tale soon goes round, and other classes will soon be asking for Speeches also. We have found it a good plan when beginning Speeches with a new group to admit them as audience to a practised class.

This gives them the chance of profiting by the experience of the proficient ones, and of adopting straightway the essentials of the procedure, without the need of inventing it all again. This plan also gives the beginners something of a standard to aim at.

It is also very helpful to a class of beginners to bring in as a visitor a proficient lecturer from another class. The Belgians, after they had exhausted their first fund of stories, devoted a period or two to problems, riddles, tricks, and Mixed Grills. It seemed to me that they were now at a juncture where they would find a difficulty in getting into the swing of regular subject lectures. So I requested the woodwork master over the way to lend me three of my best lecturers for a few minutes. As we entered the lecture-room I asked, " What will you speak on ? " " Oh, anything," the boys replied.

If an opportunity for Speeches suddenly arises there are always several boys ready to speak at once, and while the first few lectures are going on most of the other boys can prepare themselves. Even with those weaker brethren who need much encouragement and speak but rarely, the difficulty is not so much a need for preparation as the inability to think of a subject.

This raises the question of compulsion, for it may easily happen that some boys, lacking initiative, or having found themselves not very good at lecturing, may prefer to listen to the willing speakers and take no part themselves. In extreme cases a boy may be really so nervous that it is a positive torture for him to have to stand up on the platform before the rest. I know very well what such feelings mean, having suffered from the same sensitiveness myself as a boy. And it is not very helpful to give such a boy ample notice, in order to give him time to prepare, saying, " You will have to speak next Monday." This may only fill him with dread apprehension. He makes earnest, almost feverish preparations to avoid disaster, as it seems to him, and all the time his heart sinks at the thought of the approaching ordeal on Monday. Many a kindly intentioned teacher, genial and encouraging, is in reality, for lack of a truly sympathetic understanding of Littleman, nothing better than a blind, blundering fool. And when I say that many a small boy, all

116

unknown to his smiling teacher, sometimes goes through what can only be described as mental agony, I am not speaking without knowledge, for I have felt how

> Between the acting of a dreadful thing
> And the first motion, all the interim is
> Like a phantasma or a hideous dream.

Let us avoid at all costs the imposition of this torture upon any Littleman. If a boy has spoken several times already, he may in his present retirement be considered merely slack. The mister can generally get him to resume activity. But those who have not yet ventured must be given time. The master may encourage them to make criticisms first, and after a while they will offer to make a speech. So long as a boy is left to take the decisive step of his own accord he is not suffering any mental agony. It is having the ordeal thrust upon him which causes him dread. Therefore refrain from persuading Littlemen to swim by throwing them into the water.

I do not wish to give the impression that the making of Speeches is ever a trial for boys. But before they have tried it some of them are apt to *think* it will be. That is my point. Any one who sees little boys diving from high places and sporting in deep water may say, " These little beggars don't know the meaning of fear." But the teacher who a week or two before stood for half an hour waist-deep in the water, gently persuading the same little beggars to get wet above the knees, knows this cheery point of view to be both false and mischievous.

From this aspect there is something to be said for the question of that American visitor, " How do you teach them to be natural ? " And the answer is still the same, " Leave them as much as possible to do things in their own time and in their own way." Of course the teacher must see to it that there is always something before the boys ready and suitable to be done. In saying that the master may encourage a shy boy to make criticisms first, I do not mean that the master should stand up and say cheerily in front of the whole class, " Now come along, George, old chap." Nothing could conceivably give a shy boy a more difficult opening. He imagines that all eyes are upon him, and, if he hesitates at all, they soon are. As the master is merely an intelligent onlooker during Speeches he may sit among the boys—like the Village Blacksmith. Then, as some error or obscurity arises in the Speech the master may comment on it quietly to the retiring fellow beside him, and at the end of the Speech, when opportunity for criticism is given, say, " Ask him what he meant by that." Without thinking about himself the boy does so, and having thus found his voice in a question will in a day or so make criticisms from the rostrum—and so to Speeches.

The master must at all times be very sensitive of any faltering due to nervousness in any boy, and " help him out " in an easy matter-of-fact tone.

A fact which seems to have escaped the notice of many is that most nervous speakers are only really nervous at the start of a speech. His fumbling and stuttering makes the speaker worse, and even though he may not in his mind feel any occasion to be nervous, he finds that some strange physical infirmity is interfering with his breathing operations. But if some diversion should occur such as prolonged applause or laughter, the speaker is able to collect himself in the interval, and can then speak afterwards without a trace of nervousness. In public places this useful diversion cannot be planned, and so the poor nervous starter must get through as best he can. But in the classroom it is possible for the master, when a speaker on mounting the rostrum is momentarily upset by the expectant silence, to create a diversion in some way, in order to give him time to collect himself and to get his breath. Many a time I have made apparently senseless interruptions just as a speaker was about to start, much to the annoyance of the mister. But these officious interruptions were deliberate.

Many boys will not need such a tender thoughtfulness from the master. But a little boy's sensibility is a frail mechanism, and infinite tact is one of the chief qualities required in a playmaster. The Littlemen are only children after all.

But when most of the class have found their legs what is to be the arrangement of the Speeches ? Do the boys each speak in turn until the round of the class is completed, or do they speak or remain silent at their will ? Neither plan would be satisfactory. On the first method some one would certainly be out of his order when he wanted to speak, and another would be called upon when he didn't want to speak. On the second method some of the boys might never volunteer at all. It is best to leave the solution of such a matter to the boys. If you give them self-government during lecture-lessons they will soon settle the procedure with perfect fairness and to the satisfaction of all. For though a master may try to satisfy the class, a mister *must* satisfy them, for his position depends upon it.

With us the best speakers were ready at all times, and in fact were called for on almost every occasion. Others came out frequently enough of their own accord. A few were persuaded by the canvassing mister when he thought they had been silent long enough. And only a very small number remained to be " dealt with." The boys' system of dealing with the laggards was to announce the names of those who had not spoken for three weeks or so, and indicate that they would be expected to make an appearance during the current week. But such was the goodwill among them that the culprits would often turn the tables upon the ruling caste, and protest, amid cheers and counter-cheers, that they had had a speech in mind for *weeks*, but could not get a word in because A, B, and C spoke on every occasion ! This was largely true, and a good mister would often have to disregard the cries for a certain popular speaker until some others had had their turn. The canvassing mister should have in hand a waiting list of at least six speakers.

Desiring to have some record of Littleman lectures I sought the services of a shorthand writer. The boys of course were not told of this, but they soon found it out. It made no difference, however, to their speaking. So little was thought of it that not one even mentioned the matter to me afterwards. But the fluency of the speakers was too much for the shorthand writer. The rule of " No *er* " was perhaps more exacting than she had been accustomed to. The result was a mere report of the lectures and not the desired verbatim record. The services of an expert were then obtained, and some of the lectures in the following pages are

the verbatim reports he made. This man, who had had
many years' experience of public speakers, said that the
boys were much to be complimented on the clearness and
fluency of their speech. " I only wish," he observed, " that
all speakers were as easy to take down. It is not a question
of speaking loudly, but of speaking distinctly." Another
virtue which I am sure must have been noticeable is that
the boys have learnt to speak in sentences which make
good English when written down. Most adult speakers I
have heard get themselves involved in periods of mixed constructions from which they can only get free by—making a
dash for it.

For the purpose of record also the boys were called upon to
write lectures following their oral style. As this was only done
in the last week or so of the last term, there is not much material
to select from. The works given here, however, may be read
as fair examples of Littleman Lectures. It need hardly be said
that there can be no comparison between the interest of these
printed speeches and the interest of a like speech orally delivered.
The words are there, but the life of the speaker is not. Unlike
essays, these pieces cannot be expected to reflect their authors.
Most of the errors which the reader will note in the following
pieces would have been corrected by the hammer-rap. The
repetition of " it " in this sentence, for example, would certainly
be noticed, " If it falls off the branch she gets angry with it and
makes it do it all over again until it can fly properly." The
fumbling in the opening paragraph about the French partridge
could not be put right with a word ; but the hammer-boy would
rap and cry, " Don't muddle," or " Say that again," and the
speaker would mend his style at the second effort. Many
sentences which will not pass in print are quite permissible when
spoken ; such as this of the shark on deck. " He struggles and
smashes about, and knocks people down for about half an hour,"
because the speaker makes the necessary pause after " down."
Many unsatisfactory turns of phrase would escape the notice of
the hammer-boy altogether ; and where it is a matter of any
subtlety the master would be wise not to break in. Time and
practice will mend many imperfections. It must be remembered
that these are boys of eleven and twelve speaking extempore,

and it is not fair to judge their spoken periods according to the canons of prose style.

Of this lecture on *Birds* the first fit is the verbatim report as taken down by the shorthand writer. The other two fits were written by the boy.

BIRDS

FIT 1. THE SPARROW HAWK AND THE FRENCH PARTRIDGE

Sir,

I am come up here to-day to make a speech on two birds which you find quite often about Cambridge.

I will deal first with the sparrow hawk. It is a rarer bird than the kestrel hawk, and builds a larger nest, and much higher, than the kestrel. It lays from three to five eggs, which are green and have brown blotches upon them. This is an egg of the sparrow hawk. [Egg handed round.] When you are climbing for a sparrow hawk's nest you will probably see the sparrow hawk sitting there; until you get within two yards of her she will not get off, and if she has young ones you will probably get pecked two or three times before you can push her off. She feeds upon mice, and very often young partridges. That is why, if you look at a keeper's hanging-tree, where they nail all the skins of their enemies, you will often see a sparrow hawk nailed to the tree, because it has taken the young partridges or pheasants. But really it does more good than harm, as it feeds on rats, moles, and other vermin. The young of the sparrow hawk are born with very nearly all their feathers on, and it only takes about two weeks before they can leave the nest. When they first leave the nest they are brought by the mother bird into some valley with grass. They then run about for some time, and are then given their first flying lesson. The mother goes to the end of a branch and gets the young one to fly to her. If it falls off the branch she gets angry with it and makes it do it all over again until it can fly properly. The sparrow hawk is rarer than the kestrel. Though you always see the kestrel taking a rat or mouse, it really takes far more pheasants than you think it does. The reason the sparrow hawk is rarer than the kestrel is because it has been killed so much by keepers, and if it goes on being killed, very soon there will not be any sparrow hawks left.

The French partridge is the second bird I will deal with this morning. It is called a French partridge for the simple reason, not that it is a French bird, but because the ordinary partridge and the French partridge vary, because the ordinary partridge is very much different.* The French partridge has red legs, and you can either call it a red-legged partridge or a French partridge, but people do not often care to say, " I have shot a red-legged partridge." They think it better to say, " I have shot a French partridge." It makes a nest of grass on a flattened-out space in the grass, and lays six to twelve eggs. The egg of the French partridge is putty-coloured, spotted with bits of red, and sometimes a smear of brown. The other distinguishing feature of the French partridge is that whereas the French partridge runs a long way, if you are chasing him, before he flies, the ordinary partridge, if he sees any one, jumps up straight away and flies away. It can go farther than the partridge as it has larger and longer wings. The French partridge's young, different to the ordinary partridge, are not born with their feathers on, but they very quickly get their feathers. About a week after they are born the feathers appear on the young ones. The mother feeds them the whole time with little pieces of wheat and other small grain. She will sit on the nest until you nearly touch her whilst she has young ones. She likes to have her nest near the roots of a tree, with holes between the roots, and if any one goes near, the young ones can run in between the roots of the tree and you will not find them. That is all I have to tell you to-day about these two birds.

Age 11.9.

E. P. M.

BIRDS

FIT 2. THE HOUSE SPARROW, THE SAND MARTIN AND THE ROBIN

Sir,

First I will speak to you about the house sparrow. This dingy little bird is seen everywhere, in and out the traffic looking

* The fumbling here is doubtless due to the change of subject from one bird to the other.

for a piece of food.   If you go to the country you will see a very different sparrow.   He will be a beautiful brown bird with a white bar across his wing and a glossy black throat, an altogether neat little bird.

The hen makes a nest in any sheltered nook in a house, where she lays six grey eggs spotted thickly with black.

When the young are gone the mother rears another brood all through the year.

I will now deal with the sand martin.   This is the smallest of all martins and is the most quaint and interesting.   This bird is a sand colour with a very delicate thin black beak and little shining eyes.   With his little beak he digs a hole in the sand about four feet long.   At the end of this he builds a mud nest and lines it with feathers.   In this four white eggs are laid.   When the young come out of the egg they are kept in the nest and you can often see them sitting at the mouth of the hole.   When you go to look at them they scuttle to the back of the hole.

I will now speak about the last bird, the robin.   This is always a favourite among mankind because he is so tame.   In April he will find a mate and, like the bullfinch, pairs for life.   The male and female robin go about to look for a nesting site.   The nesting site of the robin is a hole or a stump of a tree thickly covered with ivy.   In this the mother places a pretty little nest with moss and twigs on the outside and feathers and hairs on the inside.   The nest takes about a fortnight to build and when it is finished the hen sits on it and lays five white eggs thickly mottled on top with red.   When the young are ready to fly fierce conflicts take place between the young and parent birds as to who shall have the old estate.

I may as well tell you that if any of you wish to have a tame robin, you have only to feed him well in the winter and he will always love you and nest in your garden.   (I have one.)

Age 11.9.   E. P. M.

BIRDS

FIT 3.   THE WILD DUCK AND THE HEDGE SPARROW

Sir,

First I wish to say something about how birds' eggs are formed.   When they are laid they are the yolk just in a soft

123

skin and about thirty minutes afterwards the shell is formed. And if the sun is shining on it the colour and spots are formed.

I have a French partridge's egg which was very nearly hidden from the sun and in consequence only a little part of it was coloured and spotted. Therefore it is like this :

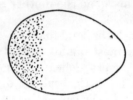

I will now tell you the most important facts in the habits of the wild duck. It makes a nest in rushes or under a hedge or bush on the bank and lays from ten to fourteen eggs, green blotched with light buff colour. The young are hatched in eighteen days. As soon as they are hatched they swim away with the mother in search of food.

I will now tell you about the hedge sparrow. It is not really a sparrow but a linnet, because it is much more graceful in its movements than its cousin the house sparrow. The hen makes a beautiful nest with moss on the outside and hairs on the inside. Four to six pale sea-blue eggs are laid. In seventeen days the young appear and it is twenty-one days before they venture from the nest with the mother.

Aged 11.9.

E. P. M.

The following Speech on *Gins* was fully reported by the short-hand writer. But the speaker has such a rapid delivery that a few mistakes in taking down were unavoidable. In correcting these on the transcript the boy has made a few other altera-tions, but they are so slight as to be negligible.

The lecture on *Model Aeroplanes* which follows was written by the same boy. It relates the practical experience he gained with his father while experimenting with these craft.

LITTLEMAN LECTURES

GINS *

Sir,

I am here to make a speech on gins   The simplest kind of gin is a noose.   It is used for catching rabbits or cats.   It is made of brass wire.   Steel wire will not do.   When the cat or rabbit goes through her run, she sticks her head into the noose, the noose tightens, and in a few minutes the cat is dead.

Another trap, for catching fish, is used in Australia.   Two natives wade out into a stream holding each end of a long net. One walks to the opposite bank.   Then they begin to walk down stream.   The one on the opposite bank gradually brings round his net until he is on the same side as his friend.   The net is then parallel to the bank and is gradually worked into a small circle containing the fish, the natives being careful to press the edges of the net close to the bank or else the fish would escape.   The women then arrive and throw the fish on the bank.

I will now tell you about a hippopotamus trap.   The first thing they do when they start to make a hippopotamus trap is to dig a big hole in the ground, driving large spikes into the bottom.   They then cut some young trees and place them over the top.   On this they place brushwood covered with grass

When the hippopotamus comes blundering along he walks over this and crashes in ; falling pierced on the spikes.   The natives come clambering down the sides by means of rough ladders and feast on him, often getting right into his inside.

Another trap is a mole trap.   Here is the earth thrown over a mole burrow.   You get a piece of wood about 2 ft. long and 6 in. wide, with a stone lashed on the top and two or three spikes underneath.   It is supported at the top end by two sticks which have been lightly driven into the mole run.   As the mole comes strolling along the run he disturbs the sticks, which give way, and the spikes fall on his head, fixing him into the ground.

You all know an elephant's trap.   It is simply a hole dug in the ground exactly like the hippopotamus trap and is covered with brushwood.

Another way of catching elephants is to form a keddah, that

* The rapid description of each gin was made clear by a blackboard illustration.

is to say, a strong enclosure with an entrance at one end barred by a gate. To this are attached long lines of ropes in the shape of a V with flags attached. When a herd of elephants is discovered a large party of natives go out on elephants and on foot and drive these wild elephants towards the enclosure. When the elephants find themselves penned in by the ropes and waving flags they become terrified and rush madly towards the keddah. The big gate is swung open and the herd dashes madly in. The large bulls of the herd hurl themselves against the stockade, generally without effect, although sometimes a savage old bull will smash his way through. When the wild elephants have quieted down several tame ones with keepers on their backs enter the stockade—they hustle a wild elephant towards a large post to which it is firmly attached by its legs with ropes. Then they are tamed in the usual way.

Another way to catch mice and rats is to get a big wooden box. You reduce the size of the lid until it just loosely fits the inside of the top of the box. You then balance it by means of two rings which are passed over a steel rod which runs right through both sides of the box. You then place your bait in the centre of the lid. You next lean a piece of wood against the side of the box as a ladder up which the rats can run. When all is ready you place a brick upright on the bottom of the box and fill with water up to the top of the brick. The first rat comes running up for the bait and collapses into the water and swims for the brick. He sits there squealing until a second rat comes to see what is the matter and he too falls into the water. Finally, if you are lucky, you have the whole box full of struggling rats, and then you can fill up with water and leave them there comfortably to be drowned.

Another way of catching rats is to get what is called a steel trap. Two pieces of steel are fixed with a spring on each side attached to a solid frame. These are kept open by a small steel rod upon which is placed some cheese or tempting bait. The rat comes along, nibbles the cheese and disturbs the steel rod, the jaws of the trap then close together and hold the animal's nose, generally with fatal effect. When caught by the legs they have been known to gnaw them clean off in their efforts to escape.

There is another trap, the ibex trap. In the same way as for elephants there are long lines of ropes with coloured tapes and flags attached to them placed in the form of a V. The hunters surround the unfortunate little animals, tearing along screaming and shouting, with waving of flags and sometimes firing of guns. At the end of the enclosure there is a marshy piece of ground into which the animals prefer to jump and be choked rather than be killed by the spear.

Another trap is a shark trap. The hook is large, somewhat resembling a butcher's hook, and it is fixed on a piece of fine tempered steel chain, generally about eight yards long. On the hook is hung a fat piece of salt pork. Then they have a very strong rope fixed round a belaying pin at the stern of the ship, with plenty of slack on the deck. They then drop the bait into the water, lowering it about three feet deep. Here comes the shark with his mouth open, and generally he has a cruise round the ship at first, and finally decides to take the bait. He opens his horrid mouth, turns slightly on one side and makes a grab at it. Then comes a jerk on the line, and the line is let out. Soon the line is drawn in again, but he makes another bolt, and finally he is too tired to do anything else. The crew hold on, a rope is thrown over the shark's tail and pulled tight, then it is fixed to the main boom, the shark is pulled up and he struggles on the deck on which he is thrown like a log. He struggles and smashes about, and knocks people down for about half an hour. It is advisable not to go too near the tail of a shark for a shark has two business ends. The tail can knock a man flat. After a desperate struggle they succeed in cutting off his tail, and finally his head, but he will still continue to jump about after his head has been cut off, and an account tells of how two hours after a shark's head was cut off he was still jumping about and his heart was still beating. I think this is all I have to say for the present.

Age 11.   G. M. J.

MODEL AEROPLANES

Fit 1

Sir,

I am here to make a speech on the model aeroplane. It is a pretty sight to see the model aeroplane gliding about in the air.

THE PLAY WAY

There are several points to be considered when you start to make a model.

The first and most important is the type. The best type for all-round work is the Wright type monoplane. This type has an elevator in front and a large main plane about six inches in front of the screw. The size of the plane must be according to the size of the machine.

The best kind of wood for the frame of the plane is American white wood. The wood for the stick is deal. For this you take a strip of wood about two feet six inches long and quarter of an inch square. At the end of this you lash a piece of brass (see Diagram I). Through one end of the brass you drill a small hole. You then bend the brass until it forms a right angle (see Diagram II). or better, bend it before attaching it to the stick. The brass is attached to the stick as shown (see Diagram III). At the other end of the stick you lash a hook (see Diagram IV).

Now I will tell you about the making of the plane. You take two strips of wood about eighteen inches long and half of an inch broad and one-sixteenth of an inch thick You lay these side by side. You then take two small pieces of wood about three and a half inches long, three-eighths wide and one-sixteenth thick and lay these so that each end touches one of the strips and nail them together. You then nail two others in the same way at equal distances from the middle (see Diagram V). Now your plane is ready for the aero silk. The silk may first be stretched on a stretching frame to enable you more easily to stick the frame of the aerofoil on it (see Diagram VI).

Having thoroughly covered the top of the frame with thin glue you place it top down upon the stretched silk and press down until it sticks tightly. You then cut round the silk with a sharp pair of scissors. Having done this you bring the overlapping pieces round and glue them underneath. Let this dry thoroughly and there you have your nearly finished aerofoil. The next thing is to put some camber on the wing (see Diagram VII) and also give it some dihedral angle (see Diagram VIII) or perhaps it is better to bend the angles before gluing on the silk. Then your plane is ready for use.

Now I will tell you how to make the screw. Take a piece of birch wood one-sixteenth of an inch thick, seven inches long and ten-sixteenths of an inch wide. Put this in boiling water for about ten minutes and then take it out and twist it into the shape of a propeller. Hold it in position for about ten minutes over a flame and it will still remain in position. Then you fix a piece of wire (with hook on end) to the screw (see Diagram IX).

Pass the hook of the screw through the hole in the brass on the one end of the stick, and stretch eight strands of elastic from hook to hook. Then fix the plane to the stick (see Diagram X). Wind up the elastic a number of times and launch it (see Diagram XI). It will probably crash down on its nose. If it does push the elevator (see beginning) forward and by and by it will go sailing away in a circle. It is a poor machine that will not fly 100 yards.

MODEL AEROPLANES

Fit 2

Sir,

I am here to continue my speech on model aeroplanes.

The model aeroplane of which I am going to tell you to-day is the racing type.

This type can travel at about thirty miles an hour. It has a long stick and a rear elevator. It is sometimes strengthened by wire lashed to the stick to strengthen it. The planes of these are sometimes made of wood planed very thin with the smoothing plane. This plane can be stained any colour, but it must not be painted. The prettiest colour to stain these planes is blue.

These machines will not travel very high. Sometimes the stick can be strengthened by lashing bow-shaped pieces of wood to it. You can buy little rings to put on the screw to prevent it from scraping against the brass. These machines are capable of flying 150 yards if wound up 500 times, but it is difficult to start them and requires a good deal of practice. If there are many people about it is dangerous to fly them as they might easily spear some one. This type of plane is easy to make, but they do not always glide down so well, and sometimes come down on their noses. Their screw is much the same as the Wright type.

Now I will tell you about the single plane machine without

any elevator. This type has the plane in the centre of the stick, but it will not rise high and will not glide very well and is very difficult to manage. The planes of this type, like all wooden planes, are very liable to split, and sometimes they will split clean in half. During the four months in which we were experimenting with wooden planes no fewer than twelve planes split at the ends.

Now I will tell you about the two-screw type. The sticks of these types are of two kinds. The first kind has cross-pieces at one end (see Diagram XII). This type is capable of travelling 200 yards and twenty miles an hour. They have built-up aerofoils and are good all-round machines.

Another type is in the form of a triangle (see Diagram XIII) with the screws at the broad end. They can be made extremely long and fast flyers.

This is all I have to say to-day about model aeroplanes, for an ounce of practice is worth a pound of theory.

Age 11.   **G. M. J.**

[*Written Lecture*]

RAIL MOTORS

FIT 1. A LECTURE ON A RAIL MOTOR ON THE KENT AND EAST SUSSEX RAILWAY

Sir,

I have come up here this morning to tell you something of a very interesting Rail Motor. The owning company, which only operates twenty-four miles of line, is wonderfully modern in most of its rolling stock, and this little Rail Motor shows that the company is not afraid to make experiments.

The boiler is at the front, and is vertical to economize space, as you find in steam road wagons. The cylinders are five and a half inches in diameter, and operate on to the front axle. The car runs on four wheels, the front pair being drivers. It seats thirty-seven passengers, and the seats are arranged like those on the top of a 'bus. At the end there is a compartment for carrying churns of milk, as this railway serves an almost purely agricultural district. In this compartment the passengers' luggage—usually of a very light character—is carried.

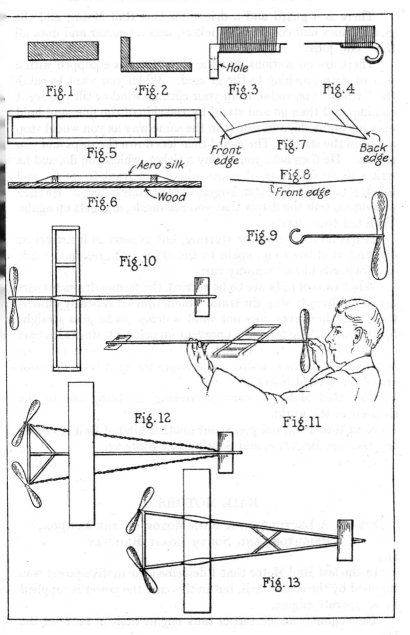

Fig. 1

Fig. 2

Fig. 3 ←Hole

Fig. 4

Fig. 5

Fig. 7 Front edge Back edge

Aero silk

Fig. 8 Front edge

Fig. 6 Wood

Fig. 9

Fig. 10

Fig. 11

Fig. 12

Fig. 13

There is a guard and a driver for this Rail Motor, and the guard issues and collects the tickets, acts as porter and does all the " odd jobs."

There are no stations, but the Rail Motor is equipped with a pair of steps reaching to the ground. When you want to catch the " train " you watch from your cottage window till you see it coming, and then go and stand by the side of the line, and hold up your umbrella, and stop it in the same way as you would stop a 'bus in the street. The guard then lets down the steps and you get up. He then asks you to buy a ticket, which you do, and he writes down on a slip of paper where you want to go to, and hands it to you. He often forgets to take your money. He then gets down, tells the driver that you are inside, and gets on again. Then the train starts.

It has no fixed time for starting, but as soon as it arrives at one end, it starts to go again to the other and goes backwards and forwards like a tramway-car.

When cans of milk are to be carried, the farmer draws his cart across the lines to stop the train. Sometimes it is nearly dinner-time, and the driver does not want a delay, so he goes straight for the cart. The farmer, to prevent an accident, draws his cart off the rails, and the train goes on, leaving the farmer to swear and wait for the next train. Sometimes the next train does not arrive for several hours.

This Rail Motor is very interesting, as being one of the smallest in the world.

Next time I will tell you about another kind of Rail Motor on the London, Brighton, and South Coast Railway.

Age 12.2. F. G. C.

RAIL MOTORS

Fit 2. A Lecture on a Rail Motor on the London, Brighton, and South Coast Railway

Sir,

In the last Rail Motor that I described the motive power was supplied by the coach itself, but in this case the power is supplied by a separate engine.

The engine is an old terrier tank engine built in 1872 for the

South London section of the line, which was then in very bad condition, and quite unfit to bear a heavy locomotive.

The engine has 4 ft. drivers, and is a 0-6-0, though the engine which I have chosen as my example has the front drivers removed and a pony truck substituted. Thus it is a 2-4-0.

It is so small that when you see it coming into the station the coach towers over the little engine.

It is so small that the driver could not see the signals when going the other way, so a compartment is supplied for him at the other end of the coach, where all the levers are duplicated. When he is in that compartment the fireman is still in the cab of the engine.

The coach is divided into two compartments, smoking and non-smoking. The seats are arranged as those on the top of an omnibus, and are cane-covered.

The stations at which the trains stop are called halts. They consist of a plain platform without any shelter. They rarely have even a seat. When the coach comes along there is a train attendant who gives out the tickets. If there are no passengers waiting at the halt, the train does not stop.

These little motor trains have vacuum brakes fitted, and a Rail Motor going at full speed can stop in the length of one of these halts. The regular trains do not stop at these halts. Sometimes when there is much traffic on the line they couple a coach on to the front of the engine, and the engine driver, when going forwards, has to lean out of the cab to see the line ahead, so small is the engine.

This engine and coach form one of the most interesting of all Rail Motors, and any one staying in the suburbs served by the London, Brighton, and South Coast Railway will often have seen these little trains.

This is the second kind of Rail Motor, having the motive power in the form of a separate engine.

These are the chief forms of Rail Motors, and I will not tell you anything more in this lecture.

Age 12.2.   F. G. C.

THE PLAY WAY

[*Written Lecture*]

METHODS OF DEFENDING A SHIP FROM
TORPEDOES AND MINES

Sir,

As I have told you about torpedoes and mines and how deadly they are, you may think that there is no adequate way of defending a ship from them. As a matter of fact there are many ways, especially in the case of mines, which we will deal with first. The first way of defending a ship against mines is by sweeping. This is done in several ways. Two boats may go out with a chain between them and in company with a torpedo boat. When a mine fouls the chain it either explodes or gives a jerk to the chain. In the latter case the ship tells the T. B. by signals where the mine is and the T. B. fires at it and explodes it.

The mine sweepers have a kind of framework sticking out all round them as they do not need to go fast. Sometimes this framework is only in front of them and in a few cases it is not there at all. This framework explodes the mines before they are able to reach the ship. Much time, is however, wasted by sweeping where there are no mines.

Now objects just under the water can be seen better from a height, so an aeroplane, captive balloon or airship is often sent up. Then the craft in the air signals to the boat where any mines it can see are. The mines are then exploded by rifle fire from the ship on the water, or they are dragged, poked, or exploded in any other way. Sometimes the aircraft goes out alone and explodes the mines itself.

If a liner or big ship gets torpedoed or strikes a mine all the water-tight doors leading from one room into another are closed. The ship may then be regarded as a structure composed of water-tight boxes. Several of these boxes are flooded owing to the hole blown in the side. More may have small leaks burst in them by the explosion. If the ship floats the pumps are set going and measures are taken to stop up the hole, and to get to the nearest port as quickly as possible. (Of course the nearest port with a dock.) The most powerful mine could not sink a

134

large British super-dreadnought in under eleven hours, so she would have a fair chance of getting *somewhere* before she sank.

When a ship is attacked by a submarine she turns her stern to the submarine as the wash of the propellers will usually alter the course of a torpedo. The ship's stern also presents a smaller target to the enemy. The ship zigzags, and may raise a cloud of black smoke to hide its movements. If several fast boats are travelling together, there may be a chance for one to ram the submarine. Destroyers and ships of war mounting small guns will fire at the submarine. A submarine has more than one periscope and when these are in a line with you the submarine is ready to fire. When the torpedo is coming only a quick man is able to put the helm over to avoid it, as the torpedo runs about as fast as a first-rate or " crack " British express train. It looks like a white flash as it whizzes past. Needless to say a boat must be going at full speed all the time it is fighting a submarine. Torpedo nets are hung out about thirty feet from the ship's side on those slanting rods you may see on battleships. Torpedo nets are not fitted to small boats. Some torpedoes can get through the nets without exploding, and the speed of a ship must be under five knots when she has her nets out (for fear of the nets and torpedo booms being washed away). Torpedo nets are seldom *used* in British ships though all the ships are provided with them. The Forth and other large bridges that are in reach of German submarines are defended with them, and other nets for catching submarines of which I will tell you later. I am afraid that I have trespassed on the grounds of my next speech, which will be, " How Submarines are Fought." But prevention is better than cure, and a sure way to defend yourself from torpedoes is to fight the submarine which sends them.

Age 12.   J. B. W.

[*Written Lecture*]

CONDITION OF AFFAIRS IN GERMANY FROM THE GERMAN POINT OF VIEW (JULY 1915)

Sir,

I wish this morning to show you that Germany is not beaten and run out as most people suppose.

THE PLAY WAY

When Germany instituted bread tickets it did not mean that she was short of bread or ever expected to be. It was only a wise precautionary move to prevent waste. The great German agricultural firms negotiated with the manufacturers of artificial manure and the result will probably be a record harvest for Germany. Manure is to be made by the hundred tons, and some areas of land will be taken over by the Government. There will be a huge demand for manure, because the German Government have decided to put the brake on the price of manure and offer it at a price within the reach of the poorest farmer. " Grants " of manure will probably be made in certain circumstances.

Then the nationalization of foodstuffs was a wise measure, and certainly ought to be copied. Here however it would not work as we treat our men as men ; while in Germany the men are treated as parts of a machine so to speak. The whole of Germany is now a great nation-wrecking machine with the Government as the engine which supplies the motive power.

Then take the case of the armies of Germany. In the western theatre of war they enclose practically all Belgium with its manufacturing cities and the richest part of France. From the products of this alone a large portion of the German people could be fed.

In the east the forces of the Kaiser and the Archduke Charles of Austria enclose a big piece of Russian Poland. They have hurled back the Russians and are advancing on the capital of Russian Poland. Warsaw is very important because it is the centre of one of the few railway systems the Russians have.

It is true that the Indians have been splendidly loyal, but, so thinks the German, Time and knowledge of the English meanness will cure that.

At sea the submarines are " starving out the English." When the English fleet is reduced to about one and a half times the size of the German fleet an engagement will take place the result of which of course will be the annihilation of the English fleet. You must remember of course that this is the German idea.

The Germans appear to be very confident of getting American help. A more serious problem to them is how to lure Roumania and the other Balkan States to their side. These States seem to favour the cause of the Allies too much.

Then as to the much discussed question of cotton. This is the only commodity for the manufacture of shells which the Germans cannot produce. Realizing this years before, they set about storing up cotton in huge quantities. Now their foresight is rewarded by enormous warehouses stuffed as full as they can with cotton.

Germany has immense reserves of copper and the confiscation of old copper pots and kettles was only to prevent waste. Kettles and pans can be made of tin plate, which is thin sheets of iron dipped in or coated with tin. By using first scrap copper they leave the Government supplies untouched and still make shells just as good as would be made with any copper.

The damage to German overseas trade is, according to Germans, temporary, and German ships will be able to run with even more safety than before the war. The Germans always avoided our warships as far as possible. The Germans always hated us, and believed that we stopped their merchant ships unnecessarily.

The average German believes implicitly in the press bureau, which does not tell so many lies as some people imagine. There are various post-card photographs used to hearten the Germans , but these are of cinema actors usually. Of course the Germans do not believe that these are actors. They never suspect anything.

From these remarks I think you will see that the war is going to be a long and fierce one. Maybe we shall fight in it when we grow up.

Age 12.1.   J. B. W.

How to make a Speech or Lecture was written at the very end of the course by our best lecturer. It is a pity that it did not occur to the boys to make a little book of directions earlier, and then to add to it as their experience grew. It was this boy's own idea to write this lecture, and the rules and suggestions are all his own. I carefully refrained from giving the class any teaching in the method of speech-making just to see if practice bore out my theories. The fact that the conventional opening,

137

" I have come up here to tell you about . . .," survived for a whole year, in itself shows that the master did not interfere, for a good beginning is the first thing a teacher would insist upon. I believe the plan of writing down stock beginnings was never tried. If it had been it would soon have been abandoned. The only point which the writer has borrowed is a recommendation of mine about the best way of obtaining silence in a noisy assembly.

[*Written Lecture*]

HOW TO MAKE A SPEECH OR LECTURE

Sir,

I propose to show you my rules for making good speeches. Of course there are several ways and this is only one. But first as to beginnings. If I shut my eyes and Johnny got up and spoke a speech through a gin to alter people's voices, I should know him by his beginning : " Sir, I am up here this morning (or this afternoon) to make a speech on so-and-so."

Now Johnny would be " floored " in more senses than one if he was called upon to make a speech from where he sat. So study good beginnings, don't use the same beginning for each lecture. It is a good thing to think out about two or three really good beginnings and write them down on a piece of paper. Then write down developments of these beginnings below until you have about six beginnings. Then take another piece of paper and think out two or three beginnings on a totally different line. Then write developments of these and so on. You will find now that you will have enough beginnings for a week or so, Don't be always telling the class that " You are up here this morning to make a speech " on this, that, or the other. They can see you are on the platform, they know it's this morning, and your speech has been, or ought to have been, announced properly.

The next thing to remember is not to be lengthy. I am afraid I am often far too long. The Chinese have a proverb, " Blessed is he that maketh short speeches for he shall be asked to come again." A good way to make speeches short is to make it a rule not to have more than a very few " by-the-bys " in your speech.

If you are always by-the-bying and by-the-waying the audience are apt to miss the point.

Mention of " by-the-by " brings us to the most important point of clearness. It is best not to talk with your hands, for if you say " about as big as this " and stretch out your hands, the class will not remember half as well as if you said " about two feet six inches long," or something like that.

Speak slowly. There is no hurry. Pronounce every word clearly and distinctly. Speak according to sense-groups, that is do not gulp out your phrases in inarticulate gasps but pause at the right places. Remember it is better to speak too loudly than not to speak loud enough. It is very irritating for the people at the back to see the misters enjoying a speech in all other ways good, and not be able to hear a word. Do not flourish about, and if the other side are shouting at you, wait till they have stopped.

This last remark of course applies to committee-matter speeches only, but if there is any disturbance the best way to put a stop to it is to be perfectly quiet and motionless yourself until there is silence again.

For the most part keep your eyes fixed on a point in the middle of the back wall about a foot above the head of the middle boy. Occasionally glance round the class and see how your remarks are catching on. If the audience are getting bored, conclude.

If you are simply lecturing, your object ought to be to please your audience ; if you are speaking on committee mattes ram your point home through anything. Though if you are clever enough to " hold " the class, a quiet bringing home of the point is often more effective than any amount of roaring. Mind by ramming a point home, I do not mean creating a species of thunderstorm on the platform, but speaking with great force and weight.

Always stand still when you speak. *Never* run about and stamp. That does not force home your point at all. It is best to stand with your hands behind your back and not fidget at all. If you have apparatus arrange it all neatly on the desk or table in

139

front of you. I think a feeble speaker should not have apparatus- as it is apt to divert the attention of the audience.

When you feel you have no more to say conclude at once. Never repeat anything, and never spin out your speech. Spun-out speeches annoy the audience, and selfishly steal time from the next speaker.

Then about conclusions. Never, never say "I think this is all I have to say." Make a different ending to every speech. Sometimes briefly sum up your points and place them in a clear and concise form before the class. Sometimes you may mention your next fit or speech, but do not do this too much. Then again you may hope the class have enjoyed the speech. Never allude to your marks in your ending. It sounds bad. If you have notes, hold them in your left hand and occasionally glance at them. If you are answering another person make mental notes of the weak points in his speech. When you get up compliment him first and then attack him on his weak points. Sum up for an ending. If anybody is drawing on the board and goes wrong, quietly correct him and do not make a great fuss about it.

Now we will talk about notes. I for myself think no one should have notes. Certainly no one should read his speech unless he is called upon to read a written lecture. Never take books up with you. If you speak on a subject, you ought to be proficient enough in it to be able to speak without a book. Never read extracts from books, or quote at any length poetry or prose. Never read newspaper cuttings. The less you read to your audience the better.

And now in conclusion I think that if you will keep these rules you will make very good speeches with ten-tens and VGs showering round you.

Age 12.1.

J. B. W.

CHAPTER V

ILONDS AND CHAP-BOOKS

My travels' history :
Wherein of antres vast and deserts idle,
Rough quarries, rocks, and hills whose heads touch heaven,
It was my hint to speak,—such was the process ;
And of the Cannibals that each other eat,
The Anthropophagi, and men whose heads
Do grow beneath their shoulders

" Othello "

See, at his feet, some little plan or chart.
WORDSWORTH

GROWN-UP people who cannot draw usually do one of two
things. Either they pretend they can, and make horrid pictures on their holidays, or they make no attempt at all. But
every one should draw sometimes, whether he is any good at it or
not. There is a world of entertainment in rapid sketches made
on the back of an envelope or in thumb-nail caricatures drawn on
the table-cloth during dessert.

Most people in their hearts love to make pictures, but they
resist the temptation for fear of " doing it wrong." The " art "
master with his models and his casts and his rules of perspective
has frightened away the practice of sketching for fun. The art
master is like all other school-teachers, he does not base his
teaching on anything which it interests you to do, but sets all
that aside and compels you to go through his course of formal
study.

But if Littleman does not find his natural desire for play
recognized officially he will satisfy it unofficially, and there are
few boys who have not at one time or another risen to the temptation offered by the margins and fly-leaves of their school books.

141

THE PLAY WAY

Those who are denied the privilege of this literary expression draw on whitewashed walls.

Most people who have to attend lectures with notebooks in front of them will draw while they listen. Many a schoolmaster at a round-table conference will amuse himself by fidgeting with a pencil and making strange patterns and geometrical designs on the paper before him. He would not understand what you meant if you accused him of not attending to the speakers; and yet many a small boy in his classes gets a smart rap on the knuckles for doing precisely the same thing.

An Ilond is one of those dreamlands which all children imagine, and love to tell stories of. We use the older form of the word, and call our thing an Ilond, to distinguish it from a piece of land surrounded by water. For an Ilond has no geographical situation. It is rather a region of faery, a country in the clouds.

It needs very little encouragement to persuade a playboy to make a picture-map of an imaginary country. There is a delight in making a creek just where you want to land, affording good shelter for your boat. Far inland you see a chain of mountains, and there must needs be a river up which you may paddle on your explorations. A volcano, a trackless forest, and a lagoon will be good things to find, so you put them in. A grotto seems a secure place to live in, so you put that in too. There you may be safe from surprise by the native inhabitants, whose huts and fires soon make their appearance. There is a fascination, too, in naming features of the Ilond, such as bays and capes and passes.

With such a game as this in hand a boy will work industriously for hours. " To what end ? " I may be asked. I don't know. It may end in anything. Certainly, you cannot claim to have definitely *taught* a boy something. But you may have set him going strongly on the path of that self-expression of which we hear so much. It is possible, too, that by going the same road in pursuit of the same goal he may shortly find himself in company with certain other adventurers not unknown to students of literature or science or geography.

Of course we don't know what will happen if we give Littleman pencil and paper and a free half-hour to draw an imaginary
142

island. He *may* draw another plan of the school playground ; or he may attempt another version of Great Britain ! On the other hand, he may give free expression to his playful fancy. It all depends upon what Littleman has learnt to think of his teacher.

A word or two will be enough to show the Littlemen what you propose they shall do. As Othello says :

> It was my hint to speak, such was the process.

Every boy is full of Ilonds. You may ask the boys if they have ever imagined themselves cast away upon a desert island. Have they, indeed ! Or you may recount the opening of a dream which broke off disappointingly just as your boat overturned on the reef and . . .

An introduction to the making of Ilonds would in itself make a fascinating essay in imaginative literature. But in this matter the playboys require but the merest suggestive beginning ; and the wise teacher will not go beyond a certain point. That point is reached when every Littleman is wide awake, almost painfully interested, and anxious to help the story along by every means in his power. One jumps about in his seat and cries, " O, yes, sir," in excited corroboration of a proposed shark waiting by the coral reef. Another adds, " And the sea is deep blue and there are palms and a sandy shore " ; and another says, " You've drifted for days in an open boat and your lips are swollen and black with thirst."

> This only is the witchcraft I have used.

To proceed is more than unnecessary, it is almost a denial of right. The boy who cannot make an Ilond after such a beginning really deserves to be spoon-fed on Mungo Park and Marco Polo.

Ilonds themselves are not the invention of the playboys or their master. We have simply borrowed a word and given it a special application. We do not so much invent as remember things, and devise ways of playing them. The interest in what we call Ilonds is world-wide, and the love of them lies deep in the hearts of men. Consequently some of the greatest players have turned their hands to the making of Ilonds.

143

THE PLAY WAY

When Robinson Crusoe was wrecked, he came ashore upon an Ilond. However many unread chapters may lead up to it, that event is the beginning of his book. Robert Louis Stevenson's chief work, according to his own estimate as well as in the judgment of his readers, is " Treasure Island." And to-day we have Peter Pan's Neverland, which is already a classic among Ilonds, and can never grow old and civilized so long as Littlemen delight in Redskins and Pirates and Mermaids, and in building houses underground or up in the trees. From the " New Atlantis " of Bacon to the short stories of H. G. Wells, Ilonds have been so numerous that they might almost form a branch of literature in themselves.

In addition to the element of adventure in Ilonds, which is concerned with perils which might actually beset the traveller by land and by water, there is the magical element. The most famous authority on this is Sir John Mandeville, who tells of such wonders as a sea " called the Gravelly Sea, which is all gravel and sand, without a drop of water." This may well be just an interesting way of describing a desert, for even of a desert it is true that it " ebbs and flows in great waves, as other seas do, and is never still." But Sir John adds that " men find therein, and on the banks, very good fish, of different nature and shape from what is found in any other sea ; and they are of very good taste and delicious to eat." Again he tells us of small trees which " every day at sunrise begin to grow, and they grow till midday bearing fruit ; but no man dare take of that fruit, for it is a thing of faerie. And after midday they decrease and enter again into the earth so that at sunset they appear no more ; and so they do every day."

Again, Sir John Mandeville tells how " In many places of the sea are great rocks of stone of adamant, which of its nature draws iron unto it ; and therefore there pass no ships that have either bonds or nails of iron in them ; and if they do, anon the rocks of adamant draw them to them, that they may never go thence. I myself have seen afar in that sea, as though it had been a great isle full of trees and bushes, full of thorns and briers, in great plenty ; and the shipmen told us that was of ships that were drawn thither by the adamants, for the iron that was in them."

144

There, indeed, is a strange thing for a man to have seen. But he knows also of a river that " runs only three days in the week,"* and of " many wild men hideous to look on, and horned ; they speak nought, but grunt like pigs," and of many other wonders. It is difficult to cease quoting Mandeville to your playboys. Certainly they have a right to know that " Nigh to the river of Pison is a marvellous thing. There is a vale between the mountains which extends nearly four miles ; and some call it the Enchanted Vale, some call it the Vale of Devils, and some the Perilous Vale. In that vale men hear oftentimes great tempests and thunders, and great murmurs and noises, day and night ; and great noise as it were of tabors, and nakeres, and trumpets, as though it were of a great feast. This vale is all full of devils and has been always ; and men say there that it is one of the entrances of hell. In that vale is plenty of gold and silver ; wherefore many misbelieving men, and many Christians also, oftentimes go in, to have of the treasure ; but few return, especially of the misbelieving men, for they are anon strangled by the devils."

Let us not be numbered among the misbelieving men. Sir John tells us that it is the devils who are " So subtle to make a thing to seem otherwise than it is," and he makes it quite plain that those who " went in for the treasure " but had " overmuch feebleness in faith " never came out again to tell the wondrous tale. Therefore let us venture into the Enchanted Vale to bring away the treasure, being full of faith and not troubled in conscience as are misbelieving men.

But perhaps, of all models, our best Ilonds most closely resemble those old maps made by voyagers in the days when discovery might still bring to light a new continent or an uncharted sea. Much of Asia was unknown then, and there must have been many maps drawn " with the augmentation of the Indies." These old charts are full of pictures with comments

* The Littlemen combine fact and fancy to a remarkable degree (just as when they were little children they would have related imaginary adventures of their own and almost thought they were real). When I read of these rivers to the boys one of the most imaginative of them observed, " Merely an exaggerated [i.e. romantic] description of intermittent springs, I suppose." There can be no sharp dividing-line for a Littleman between science and poetry.

to them such as, "Here lives the Great Khan," "These are the realms of Prester John." In the sea figure many ships, and other voyagers of the deep such as "Mermaids," and "Whales" and "Delphines." And "Here be fissches that fly." Some of the pictures are so quaint, and the comments so naïve, that it is difficult to imagine a state of knowledge in which such things were taken seriously. Perhaps, however, they were not taken so seriously as we think, for, before the coming of the exact sciences with their fancy-killing quest of bare fact and their arid terminology, mariners and explorers seem to have been just like boys out upon an adventure. Even the merchant bowed unto the seaman's star.

In Elizabethan times there was more romance and poetry in the daily life of an unlettered prentice than most schoolboys get out of Shakespeare himself in these days of dead learning.

Without questioning the wisdom of the scientists, one must regret the loss of those old pictures. Scientists themselves must admit that cartography—or whatever it pleases them to call map-making—has taken most of the romance out of maps. Then let all the wonder and romance of voyaging find refuge in Ilonds. Here at least the Great Khan shall rule on, and Prester John keep his wonted state from the East to Western Ind. Devils shall dance round fires to the terror of misbelieving men, and syrens shall sing upon the rocky places and make a tale of wrecks.

The Play interest is still seen in the names given by Antarctic explorers to the capes and sounds and islands they find : Hut Point, Mount Discovery, Razorback, Inaccessible Island, Mount Terror, Butter Point, The Cloudmaker, the Bay of Whales. What a freshness there is about these when compared with the stay-at-home names of our streets and villas, "Acacia Road," "Victoria Avenue," "Sunnybank," "Brookside," and "Hill Crest."

For the sake of cheapness we have sacrificed man's pride of home to live in the cardboard shanties of the jerry-builder. But a sense of humour might have saved us from allowing the ignorant scoundrel to name them. Better be plain No. 64 than "Verbena Croft." But perhaps the shrewd builder foresees what would happen if the names were left to the residents. One wag with a friendly circle of neighbours could spoil the whole

" Estate." Fancy such appropriate names as " The Rabbit Hutch," " Topple Down," " Chimney Row," " The Hat Box," " Ditto Villa," " The Cubic Foot," and so on.

Playboys often have a very apt fancy in naming places and things. Witness the nicknames they find for masters and the less popular articles of diet.* This knack is given a wide scope in the making of Ilonds. The outline is drawn first without much care for anything, save to get in a few exciting capes and one or two comfortable bays, and to allow for a river-mouth. Many names are then suggested by the shape of the land, such as Knee Cape, Toe Point, Horseshoe Bay.

In " The Art of Writing " Stevenson tells us how he made the Ilond which was the genesis of his greatest book. He tells of a schoolboy who was staying with him in a cottage, " and with the aid of pen and ink and a shilling box of water-colours, he had soon turned one of the rooms into a picture gallery. My more immediate duty towards the gallery was to be show-man ; but I would sometimes unbend a little, join the artist (so to speak) at the easel, and pass the afternoon with him in a generous emulation, making coloured drawings. On one of these occasions, I made the map of an island ; it was elaborately and (I thought) beautifully coloured ; the shape of it took my fancy beyond expression ; it contained harbours that pleased me like sonnets ; and with the unconsciousness of the predestined, I ticketed my performance ' Treasure Island.' I am told there are people who do not care for maps, and find it hard to believe. The names, the shapes of the woodlands, the courses of the roads and rivers, the prehistoric footsteps of man still distinctly traceable up hill and down dale, the mills and ruins, the ponds and the ferries, perhaps the *Standing Stone* or the *Druidic Circle* on the heath ; here is an inexhaustible fund of interest for any man with eyes to see or twopence-worth of imagination to see with."

But the pedant's eye is not on the look-out for a " fund of interest," nor does he care twopence for imagination.

The first Ilonds we made were simply pencil-sketches

---

* Instances, of course, abound, but I have just heard two most appropriate and typical schoolboy names for roly-poly jam-pudding —" Dead Baby " and " Sore Leg."

made in a few odd minutes at the end of a lesson. The experiment proved so interesting that the boys asked for Ilonds to be set as homework. This not only gave the opportunity of getting them painted in colour, but it meant almost unlimited time. An Ilond requires unlimited time, because each thing you put in suggests something else. After the coast-line is made, the first thing that suggests itself is a river. If you have left no estuary in your coast-line for the river-mouth you generally begin again. The next essential is mountains for the river to start from. Mountains are rarely indicated now by the old herring-bone design so familiar twenty years ago in the maps of schoolboys. Some boys use the atlas convention of varied shadings according to different heights. But others quite frankly draw their mountains as little cones. Ilonds differ from maps in many respects, but chiefly in this, that they give you the elevation of mountains, castles, woods, and so on, instead of the mere plan. The prospect map, such as the illustrated newspapers often use for battle areas, is perhaps the most attractive method of all. But the exigencies of perspective make this far too difficult for small boys. Consistency is not looked for in Ilonds, and, while lakes are always given from the bird's-eye view, trees are regarded from the ordinary human standpoint.

It is impossible to guess what a boy will put on his Ilond. Some features will be obvious, such as "Salmon River," or "Here is the Sea-serpent." Other points and places will be beautifully named by sheer luck of fancy. I find, for instance, "The Bay of Nothing," "Straits of Guidance," "Legend Lake," and "The Village of Mountain Guides." No traveller could find names more fair. Again, we have "Mount Goodwill," "The Bay of Moths," and "Memory Town." To me these names suggest some earthly paradise, or the voyaging of dreams. It is phrases such as these that Morris sought for the titles of his books. But we come into touch with Poe and Stevenson with "Mad Desert," "Fool Forest," and "Victim Glade." These names are surely an eloquent record of things which happen. How anxious the mariners must have been at "Point Ructions," how troubled was the captain in "Grumbles Sea." If you want the story of these places you have only to ask the boy who made the Ilond. He will soon make a story to fit.

148

ILONDS AND CHAP-BOOKS

In making of Ilonds there will be borrowings, imitations, the use of conventions, and also sheer originality. Here and there you get glimpses of what has passed through the boy's mind. Stray hints and chance associations will show you much of the directions in which his interests lie. For Ilonds, as I have said, give great opportunities for self-expression in one way or another.

The conventions borrowed from the old maps are sometimes very amusing. Often these amount to no more than " This is where the King lives," " Eels caught here." But there are certain conventions which have arisen among ourselves. Nearly every boy, of course, will put on his Ilond " Here I live," or " This is my boat." And not a few draw busy little figures hunting, or killing a dragon, or cruising about, and label them " This is myself," or simply " Me." Most of our Ilonds have the devil's own fire somewhere. This originated in a certain success of mine with coloured chalks on the blackboard in the only Ilond I ever made. The back view of an elephant has been common also, ever since one of the boys showed how simply it could be sketched. Another item which had a certain vogue was a large yellow patch with a camel on it and the legend, " Here a big desert which only camels can cross." On every Ilond you may expect elves and demons, and probably a giant or a witch. Gibbets appear frequently, and there is usually a tree bearing strange fruit. There is nearly always some horrid animal such as a man-eating spider, a great horned beast or a gigantic insect to shock the master, who is disgusted with all such things. In the surrounding sea, watched by the rising or setting sun, you will find ships of all kinds, and often a derelict. There are whales and mermaids of course, and nearly always a little shoal of Lulla fish. The Lulla fish is an invention of our own. He originated in this way : While reciting poems in chorus we wave sticks to keep us together and to express the rhythm of the verse. In our recital of the line in Shakespeare's " You Spotted Snakes."

Lulla, lulla, lullaby,

the movement of the stick follows the outline of a dolphin's back ;* and thus the dolphin came to be known as the Lulla fish.

* See Perse Playbooks, No. 5.

THE PLAY WAY

A feature may arise any day into sufficient favour to make it a convention, but for the most part they are things of fashion.

But the demons are a permanent race, and Hell in one form or another is constantly recurring. Sometimes it is, " Here is the mouth to the Pit of Hell," and sometimes just the big fire already mentioned. In one case there was a drawing of a brick oven with two parboiled victims in it. Near at hand stood a group of implements labelled " Torture Gins." There was quite, a mediæval suggestion about it all, and the legend above said. " Here be Hell." On the same Ilond is depicted an " Exhaust-pipe through which repenting people are blown to Heaven." A little soul in bright yellow is making the belated ascent, while a demon with a trident regards his loss with evident dismay. In this, which is called " Mixed Grill Ilond," there is another demon figure, " My host of the Ilond, a retired devil, but still dressed red." In the " Isle of King Wumpus " there are " Devils fighting " and " Baby devils doing tricks " ; and in " The Ilond of Dreams " there is a " Wicked Fairies' Maze where they cast their Christian prisoners."

In other boys' Ilonds are to be found such incidents and features as " The good witch of the Ilond with her blood and milk pails," " Runaway Cat," "A Fesaunte," " Walrus," "A Beetle Dragon," " Miser's House," " Milestone," " Fairies who do play in the Sun," " Giraffe who walks nine miles a day," " Freaks," " The Baxx, very fierce," " Idol which the natives worship," " Nunul, who holds a lantern for the Idol to see during night," " Mrs. Noah waiting for the animals," and " The Mayor's Hut."

Explanatory and helpful comments abound—" A thief was hung here," " Barley never ripens here," " Here be a large brass trumpet," and " Witches tell other people's fate by their fire." This last has a parenthetical acknowledgment " (from Macbeth)."

Nearly every Ilond will have some feature in it which is entirely original. In " The Ilond of Mieke " (pronounced Meeky) there is a man pulling the top of a tree to the ground, and he is called " The Pine Bender." In another, looming larger than the mountains, is a " Monkey sucking water through a tube." " Wonder Ilond," can boast " a town on wheels " and an invisible castle. And as " very big animals lurk here " it is not surprising that " The King lives by himself under the sea in a ginger-bread house." But he doesn't look very contented. There have been a few allusions to the war, such as " Zeppelins drop bombs here," but they are generally given some tinge of literary reminiscence such as " Bombish exilations (*sic*) whizzing in the air." There has been but one Kaiser Ilond and that was a kind of Rake's Progress. In one place he grew his " moustarche," then proceeded along the " Road to Ruin *via* Belgium," and ended in the " Slough of Despond." We shall perhaps not discover until this war is over how very little romance of any poetic kind there has been in it.

In the making of Ilonds a Littleman's imagination is so active and his attention taken up with so many things that spelling is apt to suffer neglect. Letters frequently drop out, and you find Kangroo, Grillars, Stgnant Pool, and Wods.

The earliest Ilonds, as I have said, were just rough pencil sketches. The next step was the use of a large sheet of drawing paper and very bright colours. It is better to cover the Ilond with some pale colour before putting in the geographical features and the people and the wonders. This makes a clear distinction between the Ilond and the sea. But best of all is the use of a sheet of stiff coloured paper as the sea. The coast-line is then drawn on white paper, and the Ilond cut out and stuck on to the large coloured sheet. When it is dry the painting proceeds as usual. The ships, Lulla fish and other sea-dwellers are drawn upon the coloured background, or cut in outline and affixed.

There may be some difficulty in obtaining the stiff coloured paper. Brown paper will do if it is not too dark, but the appearance of a finished Ilond on brown paper is not very lively. I cast about for some time to find stiff coloured papers. Stationers could supply nothing useful, so I had recourse to the grocer. From him I obtained a maroon and a dark blue paper which he used for wrapping up tea and sugar. But this did not satisfy us for long. At length a happy idea struck me, and for a shilling I purchased remnants of self-coloured wall-papers in great variety. Thus we obtained scarlet and bright yellow, many greens and mild blues, and even a deep purple. It is worth remembering the remnants of wall-paper, for they can be put to many uses. But for Ilonds we found wall-paper of scant avail.

THE PLAY WAY

The preparation on the paper caused the ink to be absorbed, and anything one wrote or drew in the sea became blurred at once.

Eventually I hit upon " cover " papers such as are used by printers and bookbinders. I avoided all the muddy nondescripts or " art shades," in the sample-books, and chose a range of bright colours. This included true green, blue, red, orange, and purple, a maroon and a light brown. I ordered " 21 quires assorted colours," and a few days later a great stack of paper arrived at the school on a hand-cart. The size of the sheets was about twenty-five inches by twenty inches. Half a sheet is just a good size upon which to stick an Ilond. Later I obtained some thinner paper coloured only on one side, and this the boys used to stick round the outer edge of the great sea, cut out as sun and moon, planets, many-pointed stars, and signs of the zodiac.

Some boys adorned the outer edge of the sheet with small bright labels in which the scenes and important features of the Ilond were reproduced in miniature. This touch was very telling.

It is essential that an Ilond should be clear to see and to read. Everything should therefore be drawn or written upright so that it can be understood without any need of turning the Ilond sideways or upside down. For the drawing it is best to use a decorative style with a distinct outline. Some of the boys outline their painting figures in black, which makes them very clear. It is, of course, better to use indian ink than the anæmic blue-black liquid common nowadays for writing. The legends should be neatly printed in a compact space, not scrawled wildly over the landscape. An imitation of italic print makes a neat script. A good Ilond is very neat, very clear, and generally highly coloured. It is, in fact, a bright and satisfactory piece of work altogether. The final touch is to put a red or orange label in one of the bottom corners, and to print on it the name of the Ilond and your own, thus, " The Ilond of King Wumpus, by Jack Jingle," or " Dreamland, an Ilond by Richard Wilding."

Most of our Ilonds have been wholly imaginary, but sometimes the boys take their subjects from a book read in class. The Ilond is then a kind of epitome in illustration. " A Midsummer Night's Dream " makes a beautiful Ilond.

ILONDS AND CHAP-BOOKS

It is to be presumed that most teachers of junior classes allow their boys to draw and paint pictures of the stories and ballads they read, in addition to recounting them in class or as written homework. Ilonds are very useful in this connexion, for they enable a boy to illustrate all the incidents of a story upon the same stage, instead of having to choose out some isolated episode for a single picture.

Beowulf Ilond, for instance, consists of two isles. On one is the home of Hygelac, whence Beowulf with his fourteen picked men starts out across the sea on his expedition for the relief of Hrothgar from the fell demon Grendel. The ship with its curved prow is upon the waters, going over the gannets' bath. Many whale-fishes and sea-nickers follow the men upon their voyage. Soon they draw near the land of Hrothgar, and meet the coast-watcher riding down from the cliff. He speaks bold words to Beowulf on his landing, asks who he is and what his errand. A little stone path runs inland to Heorot, the hall of Hrothgar, The roof is horn-gabled and shining with plates of gold. Hroth-gar sits upon the gift-stool. The men of Beowulf beach their ship, and bring out shields and byrnies and war-gear. Yonder in the marshes is the lair of Grendel, the lone-goer, he who walks by twilight and snatches up men as they sleep. In a cavern beneath the mere lurks Grendel's dam, grisly, awaiting her death-blow at the hands of Beowulf.

For the telling of a story in pictures it is allowable, or rather, necessary for the persons to appear several times over. Consequently Beowulf will be represented once in his ship, again in the fight with Grendel, and a third time in the struggle with Grendel's dam under the mere. But some stories are too long or too full of incident to be shown fully upon one Ilond. These are best illustrated in a series of pictures. The tale of Big Claus and Little Claus, for example (one of the best stories ever collected), can be admirably told in about a score of pictures ; and among ballads, " King Estmere," " The Gay Goshawk," and " Young Bekie " are best illustrated in this way. The pictures should be made contiguous by pasting them on a long scroll of calico. Or they may be painted on the stuff itself ; but then one blunder is fatal. The legend, most tersely worded, runs along under the pictures. The best model for this picture-narrative is, of course, the Bayeux Tapestry, a great favourite with all playboys.

Just as Ilonds can be made in illustration of an existing story, so can a story be devised to tell the tale of an existing Ilond. I mean that you may draw an Ilond first, and then make up a story to fit your pictures. This may seem a strange procedure, but such things are by no means unusual with us.* I will not say that this plan gives a stimulus to the imagination, because a playboy's imagination, if unrepressed, is already active enough. But this plan does afford a great opportunity for the imagination to express itself. The exercise of ingenuity is also required, for he who draws his pictures first, and then sets about to make a story of them, must give some plausible account of what he has drawn. Of the numerous ways of " teaching composition " the making of Ilond stories is the most conducive to originality and ingenuity, and therefore one of the most enthralling.

Speaking of his Ilond story Stevenson says, " I have said the map was the most of the plot. I might almost say it was the whole. A few reminiscences of Poe, Defoe, and Washington Irving, a copy of Johnson's 'Buccaneers,' the name of the Dead Man's Chest from Kingsley's 'At Last,' some recollections of canoeing on the high seas, and the map itself with its infinite, eloquent suggestion, made up the whole of my materials. It is, perhaps, not often that a map figures so largely in a tale, yet it is always important. . . . But it is my contention—my superstition, if you like—that who is faithful to his map, and consults it, and draws from it his inspiration, daily and hourly, gains positive support, and not mere negative immunity from accident. The tale has a root there ; it grows in that soil ; it has a spine of its own behind the words. . . . Even when a map is not all the plot, as it was in ' Treasure Island,' it will be found to be a mine of suggestion."

* Once while designing covers for chap-books I happened to make up a green cover with a band of mixed colour running across it. The design pleased me, and it next occurred to me that a suitable title for a poem to go in this cover would be " Greenwood and Arras." My friends were amused to see the cover made and the title written upon it, while yet there was no poem. But later on I made the poem to fit, and liked it even better than the chap-book cover.

ILONDS AND CHAP-BOOKS

This passage from Stevenson should be sufficient proof, if proof be needed, that in recommending the use of Ilonds in the teaching of English, we are talking, not only sense, but a sense above the common.

When the story of an Ilond is written it is bound up into the form of a chap-book. If it is your intention afterwards to write the story you should be careful not to draw the Ilond on too large a sheet ; for it must go in as the frontispiece to your chap-book.

The book itself should not be too large ; yet it cannot be very small, because writing takes up so much more space on a page than print. The paper should be white and not ruled.* The book is covered with one of the stiff coloured sheets, and tied with a bright but very narrow ribbon. A boy beginning on his second chap-book should be counselled to make it uniform with the first, but in a cover of a different tint. Thus he will make the beginnings of a series. Some design should appear upon the outer cover. If the cover paper is too dark, the design and title may be set upon a label.

The use of the chap-book is, of course, not restricted to Ilonds and their stories. Any tale can be bound up in a chap-book with its own illustrations. A long ballad, a short play or a collection of little poems will each make a chap-book. For short poems, generally light verses, we use the broadside. This is nothing but a single sheet of coloured paper of a fairly large size with the verses neatly inscribed upon it, and a gay picture on the top. Sometimes there is another picture at the bottom. Although little is said here of broadsides they will be found a very useful means of keeping the boys actively interested in the making of verses and pictures. The broadside, being but a single sheet, may be considered as a first step towards chap-books.

Here is the first chapter of an Ilond ballad-narrative by a second-form boy aged twelve. He would be a sour and unresponsive reader who would not be tempted by the last verse to turn over and read the second chapter.

* The boy will of course make his own pencil ruling which he can rub out after writing.

I requested a copy of this ballad for my album and received it with the title :

FAIR COPY OF CHAPTER I OF MY ILOND

A village there was upon my Ilond
   In the middle of the ocean blue,
And I, the king in this wondrous land,
   Dwelt with my courtiers true.

With gables high and towers strong
   In the midst of a land so free,
My palace stood with windows of gold
   Looking out o'er the fairy sea.*

The Ilonders had all their wants,
   No fighting for this and that ;
But all exchanged with a very good will
   And called it tit for tat.

But a set of rogues spoiled all our sport
   And made a great to-do.
But here is the end of Chapter I,
   The rogues are in Chapter II.

D. H.

The ballad quoted next is a description rather than a narrative. The Ilond of which it tells was not one of those finished works affixed to a coloured background and carefully painted, but merely a very rough sketch drawn in an odd moment. The sketch was only preserved because it chanced to be drawn on the wrapper in which the boy carried the bulky manuscript of a book he was writing. Considered as verse the following ballad is worthless. But its very crudity perhaps makes it more useful as an illustration. It represents, as it were, a " first step in Ilond balladry."

LAUGHING ILOND

There is a little Ilond
   Upon the Spanish main,
Its name is Laughing Ilond
   Where boys never get the cane.

* The reminiscence of Keats's " magic casements " may be very faint, but the reader has my assurance that this is a reminiscence.

To the northward is Cape Caldwell,
　　Below it Nig-nag Bay,
On its shore there is a village
　　Where the little people play

Just by it is a nigger boy
　　A-dancing on the sand.
And then a Pirates' cavern
　　On the salt sea strand.

Then there is a polar bear
　　That breathes out fire and smoke,
And the lone pines are a-swaying,
　　But the tallest tree is broke.

And then there is a greenwood
　　And it hight Ding-a-dong,
And there you see a funny tree,
　　On wheels it runs along.

Then comes the King of the Ilond
　　Who dances on the shore,
He has a crown which when he puts on
　　You see his face no more.

Then there is the Rippling Shore,
　　At one end Kaiser point,
At t'other Austrian headland
　　That looks like a thumb-joint.

That finishes the mainland
　　Except for a Redskin tent,
Which is pitched on the shore of Nig-nag Bay
　　Where the Redskin Injuns went.

To the north is Wee-wun Ilond,
　　In the centre is a hill
From which smoke is arising
　　Which is thick and makes you ill.

On the east you find the Lulla fish
　　A-basking in the sun.
On the West the Wee-wun people
　　Who sport and have much fun.

THE PLAY WAY

To the south of Laughing Ilond
  The Wa-wa fish doth sup.
My eye, an' he is big enough
  To eat the Ilond up.

There is the end of the balloon-man,
  He who failed to fly,
Eaten by the Lulla fish—
  A fearful death to die.

Age 12.

F. G. C.

The reader who is interested in Ilonds and what may come out of them will agree that this ballad, for all its weakness, was worth quoting. Many of the touches mentioned in the foregoing pages will be found illustrated in it. The writer is not one of the weaker brethren, he is one of our best playboys, but it happens that in this case he has spoken too much in the character of a guide and has not done himself justice as a poet. The following ballad, however, illustrates Ilond balladry at its best. One would think, perhaps, that the boy might have been content with such a work, but the truth is that even this ballad is but an off-shoot, while the Ilond itself has from first to last been the chief interest. The boy's father was telling me one evening how the interest of the whole household was centred in the invention and development of this Ilond ; and yet I found that the father did not even know of the existence of this ballad, which was already in the printer's hands. The Ilond itself was brought to school at my request, and the mister hung it up for all to see. But when term ended the maker of the Ilond took it away with him, explaining that he intended to make a chap-book on it. There is as much potentiality in the way of story-making in this Ilond as there was in Stevenson's map. We may yet hear more of the adventures of the new Hogginarmo and his enemy the King and those Pirates.

THE KING AND THE COUNT AND THE PIRATES

This Ilond's king is a noble man
  And hath a fine stronghold.
The domes upon his palace roof
  Are all of burnished gold.

158

When he goes to his senate house
  His flag is unfurled then,
And with the help of his soldiers
  He punishes bad men.

On a large, far-distant Ilond
  Count Hogginarmo dwells,
And north of him a burning mount
  And boiling water wells.

Hogginarmo is bad and bold,
  A mighty man is he.
When the king sent to say, " Obey ! "
  He cried, " Obey, not me ! "

" Now have I not a walled town
  And a castle on the hill ?
I'll run him through with my good sword
  Right readily I will ! "

Then bugles, trumpets, lutes and lyres
  Struck out a martial tune,
And in the town were music-men
  Who played the loud bassoon.

" Now rede me, rede me," said the king,
  " My rede shall rise at thee."
" I'd have the good and strong sea-wood *
  And quickly put to sea."

The king put out with five good ships,
  And staunch and strong were they.
And he came to the Straits of Indigo
  Upon a Saturday.

Count Hogginarmo's men came forth
  And stood upon the wall,
With gunners, bowmen, musqueteers,
  At one loud bugle call.

Then the king attacked the castle
  And smoke and dust flew high,
And all along the shrieking sound
  Of round-shot tearing by.

  * " Rede me " is from " King Estmere " ; " Sea-wood " from a
translation of Beowulf.

THE PLAY WAY

Then the king landed his soldiers
   And charged the castle wall,
But in face of Hogginarmo's guns
   Full many men did fall.

At last the top of this great wall
   Was gained by only two.
They slashed out right, they slashed out left,
   And many men they slew.

Count Hogginarmo's cowards fled
   Before the doughty twain,
And they pursued them all alone
   And struck and struck again.

And quite alone they cleared the wall,
   And when a man was found
That turned his face and tried to fight
   One smote him to the ground.

At last a fearful oath they hear
   And the great Count they see,
Who rushed on one and with his sword
   Bashed his brain-pan in three.

The other dealt the Count a blow
   As made him reel full sore.
Alas ! the Count pierced him right through—
   He died upon the floor.

Three of the king's good ships were sunk
   And one so badly hit,
That when they tried to go a-speed
   The water entered it.

Then Hogginarmo ruled the land
   For full a month—but anon
The king thundered down with might and main
   Upon the bad Baron.

Then said the king to the Pirates,
   " If you storm his stronghold,
I'll give you jewels by the pound,
   And tons and tons of gold."

The Pirates then they sailed around,
    And all along the shore
They set up guns, and many guns,
    And guns and guns galore.

Then the pirates fired red-hot shot
    And made a fearful charge
Upon the town ; whose walls were strong
    And very tall and large.

The pirates soon had won the town,
    They spared no single bit,
But plundered right and plundered left,
    And then set fire to it.

So Hogginarmo sulkily,
    Though he hated the thing,
Was forced to pay a fine and do
    Low homage to the king.

Age 12.   J. B. W.

After the Littlemen have played at Ilonds and chap-books for a while many of them will be anxious to make a book entirely by themselves ; to do the composition, painting, writing, binding and all, even as did William Blake with his books. They like to keep the matter secret until they can approach triumphantly with a finished work. But the teacher should insist upon seeing a rough copy of the proposed story or ballad or poem before the making of the broadside or chap-book begins, because there will always be some little faults of spelling or sentence-structure or metre to be amended. And nothing is more distressing to a boy—and consequently to his master—than to find the result of his joyful labour marred by trivial errors that might so easily have been corrected.

The question of the handwriting for broadsides and chap-books must have occurred to the reader. Any boy who takes a pride in his handiwork will soon be dissatisfied with writing a book in his ordinary hand. Modern handwriting has so many decorations, so many ugly curls and unnecessary links between letters that, however neat, it can never be beautiful. It is, for a number of reasons, most unsuitable for a book. And type-writing is, of course, altogether out of the question. You cannot mix together handicraft and machine-work, for the simple reason that the one allows the individual touch and the other does not.

There is only one way of writing in a hand-made chap-book, and that is in formal script. There are many styles of lettering, but for school use the best is the simplest. It is best for three reasons : (i) that a simple formal hand is mastered fairly soon for use in chap-books and other careful writing ; (ii) that, being simple, it is more likely to come into cursive use ; and (iii) that the simplicity of the letters is in direct antagonism to the curly, twisty abominations of the modern hand. And so the teacher should be careful to avoid any ornate style of old lettering, and introduce his pupils to the simple, severe, essential forms of the letters.

This warning is necessary, because most people foolishly imagine that present-day handwriting *is* lettering at its simplest ; and when one speaks of formal script they think at once of ornamental letters and the illuminated capitals of old missals. It is news to most people that quite half the strokes they make in their handwriting are unnecessary links. If you will look in a printed book you will find that the letters of a word are not strung together, but bunched. I shall say no more about script here, but refer the reader to an expert authority.*

Mr. Graily Hewitt says : " No doubt but few people can find time to learn and practise a formal hand ; but all might adopt and adapt a method of writing that acknowledged traditions achieved by centuries of painstaking, centuries qualified, if only by the absence of machinery, to assist in a matter where the hand is still essential. . . . To-day the connecting stroke between the letters of a word has been insisted upon till it has become a fetish. Of old it was only used when convenient, the letters were made one after another and connected automatically by bunching or clamping together. This bunching assists legibility, for we read the bunch of a word rather than the separate letters forming it. To separate these by a connecting stroke is to protract the reading. . . . The modern pen is chiefly

* See the Oxford Copy Books by Graily Hewitt, published by Henry Frowde and Hodder & Stoughton, Nos. 1 and 2, price 3d. each. Broad pens can be had of Wm. Mitchell, 3 Warwick Lane, E.C.

to blame. It is fine and pliable. The mediæval pen was comparatively broad and stiff. Thickness of down-strokes requires pressure upon a fine pen ; a broad pen does without, and the writer's attention is not distracted by such an unnecessary demand upon him. With a fine pen a child cannot make a page of writing uniform in its downstrokes. But if he use the old method he can do this at once, and attend to direction unembarrassed—a very great gain. . . . *With a broad stiff pen a child could not go far wrong if he tried to imitate printed letters such as our italics* without any copybook at all. . . . The tool that was chiefly concerned in the evolution of the Roman Alphabet up to the sixteenth century might be trusted again.''

Perhaps some teacher may feel that his own inability (or unwillingness) to master a formal hand renders him unable to introduce penmanship to his boys. It depends, of course, as every proposal in this book depends, on your view of a teacher's function. It is no use trying to teach what you are incapable of teaching, but a master can do wonders by putting his boys on the track of something which they can teach themselves. As soon as I came into touch with formal script I told the boys of it. Two of them in the sixth form took it up, and, being born with a skill for the craft, were beyond my reach within a week. Before the end of the following term these boys had executed " outside orders " for addresses for presentation. Among the Littlemen there are a few who write extremely well, and many more who can make a very fair page. All these outstrip me, for I am only just a little better than those despondent ones who say, " I'm no good at this game, sir." Yet with the joyous labour of many perspiring hours even we clumsy-fisted ones have produced some interesting chap-books. Some teachers, again, are unable to draw. What matter ? In my time I have even ventured on pictures. They may have been horrid—in fact they *were* horrid ; but some of the pictures made by the Littlemen thereafter afforded me an ample excuse.

The two passages which follow are Ilond stories written as prose studies. Both writers are boys of twelve in the second form. These quotations illustrate two very distinct styles. Neither of the boys had an atom of help in his work.

THE PLAY WAY

THE ILOND OF NUMOWAN

King Numowa lived on the west side of the Ilond of Numowan. On the eastern shore, opposite Devilton and Devilton harbour, was the harbour of Wolumbrigia, and King Wamgig's castel where King Wamgig lived.

One day as King Numowa was out watching his fleet fishing he fell overboard and a shark swallowed him up. His fishing fleet then ran back to Numowton harbour and told the poor Numowtonians the sad news of the death of their good king for whom great regret was felt and many people wept.

In the middle of their sadness news was received that the devils had invaded the land of Numowa and were pouring through the pass in the mountains which separated the two lands. So the Numowtonians went out and fought with the devils. The devils were soon beaten and were put to flight and chased as far as the pass by which they had entered the land of Numowan. Meanwhile strange things had happened at Devilton harbour. One of King Wamgig's boats had put into Devilton harbour by mistake and had been captured, and the king of the devils told the devils to take King Wamgig and take his robe off and burn him, and he said he would come along later to see that his work was done properly.

The devils did as they were told and took King Wamgig's robe off and burnt him. The king of the devils was true to his word and came down to see the fire and that the work had been done properly. When the king of the devils came to the fire he saw that everything had been done as he had commanded, but he was very cross when he saw King Wamgig's legs sticking out of the fire so he ordered the men who put him in to be put in also.

H. C.

IN THE ISLE OF KING SHACK

It is in the Isle of King Shack that fiery dragons do reside. And it so happened once that a brave knight did attempt their killing, but the wicked witch Wyrd, who doth reign o'er all the world, did give the dragons power to master him, and they

164

imprisoned him in the Cave of Darkness, which is their resting-place. And so the knight's bones did gradually decay, till they gave way from under him, and he died. Then demons and devils came unto his corse, and did eat of it. But as he was a good man when he lived, they liked not his flesh.

Then came a young man, who had done no sin, unto an aged man, and said :

" Now I have heard how my father was slain by the dragons, and I would avenge his death. If thou wilt give me counsel. then will I be to thee a trusty squire." Then the aged man said, " If thou wouldst do as thou sayest, lad, then go now into my cabin and fetch me my staff." Then the young man went in and fetched the staff. " Now," said the old man, " When thou comest unto the dragons, lie down as if thou wert dead, then the dragons will go away, and as they depart, strike them with this staff.

When the lad came unto the Cave of Darkness, he lay down on his back. Then came the dragons out, and when they looked on his face that was so pure, for he had done no sin, they were affrighted. Said one : " This is the man who has done no sin, and who it is prophesied shall work our destruction." Then they turned away, and the lad sprang up, He struck the first dragon upon the head, and looked hard upon him. The dragon shrank before his glance, and fell upon the ground. Then the second dragon sprang upon him, but he was light of foot, and sprang him nimbly aside. The second dragon fell upon the first, and killed him.

The lad returned to the aged man, and was faithful unto his death.

G. S. S.

A complete chap-book is too long to quote by way of illustration, but some account may be given to show how in these longer works the story becomes of more importance than the original Ilond, as happened in the case of Stevenson. " The Isle of Adrian " is the work of a boy of fifteen or more in the fifth form. He is one of those who " never grew up." Several senior boys, such as sixth-form prefects, and those who had already entered the university, took a keen interest in the play-productions of the Littlemen. But that was an adult interest, the interest which teachers will show in the course of time. But the author of " The Isle of Adrian " really wished himself back in the second form. " I wish I had a chance to do these things," he often said. He was a playboy to his finger-tips. " The Isle of Adrian," opens with a prologue : " A happy Littleman am I, and in these few pages I shall explain to Uncle Joe the joys of my Ilond."

There is a large coloured picture showing the slippered Uncle Joe sitting in his armchair smoking a long pipe and reading the paper. On the floor a small boy is kneeling. A box of toys lies open beside him, and he is setting out upon a square board, which represents his Ilond, some trees and men and Noah's Ark animals. On the next page appears a real Littleman Ilond, showing the Ilond full of life as it was appearing in fancy to the nephew of Uncle Joe. The thirty pages or so which follow give an account of the inhabitants of the Ilond, their habits, their haunts, and their goings on. Almost every page has a picture, and some have three or four. The first chapter is a general survey, and the others give particulars of chosen characters.

" King Carranzabar, the noble ruler of this land, lives with his family and court of all-valiant knights in his stately castel, which stands so proudly, sporting its red minarets here on the hill. We see him at present driving in his state coach, with footmen in cocked hats. . . ."

" Two knights we see jousting in friendlike mien. The shaggy lion lays aside his kingly state and watches the fun with undignified interest, while the glowing snake wriggles up to his side. Jumbo, the grey elephant, has strolled from the wood on to the cliff, and gazes over the blue scape of water at a ship dim on the horizon. High in air we see Bavieca the witch, astride her broom, floating down through the fresh morning air. . . while Fender, the green Dragon, is keeping up his morning practice of hurling forth red-hot abuse at some imaginary foe. On the side of the grassy slope the Flat-foot bird is flapping his wings to brace him for the day, while on the grass many little elves are prancing, prancing merrily. Over the palm-tipped crest of the hill, Lout, the Giant, is looming."

" Look, Uncle ! here in the offing you may find the king's

two sons fishing from a neatly rigged little boat, and the Sea-serpent follows the Royal yacht, perhaps in playful chase, or perhaps on the off-chance of a sympathetic crumb. But I fancy a whole loaf would be more to his liking, and not even the Royal yacht with a pattern on its sail can afford whole loaves for ordinary coily sea-serpents. You must understand, Uncle, that these beings on the isle are well-intentioned. . . . As for Fender his appearance is most misleading, for one could scarcely be fond of a being who breathed forth fire and chewed cinders. But in his less energetic moments he is a sweet old thing. He would not intentionally hurt a soul. In fact the childer of the ilond love him so much that they may be seen every afternoon toddling off to him, each with a piece of house-flannel to polish up his scales. This kind attention the dragon well enjoys, and during the operation lays himself out flat and tells stories to his gay little troop of polishers."

At this point there are two very pleasing pictures, one showing six " childer " running out with duster in hand, and the other showing them all grouped on and about old Fender busily polishing him.

The second chapter consists of the autobiography of this genial monster as " told to the blithe young children who were rubbing his scales to brightness." The chapter is long and ends with these words, " Here the dragon ceased. The little children had stopped polishing and were sitting round him, enraptured of his telling."

" Surely the most wonderful of the beings on the Isle of Adrian is Gorger, the red beast to the left of the wood. Gorger is not his real name. He is really a very fine relic of the Model-in-plasticine tribe ; but as his chief virtue is his marvellous eating capacity, the islanders gave him this name."

There is unhappily no space to relate the legend of " Ten-Three, the Gayest Bird that ever bore a Tail," nor the spell of " The Fat Pink Pig with the Big Black Spots," nor even to quote the descriptions of the other residents in the Isle of Adrian. A passage from Chapter IV must conclude these extracts :

" You must know, Uncle, that the brave walls and lofty towers of the castel enclose many fair ladies and many doughty knights. There are beautiful terraces hidden behind those solid battlements, where flowers grow, and knights court ladies in the sunlight. Each day at noon the warriors parade in line on their frisking steeds and charge down the winding road on to the Lower Island, there to rehearse the arts of war. Meanwhile His Majesty the King, dressed in shining armour with breeze-blown plumes a-fluttering, strides proudly round, attended by his equerries, clapping the gests of his knights. . . .

" When the knights have shot their arrows and given practice to their sword-play for a space, a herald, at the word of the king, raises his brasen horn to his lips and blows a mighty blast with great pouting of cheeks. The knights on hearing this signal form themselves full briskly into two equal companies. They then disarm and provide themselves with wooden swords, each man having a tuft of paper plumes stuck in his helmet—those of one side a red tuft, those of the other a white. Then a second blast is blowen and the knights, ranged in two opposing ranks, give eye to the King who is now holding aloft a purple kerchief. This he duly drops and the knights, digging their spurs into the flanks of their white chargers, dash to meet in mock battle. Then the ranks crash together as two roaring waves that meet. The chargers rear on their haunches and each sturdy fighter strains his abilities to flay his adversary's plumes from his polished helmet.

" Vigorously he slashes at them with his wooden sword, at the same time struggling to safeguard his own. Fierce waxes the fight with the cracking of swords and the clanking of armour, till at length when the ground is strewn with paper plumes, and those who have lost them are many, the king again gives word to his herald, who sounds his horn yet a third time. The knights on hearing deliver no further blows, but retire to their order. His Majesty proclaims in his clear ringing voice which company has triumphed. The announcement is received with long cheers and hearty.

" These things done, all retire to the castel. . . ."*

Throughout the whole chap-book Uncle Joe does not vouch-

---

* A hypercritical reader may complain of the artificiality of this style. But the writer is consciously aiming at style, and the *conscious* efforts of beginners must always look artificial.

168

safe a word, and the writer does not tell us whether he listened or read the paper, or fell asleep.

This is very true to life, for Littleman play requires no audience. It is not a show, but a rehearsal. While Uncle Joe sits in his chair before the fire Littleman camps on the hearthrug, and sets out his wooden toys in a pattern of life. And all the time he prattles away to himself. He is only half aware of the presence of Uncle Joe. He may from time to time feel dimly sorry that the old gentleman is missing so much. But Uncle Joe is only in the margin of his consciousness. His mind is really concentrated upon this realm of fancy he is creating, this Ilond. It is to himself that he is prattling of dragons and witches, of kings, castles, and knightly combat.

All this the writer of the " Isle of Adrian " knows as well as any of us, you may depend upon it. For as the artist creates in a flash that which critics take years to expound, so the playboy gaily produces innumerable works of self-expression, while his teachers are fumbling blindly in the murk of theoretical psychology.

Education will always be the stodgy process it is to-day, until teachers throw the pedagogical professors overboard, and turn their whole attention upon the boys. Pedagogy, forsooth ! The very word reeks of humbug. Play, sir, is what you need for boys.

If the painting of the prologue-picture to the" Isle of Adrian " had been left to me I should have put in the hands of the preoccupied Uncle Joe, not a newspaper, but a volume of " Education in the Home." But sarcasm is an adult vice.

The reader must not expect me to reason him into a belief in Ilonds considered as a device of educational method. There has already been far too much vague nonsense talked about " training the imagination," " exercising the boy in self-expression," and so on by people who haven't a notion how to set about it. There have been whole conferences and books without number devoted to such theoretical recommendations. It is high time to suggest something in the way of practice, and let psychology be a while.

Many teachers, it is to be feared, will consider Ilonds a childish game, appropriate only for leisure hours in the nursery.

THE PLAY WAY

Others, possibly, will allow Ilonds in the schoolroom, and then spoil them by making them properly *instructional*. And many teachers of English will cast these proposals aside as a waste of the all-too-brief time allotted to literature. If so, I hope that one day, when in search of out-of the-way words with which to puzzle their pupils, or " stiff " pieces of poetry to be paraphrased into a prose mince, these good people may light upon a certain book which, though inappropriately named, is yet the supreme masterpiece among Ilonds. A king with his son and their attendant lords are cast ashore upon an Ilond. There are also a few shipwrecked mariners. In a cave there lives a strange beast, whose mother was a witch. The Ilond is full of little elfin people who spend the hours in play, now mock the travellers, and anon sing and dance to the waves upon the yellow sands. The master of the Ilond is a sorcerer, and at his bidding an airy sprite, whom he freed from a cloven pine, does many wonderful magics.

The homework for teachers will be to analyse the last sentence.

CHAPTER VI

PLAYTOWN

This is the best fooling, when all is done.
"Twelfth Night"

IN a book concerned with educational method—for this is a book on educational method, however remotely it may be connected with modern classroom practice—the subject of Playtown must be treated but briefly. For Playtown is essentially an out-of-school occupation, and most teachers will not consent to be bothered with it. But there are some who will take any amount of trouble to cater for their boys' real interests, and some who themselves are players by nature, and it is to the ear and to the fancy of these that the following notes on Playtown are commended.

For the site of your Playtown you take a spare piece of land. It may be a waste patch near the scullery, or an unused corner of the kitchen garden, or, as in our case, a mere back yard. This terrain you will transform into a model countryside. It may be that you have soil and sand and sods of earth at your command, and if so, your way is made more easy. But we had nothing to work upon but a concrete back yard. The only encouraging circumstance was the opportunity of water-supply from a tap ten yards off and round the corner of the house.

First a load of coarse gravel and a load of sand were procured. These were dumped in the middle of the yard, and for lack of a shovel I distributed the heaps with a broom. It is perhaps worth recording that a heap of sand can be shifted more expeditiously with a broom than by shovelling it about in spadefuls.

The yard sloped gradually towards a drain. So in plotting the river-course I began at the far end from the drain; and added length to the proposed river by setting a hill in the direct route to the drain. This made it necessary for the river-course to go up and round. The river was to be supplied by means of a hose from the tap round the corner.

To keep the water within the gravel banks it was of course necessary to cement them. So I ordered a sack of cement, and we sifted the sand from our hills. We soon grew proficient in the craft of mortar-mixing and cementing. The river banks were made about four inches high at first. But as soon as the water was put in it became apparent that the banks near the drain would have to be built some inches higher. For the water of course did not run straight down the drain, but was dammed just above it to give us some depth. But while the depth at the end of the course was over six inches there was (owing to the slope) no water at all in the upper reaches. It was therefore necessary to put in a lock. For the gates we took two small square tiles (only one for each end of the lock), and made cement grooves for them to slide into as a window slides up and down in its frame. There was some skilful trowel-work about that lock. A similar single gate at the lowest part of the river kept the water above the level of the drain.

We kept our railway dead straight with a view to running the trains on a cable system. The advantage of the cable system in toy trains is that it enables you from either terminus to stop the train at any point. The disadvantage is that it is very difficult to avoid getting the cable, or belt, either too tight or too loose.

We decided that our railway should encounter and overcome by means of embankment, tunnel, bridge, and cutting all the difficulties it was possible to contrive. The track started on an embankment with a station. Then it plunged into a tunnel under the hill and emerged upon the second station. A bridge spanned the river, intentionally at its widest point, and an islet mysteriously sprang up in the middle to facilitate this engineering feat. There was another station cut precipitously out of the far hill-side, and the track terminated just beyond.

It is impossile to do any practical surveying on such a diminutive scale, and so everything was done empirically. What did not fit was done all over again in the light of experience. The most foolish mistake we made was to measure for the

Gareth Hostel, Green Hill, Upper River, and Lock

The Market-Place, St. Nicholl's Station, and Castle Hill

height of the bridge from the *bed* of the river (the water was turned off while we were working there) instead of allowing for the height of a ship from the *surface* of the water. The level of the whole railway track could not be raised to correct this error, because the tunnel was already finished, and a strong cement castle had been built on the hill over it.* And of course the whole river level could not be lowered. So the railway bridge was only some three inches above the river surface instead of a good six, and no boats other than barges could pass beneath.

It happened at this time that two inspectors came specially down from Whitehall to see what all this Play Way business was about. After they had seen all the things we did in the classroom they were suddenly taken to a back yard and confronted with Playtown. Both were surprised of course, but while one stood and nursed his amazement—stood upon a farmyard and made great ruin—the other grasped the Play idea at once, and, setting aside officialdom and pedagogy, went down on his knees and endeavoured to solve the problem of the bridge. The Tower Bridge device and all sorts of swing-bridges, such as he and others suggested, were impracticable, because toy railway lines are made in sections which must remain joined. In the end we had to make a steep gradient from the tunnel and onwards to make room for boats to pass under the bridge. This steep gradient has been a nuisance to us ever since.

In the beginning the first form was admitted to Playtown for one period a week during school hours. But there were too many boys for the small yard, and as the game was new to them they all needed direction, and careful watching lest they did damage. So classes were abandoned, and Playtown became the haunt of a chosen few out of school hours. There were generally about six or eight there at a time. In all, some fifty or sixty

* The photographs show the castle on the hill over the tunnel, but the plan of Playtown shows it in another situation. This is because the photographs were taken in 1913, and the plan represents the countryside as it was in 1915. Various other discrepancies are to be explained by this fact, the principal ones being the disappearance of Gareth Hostel, and the coming of a Netherland with a Tramway in its place; and the conversion of the whole hill above St. David's into one tremendous citadel.

boys of all ages ranging from nine to nineteen had their part in the building up and carrying on of this miniature countryside.

The making of the river and the railway (and playing with them) occupied all our spare time during the first summer term. The following season we covered the gravel with a layer of soil and planted grass and the cuttings of trees. Little wooden houses were made, and meadows and farms were fenced in and filled with a great variety of live stock. Roads were driven across the land, wharves appeared here and there along the river banks, with cranes and warehouses for the merchandise, and the railway stations became little centres of civic life. We found the cable system too difficult to work with any certainty, and abandoned it in the second year for clockwork engine power.

Most of the inhabitants were perforce military. It is possible to obtain from toy-shops a railway staff and a box of civilians. But in the experience of toy-makers there are only eight civilian types. Two of these are the same female figure, but painted in different colours, and three more are men in uniform, a policeman, a yachtsman, and a chauffeur. There is no shopkeeper, no workman, no newsboy, no loafer. Just two clerks, one man in a sun-hat, two identical women, and then back we go to uniforms. The public in this matter, as in all its dealings with manufacturers, must just take what it can get or go without. The commercial man's idea of service is to follow his own limited notions, and then to thrust his shoddy wares down the throats of the community, shrieking aloud to them all the while to avoid imitations. If this were true only of children's toys it would be bad enough, but it is very much the same with all the things we have to buy.

As time went on certain boys claimed estates of their own and colonized them. There were many residences, a few farms, two fortresses, a coal-mine, a builder's yard, and a market-place. The builder's merchant supplied gravel and sand, and stakes for palings. He also kept little cement bricks, which, however, every one made for himself, and no one ever used. The " Deep Drop Coal Mine " was owned by Digging Bros., and worked by some boy scouts, a wounded soldier, and a chauffeur because he had a lamp. There was a superstructure of " meccano," and a cage which went down into the pit The usual stock of merchandise upon a wharf consisted of little sacks filled with and. These could be grain in times of peace and protective sand-bags in time of war. Cats and dogs were to be found near the houses ; and rabbits, pigs, cows, horses, and even a few wild boars lived in the fields. Every household had its baby, but sometimes exigency of circumstance compelled a white mother to adopt a black piccaninny.

During the third season many improvements were made. The countryside was extended by the addition of territory, and became half as large again. The railway was also extended by the addition of a branch line with another station. The grass was now well tended ; and the little roads, just wide enough for a boy to walk along by putting one foot carefully before the other, were kept neat by frequent sprinklings of fresh sand. The introduction of paint made the whole place look much brighter and more toy-like, for houses, wharves, station platform, bridges, and fences, as well as the boats and trains, were painted all manner of gay colours.

The general lines of play as it is carried on with toy trains and boats and lead soldiers must be known to all. There is no space here to go into the details of floor-games. But a few particulars of our especial play may be given. We rarely went to war, for the boys found ample occupation in the ordering of each his own domain and in commercial transactions. As a genial onlooker once observed, " Here is citizenship in the *concrete.*"

Little clockwork tugs pulled laden barges up the river, bumping first into one bank and then into the other, and some-times wasting so much power on the journey that they could not face the outrush of water when the lock was opened. Trains ignored the signals, ran off the rails, stopped dead in the tunnel, or came in collision with one another, as they do in nurseries and playrooms everywhere. Boys shouted up the river or down the line, " I'm sending you a ton of coal for Mr. Orkney," or " The guard has orders to wait for the key of the small engine." There were excited shouts whenever accidents happened, and shouts more excited still when they didn't. Cries of " Just look at *The Little Beast* coming into my wharf ! " " Mind your silly head out of the light," and " Sir, sir, *sir* ! " were heard on all sides. There seemed to be enough to do in this little world without any need of war.

THE PLAY WAY

In a small shed the work of fretsawing and hammering and painting went steadily on. And while some were indulging in mere fun others took it in turns to cut the grass on the common land, to tidy up the roads, and to renew paint-work that didn't need renewal. These gatherings took place after school in the summer evenings, and occasionally during half-holidays when the citizens were not " down " for compulsory games.

At first we used to repair to the house for an interval for tea, but the boys were so absorbed in Playtown that they actually asked, not without some fear of seeming rude, that tea might be abolished, because " it takes up time." The refreshment, however, was not entirely abolished, but adapted to the circumstances, and we had set out upon one of our benches a bottle of lime-juice with jugs and glasses, and a round tray piled with buns. Thus we were able to eat and drink without interrupting the play.

The features of the landscape were soon named, there was Green Hill and Castle Hill, and Adrian's wharf with the Deep Drop Coal Mine (Digging Bros.). The harbour and railway station adjoining the river *sluice* were called St. Louis on that account. The places at the other termini of the railway were called St. Nicholl's and St. David's after their respective founders, who, however, had not previously been canonized. The river had its source in a waterfall (of which, by the way, any " landscape gardener " might have been proud), but this waterfall was not named, because it was in the " Undiscovered Country."

> These are the hills, these are the woods,
> These are my starry solitudes ;
> And there the river by whose brink
> The roaring lions come to drink.

The lake into which the water fell was called " The Lake of Magellan " after another boy, until an explorer was drowned in it, and then it became " Dead Man's Lake."

The body of the explorer was recovered and conveyed down the river in a barge with much funeral pomp. He was buried with military honours on the slopes of Castle Hill, and a monument erected to his memory. Here the intrepid one lay in peace for two years, until, being exhumed by chance one day

176

during excavations, he was resuscitated and restored to his rank in the army. His cenotaph remains—a hollow mockery.

The reader may recall " The Dumb Soldier " of Stevenson, who had the enviable experience of lying buried for a season.

> Under grass alone he lies,
> Looking up with leaden eyes,
> Scarlet coat and pointed gun
> To the stars and to the sun.
>
> I shall find him, never fear,
> I shall find my grenadier ;
> But for all that's gone and come,
> I shall find my soldier dumb.

When a man falls into the water a crane is hurried to the spot. If he can be fished out at the first angling he may live, but if not, he is presumed dead, and becomes for the time being a thing of naught.

The " Undiscovered Country " is known to be inhabited by various tribes, whose history would make an interesting study for an ethnologist. For it is said by those who live at " The Last Post " that one of these warring factions is led by one Hullabaloo the Zulu, and another by a certain Hitchy Koo or Bread upon the Waters, a Red Indian Chief. Another attractive personality, who made his first and only appearance at a War Council of the Powers, was Tin Can, the Chinese ambassador.

We have made so little of wars that the subject need not be treated here. The reader is referred to Mr. H. G. Wells's " Little Wars," upon whose rules of campaigning we based our own. Of the many interesting civil events which occurred during our four Playtown seasons I have space to record fully but one.

Sir George Thorpe, a landowner of local importance, was asked by Mr. Flaggy, the station-master of St. Nicholl's, to plant a tree, in commemoration of some event not stated. The occasion was an important one, and the whole countryside made ready to attend the ceremony. But a difficulty arose from the fact that each household seemed to have a double in every other household. The station staff at St. David's could not be distinguished from those at Castle Hill Station. And Mr. Orkney so closely resembled C. Tain, the builder's merchant,

M

that Mrs. Orkney refused to let her husband travel in the same train, for fear of " mixing him up."

Matters came to a head when Sir George Thorpe declared, with some heat, that unless that journalist fellow, Mr. Noseabout, ceased to duplicate him in every particular he would plant no trees—no, not though the military paraded six regiments, and all the military bands in the country played " He's a jolly good fellow." Things were looking very gloomy, and it seemed as though the public holiday would have to be abandoned, when suddenly one of the trolley porters of St. David's fell into a pot of white enamel, and was fished out *a milkman*! The solution of the difficulty was hailed with delight, and every one hurried home to change his clothes. Sir George left the journalist fellow to wear navy blue and himself appeared in a rich brown —of which trouble was to arise. Train after train now arrived at St. Nicholl's bringing families hardly yet dry in their new clothes, and with them their domestic pets. Army and Navy were both represented, and it was rumoured afterwards that even Hullabaloo the Zulu had painted little white buttons on his brown skin and come to the great tree-planting.

Speeches were made, the tree was duly planted, bands played, and the soldiers fired what some one in the crowd called a "Few de Joy." And then discord arose. Sir George having had the bad taste in his third speech to make some scathing remarks about journalists, Mr. Noseabout, the reporter, clad in neat blue serge, referred impudently to Sir George as " that chocolate eclair." The crowd began to shout and to take sides, and soon there would have been a tumult, had not the captain of the garrison, with admirable presence of mind, opened fire with his guns upon the populace.

Now it happened that in the assembly was a quiet little woman, Mrs. Bimbo by name, a lodging-house keeper. Finding that it was growing late, and not being particularly interested in the quelling of riots, Mrs. Bimbo decided to go home " and cook the chops for her young gentlemen's dinners." But when she arrived at the station there was no train and no staff.

> It was all deserted around,
> For they all had gone to the fair, sir,
> And there was no one to be found.

PLAYTOWN

It was a long walk home to the other side of Castle Hill by road, so Mrs. Bimbo decided to take a short cut through the idle tunnel. A few minutes later, the riot having been cut short by the death by misadventure of Mr. Noseabout, the return excursion train started from St. Nicholl's. And the young gentlemen had no chops for their dinner that night, for little Mrs. Bimbo had been decapitated in the tunnel.

There have been, of course, many tragedies and romances connected with the railway. One of the most remarkable was the case of old Mr. Peaky, the railway official, who spent a whole winter in the tunnel. On his being recovered in the early summer it occurred to some one, apropos of nothing at all, that poor Mr. Peaky in his present state was " the image of Ibsen." None of us understood why, but Mr. Peaky was honoured accordingly, and placed on a pedestal in the market-place.

While Playtown is in full activity every one has to be careful where he steps, and to walk only on the appointed " treads." For one is a Gulliver in this Lilliputian land. But towards the end of the season we relax care, and take less interest in the minute things. We even run up and down by the river in sailing our boats, as though it were a dyke and had no roads, fences, buildings, and wharves along its banks. Thus it happens that with the restoration of each returning spring, many relics are excavated which were trodden into the ground in the autumn. A boy digging the foundations of his new house, or making a cutting for a railway extension, will unearth old walls, pieces of machinery, bits of forgotten people, and all manner of treasure. These we carefully preserve in a Playtown Museum kept in the shed. The finds are labelled with the most romantic ascriptions : " Roof beams of a manor house of the last century unearthed on the site of the present Gareth Hostel." " Rim and a few spokes of an old cart-wheel found when digging the Well of the Lady Oliver." * The query sometimes seen on museum labels is also quaintly mimicked : " ? Skull of a Zulu warrior." " ? Funnel of a primitive steam-engine." And so on. This may be poor fun for the adult reader, and offensive to an archæologist,

* This name was not a corruption of Olivia, but had a separate origin.

but it is excellent play. For who that knows boys will deny that they love excavations, and can appreciate the excitement of a find as keenly as the most learned geologist? And surely it is better for them to dig up something which really is exciting than to fall back always upon unsupported make-believe. But I must not argue here, for an understanding of Playtown, more than of all these other schemes, depends upon one's having a player's instinct. And that is uncommunicable.

Our Playtown in shape is an irregular oblong, and in size some four yards by fourteen. There are four hills, the largest of which is about two feet in height. Those who wish to make a Playtown are recommended to go where soil is available, for in our yard more than a dozen loads of gravel, sand, and soil have been required to form the land. Cement is necessary if you propose to have any water. We used about a sack and a half of cement each season, for the banks of the river need occasional repair, and new cement is always being laid for wharves and station platforms and to support the sides of cuttings on roads and railway. Cement-work can be painted, but the colour fades rapidly until several coats have been applied. Battlements can be cast or carved in cement, but the operation is difficult. The round towers of our castle were made by filling coffee-tins with soft cement and ripping the tin away when the cement had hardened. For the water, a large lake would probably be more convenient than a river. The river current makes navigation difficult for tiny clockwork boats. Also a flowing river, if not given constant attention, will overflow. We had many floods. If possible your whole Playtown should be raised three feet or so from the ground. It would thus be easy to handle things without sitting on the ground or stooping, and, more important still, the countryside would not be constantly trodden upon. We were always having to repair damage done by our careless feet. One way of getting the Playtown three feet above ground level would be to build a wall all round the proposed coast-line and then fill the space enclosed. But a simpler plan would be to make your Playtown on ground level, and then dig trenches round it to walk in.

Adrian's Wharf and the Deep Drop Coal Mine

The Capture of St. Nicholl's

PLAYTOWN

The country itself is permanent—for the season. Houses and stations can also be made to stand the weather. But railway lines, trains, boats, and the inhabitants should be put away in a shed for the night.

A Playtown of course demands a certain amount of attention. You cannot keep the little country in trim if you bestow no more care on it than you would upon nursery floor-games. But there is no reason why a man or a boy should not spend as much care and attention upon such a thing as this as he would upon his garden. During the summer term I was accustomed to give ten or twelve hours a week myself to working at Playtown, though this of course included building new features and repairing old ones, as well as tending the place in a general way.

Needless to say we do not anticipate that there will ever be many Playtowns. But those few players who like the idea may be glad of the above hints.

The Play Way, let it be said again, is not the easy way. You cannot just throw a few materials to the boys and leave them to amuse themselves. They will find enough sheer amusement in their own free time ; but where a teacher takes part the play should be something of pith and substance. There is more hard work, even actual labour, attached to the Play Way schemes than there is in classroom " work." And the driving power, which enables both the boys and the masters to undertake the arduous duties which are *always* part and parcel of real play, is interest. If it chance that you are so made that you could never take an active interest in Playtown, then of course you will leave it alone and try something else. But if any one fancies that grown-up people (grave and reverend signiors as we all fancy we are) cannot be thoroughly enchanted with such toys as clockwork boats and trains, then he is blind. Men and women do not play with toys, simply because they are too busy or because toys are not at hand. But while Playtown has been available many grown men and several women have spent hours playing there. And on more than one occasion, when the Littlemen had all gone home to bed, three or four staid and responsible adults have left care behind them in the house, and come out with me after dinner to sail the boats and to run the trains. When it grew too dark to see any longer we did not go in, but brought out lighted candles and still pursued the game. Sometimes we have played away the length of two whole candles after dark.

"But what has all this to do with education ? " you may ask. Yes, you may well ask ; but, like Shylock, " I'll not answer that ! "

CHAPTER VII

ACTING SHAKESPEARE IN THE CLASSROOM *

Within this wooden O.
"Henry V"

A TEACHER who is desirous of adopting play-methods with his
boys in connexion with at least some of their lessons will perhaps
at first find some difficulty in devising schemes of play. It is
too much to expect that the boys or the master should start
suddenly from their desks and say, "Go to, we will now study
in the Play Way." For the teacher of English the easiest way
of making a start is obviously to let the boys act some story or
portion of a book which they are reading. It is of course out
of the question for any one to sit down and write a dramatic
version of the story. The thing must be acted extempore in
the classroom. But unless you happen to have a special knack
of casting stories into dramatic form you may find yourself in
difficulties at the very start. And it is very disheartening to
the boys if their experiments keep falling through, and the play
of which so much was expected turns out a failure.

We early formed a habit of dramatizing almost everything
we read. But at first I used to give the boys suggestions of a
scheme of action. This was a very simple aid, but without it
the boys never would have found the acting successful.

What is meant by planning the play will be seen best in an
actual illustration. In dramatizing the story of Beowulf, the

* This chapter should have been on "Acting in the Classroom,"
but in writing it I found that apart from matters in connexion with
Shakespeare, there was very little of importance to say, which is not
dealt with in the chapters on "Miming" and on "Playmaking."
After all, if you can act Shakespeare you can act anything, and if you
cannot act even Shakespeare you might as well sit down again.

boys would be quite likely to begin with the coming of Beowulf
to the land of Hrothgar. But as Beowulf is coming to help
Hrothgar against the demon Grendel, who has been carrying
off his men, it is obvious that earlier scenes must show Hrothgar
in his difficulty. Accordingly one would take as the first scene
the building of the hall Heorot, and the holding of a beer-
drinking there as a celebration. The building of the hall,
presents no difficulties in the classroom, as it may be thought
although it is best (if you have to avoid making a noise, out of
consideration for the neighbouring classes) to repair to the
gymnasium or some empty place afar off. Of course you do
not dwell in the hall you build ! We simply stood a few benches
on end to represent the trees of the forest. Then the king
entered and, after announcing in a fine speech his intention of
building a great hall, directed his men to hew down the trees.
This they soon accomplished, and then two men to each log
bore away the timber, chanting a song as they went. If you
wish to show the actual building operations they are easily
represented by going through the motions of sawing, planing,
and so on, but as there is but small opportunity for anything
of purpose to be *said* at this point it is best to set your second
scene as the interior of the finished hall. But note, in passing,
that when your playboys become expert in acting and playmaking they will, at such a juncture as this, interpolate a comic
scene in which the builders rag one another and make comments
upon life in general. This interpolated comic scene is of course
borrowed from Shakespeare as instanced in the porter in
" Macbeth," and the grave-digger in " Hamlet." But the
tradition goes back to the Miracle Plays, and further.

During this second scene Hrothgar, the king, makes a great
speech, inaugurating the hall and foretelling many a feast
therein and the prospect of long and happy days. Then the
minstrel comes forward and chants a lay* in praise of Hrothgar

* As all this actually took place it is possible to state that a boy
can chant an extempore lay. Beowulf was dramatized in the first
instance by Form IIb (average age about 12). No book was used.
The story was told by the master, first as a whole and then in the sections
as required in detail for each scene. Certain simple elements of the
style, such as alliteration, were explained. And for the purposes of
the lay balance of phrasing was also mentioned. This and other chants
184

and the new dwelling, tells of other noble kings and other fine halls, and praises Hrothgar and Heorot above them all. A touch of irony may fitly be introduced here. It would be well in keeping with the spirit of a minstrel's lay, if he should refer to the troubles and disasters which had overcome those kings and those castles. This touch will actually be found in the epic, where it is foretold that Heorot would end by fire.

Now, of course, the boys prepare to sleep upon the benches, and Grendel draws on his huge fur gloves (his claws) in view of a predatory onslaught. But the master intervenes. This is not the way to tell a story dramatically. They are in too much of a hurry to reach the climax. But how are we to delay the coming of Grendel and give Hrothgar and his men at least a few days of peace in their new hall ? Obviously by interpolating a scene in some other place, and introducing some other characters of the story. It might be well to show Beowulf at home in the court of Hygelac ; or even to have a scene of the mumbling and grumbling of Grendel and his dam over a few well-gnawed bones, which would prepare us for the coming raid upon Heorot.

Some such *planning* and direction of the dramatized story is essential. But, as I have said, it may be that the master has not a previous knowledge of this craft nor a ready knack of invention. In that case the affair will be a fiasco, or at best a muddle-through on the part of the boys.

Well, these things can be learnt. One is not born with a working knowledge of playmaking and dramatic conventions. We have learnt all we know in this kind from Shakespeare. The best way to make a start in classroom acting is to take a play of Shakespeare and act it. The boys will there find that everything is set down for them in the book.

After having performed but one play they will be more at ease in moving about the classroom, and consequently more able to devise play-methods of studying matters which are not in themselves dramatic.

were distinctly rhythmical, but we used no melody at this time. Folk-airs, especially chanteys, might be introduced with excellent effect. For an example of the style of speech attained by the boys in this experiment see Perse Playbooks, No. 4, pp. 124, 125. The other Beowulf pieces in that book belong to a different occasion.

185

THE PLAY WAY

However young the boys may be, provided they are over ten, a Shakespeare play is the most useful beginning.* Some teachers are afraid of the difficulties of the language. This is perhaps because they have been accustomed to look out for difficulties in the subjects they teach, and to base their instructions principally upon such things.† If the teacher has had to prepare his boys for examinations this will certainly be the case. But if the chief interest of the boys is centred in the story of the play as shown in the action and the speeches of the characters, it will be found afterwards that the plot of the play has been perfectly well understood, and that the characters have become familiar friends. And what, after all, could you desire further of a small boy's first study of Shakespeare ? Of course there may be scores of matters left untouched which might have been made the subject-matter of the whole term's lessons. But if your time is limited you must decide between the play and these unessential matters. If you decide on acting, then "the play's the thing," and the "might have beens" can for the moment be disregarded.

If time allows, the numerous matters of study connected with a play of Shakespeare can be dealt with afterwards. Although we have always made it our *first* care to act the play simply as a play, even the lowest forms have been taught many things connected with the life and times of Shakespeare, either in a few words in passing or in lessons set apart. We have of course made a point of understanding the historical events upon which " Henry V " or " Richard II " are based ; and the boys themselves have given lectures on such subjects as " The Colossus," " Tudor Architecture," " Domestic Life in Shakespeare's Time,"‡ " Nine Men's Morris," " Fairies and Witches," " Rogues and Vagabonds," " The Globe Theatre," and so on. We have even on occasion gone very thoroughly into the study of the three authentic portraits of Shakespeare. The study of blank verse metre has also been undertaken in connexion with

* For boys under ten the traditional ballads afford the best material for dramatization.

† Cf. p. 195.

‡ A verbatim report of this lecture is given in Perse Playbooks, No. 4.

every play, not idly, but for use in the boys' own poems and playmaking. So far from overlooking or ignoring the intellectual and learned side of Shakespeare study, we have gone most thoroughly into every branch of it, whether in the literary aspect, the archæological aspect, the aspect of the craftsmanship of dramatic art, or the mere technicalities of stage procedure. But these things were not all huddled together in a mess during the study of one play. Whatever the master knew in this " subject " he taught, sometimes discoursing throughout a whole period to the fourth form on the meaning of tragedy, sometimes entertaining IIIa by comparisons between the art of Elizabethan days and the music-halls and cinemas and concerts of our own time, sometimes merely chatting about living actors and their ways, and what they had said in this or that Shakespearean connexion. But all this was based upon, and most intimately bound up with, the actual living familiarity which the boys had made with the plays by *acting* them. A man or a boy who has acted through a play of Shakespeare will not require any bidding to listen to a learned discourse upon that play, its characters, its plot, and its illustrations of the dramatist's skill in the use of stage conventions. A fellow so primed with the means of appreciative study as this acting gives simply *demands* lectures by a master. But the lectures to be interesting, to be understood, to be effective as instruction, must be given in response to a demand. They must come after a familiarity with the subject-matter of the play has whetted the appetite for closer study. Hunger is the best sauce, but surfeit ruins the digestion.

With a play to act and all these humanist studies to be undertaken in connexion with it, it will easily be understood how a playmaster is not only willng to ignore parsing, paraphrasing, and the cramming of notes and introductions,* but feels himself in a position to dispute with (and even to ridicule) those who give all their attention to such things. The important thing about the study of Shakespeare on the Play Way is

---

* I need hardly say that I have obtained much help from the scholarly notes of the late Dr. Aldis Wright. But such notes are not adapted for class use. They should be studied by the teacher, and only put into a boy's hands if he is preparing for a lecture or an essay.

187

that the play must be acted first, acted two or three times if possible. And while this acting is going on all matters which do not forward the acting must be held in suspension.

But one must not too hastily cast aside in the acting lessons all that does not immediately concern the story of the play and the actors. Although we shall at first refrain from any detailed study of words and phrases, and any pedantic investigation into the meaning of every allegory, allusion, metaphor, or reference to mythology, we must nevertheless remember that this is a play which we are acting, and not merely a tale which we are reading aloud. And the acting of a play demands the consideration of many things in addition to the story and the persons. So long as the boys were only allowed to sit in their desks and read in turn, even the stage directions were of no account, but so soon as they begin acting everything is changed.

There must be a stage of some sort, even if it is but a space cleared of desks and left quite bare. There must be recognized entrances and exits. Then you must consider what you propose to do about scenery and costume and properties. Above all there is the acting itself, for the performance of a play does not consist of reading speeches in rotation.

Now it happens that the study of Shakespeare is full of helpful instruction in these very matters; and this, quite apart from their unapproachable literary value, is an excellent reason for starting with the plays of Shakespeare, however difficult they may seem at first sight, rather than pottering about with that feeble amateur rubbish which is sometimes sent to one on approval.

Since " the dramatic method of teaching " first came into notice, publishers have turned out numerous books of " Plays for Schools," not so much to meet a demand as in the hope of creating one. The playlets thus offered to us are generally written by inexperienced schoolmistresses, and have no spark of literary value nor any dramatic power whatever. To shun Shakespeare for his difficulty, and fall into the accommodating laps of these dear ladies would indeed be a sorry descent.

In discussing educational method one ought perhaps to take for granted that the teacher at least knows his subject. But there are many ways of being learned in a subject so extensive as Shakespeare. The Shakespearean learning of most school-masters is of an exclusively literary kind, and in consequence they find themselves none too well equipped to direct the study of a Shakespeare play in any active form.

Indeed, it may be stated (for there is nothing to be gained and much to lose by concealing the fact) that most teachers bother their classes with word-study, and the pursuit of references to gods and heroes, and the solution of other riddles, simply because they have not the requisite knowledge safely to leave these academic questions and deal with what really *is* proper to the study of a Shakespeare play.

It will therefore be in place to describe fully the manner in which our playboys have been trained to look to the play for most of what they require, and in all things appertaining to the production to trust to Shakespeare himself. For though he is generally regarded as a happy-go-lucky playwright who achieved all his success by some slapdash method vouchsafed only to genius, Shakespeare has nevertheless stood ever before us players as a model of the most perfect yet unobtrusive crafts-manship.

The chief point about a stage-play is that it is meant to be played on a stage. Therefore, whether you are studying some-one else's play or making one of your own, you at once seek after a stage. And if a wicked generation determine that no stage be given you, you fall back upon the natural resources of the player, and make-believe a stage : fashion a heaven in hell's despite, and proceed with your playing maugre the un-godly.

Acting on an imaginary stage is not so impossible as it may appear. It is in fact the invariable custom of the playboys in the classroom.* We invented the imaginary stage because our thorough study of Shakespeare on the Play Way demanded

* For the last two terms of our four years' course we did have a little school stage. We designed it to suit our Elizabethan methods of production, and made great use of it. The story of our experiences with this playhouse, which we called *The Mummery*, would be very interesting to tell, but as the work of most of my readers is necessarily confined to the classroom, only classroom acting shall be considered in this chapter.

an Elizabethan setting, and this we could only supply in our imagination.

The imaginary stage we use for the study of Shakespeare in the classroom is naturally that of an Elizabethan playhouse. This was not the *picture* stage familiar at the present day, with its picture-frame proscenium arch, its front curtain, and its footlights, but the *platform* stage, which happily is being re-introduced, with its natural accompaniments of diffused lighting, and with hangings and other decoration in place of painted canvas scenery.*

All the while the boys are playing Shakespeare in the classroom they consider themselves subject to most of the conditions of an Elizabethan playhouse stage, and they observe the conventions which such a setting would require. This method of acting Shakespeare is carried out very thoroughly. Yet the reader must not hastily conclude with a chuckle that we are as academic about our stage conventions as are any of the pedants we abuse about their book-lore.

Some one may say that the conventions are of small account, and that a Shakespeare play is just as valuable a literary study when these are ignored. This is a false and ignorant view. For the Shakespeare plays were wrought with such care to fit the Elizabethan conditions of stage production that to leave this fact out of account is to produce nothing but a travesty of the plays. Without a full respect for these conventions you do not get the real Shakespeare at all, but a modern translation. The truth of this will be made apparent later.

That is the first reason for acting the plays in the Elizabethan manner. But from the point of view of classroom production there are many other reasons. When one of the Littlemen is cast to play Titania, he and his companions will realize the

---

* The researches of E. K. Chambers, William Poel, W. J. Lawrence, and many others have established beyond any reasonable doubt the shape of an Elizabethan playhouse stage and the conditions that governed it. Many readers will have seen Granville Barker's recent London productions in which a front stage was used, though the shows were not Elizabethan in many other respects. The above-mentioned writers should be consu'ted, but the reader is warned against unscholarly treatises on the subject. The chapter in the "Cambridge History of Literature," for example, is of little value for our purpose.

The Witches and Hecate in "Macbeth"

[See foot-note on p. 191

The Three Murderers in "Macbeth"

[See foot-note on p. 191

airy queen more truly in the rich robes woven of their own fancy than they could do were she decked out in the poor tinsel makeshift so painfully familiar in school performances.*

A boy reading a play from the book for the first time might be expected at most to understand the sense of the words, but not to express it at all. And this is what happens when the play is undertaken in the spelling-bee manner of a literary society, the boys all sitting in the stocks and spouting in turn. But by letting them act the scenes you will find that they not only take in the sense, but bring it out.

Action requires its fit setting. Shakespeare, having no artificial stage pictures to rely upon as a background, described the necessary scenery in the words of the play. The classroom has no painted canvas background either, and so the boys welcome and appreciate that wonderful word-painting. For the active imagination of the poet-player the beauty of the lines calls up a far more satisfying surrounding than a painted cloth can do, even when aided by lights and music.

A good playwright not only realizes that he must build his play in accordance with the conditions of the stage, but, what is far more important, he relies for some of his neatest touches, and some of his finest effects, on those very conventions which would hamper a weaker craftsman. A playboy who has been trained to observe this in the models set before him, and to try it for himself in his own work, will never consent to make sensational departures from accepted rule, nor to lean upon empty artificial aids. Consider the question of scenery. I do not say that Shakespeare would not have used

---

* In *The Mummery* we had a grand collection of costumes and properties, but while we were confined to the classroom we made use of anything we could lay our hands on. One or two boys brought short cloaks, a blanket turned up from somewhere, and some scout hats were lent. There was also an indescribable piece of red cloth which did duty as every imaginable class of apparel. For properties we had our Morris-dancing sticks and swords—the iron swords of the Kirkby dance were especially favoured—and all the usual appartus of a classroom, such as desks, benches, books, chalk-box, easel, blackboard, wall-map, window-blind, cord, duster, and waste-paper basket. If any class of playboys cannot stage a play with such a wealth of material they *deserve* to be spoon-fed.

191

painted scenery if it had been obtainable. I believe he was
the kind of craftsman who would be glad to make the best use
of any likely aid that came his way. But I do say, that it was
more fortunate for a man of his poetical powers, and incal
culably a greater gain to poetry and to drama, that there was
not any realistic scenery available in the form of painted canvas
Shakespeare's plays contain almost as much descriptive poetry
as they do speeches in character—the third element being the
proverbial reflections and moralizings which so disturbed Mr
Bernard Shaw. There is a two-fold reason for this full flood
of poetry. In the first place, the man Shakespeare was full
of that power of imagery and melodious expression which kept
overflowing in the splendour of rare description and the majesty
of high-sounding lines. And, secondly, it was necessary to
supply the " scenery." Had the stage been set about with
great drop-curtains, frameworks of canvas, and painted cloths
upon which the scenes were represented, the descriptive
passages which now stand as half the beauty of the plays would
have been either unnecessary or incongruous. Perhaps I shall
be reminded that those same plays are staged to-day in a full
setting of realistic paintings, and lighted by an ingenious
mechanism. But, for those of us who can still hear with our
ears and see with the eyes of imagination that far finer setting
which is given in the lines, it is all this scenery and lime-
lighting which are now both unnecessary and incongruous.
When Horatio says :

> But look, the morn in russet mantle clad
> Walks o'er the dew of yon high eastern hill,

is not all said ? Is it not unnecessary to flash about with
pink limes—incongruous, moreover, to a ridiculous degree
to those who know that " russet " here means grey, and
not red at all ? And what of the " mantle " and the " dew " ?
Since the thing cannot be adequately done with scenery,
why not rely upon a simple decorative setting and permit
the onlookers to do as Shakespeare directed in the prologue to
" Henry V " ?

> Piece out our imperfections with your thoughts.

Again, what artificial representation can do more than spoil Romeo's despairing note :

> Look, love, what envious streaks
> Do lace the severing clouds in yonder east :
> Night's candles are burnt out, and jocund day
> Stands tiptoe on the misty mountain tops :
> I must begone and live, or stay and die.

It is noteworthy that there is here as much of the gladness of dawn as there is of despair. " Candles," " tiptoe " ; strange that these actual words should widen and extend the bounds of the imagined scene, while a back-cloth streaked with painted clouds can only narrow it. Not strange at all ; these words, though one is a metaphor of indoors, and the other a personification, are bred in the bone of the play, while the canvas back-cloth is a piece of stupid impertinence.

Of course it is not *easy* for a modern audience thus to fancy for themselves the imagery from the words. But contemporary stage productions give us no chance to try it Who can enjoy a soundless rehearsal of a symphony in his head while a restaurant band is celebrating musical comedy airs ? But if some one should kill all the professional managers, producers, and scene-painters, our living actors could at once play Shakespeare to us as he should be played It has been done in a hole-and-corner sort of way, time and again. The present duty of all who are interested in the restoration of the real drama is to fight in favour of some such training as I have advocated in connexion with the Play Way in the classroom.

The putting of all these passages of descriptive poetry into the mouths of the persons of the drama has naturally had a noticeable effect upon the characters as they appear to us. Thus, many literary critics, not being aware that stage conventions have an influence upon the plays, have conceived a very lop-sided view of Shakespeare's characters. Shakespeare himself was a poet, and many of his chief creations are poets too ; but not by any means can every one in the plays who utters poetry be claimed a poet. For its own sake the romantic drama cannot stoop to represent in a realistic manner the speech of all its minor personages. And in many of the lines the characters, both high and low, are but serving the office of scene-shifters, so to say.

In contrast to such a scene-painting as Oberon's description of the bower of the Fairy Queen,

> **I know a bank whereon the wild thyme blows,**

consider those gentlemen in shirt-sleeves whom one sometimes sees rushing on just as the scene-drop comes down. How flurried they are about their packing-cases, and their shrubs and their ivy twigs. Dear souls ! so eager, and only to spoil the play. And as the curtain goes up again *twenty minutes later*—that curtain with its pretty chocolate-box picture of fountains and naked nymphs—there again we mark a pair of aproned legs scuttling away into the wings. Pathetic pretence at art.

The boys may safely be left to body forth the fancies of Shakespeare without any but the most simple appliances. One of the Littlemen in shorts and a jersey showed a charming appreciation of Titania—always an unsatisfactory part when seen on the stage. By the very enchantment of his bearing one could see that he pictured for himself the green woodland sunk in the deep blue night, and went not unattended by a meiny of his own calling up, a retinue of sprites and fays.

Many who have forgotten their childhood will be surprised to see from the following how completely the Littlemen identify themselves with the persons they play. We were turning over Arthur Rackham's illustrations to " A Midsummer Night's Dream " and nearly every page called forth some arresting comment, such as this from Titania : " O, look at the tiny pages holding up my train " ; or this, " O, sir, surely I shouldn't be wearing a kind of ball-dress in the woods " ; or this, with delight from the whole group when one of Bottom's fellows was found pictured with a comical grimace, " Just *look* at Billy ! " This interesting trait of child psychology (really to imagine oneself living as a character seen or heard of in a picture or a story) is the subject of that chapter " Its Walls were as of Jasper " in Kenneth Grahame's " Dream Days."

A visitor inquired of me recently, " What do you do with a play of Shakespeare ? " " Act it," I replied. " What else can you do with a play?" What the old-fashioned pedant could do to a play of Shakespeare is too well known to bear relation, but, incredible though it may seem, it is still rare to find acting the principal means of dealing with plays in school. Teachers still compel their pupils to examine minutely a play they have not even read as a story. Here is a paragraph from "Notes on the Teaching of English in the Lower Middles," at Rugby, published in 1914 :

"A reading lesson, when the book is a play, proceeds as follows : the Master reads aloud himself, the boys all following. He reads as dramatically as possible, exaggerating his effects, taking ells himself in order to encourage the boys to try an inch. When he has read twenty or thirty lines the work begins. The meaning is examined : dug out of the words, torn out of the idioms, enticed out of the allusions. Every bush is beaten, and hares that start up, whether historical, mythological, moral, geographical, political, etymological, architectural, or ecclesiastical, are pursued, and, if possible, caught. All this must be done by the Form, and the Master should play the part of huntsman while they are hounds. . . ." Doubtless, these hounds are bred out of the Spartan kind. Alas, poor " Lower Middles." " As soon as a scene has been read intensively in this way, the parts are assigned to readers, the others shut their books, and it is read dramatically with any amount of coaching in emphasis and inflexion by the Master. . . . When, in the course of a fortnight or ten days, a whole act has been finished, it is read right through dramatically." But then, surely, it is too late. As well hand over your dog to be hanged, drawn, quartered, tarred and feathered, and then whistle him out for a run ! One play vivisected in this manner at the school referred to was no other than "Twelfth Night." One recalls Toby's " Tut, there's life in't, man." And we can fancy the " Lower Middles " overlooking the opening line,

> If music be the food of love, play on,

and chanting in chorus :

> Give me excess of it ; that, surfeiting,
> The appetite may sicken and so die.

195

THE PLAY WAY

If the meaning has been "enticed" out of the allusion to "fell and cruel hounds" which occurs in Orsino's second speech, this Master at Rugby knows what he risks as huntsman of such fearful wild-fowl. Ecclesiastical hare, forsooth!

When a teacher says that in his treatment of Shakespeare "the parts are assigned and the play read dramatically," this generally means no more than the boys reading in turns while seated in their desks. I insist that to ignore action is to ignore the play. A book in the hand is not a very serious impediment to a boy who has the chance to stab some one, or to storm a city wall. The writer I have quoted actually applies to school lessons what Disraeli said of public dinners, "They are meant to be dull." So we must allow that he is not unaware of the boredom necessarily incurred by his strange partiality for pursuing the architectural and political hare in the study of a Shakespearean comedy. The Play Way on the other hand, desires to avoid unnecessary dullness, so the playboys are allowed to make their first acquaintance of the play in the manner that most appeals to them. Thus they do all the necessary work of their own accord.

Two episodes in class one day were the occasion of great merriment. Evidently the mister was slack or overfull of self-affairs, for Portia, about to enter with the Prince of Arragon, found herself unattended. Thereupon, striking a most comical attitude to suggest the offended dame, the playboy observed in character, "And *where's* my train?"—just as a prim lady on finding the servants in bed in the morning might ask, "What is the meaning of this, pray?" But the mister got his own back before the end of that scene. When Arragon opens the silver casket he should start back amazed; and Portia should say, "Too long a pause for that which you find there." The mister had looked ahead; and when the lid of the chalk-box was drawn open there appeared such a startling "portrait of a blinking idiot" that Portia's whole retinue burst into shouts of laughter. Such episodes do not spoil the comedy for the boys, but add to its fun; and there is no need to dig the meaning out of the words, tear it out of the idioms, or entice it out of the allusions. Anything not readily intelligible is suffered to go by at the first reading, unless the players get

196

hung up over a difficulty. In that case the master gives a brief explanation, and on they go.

In support of my contention that the boys do really feel the play when they act it in school, it may perhaps be allowable to quote the report of an onlooker which appeared a while back in a London paper. " Remember how you were taught Shakespeare at school, the dreary reading of a dull play, the dreary explanations of the meaning of obscure words, the lifeless recitation of speeches, and then consider this : ' Well, Jones,' said the master, ' you're producer, I'll leave it to you.' Then the master retired to the back of the room, while the sacred area round his desk was invaded by Jones and his cast. And then they put their backs into it with a vengeance. They read their parts from the book so well that they had to be pulled up only occasionally by the master or by the youthful Jones. They acted too, and uncommonly well. The great scene was the charge into the breach of Harfleur. To my astonishment I realized that there was actually going to be a fight in the classroom of a school. I saw half a dozen boys armed with sticks take up a position behind the master's desk, and then I saw Jones mounted on a bench urging his followers on to the attack. In a great voice he reminded them of their duty, and at the word of command a dozen boys charged the little force holding the master's desk. In a moment the classroom was filled with the sound of blows, while the master looked on smiling. Twice the charge was repeated, and even a third time did the enthusiastic Jones cry aloud :

> Once more unto the breach, dear friends, once more,
> Or close the wall up with our English dead !

But at last the master thought there had been fighting enough. ' Steady, Jones,' he said. ' You can make the speech, but we don't want another charge.' Jones looked round reproachfully."

It is only to be expected that the boys will do justice to noisy heroics. But it is not generally recognized that by letting them act the plays from the beginning you make it possible for boys under fifteen to appreciate some of the most difficult and moving passages of tragedy. To know this as a fact surely gives great support to my belief that *a true feeling*

THE PLAY WAY

for art values may be expected to arise out of the trial practice of the arts. Two instances may be given.

The fourth form having read most of the Shakespeare plays usually done in school, the bold experiment was tried of introducing " Hamlet." It is not so bold if you are to treat it as archæology, but as a *play* for boys of fourteen there is a fair risk of the motive, the passion of Hamlet, being unappreciated. We came to Hamlet's interview with his mother. The fourteen-year-old boy who played Hamlet had read over the scene beforehand, but there had been no coaching. True, he had been with me to see Mr. Poel's production at the Little Theatre, but his rendering of the scene was quite unlike Mr. Esme Percy's fine interpretation. There is no doubt in my own mind—and this is the remarkable thing—that the boy interpreted the words spontaneously. In fact he said afterwards that he " made it up as he went along." Hamlet began the scene with an air of assumed madness, snapping out the words in a high-pitched voice. But with " Come, come, and sit you down," his whole bearing changed to suit his altered purpose. He became outwardly calm, but spoke in a tense voice full of restrained excitement. Just that voice, in fact, which so frightened the Queen that she cried out on murder. At this point the death of Polonius provided, of course, an exciting sensation for the class. But, after that, nothing else was thought of but the passion of Hamlet. The boys all watching in breathless interest. No one moved in his seat It is a pity that the boy playing the Queen became unconsciously an onlooker also, and simply walked through his part. A change from pathos in " This *was* your husband," to contempt in " This *is* your husband "—no easy thing for a boy to express —was very effective, and the tone in " Ha ! have you eyes ? " rose to a kind of shriek, which seemed to make clear once and for all that the madness of Hamlet was neither real madness nor assumed, but hysteria. Just before the Ghost appeared Hamlet was openly ranting, shouting and throwing his arms about. But now he fell suddenly to his knees, bent low his head and prayed in a hushed voice :

> Save me and hover o'er me with your wings,
> You heavenly guards !

And when he crouched right low upon the ground and moaned appealingly, " Do not look upon me," I really almost wished Polonius might have come to life to break the tension with " Look whether he has not turned colour, and has tears in's eyes.—Pray you no more."

Yet when the Queen said,

O, Hamlet, thou hast cleft my heart in twain !

he had spied enough of Hamlet's next attitude not to speak sympathetically ; but assumed again his high-pitched tone of madness, and rapped out his lines as before. A school edition has to cut most of what remains of this scene. But the concluding words appealed to me as much as anything. The dead body could not be dragged along the floor, but though Polonius arose and walked out by Hamlet's side no one laughed. And Hamlet, all his excitement gone, piped in a high, mad, jaunty voice, " Good-night, mother." It was diabolical.

The other boys remained sitting and no one spoke a word. The atmosphere showed that no comment was needed, so I simply praised it as the finest piece of work I had ever seen in the school ; and the class dispersed.

Another instance of the playboys' appreciation of both comedy and tragedy was seen in " Richard II," a play which they thoroughly enjoyed in Form IIIa (age 13). A favourite scene was the lists at Coventry, which they played quite half a dozen times. The King, surrounded by his court, was seated high aloft on a chair perched on top of my desk, and there was much heraldic display. The champions had each a squire to bear his shield, and a herald with a scroll to read his challenge. The mister, acting the part of the Marshal, elaborated the business every time, and required more and more performers, until at last the master alone remained sitting in the stocks. They had much fun out of old York, who was played as a fussy old gentleman, and nicknamed " *Boots* " from his idiotic behaviour in the fifth act. The murder of Richard was carried out with some vigour. After the King had slain the two servants, and Exton was about to run him through, the mister, who had consulted Holinshed's account in a note in another edition, interrupted to insist that Exton must stand on the

199

chair and smash the King's head from above. Richard in his turn insisted, for the sake of the climax, on the two servants rising to be slain again. The menials rose and dusted themselves. Exton blundered again, so Richard, who resolutely refused to be dispatched unless the deed were done well, had the whole business repeated, servants and all—he had now contrived to get in six slaughters for the two of them! Last of all the King died also.

The triumph came at the very close. While Bolingbroke was winding up his affairs, and collecting the heads of traitors, the ingenious mister made ready the funeral procession. A blackboard easel was brought out, and thereon, to be borne in by four stalwarts shoulder-high, was laid the body of King Richard. It was supremely ridiculous, because the bearers were of different heights, and the body much in peril of rolling off. But I called a hush, and we all proceeded to play the finale seriously. Exton and Bolingbroke spoke with feeling, and the rest were now perfectly solemn. On the words,

> March sadly after ; grace my mournings here,
> In weeping after this untimely bier,

the bearers elaborately turned about, and the coffin was borne away foot foremost. Bolingbroke stepped down from the dais sceptre in hand, and the lords attendant followed in pairs, each with his bare sword resting on his arm. Poor Exton shuffled hopelessly on behind. The door was opened, and very slowly and solemnly the procession of twenty passed out of the room. I was left alone with a visitor. We were both absurdly impressed. Without scenery, lighting, costume, music or any other aid but the thoughts which are able to piece out all imperfections, and even to deck the obsequies of a king, these playboys out of the spontaneity of their hearts had staged us a tragedy.

A moment later in the passage the dead King came to the ground with a flop, and as the easel was replaced in the corner they all rushed in to know what I thought of it. " Stop this noise," said the mister. " Shut, the door, and sit down at once."

Stage conditions must of course be studied in connexion

with the acting of a play. When the third form say,, begins
to act "The Merchant of Venice," their attention is called
to an imaginary line drawn across the floor-space they are
using. This line divides the two-thirds in front from the third
at the back. It soon wants a name, so you call it the " curtain
or " traverse." Some boy is sure to protest that the curtain
ought to be in the very front. He can then be told, not only
that the stage for which Shakespeare wrote was different from
those we have now, but also that this fact made a great difference to the plays themselves, as he shall see. Many questions
arise at once, but we undertake that such of them as the
performance does not answer for itself shall be dealt with at
the end of the lesson. All the rules of the game are at first
known only to the master. If he insists on the actors keeping
in front of the traverse line throughout the first scene, their
interest is at once aroused. Whenever I have opened the
performance in this way—and we always read " The Merchant "
in IIIb—several boys not acting at the moment have, by
turning over to the next scene, discovered why the imaginary
curtain was kept shut. Once a boy called out excitedly, " O,
I see, Portia's house is hidden behind there." " There " was,
of course, nothing more substantial than the imaginary curtain.
Then while Bassanio is telling Antonio,

> In Belmont is a lady richly left,

the mister quietly ushers his Portia and Nerissa into a corner at
the back, whence they are ready to walk on as soon as the first
scene is ended. The class easily understands that no curtain
comes down at the end of Scene I. Instead, the traverse
is now declared open, and the master explains that the
Street in Venice disappears and the whole stage becomes
Belmont. The boys are not quite ready for this. Some have
convinced their imaginations that this is a street. They have
fancied houses, and the canal, and the masts of shipping in
the distance. If any teacher doubt this—and many teachers
behave as though they doubted all the powers of their pupils
—let him get this opening scene played thus by a group of boys,
and then allow them to talk about it. After they have been
at pains to construct such a complete setting it appears rather

201

cool to clear this picture all away upon the opening of an imaginary curtain behind; and start all over again, this time to picture the interior of a palace. For a moment it seems as though they might dispute the plausibility of the change demanded. For, strange to relate, the playboys are permitted to have a say in the conduct of a lesson which, after all, is being given solely for their benefit. It seems as if they might be indisposed to grant what Coleridge calls " that willing suspension of disbelief for the moment, which constitutes poetic faith." So the master seeks to justify the dramatist by asking the boys whence they obtained their picture of the first scene. They admit that Antonio and his friends suggested it in what they said, and one boy actually gives Salarino all the credit for the ships; which, if you know the play well, you will easily understand. It is now a simple matter to suggest that the gentlemen have taken away with them the street-stuff they had brought. They think. One presently asks: " Is the scenery mixed up with the actors ? " And another, not necessarily the master, replies : " No, the scenery is given in the lines."

On the opening of the curtain, Portia and Nerissa are expected in their turn to suggest another setting. But they do not seem to give any very definite help; and the onlookers are clearly more sparing of their fancy over the second scene, and do not localize it at all definitely. Some are for a boudoir, some for a garden. Discussion springs up again. At such an early occasion in the play discussion should not be too ruthlessly checked. The playboys have still to master the conventions. One protests that neither Portia nor Nerissa has told us " where they are.' The master asks, " Where do you think they are ? " " At Belmont," comes the reply in chorus. That is all we know, and all we need to know.

Already, by the conclusion of the second scene, the master's aid in this matter of " scenery " is no longer required. The playboys have grasped the first rules of the game. While the mister goes through the motions of closing the traverse—you must " do it in action " lest the imaginary fittings be forgotten and the play marred—Bassanio walks on to the front stage in company with Shylock. At once the onlookers, already more than audience now, and almost equivalent to a chorus, smile knowingly to themselves as they recognize that Bassanio is bringing back the street, with the rigging of ships in the background. If he were not, you may be sure that Shakespeare would have made clear the change of locality. And the play boys are now ready to give careful heed to learn whether Shylock will lend Bassanio the "three thousand ducats" of which he keeps muttering to himself. For however familiar the story may be to some of us it is as well to remember that children are not born knowing the plot of "The Merchant of Venice."

But the scene-openings of this play are not by any means the easiest to cope with. I have just shown one difficulty at the very start: the audience having been prepared already for the appearance of Portia at Belmont, no more in the way of explanation is deemed necessary by the dramatist when she is shown. His concern now is to get the matter of the caskets introduced as soon as possible; which he does with no little skill. But "The Merchant of Venice" does furnish an excellent example of the alternation of scenes on the Elizabethan stage. Throughout the first three acts the scenes are laid in Belmont or in a Venetian street. Venice is always on the front stage; Belmont always on the back. This makes your exposition of the elementary principles of Elizabethan stage-craft quite a simple undertaking. A grasp of the "alternation theory" may not at first sight appear to have any particular value. But in addition to making the story clear, it directs the interest of the boys to the constructive side of the artist's work. It is also an extremely useful asset in their own playmaking.

Here, then, are matters worthy of consideration when you take up the reading of a Shakespearean play in the classroom. The pursuit of hares, "whether historical, mythological, moral, geographical, political, etymological, architectural, or ecclesiastical," not only bores the class, but distracts their attention from the very subject they are called upon to study. And the pedant alone knows how difficult it is to hold the attention of the boys by the system of teaching which prevails everywhere at the present time. The Play Way is not a collection of schemes for keeping small boys entertained during school-hours, without reference to the subject-matter of their lessons. On the contrary, it is the main principle of the Play Way that you shall get right to the heart of the matter you have in hand and then do actively *what* your interest bids, *as* the necessity of the case demands. If you have a play in hand, and get to the heart of the matter, you will find that your interest bids you act it. If you do not find this, you are not yet at the heart of the play. And the necessity of the case requires that you get some knowledge of the conditions in relation to which this particular play was wrought actable.

Accordingly the play-method allows the master or the boys to hold up the dramatic narration of the story from time to time. But these interruptions only occur often at the beginning and become less and less frequent as the boys' grasp of the Elizabethan stage convention makes comment more rarely necessary. When a proffered remark is obviously on some point now quite familiar to the whole class it may with more gain than damage be suppressed. The notable distinction between the two methods is this. The hunting method, as approved and practised at Rugby and most other schools, is off the point at every interruption. The plan upon which the whole hunting method is founded—that of taking a slice of thirty lines or so and proceeding to mince it into an unrecognizable slush—is in itself enough to kill the play. But the interruptions made by the playboys serve only, by raising the discussion of *essential* questions, to enhance the value of the whole study.

In many of the plays the scene-openings are not only very carefully localized, but they serve also to make the author's purpose clear by explaining the plot and characters, precisely at that point where exposition is necessary. Look at Act I of " Twelfth Night." * You must, of course, always ignore the printed stage directions, which, with a few exceptions, do not appear in the First Folio. Orsino partly introduces himself, and he and Valentine clear the way for Olivia. But the second scene introduces Viola. So, to save confusion, the place, the

* It is hoped that the reader will take the trouble to look up the few simple references required, and so obviate much lengthy quotation.

persons, the recent events, present circumstances, and future possibilities are all dealt with in the utmost precision.

> *Viola :* What country, friends, is this ?
> *Captain :* This is Illyria, lady.

Then they discuss her brother, and the shipwreck, the captain, the duke, Olivia again, and Viola's own position and prospects. Which being done they go off. They only came on to do that. The third scene opens with the remarks of a stout and jovial person, who is addressed as Sir Toby, referring to his niece, who is lamenting the death of her brother. This is the third time we have heard about the lamented brother, so there can be no doubt that the niece in question is no other than that same Lady Olivia, whom we are by now quite anxious to look upon. She is discussed again in the fourth scene, and only enters in the midst of scene five. In the meantime, since the play opened, no fewer than ten persons have become known to us ; and the plot is well afoot. We are all in a very good humour, and would not even notice the escape of an astrological hare when Toby says, " Were we not born under Taurus ? "

We have not fared ill, then, with our imaginary line called a traverse, and our scene-openings. If " Shakespeare wanted arte " it was doubtless the kind of art typified by rare old Ben himself, who was so stuffed up with much Greek and more Latin that he applied the critical standard of one age to the creative production of a totally different one, as though the influence of intervening time (during which, as a matter of fact, the drama of his day actually took its rise) were of small account, and the whole *new* character of contemporary life and art, including his own, of no account at all. The critical standpoint of such craftsmen as Jonson, who himself confessed that he wrote his poetry first as prose and then translated it into metre, is not unknown among us at the present day. Any work which shows abounding vigour and joy is, without respect to its intrinsic worth, held *undisciplined* by those whose own uninspired productions reveal their laboured mechanism at every joint. Am I not right in saying that Shakespeare is indulgently regarded as a rare genius who was able to rely with glorious abandon upon the first fine careless rapture ? Yet did he not actually copy out his lines with such a finished care that his editors received of him scarce a blot in his papers ? At all events, the craftsman who had that skill, in scene-openings alone, which I have been able to illustrate, will serve well enough as a master for my playboys. But the most remarkable fact about Shakespeare's skill in stage-craft is the way he tells his actors at every important moment exactly what he wants them to do. Could anything be at once so interesting for the boy-players to notice and so helpful to them in their acting of the plays ? The mister in charge has only to read the book with care to find all the directions literally waiting for him.

In Shakespeare we have everything given, as any one may find for himself by studying the text with a purpose. Over and above the plot and characterization Shakespeare gives us poetry that is not mere gush. Lorenzo brings his moonlight with him, Macbeth wraps himself in darkness, and Romeo points out the dawn. It is the moonlight and darkness they want, the dawn he dreads. Who more fitly then may indicate their presence ? As a model for playwrights (as opposed to play-writers) it is the greatest of Shakespeare's merits that his plays *seem to have been written after rehearsal*. He never forgot his stage. You could almost " dress " the whole play " Julius Cæsar " correctly in the Elizabethan manner out of all the hats, cloaks, shoes, daggers, nightcaps, leather aprons, kerchiefs, tapers, letters, tools, and musical instruments that are mentioned. And as for Cæsar, are we not told both of his nightgown and of his doublet ? Again, just before the entry of the conspirators, Lucius tells Brutus,

> Their hats are pluck'd about their ears,
> And half their faces buried in their cloaks,
> That by no means I may discover them
> By any mark of favour.*

Our playboys in consequence always enter in the muffled

---

* A knowledge of Shakespeare's use of the word *favour* by the way and of many other apparently simple words, such as *fancy*, for example, is essential to a right understanding of the plays.

guise of the traditional stage conspirators. But always in the representations seen on the modern stage, this secretive company strolls on bareheaded. And of course every man of them wears a toga!

The very stage-directions and " business " of Shakespeare's plays can be found in the text, to say nothing of what we now call the " programme." The mister has only to keep alert and he will find (quite apart from the modern editor's stage-directions, which we always ignore) that the knockings, the drawing of the curtain, the sewing of banquets and the taking up of bodies are all clearly indicated. At the very first knock on the door Macbeth says, " Whence is that knocking? " Presently Lady Macbeth says, " I hear a knocking at the south entry," and again, " Hark, more knocking." The porter comes in with " Here's a knocking, indeed! " and throughout the scene with his " Knock, knock, knock " he makes it quite plain that the knocking must continue.

Both Lorenzo and Jessica mention, on the occasion of her flight, that she is dressed in boy's clothes. The curtain which screens Portia's caskets is scarcely ever drawn apart or together without some one saying, " Draw the curtain."

And for the current aid of the actors themselves, " Here," " Thus," " Yonder " are frequent hints. Characters are often named as they enter, or they announce themselves. This is so usual that we might almost dispense with " Enter So-and-so." The custom reminds one of the Mummer's Plays where the persons nearly always announce themselves with, " In comes I King George " or " In comes I the Fool." The familiar observation of the clown in the Harlequinade, " Here we are again! " is in the direct tradition. Of course the purpose is to make everything quite plain to the audience, but there is more in it than that, I am convinced. A study of these old stage conventions would make an excellent subject for a thesis.

It is in fact difficult for the boys to miss an intended action, for curtsies, handskakings, pointings, and the smallest movements and gestures of all kinds are actually described in the doing. A few illustrations will make the point quite clear : " Sit, Jessica," " Here, catch this casket," " Why dost thou whet thy knife ? " " Eat, look you, this leek," " Nay, never shake thy gory locks at me," " Look where it comes again," " There's blood upon thy face," " Who did strike out the light ? " " This is the door—I'll make so bold to call," " Here is the scroll of every man's name," " Here come two noble beasts, in a man and a lion," " Well moused, lion ! " " This thorn-bush my thorn-bush, this dog my dog," " My tables— it is meet I set it down," " Leave thy damnable faces and begin," " Look here upon this picture and on this," " Take up the bodies," " Go, bid the soldiers shoot."

The words themselves tell the actor what to do, and what properties will be required. In fact Shakespeare is so much at ease in instructing his players in the very text of their speeches that he even puts stage-directions into the body of his songs ! The reader will possibly think that such a state- ment is pushing the case to a ridiculous extreme. But most convincing instances of these stage-directions in the songs are easily given. Ariel's song, " Come unto these yellow sands," is from start to finish nothing but a little pageant-mister's direction to his troupe of fairy dancers.* They are all invisible to Ferdinand, of course, but they should appear upon the stage nevertheless, and do as Ariel bids. They foot it featly here and there, and cry their nursery rhyme at one another across the stage. Instead of saying " Chorus " the mister says, " Sweet sprites the burthen bear." Then the group which is footing it featly " here " cries " Hark, hark ! " and the group which is footing it featly " there " answers " Bowgh-wowgh ! " Then the fairy mister suddenly stops his nimble prancing and says ,

> Hark, hark ! I hear
> The strain of strutting chanticlere.

And then some little fellow behind cries " Cock-a-diddle-dowe ! " The song is a miniature Littleman play.

He who has not tried putting himself and his players entirely into Shakespeare's hands, and playing all his games exactly as he directs they should be played, has missed half the fun so generously given by this amazing craftsman.

* Cf. Perse Playbook, No. 3, Introduction.

ACTING SHAKESPEARE

Ferdinand now speaks. But he has hardly uttered ten lines before Ariel begins again his enchantments. He sings his song about the underwater world, and then gives his chorus off stage the cue when to join in with their "burthen." He says,

Sea-nymphs hourly ring his knell,

and the chorus chimes its "Ding-dong." Then he repeats his chanticlere phrase, "Hark, now I hear them," and the whole choir breaks into a round of "Ding-dong, bell."

If the music were treated in a true Elizabethan manner, and the dancing and play-business carried out as Shakespeare most clearly directs, these two little songs would make in themselves a most enchanting performance. All the business is actually given in the words of the song; but as Ferdinand truly says, "This is no mortal business." Nowadays musicians don't care, producers don't understand, and —most unkindest cut of all—boys don't have the run of the stage. When children appear at all in modern Shakespeare productions the most you will see is a group of badly drilled amateur girls jumping about in tennis shoes.

But my illustrations of stage-directions in the songs are not confined to those two songs in "The Tempest." A boy sings a song in "The Merchant of Venice" while Bassanio is making his speech before the caskets. It is a good plan to have the song going on while Bassanio is speaking, in order to drown his stodgy moralizings. At the close of his song the boy calls for the chorus, just as Ariel did. It must have been a boy. It was probably Ariel himself. He says :

Let us all ring fancy's knell,
I'll begin it,—Ding-dong, bell.

And the chorus, either on or off the stage, takes up the cue, and sings "Ding-dong, bell."

Remember that all the ladies-in-waiting and Portia herself were played by boys. Is it too much to suppose that it was the same group of boys as played with Ariel, and that they may even have sung the same round for this "Ding-dong, bell," as they did in the character of sea-nymphs ?

o   209

"I'll begin it." Could you think of any statement so obviously a conductor's direction. It is equivalent to "Now, all together." Yet the one is lyric utterance here and the other is not.

In "A Midsummer Night's Dream" Oberon and Puck spend most of their time in painting scenes, giving directions to the actors, or explaining the play to the audience. Titania need never be anxious whether her band of little fairy people has been sufficiently rehearsed, because she tells them what to do at every turn, "Fairies, skip hence," "Fairies, away." "Come now, a roundel and a fairy song," "Come, wait upon him ; lead him to my bower," "Fairies, begone, and be all ways away" And when she goes to sleep they direct their own play, as did Ariel and his troupe, in the words of their fairy song. At the end of the play all the little people come in with Oberon and Titania, and "now are frolic." After what has been shown you will not be surprised to find that Oberon and Titania in their singing give most explicit directions to their meiny of Littlemen.

> Through this house give glimmering light,
> By the dead and drowsy fire :
> Every elf and fairy sprite
> Hop as light as bird from brier :
> And this ditty after me,
> Sing and dance it trippingly.

Here, then, once again, the cue for the chorus is given by the chief singer.

The modern editor's final stage-direction, "*Exeunt Ob., Tit., and Train,*" is not only hideous, but ludicrously out of place, following, as it does, on the heels of Oberon's.

> Trip away,
> Make no stay.
> Meet me all by break of day.

Such mastery of a craft is wonderful. But it has escaped the knowledge of the general, because it is "set down with as much modesty as cunning."

The fact that Shakespeare puts into Hamlet's few words

" *Antony :* You all do know this mantle "

[Cf. p. 211

" *Marullus :* And do you now put on your best attire "

[See foot-note on p. 19]

of advice to the players such explicit warnings against stage-mannerisms and faults of overacting, tells the actors not to mouth his words, not to saw the air with their hands, not to tear a passion to tatters ; and the fools not to prolong the patter of their interludes and so spoil the continuity of the play—all this put in so few words shows that the dramatist had very decided opinions upon what should and what should not be done in the acting of his plays. Is it not more than likely, then, that all this meticulous description of actions by the characters is *intentionally* put into their lines in order to make sure they do them ? Yet actors of to-day are very casual about this. They do not observe with any artistic precision the law laid down by Shakespeare in the words of Hamlet, " Suit the action to the word, the word to the action."

Professional actors and producers may prefer to ignore this method of direction so systematically observed by Shakespeare throughout the plays. But to the boys, whether in the class-room or on the stage it is a very godsend. The mister knows that he must make ready certain little scrolls of paper when he sees " I will bestow these papers," and Lucius knows that he must enter with one in his hand, because he presently has to say, " I found this paper." The modern editor adds the gratuitous stage-direction, " *Gives a paper.*" Cassius knows when to draw Brutus aside and whisper with hin, because he himself says the cue, " Shall I entreat a word ? " The rest are also made to tell themselves what to do, " Here, as I point my sword, the sun arises," and so on. The mister, ever watchful for what is coming, is told when to strike his bell by " Peace, count the clock," and he is told how often to strike it, " The clock hath stricken three." In " Macbeth " also we find, " Go, bid thy mistress . . . strike upon the bell," and the cue a while later, " The bell invites me." When " the games are done and Cæsar is returning " Brutus describes to Cassius the appearance of the whole company so clearly that not a man of them but must know how to look.

> The angry spot doth glow on Cæsar's brow,
> And all the rest look like a chidden train :
> Calphurnia's cheek is pale ; and Cicero
> Looks with such ferret and such fiery eyes

THE PLAY WAY

As we have seen him in the Capitol,
Being crossed in conference by some senators.

If still further illustration of this characteristic habit in Shakespeare's workmanship be deemed necessary the reader is referred to Act III, Scene 1, of "Julius Cæsar." There is hardly a gesture or a movement in that important scene but is clearly directed in the text : " Look how he makes to Cæsar," " Look, he smiles, and Cæsar doth not change,"

Trebonius knows his time ; for, look you, Brutus,
He draws Mark Antony out of the way,

" I kiss thy hand," " As low as to thy foot doth Cassius fall," " Speak hands for me," " Stoop, Romans, stoop, and let us bathe our hands in Cæsar's blood," " Thus, Brutus, did my master bid me kneel "—and so throughout.

The Elizabethans loved fights and shows and all kinds of spectacular effects in their plays. The theatre supplied them with all the sensations which in modern days we may obtain from boxing, fencing, and wrestling matches, from conjuring shows, the melodrama, the cinema, and the variety entertainments. So Shakespeare filled his plays with sensations. There is always much display of clothes, much pageantry, music, the braying of trumpets and the letting off of firearms. " Macbeth " gives us witches, a ghost, apparitions, a sleep-walker, a forest on the move, a great battle, several murders and a head brought in on a pole. " Hamlet," with the ghost, the stage-play, the madness of Ophelia, the killing of Polonius, the crowd that hails Laertes king, the fight in the grave, and all the poisonings and stabbings at the end, contains more sensational elements than any melodrama you can see to-day. It is not for nothing that the very last words of this play are, " Go, bid the soldiers shoot."

All such things are the very stuff that boys delight in, so that if plays had not been available containing so much show and noise and sensation it would have been necessary to invent them. And whether Shakespeare put in such things *solely* to cater for the tastes of his hearers or not, he most certainly

212

gave the sensational element a status in drama. And so the boys can at the same time revel in din and clash and horrors, and learn to appreciate literature in its highest form.

Sir Walter Raleigh says : * " The citizens delighted in exhibitions of juggling, tumbling, fencing and wrestling ; and these also were provided by the drama. Shakespeare is profuse in his concessions to the athletic interest. The wrestling match in ' As You Like It,' the rapier duels in ' Romeo and Juliet ' and in ' Hamlet,' the broadsword fight in ' Macbeth,' —these were real displays of skill by practised combatants. The whole First Act of ' Coriolanus ' is so full of alarums and excursions and hand-to-hand fighting with hard blows given and taken, that it is tedious to Shakespeare's modern admirers, but it gave keen pleasure to the patrons of the Globe. ' The Comedy of Errors ' is noisy with beatings and the outcries of the victims. All these things, though it discolour the complexion of his greatness to acknowledge it,† were imposed upon Shakespeare by the tastes and habits of his patrons and by the fashions of the primitive theatre. It was on this robust stock that his towering thought and his delicate fancy were grafted." And again,‡

" In nothing is Shakespeare's greatness more apparent than in his concessions to the requirements of the Elizabethan theatre, concessions made sparingly and with an ill grace by some of his contemporaries, by him offered with both hands, yet transmuted in the giving, so that what might have been a mere connivance in baseness becomes a miracle of expressive art. The audience asked for bloodshed, and he gave them ' Hamlet.' They asked for foolery, and he gave them ' King Lear.' "

There is another quality about the work of Shakespeare which stands out so prominently that the boys can easily learn to appreciate it in their acting, and to try and imitate it in their own playmaking. That is the quality of being distinct and broad in treatment. Much of Shakespeare's

* " Shakespeare " (" English Men of Letters "), p. 102.

† Sir Walter Raleigh's unfortunate lapse as a critic in this phrase is happily made good in the passage next quoted.

‡ " Shakespeare " (" English Men of Letters "), p. 27.

213

greatness rests in this. He was not afraid of exaggeration. Look at Falstaff. Was ever man so fat ? And, given such an apparently obvious topic for jest as a very fat man, were there ever so many jokes made on the same subject ? Has any one ever counted the number of jokes made by Falstaff and others at the expense of his waist-line ? There must be hundreds. Yet Shakespeare was quite right ; though no modern writer would dare to do a thing like that. We are all too fearful. We never let ourselves go. Again, look at Pistol's swaggering, and Bardolph's red nose. And according to our puny modern standpoint Bottom's blunders in speaking would be an impermissible exaggeration. " The eye of man hath not heard, the ear of man hath not seen ; man's hand is not able to taste, his tongue to conceive, nor his heart to report what my dream was." Why, it is absurdly overdone, is it not ? Mistress Quickly and Dogberry and Slender and many others make the same improbable blunders. For even if we are to believe that such mistakes as " I am freely dissolved and dissolutely " were not improbable in Shakespeare's time, the fact is that they are quite unconvincing to-day. And yet we laugh still, and would not spare one of them. In fact, it is well worth while to investigate those we do not immediately see the point of, such as Mistress Quickly's " Good people, bring a rescue or two," and " O thou honeysuckle villain ! Wilt thou kill God's officers and the king's ? O thou honeyseed rogue ! Thou art a honey-seed." The good dame means " homicide." This " broad " comedy is the very essence of boy-stuff, and the playboys delight in it. The ridiculous business between Lancelot Gobbo and his father, in the matter of the beard which Lancelot grew on the back of his head, is one of the favourite features of this popular fellow. And the more outrageous you can make the antics of Pyramus and the Lion and the Moon the better pleased they all are. We have also found our audiences delighted with our broad treatment of what is manifestly broad comedy.

The question of why Shakespeare's exaggerations and burlesques are recognized by all as fitting and genuinely comic, while the tamer and more modest foolery of such turns as " Charley's Aunt " and the red-nosed, umbrella-wagging tramps of the modern variety stage are often found silly, and never for long satisfying, cannot be examined here. There is a very demonstrable reason, but the discussion would not be in place. Suffice it for the present to say that Shakespeare for all his tomfoolery somehow always makes us feel that his creations are true to life; but the aim of modern farce is to amuse by strangeness, and by the sudden introduction of the unexpected.

But it would be leaving the case for broad, bold treatment, as instanced by Shakespeare, in a very one-sided position if we did not show that his touch is just as decided, and his taste just as courageous in the serious side of his work. Laertes is hardly less of a swashbuckler than Pistol, only we are not meant to laugh at him, and so we do not find him funny. The ravings of Lear are immoderate. He out-Herods Herod at times. Othello and even Hamlet rant. And Shakespeare himself pokes fun at the bloodthirsty character of Hotspur, in the words he gives to Prince Hal. But there is a touch of subtlety in all this character-drawing which makes every one of these persons a human being for us, even while we notice the emphasis with which one side of their nature is brought out. Consider the best criticisms one reads of the characters of Iago, Goneril, Regan. The writers, although they speak of nothing but the villainy or cruelty of these people, never speak of them except as people. Goneril and Regan may be unnatural daughters, but daughters they are, and natural.

This bold, definite touch is to be seen in every side of Shakespeare's work, and I have made a special point of it here because it is this quality in the workmanship and the whole art of the plays which makes it at once so easy for the boys to " see something in them " from the first, so easy for boys to act them, and which makes the study of Shakespeare so helpful to their own playmaking.

There is always " something to get hold of " in Shakespeare. Whatever subject he took for a plot he always made of it a story you could never forget. The history we know best is the history we learn from Shakespeare. Those characters he means to draw he draws so distinctly that you cannot but feel they are as actual as any one you ever met in real life. Who will believe me if I say that Falstaff never lived, and that

215

Shylock is only " made up " ? And when Shakespeare does
not mean to draw a character as a real live person he is generally
careful not to do so, and thus avoids the blurred impression
we should get from a half-delineated figure. Demetrius,
Lysander, Hippolyta, Salanio, Hamlet's uncle, and others
merely fill parts in a plot. That is all they were meant to do.
But so creative is his touch that sometimes even minor characters
insist on coming to life and taking affairs into their own hands.
There are many instances of this, such as Barnardine in " Measure
for Measure " as instanced by Sir Walter Raleigh. But Mercutio
is another. He becomes so obtrusive that Shakespeare has to
kill him to save the play. He does not kill Sir Toby, and so
this genial old scoundrel takes the direction of matters into
his own hands and pushes Orsino and Olivia into the background. Even Falstaff was not originally intended to bulk
so large throughout the epic of Harry. " He had been brought
in as an amusement, and had rapidly established himself as
the chief person of the play."

If Shakespeare's workmanship could produce figures so
life-like as to confound their maker it is easily understood
how his most unlearned readers may at once be captivated.
You cannot confuse one play of Shakespeare with another
play, or get " mixed up " between the persons, because the
plays and the persons are *real* and distinguishable. They are
as distinctly recognizable as one's brothers and sisters and
friends.

Even in the matter of the merest accessories the same
distinctive touch is seen. Most of the plays require one or
more properties which appear in their own place and nowhere
else. There are the caskets in " The Merchant of Venice," the
skull in " Hamlet," the bear in " The Winter's Tale," the cauldron in " Macbeth," the hot irons in " King John," the mirror
in " Richard II," the deer in " As you Like It," the handkerchief in " Othello," the worm in " Antony and Cleopatra," the
ass-head in " A Midsummer Night's Dream," and the leek in
" Henry V."

Literary critics are apt to overlook the importance of these
concrete things. And many teachers of Shakespeare, not
understanding the power of association that is in them, pay

them no attention at all. But the property-master and his goods contribute very much to the reality of a play. When the playboys have in their tiring-house a cauldron, three caskets, a hand-mirror, a skull, a lanthorn, a bunch of thorn-twigs, and the masks of an ass, a lion, a dog, and a bear, they look upon each as a kind of emblem or concrete embodiment of one most distinct play.

The works of Shakespeare represent so many sides of life and study that it is possible for a man totally to ignore many elements and yet own a rich possession in the rest. It is possible to devote many busy and well-spent years solely in studying Shakespeare's use of language or to the impersonation of his characters upon the boards, or to the critical elucidation of the text. Some of the truest lovers of Shakespeare are engaged daily with ropes, hammers, lamps, and such things behind the scenes. A student of Shakespeare, sick of much study in learned books, may, even in this material and unimaginative age, find a full refreshment by spending an evening in a tavern at Oxford or Stratford-on-Avon with the stage-hands of the Benson Company. Those whose daily occupation is the traffic of the stage, even if they be simple unlettered men, are often nearer to the spirit of Shakespeare than the most learned among scholars.

No man can come to the end of all there is to learn and to feel about Shakespeare. And, in common with the rest of mankind, boys have their due part in him. What is this part? Under right guidance, I think a company of boys might well find that Shakespeare belongs more to them than to some of their learned elders. Their romantic, adventurous tastes bring them nearer to the life of Shakespeare's own day than has been possible for most adults during the past three hundred years of puritan dominion. And Shakespeare himself knew all about boys.

You may be surprised to see how few boys are represented among the crowd of Shakespeare's characters. They are generally children, and a boy is not by any means the same thing as a child. Mamillius in " The Winter's Tale " and Falstaff's page (who lives on as the boy in " Henry V") are real boys. The princes in " Richard III " and Arthur

in "King John" are less convincing. Lucius in "Julius
Cæsar" serves to bring out the gentleness of Brutus, but has
no separate being. Looked at beside that shrewd and knavish
sprite called Robin Goodfellow these lads show up for what they
are, figures for pathos. Their main function is to excite our
pity. Macduff's little son is similarly placed. He does show
some touches of nature in his prattling; but he is not meant
to live, he is meant to die. These gentle babes are after all
but food for slaughter, and the reader will not be surprised
to learn that all the sympathy of our playboys is with those
who murder them. They much enjoy playing the scene in
which Lady Macduff and her son are slain, but they refer to
it with rude relish as "the fried-egg scene." This is a nick-
name suggested to a boyish fancy by the lines,

> *Son.* Thou liest, thou shag-hair'd villain.
> *Murderer.*   What, you egg?
> Young fry of treachery !   [*Kills him.*

What is the boys' share in Shakespeare's gift to the world ?
Is it confined to their healthy appreciation of the sensational
and knockabout elements ? Most teachers have not the wit to
allow their boys even this small share in the greatest treasury
of life-lore our nation has produced. But what further can
we expect schoolboys to understand and appreciate in Shakespeare ? Can they have any real feeling for the poetry ? Can
they appreciate the subtleties of plot-development ? Can they
comprehend the characters ? These are no idle questions,
nor shall they be idly answered.

One of the best ways of teaching English to boys (whether
you mean by that word a knowledge and appreciation of
literature, or a skill in the use of language; or even if you
include as part of this study the ability to *make* literature)
is to *base all their English studies on their acting of the plays
of Shakespeare*. The first acquaintance a boy makes with
literature, after his simple reading of stories and ballads, should
be this acting of Shakespeare. And thereafter all you wish to
teach him in English can be directly or indirectly associated
with this.

On what authority can such a recommendation be made ?

218

ACTING SHAKESPEARE

Although the methods described in this book are one and all the outcome of actual experiments, the reader has only one man's word for it that the experiments have been successful. It may be thought merely a matter of opinion that Speeches and Ilonds and Playtown and Miming and these other devices are adapted to the character and preference of boys, and do really represent their natural way of learning. But in advising teachers to let their boys act Shakespeare, with full confidence that they can and will appreciate not only the sporting side but also the poetic, the dramatic, and the human aspects of the work, we have the support of the highest authority, that of Shakespeare himself.

Though there may be but few real boys drawn among his characters there were many real boys among his players. Shakespeare had with him just the same sturdy, naughty, laughing, loving English boys as you and I have with us to-day. They liked the same things, such as fights and din, and high adventure, and broad nonsense. Their imaginations were as rich in the poetry of life as your boys' are, only Shakespeare knew it and you don't. There was as much noisy chatter and heroic make-believe in the tiring-house as there is in the schoolroom, but with this difference: that the noise was greater, the laughter louder, and the fancy much quickened when the master was present. Shakespeare was familiar with the same tousled heads, the same grubby paws, the same quarrels and appeals, the same cries of " Sir ! " The little wretches left their stockings on the floor, and mislaid essential properties, and dropped their wigs into the sink, just as they do to-day—that is, if you give them stockings and wigs and a sink, and other essential properties. Can you not see Master Shakespeare in the tiring-house ? The boys knew him and loved him as all men did. They had no cause to be afraid of him, and did not hush their boy-business at his approach. They did not think him a tyrant or a bore. They did not associate him with stodgy lessons and " swot." This is noteworthy, for you must remember that the lads had to learn hundreds of his lines by heart and deliver them as he would have them delivered, neither drawling them nor mouthing them ; but speaking them trippingly on the tongue. And there was some very stiff work to be gone through in the way of rehearsals. For Shakespeare was in the midst of it all, and he would have things right. Yet the boys would do anything for him. Ben Jonson was not, by many a score, the only one who, after his death, could say in candour, " I loved the man, and do honour his memory on this side idolatry as much as any."

This first of playmasters knew the capacity of his boys. While Shakespeare was writing the lines which embodied the life of Imogen and Portia he knew that the parts would be played by his boys. He had no thought of any one to play them but his boys, and often he knew the very boy who would be cast for a certain part. It is true that Imogen and Portia and Jessica played their most important scenes in the guise of men, and that Rosalind and Viola appeared in a male habit throughout most of their parts. But Portia the wife of Brutus was also played by a boy, and so were Juliet and Lady Macbeth and Ophelia. Consider what a faith in—or say rather a knowledge of—boys he must have had who could create Cordelia and Desdemona to be impersonated by boy-players. Nowadays there is much reading of Shakespeare in the study, much regard for the plays quite apart from their representation on the stage, and rightly so. But we may safely challenge any one to produce the least tittle of evidence that Shakespeare counted upon this, or even thought of his plays except as matter for the " three hours' traffic of the stage." He requires the onlooker to

> Eke out our performance with your mind.

But he never doubts that there will be a performance.

Are Shakespeare's women dummies ? Is nothing required to represent these parts but dressing up and an unbroken voice ? Or have we not rather in these creations all the characteristics of a world of womankind ?

The only sign of any dissatisfaction is, just where you would expect it, in Cleopatra. She says :

> the quick comedians
> Extemporally will stage us . . . and I shall see
> Some squeaking Cleopatra boy my greatness.

ACTING SHAKESPEARE

One of the very few contemporary allusions made by Shakespeare is the mention in " Hamlet " of the " aery of children." Rosencrantz tells Hamlet that the tragedians of the city, those he was wont to take delight in, are on travel, because they do not hold the same estimation as they did, and are not so followed. They have not grown rusty, their endeavour keeps in the wonted pace, but they have been put out of favour by a company of children which has become fashionable. Rosencrantz explains that much of the interest is excited by a controversy, and by the introduction of personal abuse into the plays. But the quarrel and the exchange of personalities among the poets and actors does not concern us here. When Hamlet asks, " Do the boys carry it away ? " Rosencrantz replies, " Ay, that they do, my lord ; Hercules and his load too." Which shows that the success of the boys had even troubled the company at the Globe.

So long as Shakespeare's work is thoroughly studied and whole-heartedly played by boys, not only will the boys themselves profit, but the fine traditions of Elizabethan drama will be carried on. " For," as the boy says in " Henry V," " there is none to guard it but boys."

The study of Shakespeare in schools to-day should be not only a means of encouraging self-expression but the medium of much learning in literature and in life. If it cannot be made so, the fault lies not in any want of appreciative power on the boys' part but in the ignorance and incompetence of narrow-minded teachers. To these, and to many who are not teachers, may be commended for reflection Sir Walter Raleigh's deliberate statement, " With the disappearance of the boy-players the poetic drama died in England, and it has had no second life."

CHAPTER VIII

MIMING AND THE BALLADS

And then bespake the schoolmaster
Unto the Lord of Learne said he,
" I think thou be some stranger born
For the Holy Ghost remains with thee."

He said, " I am no stranger born,
Forsooth, master, I tell it to thee,
It is a gift of Almighty God
Which He hath given unto me."
" The Lord of Learne "

MIMING, the language of gesture, is as old-established a form of expression as any other language, and it can be made of much educational value. There must be books on the subject, and they should be both learned and entertaining, but we did not happen to come across them, and all that is said here springs directly from our own original and unaided experiments.

In miming, the first thing to note is that you have to make yourself understood without uttering any words. We have used two classes of gesture. We communicate our thought to others (i) by the use of those signs, gestures, looks, and actions which every one understands ; or (ii) by the use of certain conventional signs and gestures previously agreed upon. These two means of expression we have always combined, using our own conventional signs only where there was no commonly accepted way of expressing a thing.

The first class includes such easily intelligible action as extending something towards a person to *Offer* it, or holding out the hand to imply " Give it to me " ; a nod of the head for *Yes* and a shake for *No*. *Eat* and *drink* are easily shown ; and most people without using any words can say, " Come here,"

222

"Go," "Good-bye." Facial expression alone can easily put a simple query, "Is it?" "Does he?" "May I?" "Shall we?" "Who?" "Why?" And in conjunction with a shrug of the shoulders (and a context) facial expression can indicate more particular inquiry such as, "What am I to do with this?" "Where shall I put it?" "What shall we do now?" A look and a simple movement are all that is needed to say "Get out of my chair," "Put that back where you took it from," or "Dare you push him in?"

Momentary hesitation, with a pursing of the lips, shows *Doubt*. *Perplexity* is shown by placing the forefinger on the temple and frowning. *Recognition* of the solution of a difficulty is obviously a silent "Ah!" Those who think they have never tried miming will perhaps be surprised to hear that all the instances given above and hundreds of similar expressive gestures are exchanged daily by all ordinary people—even in England.

Even in circumstances where movement is not the usual medium of expression, any one can invent it, if necessary, for such meanings as "Where shall I hide?" "Where did I put that letter?" "Good luck, old fellow," "It's getting late," the last, of course, by simply looking at one's watch.

There are many other gestures which those good people we call foreigners use to express a world of meaning which could scarcely be put into words at all. A Frenchman or an Italian can keep up his side of a conversation for a long while merely in gesture. In his gestures he can say, "Ah! my friend, why have you not told me this long ago?" "True, true, but what is to be done?" or, "'She is a woman, after all."

If you should take up miming it is well that you should remember it is not a mere matter of *descriptive* dumb-show. Although you have no words, you have the use of all those varied *expressive* movements which went with words.

Apart from these there are gestures which, although perfectly intelligible, are never used (by Englishmen at least) when words are available, because the gesture, save for emphasis, means no more than the word. Such are pointing to one's chest to express "I," and to the other person's chest to express "you"; pointing to the mouth as a request for food; going

223

through the motion of drinking off a bumper to indicate thirst, and drawing the hand across the throat to express either a fear of, or a threat of, assassination. Englishmen at home are not prone to expressive gesture. An Englishman feels a fool if he makes any hand-movements. But since he has colonized half the world without learning any foreign languages he must behave differently when away from his friends!

If these various kinds of expressive gesture be considered it will be seen that, although I have divided the gestures used in our mining into two classes only, it is possible to make numerous subdivisions. But a twofold division at least is essential—into *signs universal* and *signs conventional*. The sign universal has been sufficiently described. Let us consider the sign conventional.

When in your miming you wish to signify " day " or " night," or " yesterday," " to-day," or " to-morrow " you find yourself " stumped " as regards signs universal. And if you meet a Russian who cannot speak English, you cannot make him understand in gesture " I arrived," " He came on horseback," " You go by boat," " It is ten miles away," or " That is the King." Gesture as universally understood will not convey " Where is your mother ? " " This is my son," " Can you hear the Cathedral clock ? " or " Over the hills and far away." Without using any words you *can* express simple ideas such as " Come," " Hush ! " " Look " ; and you can ask for things, such as a knife, a fork, or a spoon. But you cannot express equally simple ideas, such as " Begin," " Stop," " Hurry up," " More slowly," " Wait for me," " Look out ! " or " Give me a bed."

The Play Way is happy to have realized from the beginning that a necessary thing which does not exist can be invented. But this fact is proverbial. Necessity, they say, is the mother of invention. It would be a sorry thing if those who invented an imaginary stage to act on could not also invent miming signs for a few common objects. So we found no difficulty in devising conventional signs for meanings which did not seem to be covered by the universal language of gesture. There is no doubt that our signs could easily be improved upon. We have endeavoured to make them simple and direct so that they might be understood by all. But all innovations grafted on to an old stock are subject to grave disabilities. As innovators we have recognized this difficulty, and we have coped with it. The question of the rights and duties of an innovator will be discussed in its place, but some of our new conventional signs must now be described.

The description of gesture is a thankless task, because gesture chiefly exists to save description. Words, in any case, are cumbrous to explain movement. A simple wave of the hand may be talked about for a whole paragraph, and still not be made visible. An action may express hope, desire, anger, fear, despair. Words also may express hope, desire, anger, fear, despair. But the attempt to describe in words the feeling as shown in the action is hopeless.

Novelists say, " ' Damnation ! ' said Travers, with a gesture of impatience "; or, " ' Leave it all to me,' replied Miss Phipson airily, indicating with a sweep of the hand that she was perfectly capable of managing the whole affair." But they have to leave the gesture of impatience and this comprehensive sweep of the hand to the imagination of their readers.

So I will not attempt to give descriptions of those gestures which we have used to express feeling of any kind, but will confine my detailed illustrations to those signs and symbols which we have devised to represent persons and things and simple ideas.

King is indicated by making a plain circle round one's head. Preceded or followed by the sign for " woman," this means " queen "; and in conjunction with the sign for " boy " it means " prince."

Day is indicated by making a circle on the right with the finger, then carrying the line over in a curve to the left and making another circle there. This figure, not unlike a pair of spectacles with an exaggerated bridge, is designed to represent the sun in the east, going over, and in the west—hence a day.

Here is indicated by pointing to the ground at one's feet.

To-day is indicated by " Day-here," or " Day-now."

Yesterday is indicated as " Day-back-one." " Day " is done first, then the thumb is pointed back over the shoulder for " back," and then the forefinger is held up for " one." Either hand may be used. The actions are run smoothly together into one rhythmical movement.

To-morrow is " Day-forward-one."

Now is indicated by a grasping action of the hand (*maintenant*).

The action may be performed comparatively quickly or slowly according to the sense which it is desired to express in the word. The reader will be surprised to learn that it is possible to express as many different tones of " now " with the hand as it is with the voice. Of course facial expression, and the whole posture and set of the body, have part in this expression by the hands, just as they do in the expression by the voice. Consider some "nows." There is the threatening approach of a fiendish enemy who at last has one in his grasp. He comes toward his victim with a devilish leer and, instead of saying " Now ! " he holds his hand before him and slowly closes his contorting fingers. Try it. There is a totally different movement in the hand of the captain who cries to his men awaiting the signal for a charge, " Now ! " He clenches his fist and throws his whole arm upward and forward in one inspiring command. Then there is the eternal " Now " of old Omar, " one moment in annihilation's waste." What an infinitude of meaning he would express with his fingers as he closed them tenderly about the rose that lay in his palm !

But such interpretations as these lie outside the scope of the present description. We must confine ourselves to plain signs for simple meanings.

Signs such as these (for " day," " king," " here," and so on will not be invented by a boy on the spur of the moment as he needs them ; and even if some boys are able to devise such signs, the rest may not understand the movement on seeing it for the first time. Such symbols must be suggested and agreed upon in a council met together—a convention.

But we did not begin to devise these signs until we found it impossible to get on without them in miming. And we never made more at one sitting than were immediately required. Consequently there was never a long and forbidding vocabulary to learn. The boys picked up the necessary signs as need occasioned their invention.

MIMING AND THE BALLADS

When a sign for " night " was demanded we all thought carefully for a while. One boy suggested " day-not," but although this would have passed in an emergency, we decided to think out something better. I made an equally feeble suggestion. " day-blind," to be shown by closing the eyelids with the finger-tips after making the sign for " day." But presently it occurred to the youngest boy in the class that if the path of the sun was shown to curve *over* for " day," it might be shown to curve *under* for " night." This was obviously the right symbol, and so we straightway adopted it.

For some time we had found a difficulty in expressing " man," "woman," " boy," and " girl." Eventually we decided to describe them by the fashion of the hair.

Man is indicated by placing the hands flat on each side of the head.

Woman is indicated by drawing both hands down from the temples to the waist.

Girl is indicated by ringlets falling to the shoulder.

Boy is indicated by twiddling the forefinger just above the ear to imply " curly-head."

But one twiddle of the finger is not enough to show the ringlets or the curls which imply " girl " or " boy." So small an action as a hasty movement of one finger will scarcely be caught by the onlooker. These and all the other movements of the conventional signs must be done slowly, *in a measured and rhythmical manner.* Slowness is essential in miming. The fault of all beginners is to make the movements too quickly. This makes the gestures not only difficult to understand but ugly in themselves.

A teacher who is not alive to the beauty of gesture will probably not be alive to the value of expressive movement at all, and will in consequence be unlikely to introduce miming in his classes. But there may be some who will try miming either " for the fun of the thing " or at the request of a principal, without previously having realized that as much seriousness and care is required in the practice of expressive movement as in music or speaking.

Any advice or warning we are able to give is based solely upon our own short experience, but whoever will make a few serious and careful experiments for himself will at once agree that miming as a means of expression has real educational value. It is therefore worth while to undertake it earnestly. We do not wish the slang and Cockney of daily speech to have their parallel in the language of gesture, and we hope that the public taste in music, as seen in the popular sentimental and comic songs, will not be considered a sufficiently high standard for miming.

It is necessary to say a word also about the cinema. A few days after we started miming, a senior boy, who in his day had been a keen Shakespearean actor and a good mister in the third form, met me in hall and said in jest, "What is this I hear about your taste having come down to the level of the cinema? It is a great drop, after all you have said about drama." Of course our miming has no connexion at all with the moving pictures of the cinema. The representation of a story without the use of spoken words is all that is common between the two. To attempt any closer comparison would be as false as to compare the cartoons of Raphael with the cartoons in the *Daily Mirror* because both are drawings! If, as seems to be the case, the cinema has come to stay, men of taste might go to the aid of those low-minded men who are responsible for the choice of what is thrown upon the screens, and show them how to make the entertainment more intelligent and less vulgar, without lessening its attractiveness in the least. In some respects the cinema has opportunities of representation which are denied to the other kinds of stage show. The photographers can, for instance, give us coloured and moving scenes of streets in all the great cities of the world; they can show Venice, Athens, Rome, Egypt, and the great Cathedrals, the Monuments, and the Markets. Scenes may be shown by the lake of an Italian garden, in a wooded English park, or in the Rocky Mountains. But the effect of these wonderful backgrounds is marred by the rubbishy character of the stories shown; and even more by the fact that the cinema method of representation ignores all the *literary* quality of a tale, and treats it as a mere string of incidents. Even then the narration of this emasculated story has to be eked out by the periodical appearance of explanatory labels. The present cinema method

228

MIMING AND THE BALLADS

of telling a story is nothing but external show; it is a hollow sham, a mere travesty of art. But every form of representation has certain conditions proper to itself; there are things you can do and things you cannot do in painting, drawing, sculpture, acting, and so on. The cinema is not an artistic medium at all, but only a machine. Nevertheless there are certain laws and conditions which the cinema as a means of representation must obey. No one, so far as we can see, has made it his business to study the conditions which govern representation by cinematography. If the money-snatchers could be persuaded to allow some higher order of intellectual life to co-operate with them in their production, the ubiquitous cinema-show might be made quite an interesting experiment. Our position, then, with regard to the moving pictures is that we are not indebted to them in the slightest degree. But we think it quite possible that the introduction of miming in cinema representation might be found helpful in civilizing and refining that mechanical substitute for the acting of live players.

Some of the descriptions of our signs, as jotted down in words by the boys in their notebooks, are in the right spirit of taste. "King" they call "crowned one," "man" is "crop-head," "boy" is "curly-head." Thus "prince" becomes "crowned curly-head"—a charming description of a royal lad.

At one lesson we invented signs for the days of the week. They were not really necessary, but one of the boys began with Sunday and Monday, and then we decided to go through with it. We already had our sign for "day," and this was of course used in each case, preceded by particular descriptive signs to indicate the days of the week.

The sun was a circle drawn with one hand while the other described "day." The moon, for Monday, was of course a crescent. Tuesday is the day of Tiw, or Tyr, who, as the god of war in the Norse mythology, was already a familiar figure to the boys. Tyr had his right hand bitten off by Fenris the wolf. So our conventional sign for Tuesday is described in the notes as "Left-hand-sword-day," and is shown by the action of drawing a sword from the right thigh with the left hand. Thursday gave no difficulty; it was called "Hammer-

229

day," after old Thorr and his trusty Miolnir. Friday became " Lady-day " after Frigga, the mother of the gods.

But what were we to do about Wednesday and Saturday ? We knew much about Woden or Othinn, but we were long puzzled in our choice among his attributes. At last one of the boys remembered that the father of the gods had but one eye, having given the other to buy wisdom. Wednesday, then, was shown by closing one eye with a finger and drawing day with the other hand. The boy at the blackboard wrote up, " Wednesday—One-eyed's day."

For Saturday, the planet and his rings were suggested. But every one was sorry to leave the company of the Norse gods. I promised to do a little research. As a result of my learned labours we described Saturday as " Washing-day " ! The action for this was, of course, the " Rub-a-dub-dub," familiar to all in the Nursery Rhymes. To have overthrown Saturn from his place and described his ancient reign as " Washing-day " may appear to some a sad drop from the sublime to the commonplace. But if the reader will pursue a scholarly research into folk-lore he will find that tradition has not been set at naught. And fair white linen has ever been associated with godliness.

As a sign for " week," " seven days " readily suggested itself, but we bettered this by adopting " sennight." " Month " is " wax and wane." The movement of the thumbs and forefingers showing how the crescent fills out into the full moon and then thins out again into a silver bow, though beautiful to see, would be tedious in a detailed description. For " year " the revolution of the earth about the sun is shown in a movement of the two fists.

In the ballad narratives, which we very soon used for the stories of our miming, persons generally travelled on horseback or by boat. A player wishing to say " I came on horseback " would make the signs for " I-ride-here." The movement of the hands in a make-believe of riding is familiar in every nursery. Refinements which would make it possible to say " hither " instead of " here " or to indicate the past and the future tense could easily be invented. But it is better to confine oneself to the simple essential things first. In any case I am only describing here the conventional signs we did invent and bring into daily use. If you were directing a traveller to cross a ferry at a certain point you would tell him " River-you-row-over." The action for rowing is obvious.

River is indicated by a flowing line, as on a map. If you wish to describe its widening or narrowing at a certain spot you trace the course with two hands, and draw them together or apart to emphasize your point.

Hill is indicated by a slant.

House is indicated by a gable.

Castle is indicated by a line of battlements.

Scores of other necessary signs for things can be invented on this model. But verbs are more difficult.

To see is indicated by touching the eye-lid, then pointing forward and describing the thing seen.

To hear is indicated by placing a finger behind the ear.

To think is indicated by pausing with the forefinger on the temple.

To know or *to understand* is indicated by touching the temple and nodding slowly.

To ask is indicated by holding out one hand, palm upwards.

To implore or *to pray* is indicated by interlacing the fingers.

To love is indicated by placing one hand on the heart.

To marry is indicated by touching an imaginary ring on the third finger of the left hand with the thumb and forefinger of the right hand.

To lie down is indicated by a depressive movement with the open hand, as in the military signal.

To stop is indicated by the military signal for " Halt."

Slowly is indicated by a movement similar to " lie down," only this is more a stroking.

Hurry up is indicated by a stirring motion with both hands such as is used in shooing hens. But a player expressive in gesture can signify " hurry up " with a quick motion of one hand—a kind of beckoning upward.

To sleep is indicated by " folding " the hands and slightly inclining the head upon them.

No, or any form of the negative, is indicated by wagging the forefinger. This has been found in practice a more natural form of denial than shaking the head.

The making of a sign for "dead" or "to die" was a valuable experience for the players. The need for some descriptive sign arose suddenly while a mime was going on. But the boy would not break silence to voice a difficulty. He preferred to find some immediate solution and to convey his meaning, even if the sign he invented should not prove good enough to come into permanent acceptance.

According to the story they were miming, two princes were asking their father which of them should inherit the crown. When the time came to put this question the elder son fumbled a little, and could not make his meaning clear. But the younger pointed to his father, then shut his eyes, opened his mouth, and thrust one forefinger into each cheek. This was caught at once by the class to mean "You-dead"; and it was followed by the accepted gestures for "I-crowned." The newly invented sign for dead (an improvised skeleton head) pleased the onlookers by its quaint and almost comical effect. But the first comment offered when criticism was called for upon the conclusion of the mime was that a better sign for "dead" must at once be agreed upon. Nothing acceptable to the class was suggested then, and so the comic sign lived for a few days. But before long we devised a more dignified symbol of death. The eyes were closed and the wrists crossed upon the breast in the posture of those old effigies one sees upon cathedrals tombs.

The list of our new-created symbols and gestures need not be further prolonged. There is no occasion for the reader to be afraid of the number of these signs agreed upon. More than half of the new vocabulary we used is comprised in the above descriptions. And the signs are all so obvious that, once seen and understood, they are set in mind for ever. Moreover the signs conventional are so very very few, in proportion to the signs universal, that it is possible (as we have often proved) for a spectator perfectly to understand a play in mime without any previous familiarity with these set signs, even if he has never seen a mime in his life before. Even if you should find it necessary to invent scores of signs conventional, they will but appear now and then in acting, for nine-tenths of the descriptive gestures necessary for your story will always be possible in signs universal.

Nor must it be thought that there is any initial difficulty in miming. Our list of conventional symbols need not deter any ingenious person from beginning at once without any knowledge or outside help whatever. Assuredly a handy book on miming, if it were well written, would be a welcome aid. But there are no handy books on the practice of miming, and even if there were they would only be catch-penny manuals.

We started from bare nothing. The boys were simply told that to mime was to describe or relate something in dumb-show. The idea of expressing meaning by action was already familiar to them all in the parlour-game known as "Dumb Charades." It rested with the master to see that charades when imported to the classroom became a thing of value without becoming a whit less entertaining. This case affords an excellent illustration of the Play Way principles in working. Left entirely to their own devices, the boys could hardly be expected to make charades in any real sense a vehicle of learning. They would have continued indefinitely that somewhat inane occupation of rainy days—the guessing of acted words. But with a master to infuse something of value into the subject-matter and to keep a guiding hand upon the representation, the whole occupation was lifted from the level of mere pastime to the level of true play. The supersession of charades by miming, so far from lessening the fun, increased it, made a real *interest* of it.

In the beginning the boys were directed to mime the very simplest things, such as "Little Miss Muffet." They liked the notion of miming, but were not much impressed with the subject suggested. But so soon as one boy had tried to mime "Little Miss Muffet" several others sprang up to offer criticism. One of the most urgent of the critics was invited to try his skill. Some of the simplest details were omitted from the story in these early attempts. The critics were soon loudly insisting that Miss Muffet did not sit on the ground, but on a tuffet. They pointed out that, just

as Shakespeare mentioned everything in his lines, so the player
must show everything in his actions or gestures! But what
is a tuffet? Some, in recollection of the pictures in their baby
books, said a tuffet was a hassock. Some said it was a tuft of
grass. The master maintained a safe and benevolent neutrality.
The dictionary gave us no help, so we decided that "tuffet"
was a rhyme; and proceeded to the next point of criticism.

It was claimed by one objector that the last playboy who
impersonated Miss Muffet had eaten curds and whey without
ever putting spoon to mouth. A still stronger criticism was
that the mimist, although he had certainly shown fright enough,
had not made it clear that it was a spider which had occasioned
his retirement. "It might have been a bull in the field,"
said one critic. "Or even a clap of thunder," added another.
Enough difficulties were discovered to make the miming of
this simple Nursery Rhyme a task worth attempting.

Before long the master ventured a trial—a rare event. He represented the spider by wriggling the fingers of the right hand, held
high up and well back, while calmly eating curds and whey with
the left hand from an imaginary bowl and spoon. The next
movements were, to look quietly around as though enjoying
this supper in the meadow; then, catching sight of the right
hand behaving like a spider, suddenly to jump aside, throw
up both hands in horror and make a precipitous exit. This
was really a most skilful interpretation of the tragic narrative;
but even then there were some exacting critics who asked
whether Miss Muffet had taken the supper bowl along with
her, or left it for the delectation of the spider.

The next subject tried was "Little Jack Horner." It
was no easy matter to satisfy the critics about the pie. One
boy began by stealing the pie out of the oven. But the only
way of indicating "Christmas" seemed to be a rather laboured
reference to Santa Claus and gifts in one's stocking. "He
put in his thumb" is not so easy as it looks; for it is unlikely
that Jack *speared* the plum instead of using his forefinger
and thumb in the ordinary way.

"Curly Locks" proved to be one of our most successful
mimes. In the hands of two skilful and imaginative playboys
this Nursery Rhyme can afford a quaint little performance

fit to be shown on any stage. It was here that we discovered
our signs conventional for "man," "woman" "girl," and
"boy." Once we had learnt to call a little girl "Curly Locks"
it soon occurred to us to describe other folk also by the fashion
of the hair. Here also we first mimed love and the proposal of
marriage, which come into so many stories fit for miming.

The little boy says to the little girl, "Curly Locks, I love
you. Will you marry me?" The little girl ponders demurely
and remains silent. Then he presses his suit more earnestly,
and soon she looks at him and says, "You love me. I marry
you? No." He looks disappointed and she bids him, with
a motion of one finger. "Mark this." She turns on a tap,
holds a plate under it, and with the tips of her fingers takes a
nasty, greasy dish-cloth and cleans the plate. Her face expresses
her disgust at the business. Then the plate is dried and stood
on the dresser. The little boy lover begins to protest, but she
cuts him short with another "Look you"; and goes again
through the business of washing a greasy plate. Then she
tells him that there would be plates and plates and plates to
wash; and the rag would get greasier and nastier. When
her fingers and her face have shown unspoken disgust, she
concludes with, "No. I'll not marry you." It would be
meaningless if the little boy simply gave a reassuring denial
by means of the sign for "No." So, in his reply, he refers
to the washing-up by repeating her chief gestures in a
briefer form, such as "tap—plate—greasy—rag," and then
says, "If you marry me there will not be any of that nasty
washing-up." Or, to put it in the literal order of the words
mimed, "You—marry—me. Nasty—washing-up—you—No."

The little girl then says again, "But look you." She
points to where a number of (imaginary) fat creatures, who
have curly tails and say "Er," are waiting for something to
eat. She next prepares, with many indications of distaste,
a mess of kitchen-refuse in a pig-pail, and, holding it away
from her, steps daintily through the muck of the yard, and
shoots it over the gate of the sty. Of course to "feed the
swine," in this traditional verse, more probably means the
driving out of a herd of clean-bristled animals to feed upon
the beech-mast and acorns of the forest floor. But for the

purposes of this mime we thought it better to substitute the modern muck-pig for the nobler swine of other days. Well, the relish of the fat creatures who have curly tails is clearly shown, and the dainty lady's disgust at their beastliness is made equally apparent. Then with an air of finality she says to her lover, "I marry you and do all this for the fat things who have curly tails? Certainly not." The little boy replies. He makes a brief reference to her description of pig-tending, as he did to her complaint about the nastiness of washing-up. He assures her that nothing of the kind will ever be expected of her as his wife. On the contrary, he pictures a life of ease and luxury, where her hands shall always be clean: where she may sleep if she will upon soft cushions, or sew awhile at some elegant embroidery. She shall make the fruits and the flowers and the birds so real by the skill of her needlecraft that he will be content to stay from the orchard and the meadow only to look upon her handiwork. He will forgo the hunt itself, if only he may pursue the quarry in following her nimble fingers. When the time comes to eat and drink, there shall be no thought of dishes to wash, or kitchens which make refuse, but only "strawberries, sugar, and cream." And so the little girl is captivated. It may turn out that the fears of Curly Locks were well grounded. Sugar makes a sticky mess upon a plate; and perhaps she will have to keep a cow to supply the cream. But this is a digression. The end of the mime was that Curly Locks said, as all practically minded little girls eventually do say to their rosily romantic lovers, "You love me. I marry you."

Only the very best playboys could mime without previous rehearsal or instruction this story as I have described it. But if the whole class is given the opportunity of miming, the boys soon become proficient, not only in the language of gesture, but also in adapting all kinds of stories to make them suitable for miming. "Where are you going to, my Pretty Maid?" is already in the form of a dialogue, and consequently requires no adaptation. But the little play of "Curly Locks" is built up out of eight short lines which, in the Nursery Rhyme, are spoken only by the boy lover. "Baa, baa, Black Sheep," again, can be mimed without change; but "Little Bo-Peep" will afford any two or three boys an excellent exercise in adaptation. We did not really spend much time over representing the Nursery Rhymes, but a few more may be mentioned here as the easiest illustration of certain points it is necessary to make.

The following are capable of direct representation :

> Where are you going to, my Pretty Maid ?
> Baa, baa, Black Sheep.
> Simple Simon.
> Little Polly Flinders.
> How many Miles is it to Babylon ? *
> Old King Cole.

The following can be represented by turning the narrative form into dialogue :

> I had a little Pony.
> A Frog he would a-wooing go.
> There was a Jolly Miller.
> Taffy was a Welshman.
> There was an Old Woman who lived in a Shoe.
> I love Sixpence.

Skill of adaptation is needed in these exercises. For instance, in " I had a little Pony " a dialogue must be represented between the little boy proud of his pony and the lady who comes to borrow him for the second time. " No, no," says the boy. " Last time I lent him, you whipped him and slashed him and rode him through the mire. You shan't have him again at any cost." Taffy's defeat could be represented by an amusing series of visits, each party calling when the other was not at home, and describing his naughty doings in a soliloquy of gesture.

But there is one form of telling a story without word which the boys must use but sparingly. That is the acting

* Miles, or any other tokens of distance, are shown by shading the eyes with the open hand and looking far away. Thus ten miles is shown as " ten fars." This is quite definite enough.

of incident without the accompaniment of language in gesture. Many stories consist entirely of action, and nothing at all is said either in words or gestures.

The following Nursery Rhymes can be acted thus without speech of any kind.

> The Lion and the Unicorn.
> The Queen of Hearts.
> Tom, Tom, the Piper's son.
> Humpty Dumpty.
> Jack and Jill.

The first of these merely consists of a fight and a cadging run round the town. In the second the queen simply goes through the motions of pastry-making, and then the knave comes and steals the tarts. In the third, a pig is stolen and a hue and cry made after the thief. " Humpty Dumpty " and " Jack and Jill " are represented merely by getting up on something and falling down. Obviously there is little of true miming in all this. Such play with very young children has its place ; and at the very beginning of an experimental course of miming with older boys it may be useful. But the players must soon be told that talking with the hands is required.

After trying " Little Miss Muffet," " Curly Locks," " Old King Cole," and a few more under the master's direction our boys were left to choose their own subjects. At this stage the lesson was often conducted for half an hour at a stretch without a word being uttered. The mister would command attention by raising one hand as if to say " Silence." A click of the fingers called the attention of any one who was not looking. Then the mister would indicate one boy as leader of a mime, and this boy would choose several accomplices, and go out of the room for a minute or two to arrange the performance. When the players were too quick in their movements (and all the boys mimed too quickly in the beginning) the boys in the class would snap their fingers and then make the sign for " Slowly." When any boy failed to understand a certain movement, he would first call attention by this snapping of the fingers, and then indicate by a shrug of the shoulders that he could not understand.

MIMING AND THE BALLADS

Many players at first used twice as many movements as were really necessary for the expression of their meaning. But the continuous interruptions of " I don't understand that," followed by a repetition of the idle movement, soon caused the players to confine themselves to intentional and expressive gestures. The players were very keen, and often excited, and this was a fine lesson in restraint and self-control.

When a short story was spun out in mime to a tedious length (this was often occasioned by poor players repeating themselves again and again for lack of a quick inventiveness in devising the next step) the onlookers would snap their fingers and make the sign for " Hurry up " ; showing the same impatience of tiresome prolixity as they did during Lectures, when a speaker spun out his discourse beyond the limit of real interest.

In the first miming exercises made by these boys without the direction of the master the fault of acting incident only, without representing any speech, was very noticeable. One boy produced a mime of a barber's shop. There was shaving, shampooing, and hair-cutting, but, as the barber ventured nothing in the way of conversation, the show was quite unconvincing ! Another group of players presented a shoeing-forge. One plied the bellows, another was busy with hammer and anvil, and there was some entertaining by-play on the part of the horse ; but nothing was " said." And when at last another group represented a church service, the fault in question became apparent to the whole class. We were given the playing of the organ, the blowing of the bellows, the reading of the lesson ; and also prayers, hymns, and the taking of the collection. The parson then went up into the pulpit and delivered a soundless sermon, which, for vigorous gesticulation (and especially the recourse to a glass of water to mark the stages " thirdly " " fourthly," " fifthly ") would have done credit to a comic cinema star. But when spoken criticism was called for several speakers pointed out, and the rest of the class agreed, that this dumb-show merely represented externals. What lesson had been read ? What hymn had been sung ? Upon what subject had the parson preached so earnestly ?

In this practical way, by trial and manifest error, the

boys came to learn what a mime should be. They had now realized the need for speech to be represented. To make this realization quite sure I then directed that representation by the acting of players be entirely suspended for a space, and meaning conveyed in gesture by a single mimist in the form of an anecdote. This struck the boys as a very difficult exercise. And so it was. But several anecdotes were successfully narrated without a word being uttered. The performer would go through his exercise without having told the class beforehand what he was about to show. One told that chestnut of the boy who had been swimming, contrary to his mother's orders. He represented both sides of the dialogue, indicating the mother or the son in turn by making the sign for " woman ," or " boy," and shifting his position to the right or to the left. The mother asks the boy if he has been swimming. He denies it. She points out that his hair is wet. He replies that he had not meant to go in the water, but found the temptation too much for him. She preaches to him that when he is tempted he must say to the Devil, " Get thee behind me, Satan." The boy replies that he did so, but the Devil got behind and pushed him in ! The Devil was shown as " that horned one, horrid, with a long barbed tail."

An even more difficult anecdote was well told by another player. Two boys have stolen some apples (or nuts—the mimist was criticized for not making clear precisely what he meant by " round eatable things off a tree ") and have climbed over the wall into a graveyard to apportion the spoil between them. But in clambering over they have dropped two apples, and dare not go back for them because the old sexton (shown in mime as " old man of the graveyard ") is coming along, the road and they might be seen. While they are counting " One for you, and one for me," the parson and the sexton chance to meet in the roadway on the other side of the wall. After listening a while the old sexton tells the parson that in the graveyard over the wall God and the Devil are sharing out the dead. At this moment one of the boys says, " That's all." But the other asks, " What about those two on the other side of the wall ? " Consternation of the sexton and the parson !

It is not a story of any great merit, but it is an extremely difficult exercise for a boy to have chosen as a subject for miming. Yet I can assure the reader that I myself and quite half the class understood the story from the boy's gestures and signs. One of those who had understood then told the story to the class in words. The only real discrepancy between the two versions was that one boy said apples though the other had intended nuts.

There had previously been no sign conventional agreed upon for " God." The narrator's first idea, shown in gesture, after a scarcely perceptible pause, was " Crown of Prayer." That phrase, of course, is only my way of stating what I saw. The boy himself would probably have worded his gesture as " King to whom one prays." But the idea, however it be stated in words, is a beautiful idea. Those of my readers who (though not perhaps shocked at the anecdote itself) are inclined to feel that the idea of the Deity, in connexion with this story, could not have been in any sense a *noble* conception in the boy's mind, are asked to try and forget the puritan outlook, the limited and fearful notions of modern belief, and think themselves back into those days of a simpler and more childlike faith—mediæval days if you like—when belief was robust and hearty, and an honest man could without blasphemy share even his jokes with God. Later on I met a man who told me that he remembered somewhere having seen God represented in symbolism by forming the arms into a circle with the face looking through. This somehow reminded me of Blake.

One morning the boys were anxious to spend the English period in miming, but we had suspended plays in mime for the time being, and no one volunteered to describe an anecdote. So I called upon one boy to relate to the class our experiences of the night before. It was the winter term and a group of these boys had been learning the folk-carols with a view to singing them outside the houses of our friends when Christmas came near. Two of the senior boys came with us on these wanderings and played their fiddles, and several grown-up friends joined us with viola, 'cello, and voice. In all, our band of waits numbered about fifteen, and eight of the boys carried lanterns hung upon scout-poles to show a light for the musicians. We did not march in fours along the street, but trooped from house to house in a scattered procession, and the light from the swinging lanterns as the boys ran hither and thither gave a will-o'-the-wisp impression which was very pleasing. And when the company was clustered together outside some door to give its performance, the lanterns lighted up such a group of merry faces that any one could see that our charity began at home, and that the benefit of these outings did not entirely consist in the money we collected for a Red Cross fund.

The boy who was called upon to narrate in mime the happenings of the previous evening described this lantern-lighted throng of singers and musicians. He related who played, who sang; and told how a certain person, who had no skill with voice or fiddle, bore a box with a slit in it, and knocked the knockers and rang the bells of the house-doors to take toll of the good people within. The other boys were interested to learn of our good fortune in having been received with such hospitality at several houses that we actually had to decline cakes and buns and ginger-beer and coffee after the first few visits. I asked the boy if he could not tell the others what carols we had sung, and he then described in gesture, " The Wassail Song," " King Herod and the Cock," and " Mary Mother Mild." *   This boy was our chief mimist; it is doubtful if any other boy could have done this.   He finished his story by telling how one of the playboys had been taken ill at the last house we visited.   But fortunately it was a doctor's house. The doctor-man revived the boy, who had nearly fainted, and then very kindly offered to drive three of them to their homes. The conclusion of this narrative in gesture had the same effect upon me as if I had read it in a piece of well-written prose ; though of course I must content myself here with a mere description of the events related.   The first house was reached. The boy got out, shut the door of the car, raised his cap and thanked the doctor, and then went straight in to bed.   The second house was the home of the boy who had been unwell. The doctor hoped he was better now.   The boy thanked him for his kindness, said good night, and went in to go to bed.   Then

* See " English Folk-Carols " collected by Cecil J. Sharp (Novello) and Perse Playbooks, No. 5, p. 163.

the boy who was telling the story was taken to his home. He also thanked the doctor, then went to bed, and was soon asleep. But the doctor had still to get home. He started his engine, leapt to his seat, turned various corners, and at last arrived at his house. Here he put the car in the garage, let himself in with his latch-key, found that all his household was in bed, and so himself retired, and was soon asleep. " So," concluded the playboy with the customary bow, " everybody sleeping."

Not only was there much skill in the description of the night's events solely in gesture, but surely some art of peroration also.

After a little practice in the difficult exercise of relating anecdotes in gesture, the boys were ready to include plenty of speech-gesture (as distinct from mere acted epidodes) in the miming of dramatized stories. One of the best mimes performed at this period was the story of King Alfred in the camp of the Danes. The Danes were described as " Winged Hats," but we could think of nothing appropriate for the English, and referred to them simply as " Our men." A single player performed this mime.

Taking the part of Alfred, he crept up to a tent in which the Danish leader and his captains were discussing their plan of campaign. A more clever piece of acting could not be desired. The boy represented with one hand the part of the harper-king. He told us who he was and what he was about, and made clear the danger he was in as a spy in the enemy's camp. With the other hand he first showed, by touching the ear and holding up one finger, that he was listening attentively, and then described what he heard of the plans which were being discussed within the Danish tent.

As I write I can see the figure of the king in the dark, straining to catch the drift of the murmured conference ; I can see the group of " Winged Hats " sitting about the table inside the tent, while in the dim light of a lamp the leader's long finger maps out his plans for the disposition of his men and his ships. Yet there was no tent, no lamps, no darkness, no " Winged Hats " even. There was nothing but a single boy in ordinary school dress making a story live in the play of his hands.

THE PLAY WAY

While such a mime is going on the other boys sit quietly but they are by no means idle. They " play with their fancies," as Shakespeare directs, and " eke out the performance with their minds." And so it happened that, although the master was more than pleased with this piece of acting, several of the Littlemen at once sprang up to offer critical suggestions. They took for granted all the brilliant representation of Alfred the King, and began to discuss the weak points in the Danish leader's plan of campaign ! I excused the player to his critics on the ground that he was doing several things at the same time, and had but one hand with which to represent the leader and his captains and all they were saying. Two of the critics were then sent up to the platform to mime the parts of the leader and his second in command.

The leader began by showing " Here is a line of hills, and here another. The valley runs along here. Now the English will march along this valley——"

" Why should they ? " interrupted the captain.

" Because there is no other road for them to march on," replied the leader. " You will take half our men and go up the hills, here, and I with the rest will go up on the other side, here. Then as the English reach this point in the valley between us, we rush down from both sides and fall upon them."

" No," said the captain, " they will see us coming down the hills, and will make off along the valley."

" There are trees enough on the hill-side," replied the leader, " to hide all our men."

But the captain still protested. " The English are not so foolish as to march along this valley without having scouts ahead on the hills on either side."

The Danish leader was persuaded in the end to abandon his plan of campaign. The details need not be further related, but the discussion of that matter outlasted the period. And yet no one was allowed to speak a word.

We next took the stories of the traditional ballads and acted them in mime. It is very good to have many devices for use in connexion with the ballads ; for the essential thing about a ballad is that it should be thoroughly familiar. Poems, plays, stories, and essays may be read and

244

carefully studied, and then set aside. But your knowledge of a ballad is not complete, your work upon it is not finished, unless you carry it for ever after in your mind. Ballads above all else in literature must be known by heart. It is poor fun learning a few stanzas at a time for homework. And repeated readings and re-readings in class are almost as dull, once the story is known. Here then, once again, comes in the school necessity which is the mother of Play Ways.

In the first place a ballad may be read aloud by one boy while the rest listen with their books closed. This method has obvious advantages for a first reading. Then the ballad can be read again by one or several of the boys while the rest follow in their books. Any discussion which springs up of its own accord should of course be permitted. But it seems to me a mistake for a master, in connexion with such a simple thing as a ballad, artificially to raise inquiry by asking unnecessary questions. If difficulties are thus made where no real difficulties exist, the boys will be less likely to turn to the reading of ballads for their own enjoyment out of school. The matter has been mentioned before in these pages ; and the suggestion has been made that teachers still consider everything a matter for questions and problems simply because they cannot think of anything better to do.

A good way of getting a ballad read carefully time and again, without risking that boredom which robs learning of its joy and makes study a thing of naught, is, after the first two or three readings, to bring in an alternative version of the ballad. Comparisons are interesting, and the quest of them causes one to read both versions several times. By this time the ballad will already be shaping in the memory. Then many of the ballads can be read in *parts* by a number of boys, with one of them acting as chorus to fill in the narrative passages. The mister reads,

> The king sits in Dunfermline town
> Drinking the blude-red wine ;

and the king reads,

> " O whare will I get a skeely skipper
> To sail this new ship o' mine ? "

THE PLAY WAY

The mister even puts in " He said " and " She cried." Even so simple a device as this adds variety, and gives you another reading or two without boredom. Then again, we have often borrowed the tunes of the folk-ballads which have been recently collected by Mr. Cecil Sharp and others, and have used them for the ballads in our other books. Thus we have sung " King Estmere " to the tune of " Ward the Pirate," and " Young Bekie " to the tune of " The Outlandish Knight." We only did this in a rough-and-ready manner in the classroom, and without any accompaniment. Here and there the words and the music did not quite fit, but we made adjustments in passing and thus gaily sang through our ballads instead of reading them. It is only fair to the music master to add that he would not have approved of these singing lessons !

Ballads, again, can be acted without book. You have at command a good actable story and a number of keen players. Nothing more is needed but floor-space, and a few odds and ends to serve as properties. The mister plans the scenes, and the players make up their parts as they go along, using whenever possible the actual words of the ballad. My readers may fear that to attempt the performance of a play without preparation is to court failure. Of course it is. The first effort, when a *spoken* part has to be taken extempore, generally results in a shocking mess. It is this very disaster which causes the boys to read the ballad again very carefully, and to commit great swarths of it to memory against the next day when the master shall be in a good mood, and may be approached with " May we act ' King Estmere ' ? " Few teachers realize that the process of learning consists as much in failure as in success.

Finally, as a method of making ballads thoroughly familiar, there is miming. There need be no fear that the absence of words in miming implies any loss in the study of a ballad in this way. It is one of the characteristic virtues of the traditional ballads that they give the bare story without trimmings or ornament ; so that the players, by the time they know the story well enough to represent it in detail, will already have the stanzas almost by heart. And, as the story has never been thought of apart from its ballad form, the words and the phrasing, and

246

the very rhymes and rhythms, will be running in every one's head all the time.

The ballad of " Young Bekie " opens thus :

> Young Bekie was as brave a knight
>   As ever sailed the sea ;
> An' he's done him to the court of France,
>   To serve for meat and fee.

The first scene of the mime will show Young Bekie, a fine upstanding young fellow, presenting himself to the King of France, and offering his knightly service. The king accepts Young Bekie as his man, and presents him to his daughter, Burd Isbel.

> He had nae been i' the court of France
>   A twelvemonth nor sae long,
> Till he fell in love with the king's daughter,
>   An' was thrown in prison strong.

The first two lines of this stanza are passed over. The second pair supply all the material required to complete *the two opening scenes*. The king tells his daughter to entertain the young man, and then he goes out. This exit, however, did not seem convincing to our playboys ; and so the second time the mime was given, they arranged for a " little wee page " to enter at this point with a scroll of some business which required his majesty's immediate attention. The king, therefore, begs the young knight to excuse him while he attends to this urgent matter, and goes off the stage with good reason. After he has gone, the young couple chat for a while about things in general. If the mime were being represented fully as a stage performance, " music and a song " would be introduced at this point. Eventually the knight declares his love for the lady. She is on the point of accepting him as her lover when the king returns. He is very angry indeed ; bids the princess out of his sight, and straightway sends Sir Bekie to prison. The details of this sending to prison are mimed in the following manner ; the king claps his hands, and a little page comes in and bows. A janitor is summoned, and the king directs him to take a big key, open a heavy door ; then manacle this fellow and thrust him in. "There shalt thou stay for many a month," he adds to the wretched knight.

If the mime is being performed in the classroom, most of the stage-fittings will have to be imaginary. The second scene then opens with the entrance of the janitor bringing in Young Bekie with his hands crossed, as though manacled. Boys are always vivid in representation, and it is probable that the player taking the part of Bekie will hobble in as though his ankles also were fettered. Our playboy, in point of fact, after the first performance, cautioned the king always to command this ankle-fettering in future. If the janitor does his part well, there need be no one among the onlookers who does not most clearly see the key unhitched from his leathern belt, the opening of the ponderous door, the thrusting in of the prisoner, and the parting appeals and jeers exchanged through the iron grill. Yet if you look blindly you will see nothing but two boys making signs at one another through the barred back of a Windsor chair !

Visitors who casually dropped in and looked on at two or three miming lessons out of a consecutive series of fifty must have wondered how sane persons could spend so much time in making apparently unintelligible gestures. But any language sounds barbarous to one who does not understand it.

It has taken many words to describe the representation of those two lines, consisting of scarce a score of syllables. And the acting of those two scenes might easily fill twenty minutes. Yet no one could accuse the players of having added any ornament or trimmings. It happens that ballad-narrative is most condensed.

The three verses which follow tell how the lady went to the prison-house, and heard the captive making his moan. The shrewd Bekie spies her through the bars, but affects to be unaware of her presence, and makes a piteous appeal for some lady who will borrow him for a footpage, or some widow who will take him as her son. Then he cries :

> " Or gin a virgin would borrow me,
>   I would wed her wi' a ring ;
> I'd gie her ha's, I'd gie her bowers,
>   The bonny tow'rs o' Linne."

Burd Isbel visits Young Bekie in Prison

[See p. 243]

King Alfred in the Camp of the Danes

[See p. 243

She then comes to the grill, and they talk together. She tries to force the door, and he tries to rid himself of the fetters ; but of course it is of no avail. The lady then goes away deep in thought. Presently she returns on tiptoe and tells her lover that she has found her father asleep, and is going to steal his keys.

> O barefoot, barefoot gaed she but,
>   An' barefoot came she ben ;
> It was no for want o' hose an' shoon,
>   Nor time to put them on ;
>
> But a' for fear that her father dear,
>   Had heard her making din :
> She's stown the keys o' the prison-house door,
>   An' latten the prisoner gang.

The theft of the keys should be shown in the mime, and this is easily contrived. The stage must represent two places at once. Then, either the king enters on one side and lies down to sleep while his daughter is at the prison on the other side of the stage, or she meets him as she is leaving the prison and, seeing the keys at his belt, wheedles the old man into taking an afternoon doze. The second plan is the more convincing, but the more difficult. It is the plan which our playboys devised ; for they aim always at the truest and most natural representation of their story, without thinking of difficulties beforehand. A playboy pursuing the easiest way would, of course, simply go off the stage to get the key and presently return with it in his hand. But this would be depriving the onlookers of a scene they would fain have witnessed, as well as throwing away the opportunity for some good acting by two of the players.

The next few stanzas of this ballad afford the richest miming stuff that any playboy could desire. Burd Isbel liberates her lover :

> O whan she saw him Young Bekie,
>   Her heart was wondrous sair !
> For the mice but an' the bold rottons *
>   Had eaten his yallow hair.

* This is simply a metrical way of saying, " the mice and the rats."

THE PLAY WAY

Any one reading this ballad will not, of course, pause to think over that stanza, but will just give one laugh and read on. But think of it *staged*. The lady comes nimbly to set free her splendid knight, and, on the opening of the great door, out comes a pathetic figure with his lovely golden hair all nibbled by the mice and rats which have been running about in the straw of his cell. This excellent picture of comedy will always stick in my memory as it was brought to life one evening after tea in my room, when two or three Littlemen, without costume or any apparatus but one Windsor chair, mimed the story they had read in school. The players performed in a little inner room which was lighted, while the rest of us sat in darkness. For half an hour there was no sound from the whole party, save for a periodical outburst of Shakespearean laughter when a point of comedy got home. It was only later on in the evening, when the players were fast asleep in their beds, that I realized that these were schoolboys, and that their evening's amusement showed them to possess a very firm grasp of what their teacher called miming, balladry, play-making, Shakespeare, discipline, and above all, activity in their own learning.

Although we had consciously been pursuing the Play Way for some years, it came as a new surprise to me that night that so much pleasure could be taken in the exercise of learning, and so much learning shown in the sheer exercise of pleasure.

Burd Isbel followed in every detail the next stanza of the ballad,

> She's gi'en him a shaver for his beard,
>   A comber till his hair,
> Five hunder pound in his pocket,
>   To spen' and nae to spair.

The shaver and the comber had been fetched by Burd Isbel from somewhere off the stage. The " five hunder pound " was represented by a bag of money stolen from the king at the same time as the key. All these things could easily have been brought in as concrete properties ; rulers would have served for shaver and comber, and a duster could have been tied up in a bundle for the bag of money. But the player in this instance preferred to mime *everything*, to have even his properties imaginary. And, of course, having brought these things into existence in our minds, he had to account for them all, carry them to the prison, and put them down while he unlocked the door. This he did with such vividness and precision that those of us who were giving our diligent attention could have said positively at any moment which of the imaginary properties the player was handling, whether the razor, the comb, the bag of money, or the big key. Burd Isbel could not bring the rest of her gifts to the prison, but she promised her lover a steed and a saddle and a leash of hounds. Then

> Atween this twa a vow was made,
>   'Twas made full solemnly,
> That or three years was come and gane,
>   Well married they should be.

Here the scene ends, and Sir Bekie will steal away to England as soon as he can. The playboy who was acting the lady's part put in a delightful little touch of character at this point. While they were making their farewell she alluded again to his nibbled hair, and said in much distress what a shame it was that he should be so disfigured. Then, suddenly, brightening again into her practical and sunny self, she added cheerily, " But in three years it will have plenty of time to grow again ! " And so they parted with merry laughter.

The story continues,

> He had nae been in's ain country
>   A twelvemonth till an end,
> Till he's forced to marry a duke's daughter,
>   Or then lose a' his land.

The playboys can easily make a scene of this stanza if some method is devised of indicating the possession of land. A tenure-sword might be agreed upon as the sign conventional to represent Bekie's title to his estates. Then Sir Bekie, on his return from France, can find the villainous duke in possession of this tenure-sword ; and the duke can force the knight to marry his daughter by threats of dispossession. Burd Isbel is made aware of this unhappy trend of events by a vision,

in which the benevolent household sprite, " Billy Blin," appears
to her.

> O it fell once upon a day
> Burd Isbel fell asleep,
> An' up it starts the Billy Blin,
> An' stood at her bed-feet.

This makes an excellent scene. The good little demon
tells the lady in detail what she is to do, how she is to dress
herself and two of her mother's maids, and how she is to get a
boat; and he himself promises to come at her call and be
the steerer to row them o'er the sea. So this sweet and brave
princess goes over to England to liberate her lover for the second
time. The rest of the story needs no detailed description here,
for all the necessary action will be found clearly given in the
lines. Thus:

> She's pitten her hand in her pocket
> Gi'n the porter guineas three.

And again, of the porter:

> O whan that he came up the stair
> He fell low down on his knee.

Though the ballad tells the whole story in thirty-six stanzas
only, the representation of it in mime will take an hour or two.
But even if it should take a week it is well worth all the time
passed upon it. Surely any teacher who could take such a
ballad as this, and make it the subject of " literature lessons "
in which word-study was made of more importance than the
tale, would be guilty of a crime not only against literature
but against life-lore itself. How much real learning is at once
too simple and too joyous to engage the attention of schoolmasters !

Among many other ballads which will make whole plays
in mime "The Lord of Learne" and "King Estmere"
must be specially mentioned.* "The Lord of Learne"

* All these] are available for school use in the collection of " Old
Ballads " edited by Frank Sidgwick, and published by the Cambridge
University Press.

runs into more than a hundred stanzas, but it can of course, like any other story, be subdivided. King Estmere has been ever an especial favourite with us. Estmere and his brother Adler, although they set about to find a queen, and although they have " dukes and lords and knights " at their command, are essentially boys. " The king his son of Spain," that foul paynim with the kempery-men at his back, who swore to pull down the halls and castles if he could not have the lady, makes the right lusty villain of the piece. Childe Estmere might well be proud to have such a man to his foe. King Adland, the timorous old father, is a character which any clever boy can make live. And his daughter, although she does not play so full a part in this story as Burd Isbel does in " Young Bekie," is nevertheless not the colourless ineffectual maiden such as one finds in some romances, but a young lady of wit and purpose. She snaps her fingers in the paynim's face, tells her trembling father that his castles and towers are strong, and decides very definitely that she will marry the man she wants to marry, and will have " none of your swaggerers."

The ballad of King Estmere can be easily mimed, because there is very little discussion in it, and plenty of expressive action. King Estmere and his brother Adler gallop to and fro upon their horses. The King of Spain blusters in with his meiny of kempers. Every one is eager to get things done. All affairs are urgent.

> They had not ridden scant a mile,
>   A mile forth of the town,
> But in did come the King of Spain
>   With kempes many a one ;
>
> But in did come the King of Spain
>   With many a bold barone,
> Tone day to marry King Adland's daughter,
>   Tother day to carry her home.
>
> She sent one after King Estmere
>   In all the speed might be,
> That he must either turn and fight,
>   Or go home and lose his lady.

The very ring of the lines warns you that it is impossible to *walk* through such a story ; far less *sit* through it. We seized two bamboo curtain-poles to serve as hobby-horses for King Estmere and Adler young, and on these they capered and cantered through the epic ! Horses of some kind *must* be found for the boys, for time after time they " renish them to ride of two good renisht steeds." And, on his return to the castle of Adland, Childe Estmere splendidly rides into the hall where the banquet is going on, and

> The froth that came from his bridle-bit
> Light in King Bremor's beard.

The play brings in many a thing which delights the hearts of boys. There is magic, or gramary, for purposes of disguise and safeguard :

> There grows an herb within this field
> And if it were but known ;
> His colour, which is white and red,
> It will make black and brown ;
>
> His colour, which is brown and black
> It will make red and white ;
> That sword is not in all England
> Upon his coat will bite.

There is music and song :

> And you shall be the best harper
> That ever took harp in hand,
> And I will be the best singer
> That ever sang in this land.

And there is a great fight to end it all :

> Up then rose the kempery-men
> And loud they gan to cry ;
> " Ah, traitors, ye have slain our king,
> And therefore ye shall die."
>
> King Estmere threw his harp aside,
> And swithe he drew his brand,
> And Estmere, he, and Adler young
> Right stiff in stour did stand.

MIMING AND THE BALLADS

If our schoolmasters knew their business as teachers of literature to boys, this ballad of King Estmere would be known by heart in all the schools of England. And then, if the teachers objected to any acting in the classroom, King Estmere would nevertheless be played, in nurseries and suburban gardens, and even in the courts and back alleys of the great cities all up and down the country.

The stories of most of the ballads include a love-affair of some kind, and teachers might expect on that ground to find the boys not in favour of ballads for acting purposes. Your sturdy English boy considers love-making a silly business. And if Peter thought he was expected to stand out before his fellows and go billing and cooing with his friend Jack, he might well say, " I'll be blowed first." He might, with even greater justice, offer to see some one else " blowed " ; for the master whose boys regard the acting of ballads in this light has himself a totally wrong way with boys, and has given them a totally wrong idea of ballads. The love element in all these old romances, so far as their stage representation is concerned, is not a kissing business at all ; it is an occasion for the utterance of fine poetry. It is not soft wooing, but brave courting. It is not the whispering of amorous sentimentalities, but outspoken gallantry, courtly vows and protestations. In a word, it is not cuddling, but chivalry.

Littlemen know nothing at all of one kind of love, the way of a man with a maid ; and they are impatient of all kissing. But in that kind of love which is chivalry, the knight's devotion to his lady's service, they can ride at ease among the truest romantic poets.

I am anxious to make this point perfectly clear because, although the true representation of parts in character may be a matter of no account to those who confess themselves mere book-teachers, it is a matter of great moment to play-masters, and those who feel for the *life* of the study in the minds of the boys. The play-methods must not run counter to any natural feelings of the boys. Many teachers will think that it must be against a boy's instinct to act the part of a girl.

Given the least opening, the least suspicion of " girlishness," a right-minded boy is only too ready to " see you blowed first," and to resent this proposed upset of his boyishness. For when a playboy acts well he puts *himself* into his part, lives in character. How then can he, a boy, live a girl's part ? * The teacher who goes in for play at all thoroughly must soon come upon this difficulty ; and the danger is that he will at.empt its solution by permitting all the female parts to be simply " walked through." This is to sacrifice in the representation that thoroughness which alone makes any art a thing of value. If we have the women's parts casually presented " then the play is marred ; it goes not forward, doth it " ?

The solution of this difficulty, as it seems to me, lies in a master's complete understanding of his boys—not boys in general, but his very boys—and a complete understanding also of the subject he is teaching. This may seem a heavy requirement in any teacher ; but it is, I must protest, the first essential of method in playmastery. Given this understanding a master will not offend either the player or the play. " The lady shall say her mind freely," and the blank verse shall not halt for't. The playmaster with any insight will realize that the boy, being an unselfconscious little fellow is not really unable or unwilling to take a woman's part. His objection is a very simple one. He is told to act " the girl," and he fancies, without thinking, that he will have to stand up before his fellows and behave in the silly simpering manner which he usually associates with love-making and girls, unless he has been properly brought up with them.†

* There must be no confusion of this matter with the question of Shakespeare's boy-players and their acting of women's parts. The Elizabethan playboy was doubtless coached and rehearsed and put through his paces in every imaginable way, in order that he might fitly present a play before an audience. After highly specialized training a boy could represent any woman's part. But the playboys in the classroom must interpret the play as they go along (with a minimum of coaching in the acting) and solely for their *own* benefit. This is a very important distinction.

† All that is said here refers solely to those plays in which boys take *all* the parts. It would be very interesting to know exactly what is possible when the female parts are played by little girls. I have no experience at all in co-education, and have refrained from making guesses. The love-affairs of the romances would of course have to be represented in the same chivalrous manner between boys and girls as

But, as has been said, there is no silliness about the girls in these romances, nothing mawkish about the ladies and the queens, and nothing sentimental in their love-affairs. What boy could find anything derogatory to his boyhood even in the childish character of Curly Locks when treated as we treated it in our mime ? What playboy would not gladly seize the opportunity to act Burd Isbel rather than to represent the minor majesty of the king, her father ? And which of your boys have you so mistaught that he will find the vigorous love-making of King Estmere unbefitting the nature of a thorough-going Littleman ?

> Then King Estmere pulled forth his harp
>   And played a pretty thing ;
> The lady upstart from the board
>   And would have gone from the king.
>
> He played again both loud and shrill,
>   And Adler he did sing—
> " O lady, this is thy own true love ;
>   No harper, but a king.
>
> " O lady this is thy own true love,
>   As plainly thou mayst see,
> And I'll rid thee of that foul paynim
>   Who parts thy love and thee."

That is the Estmere vein. It is true that the ballad says

> The lady looked, the lady blushed,
>   And blushed and looked again,
> While Adler he hath drawn his brand
>   And hath the Sowdan slain.

they are between boys alone. Girls would, presumably, be able to act girls' parts at least as well as the boys can. But the representation of boys' and men's parts by girls, whether in the amateur shows at girls' schools or on the professional stage, gives one little hope of their acting powers. Girls have no initiative.

It is not by any means certain that even Shakespeare's female characters are best acted by women. Viola and Rosalind, at all events, can only be properly done by boys. The modern practice of giving all Shakespeare's boys, princes, and pages to be played by women is of course indefensible. To have a well-shaped young woman mincing about the stage on high heels, with her legs clad in pink tights, may be good ballet or " revue," but it is most certainly not Shakespeare.

But we may be sure that the interest of all, including not least the lady, will be so centred in the slaughter of the Sowdan that no one will look critically to mark whether or not the playboy can conjure up a maidenly blush.

A little boy of eleven once entertained us for a whole hour at tea-time by making heroic love, in the Estmere vein, to a girl of twenty. Of course he was doing it for fun; and very good fun we all had of it. But the fine ideas he struck upon were a great thing to hear, and the fashioning of his knightly vows, cried straight out in a moment of play, were pure poetry. I believe the affair ended in my being slain as a false steward, or an ogre, or a rival lover, or something of the kind.

Another boy, aged ten, was once acting at school in " Sir Patrick Spens " as " the king's daughter o' Norroway." No books were in use at the moment, and the boys were composing their parts extempore in ballad measure. This, believe me, is none too easy. I can remember but one of this boy's stanzas in the character of a princess. But the second line alone is enough to show that he did not feel that he " would be blowed first " :

> O bring to me my robe of silk
> And a girdle of rubies red,
> Go, fetch me here a crown of gold
> And set it upon my head.

This type of love and ladyship, then, as seen in our examples from the romances of Curly Locks, Burd Isbel, King Estmere's queen and the king's daughter o' Norroway, is the kind of chivalrous love which I know Littleman can appreciate. Possibly these few brief instances of high romance, and of the poetry which Littleman uses as a medium even in nursery or classroom play, will make more clear what we meant by quoting at the end of the chapter on Shakespeare the words of Sir Walter Raleigh : " With the disappearance of the boy-players the poetic drama died in England, and it has had no second life." For, with the possible exception of the Irish plays of J. M. Synge, we know of nothing in the way of *poetic* drama to-day at all comparable with the old romantic plays as acted by boys.

258

MIMING AND THE BALLADS

This is not the place to open a discussion on the whole field of poetry. But in connexion with all that is said in this chapter, I should like to record my conviction that modern poetry can only be cured of its headache by a tonic draught of boys and balladry. The poems of adults to-day are vague and sickly, or harsh, flatulent things. Before we can write again with the fullness and glory of Spenser and Milton and Shakespeare we must learn again the secret of that English freshness in Chaucer; the secret of that vision and simplicity in Blake; the secret of that merry wit, and simple, touching pathos in the folk-songs and ballads. We must learn the secret of inspiration and of play. The secret of all this is with the boys of England. I have found it there.

In conclusion of this account of miming and the ballads a description shall be given of an entirely original play which lasted three-quarters of an hour, and yet had taken less than ten minutes to prepare.

Our band of carol-singers and musicians met one evening at the house, but we were prevented by the weather from going out on our rounds. The Littlemen were eager to stay at home instead, and spend the evening in miming. But by the time tea was done the weather had cleared, and the lady director of the singing was in favour of our going the rounds, the more especially since she had promised several friends in the neighbourhood that the troupe would pay them a visit that evening. But, being now set on miming, we outvoted the lady director of the singing and stayed at home. Then I suggested to the boys that they should take a ballad entirely new to them, and see what they could make of it as a play, without any preparatory discussion or rehearsal. The ballad taken was the following.* It is the composition of one of the playboys of the school; but it was written two years before this date, and was quite unknown to the carol-singers.

* The ballad will be found in Perse Playbooks, No. 2, p. 52, under the title of " The Two Brothers."

THE PLAY WAY

THE GOLDEN CUP

The king sits on his golden throne,
  With his two sons at his knee.
" The one that fetches the golden cup
  Shall reign king after me."

The two brothers at once set off
  To fetch the golden cup,
The younger one was faster much
  When he was in the stirrup.

At last he came to the castle grim,
  Wherein the cup did lie ;
And he had started back again
  Before the sun was high.

And when he came to a lonely wood
  His brother he espied
Running to him with all his speed,
  With his long sword at his side.

He's stabbed his brother through the heart,
  And he's ta'en the cup from his hand,
And hastened back to his good father,
  To reign o'er all the land.

It happened that in the house at this time was a schoolroom
hung with curtains as a temporary stage,* and in lockers near
at hand were stored the dresses which had been used a year
earlier in the production at the school of " Baldr's Death "
and " Freyr's Wooing." The carol-party went into the schoolroom, and I read this short ballad. Then the parts of the
king and his two sons and a " little wee page " were assigned
to four of the Littlemen, and one of the ladies of the party
undertook to try her hand as the lady of the castle " wherein
the cup did lie." We soon had the players dressed very simply
from our assortment of costumes ; giving merely a crown and
a robe to the king, a tunic, cloak, sword, and coronet to each
of the sons, a tunic and ruff to the page, and a robe to the lady.

Then, to save time, instead of leaving the plot-construction
for the boys to discuss, as would have been done in school,

* This little stage only existed for one term while I was testing
various effects of design and colour before fitting up the new *Mummery*
at the school. It was not available for class lessons.

260

MIMING AND THE BALLADS

I gave a rapid outline of the story as it might be adapted for the purpose of the play. The third stanza obviously requires amplification. I therefore suggested that the golden cup should be in the keeping of a lady. She lived in a castle and was a kind of magician. She had been instructed by her father before his death carefully to guard the cup, and only to yield it to that man whom she truly loved. The idea, of course, was an adaptation of Portia's caskets in " The Merchant of Venice." The lady was to fall in love with the younger son upon his arrival, and, after a scene which the players were left to invent when the time came, she was to give him the cup, and he was to take her for his queen when he had inherited his father's kingdom. I suggested, further, that (instead of having the scene in the wood) the elder son should arrive just as the younger son was leaving his lady, and should spring from behind the curtain, stab his brother and make off with the golden cup. The younger son could either be quite dead or, better, simply wounded. In either case he would be restored by the magics of the lady ; and together they would return to the king's castle and expose the deceit of the elder brother, who by this time would be celebrating his achievement in a great banquet before the king and would, at the moment of their entrance, be on the point of drinking off a bumper of wine from the golden cup itself.

The whole scheme of the plot was put before the players, and a few recommendations made in passing, in as brief a space of time as it has taken the reader to read this account of the plan. Then the fiddlers and the 'cellist, and the remaining Littlemen and the rest of us sat down in the dark at the other end of the room, and the mime began.

The first scene of the king and his two sons proceeded straightforwardly. As soon as the quest of the golden cup had been stated by the king the younger soon took his leave. But the elder one stayed with his father and boasted of his better wit. The curtain was then closed, and the younger son at once cantered in before it, astride of a bamboo pole for his hobby-horse. He told us that he was now in quest of the golden cup, but was at a loss which way to take. He feared his brother might be first to find the cup. Presently

261

he spied a castle in the distance, and spurred his horse in that direction. The third scene introduced us to the lady-magician, and showed her brewing spells to attract errant knights. The lady should have referred to the golden cup and the conditions attaching to her possession of it.* But the lady-player had never mimed in her life before, and was indeed much to be complimented on filling a rôle at all, among such a proficient company of Littlemen. When the curtain closed again the elder brother galloped in on his piebald bamboo steed, and expressed an easy assurance of his chances of outwitting his silly little brother.

The elder son wore about his head a brass circlet fitted in the front with three jewels, and the younger wore a similar circlet, but with one jewel only. Thus the two princes were easily able to refer to one another throughout the play by making the signs for " coronet of three stars " or "coronet of one star." No latent symbolism was intended in these signs. They simply arose from the fact that we found two such brass circlets in the store of costumes, and used them. The fifth scene was played on the inner stage, and again showed us the lady-magician in her castle chamber, with the golden cup on a pedestal close at hand. Soon the prince of the single star arrived. He dismounted in a corner outside the curtain.

This detail is very interesting. The boy had it in mind to make his arrival at the castle the occasion of the traditional comic scene with the porter.† But the only thing he could do, on finding the curtain already opened, was to stand in the corner just outside the stage, in sight of the audience, but not in view of the lady and her page. Apparently the others had not expected this interpolation. In any case there was no porter available, and so the " little wee page " had to come forward and go through the business of inquiring who was there, and what he wanted. Having said this, the poor little page was at a loss how to proceed. For the whole play was unrehearsed, and his own part in any case but a small one. The

* Cf. " The Merchant of Venice," Act I, Scene 2 : the third speech of Portia and the third speech of Nerissa.

† As in " Macbeth," Act II, " King Estmere," " Young Bekie," " The Harrowing of Hell," and many another place in early literature.

particular scene he was now called upon to enact had suddenly
been sprung upon him by the zeal of a fellow who appeared
out of nowhere on a bamboo horse, and insisted on being a
prince at a castle gate, and nothing but a prince at a castle
gate. The boy who was playing the little wee page was not
of any great note as an actor, and his attitude throughout
this scene (no word, of course, was spoken on either side) was
a comic blend of the ineffectual desire to do something and a
constant surreptitious miming to the other boy of, " What
do you want me to do ? " The Prince of the Lone Star, on the
other hand, was an actor of great genius, the perfect Littleman
player ; and he took full advantage of the puzzle in which he
had involved the other boy. The bewilderment of the porter-
page exactly suited his purpose, and he treated him just as the
gallants treat the witless clowns in the old comedies. And
the more the porter-page endeavoured to carry off the situation
by nodding and smiling, and the general " Quite so " tomfoolery
which comedians at a loss always use as a gag, the more definitely did the prince indicate his lordly and contemptuous
baiting of the clown for the entertainment of the spectators.
The perfect player had the whole company of us in his hands.
We laughed heartily. The only mistake was due to the lack
of preparation in management, for this should have been
arranged as a scene on the front stage. As it was, the whole
business was conducted in a half-light, while the unfortunate
lady in her chamber beyond was left all the time with nothing
to do. Eventually the Prince of the Lone Star suffered the
page to conduct him into the presence of the lady. Here
again he took the whole scene into his own hands. Observing,
(or, rather, making us believe that he observed) the apparatus
of alchemy on every side, he affected to dread magic in all
that occurred. When the lady offered him a horn of wine
he smilingly accepted it, but secretly expressed a fear of being
poisoned (Magics !—I drink—I dead—Not I !) and surreptitiously
poured the wine away. While the lady made herself busy
about some other matter in order to give him an opening,
the little prince examined the drinking-horn, and kept the
onlookers in a roar of laughter by his descriptions of the strange
devils and horned demons which he found graven upon the

bands of metal. " Magics, magics everywhere," mimed the little Prince of the Lone Star.

From time to time I explained a gesture for the benefit of the audience, most of whom had never seen a mime before. But except in a few cases, where our signs conventional appeared, the spectators assured me they were able to follow it all quite easily without interpretation. And why not ? For I, the interpreter, had myself never seen these particular gesture-expressions in use before. However strange all this may seem, however remotely connected with what is ordinarily regarded as educational method, I feel it to be important that the incidents of this out-of-school play should be described as they actually happened. Here was a room divided in two by a curtain now drawn open. On one side, in the dark, sat a group of men, women, and boys, and on the lighted side stood this boy of twelve in a green cloak and with a brass circlet on his head. In his hand was an undecorated drinking-horn, and without using any words the boy, by his skill in the art of expressive gesture, was keeping the whole company of onlookers thoroughly interested and highly amused by his fearful discovery of totally imaginary demons pictured upon the drinking-horn. The more we laughed the more ready was the little prince to discover further shapes of sorcery. His crowning touch was the finding of a little grinning gargoyle at the very tip of the horn at the moment of the lady's re-entrance. At once he hushed his apprehensive soliloquy and became a model of courtesy, though wary still.

The inexperience of the lady-player as a mimist and the backwardness of the boy-player because he did not quite know how to set about making love to her, rendered the rest of this scene rather weak as a stage in the story. In fact, I had to break silence at this point to give a spoken direction. But if the two had rehearsed together a few times, this scene would soon have become the best in the play, for the lady and the Littleman would not have been long in coming to intimate terms with one another.

The rest of the mime requires no particular description. The elder brother, Prince of the Three Stars, after some peeping and skirmishing behind the curtains, made a dash into the chamber, smote his younger brother, seized the cup from his hands, and fled. The scene of the wonderful cure, wherein the lady, assisted by the page, brewed magic charms in a smoking cauldron, was played in a dim light and was quite effective. But, as there was little speech-gesture in it, this scene had no especial virtue as part of a mime. I told the players afterwards that a cinema could have done as much. For the rest, as time was now growing short, the players briefly followed the directions I had given at the start. The Prince of the Three Stars was exposed before the king, his father, just as he was about to drink off a bumper of wine from the golden cup. He was ignominiously banished; and the Prince of the Lone Star and his magic lady were received as the rightful heirs to the kingdom. May they live happily ever after.

The mime of the Golden Cup lasted fully three-quarters of an hour, with none of those London intervals between the scenes. Thus did the Littlemen spend the evening, after we had persuaded the lady director of the singing that it was too wet to go out on a round of carols. It was not by any means that we did not love to go trooping round the town and singing folk-carols by the light of swinging lanterns. But one has moods.

In connexion with performances such as the one just described, the boys might be encouraged to make short ballads for miming. There are, unfortunately, no examples of the boys' work in this; but the following verses which I made to fill a chap-book will perhaps afford some hints. There is, however, no plot in this. It is rather an exercise in simple stage design than a story.

KING ROLDO AND HIS LITTLE PAGE

Mister came forth in a purple gown
    Before the green curtain,
He bowed and told us some of his play,
    Then he went in again.

There came two little beadles
    And drew the curtain back;
The stage was grey with purple hangings,
    And the walls dead black.

THE PLAY WAY

The king came out in a crimson cloak
  With a crown upon his head ;
He called to him his little wee page
  To hearken what he said.

The page he did him in a purple tunic,
  Bordered it was of gold ;
Courteous he bowed and seemed right quick
  To do as the king him told.

The king he bade bring a taper
  And a bowl of wine to drink ;
And soon he called for a parchment
  And a pen and a horn of ink.

And he wrote a proclamation
  To the folk of his meadow-land ;
And ever the page in his gold and purple
  Stood fair at his right hand.

The king he sipped of the bowl and thought,
  And anon he wrote a line,
Till the whole was writ and he put his seal
  And finished the bowl of wine.

And the king he read it over,
  And nodded upon the scroll ;
And the page blew out the taper
  And took up the empty bowl.

And the king stood up in his crimson,
  And went forth out of the hall ;
And the little page followed him after
  So the place was empty all,

CHAPTER IX

PLAYMAKING

Play out the Play.—FALSTAFF

THE chapters on the Acting of Shakespeare and on Miming the traditional ballads have sufficiently shown how young boys can be taught to appreciate literature in dramatic form. In connexion with those studies certain elements of play construction were mentioned, such as the alternation of scenes, the excellent craftsmanship of suiting the word to the action, and the necessity of making the plot self-explanatory without adventitious aids. We are now to consider how the boys may put into practice what they have learnt, in the making of original plays.

But in this chapter we must also consider the necessity of setting a high standard of literary workmanship. When the boys are acting Shakespeare all the poetry is waiting for them ; they have only to appreciate its worth and give due expression to it. But in playmaking the plot and the poetry and the acting have all to be fashioned by the boys themselves. It is therefore necessary for the master to set before them the very best material and models, and to keep their work up to a high standard of literary taste.

Now as touching originality, it is, I think, a mistake to encourage boys to invent the story and characters for themselves. They will be too apt to lay the scene in the cellar of a London bank, or in a Wild West cañon, or in the boarding-house of a public school ; and to choose for their protagonist a detective or a bushranger, or one of those caricatures of boyhood who strut and fret their hour in magazines written for schoolboys, and then are heard no more. This side of the boys' interests should not by any means be neglected in school-work. But

267

we have always found place for the crude expression of this youthful taste in *preliminary exercises*, and in " asides " from the main business. In the oral exercises, for instance, with which our study of prose composition began—soliloquy, description, narrative, and dialogue—the boys were not only permitted but encouraged to choose subjects which had an immediate interest for them. There were at first no restrictions. The main purpose was that the boys should exercise themselves in " oral composition " of some kind, until they should become ready speakers. Early practice was not hampered by an exacting literary taste ; nor was self-expression at first conditioned by the quest of " art forms." But after a time the boys came to feel the inadequacy and superficiality of their exercises based upon the commonplace. They were then easily persuaded to use craft in selection and condensation. They began with some feeling to say things with an artistic intention, and to *express* where before they had been content to *describe*. The soliloquy of a man in a dentist's chair, or the description of a crowded railway station, were all very well as first exercises ; but these preliminaries were succeeded by prose studies which had the merit of style.*

Similarly, in our miming experiments, after a few introductory lessons under the master's direction the boys were allowed to practise in exercises of their own devising for a week or two. The feeble mimes of the Shoeing Forge and the Church Service have been mentioned, but there were many other boyish ventures of a similarly poor standard. But by following this natural course of gradual training we were able after a while to mime a whole ballad story as a play.

The same course should be followed in playmaking. Boys should not be plunged at once into the deeps of an expressive art without some preliminary paddling on the margin. A boy's desire to try his hand at some new thing without tiresome direction (vividly, if crudely, expressed in the words " Let's have a go ! ") may be allowed free play before sober and studious business is put under way. Football, a game played in obedience to strict rule, never begins without a free and easy kicking

---

* For examples, and an account of a full course of lessons in prose composition by the play-method, see Perse Playbooks, No. 4.

of the ball about the field. Cricket, a game of skill and precision, generally has a prelude of bat-swinging and the exchange of catches. And, if you have ever learnt to skate, I am sure you were not content for long to dodder about hand-in-hand with your instructor. " Let's have a go ! " is the right spirit in which to undertake any enterprise of play.* It is far more healthy for the beginner that he learn his earliest adjustments of balance empirically at the risk of (and better still at the cost of) a few real sprawls upon the hard ice, than that he

* I have noticed a very interesting example of this boyish desire to make free play with a new instrument, in connexion with languages taught on the Direct Method. The seniors who have attained a fair mastery in French or Latin or Greek will speak in these languages only of set intention, and to one who understands them. But the Littlemen, when they first begin to learn Latin, love to come out with the odd words and phrases they have learnt, whenever they are excited, in the playground or at tea parties. But these boys do not confine their exuberant exercise to words and phrases which they have learnt thoroughly and can repeat correctly. They will venture random utterance in long sentences composed of the most ungrammatical jargon, which sometimes resembles Latin, sometimes English ; and they will often tack Latin endings on to English words when their Latin vocabulary fails them. This gibberish is painful to hear, and, for no better reason, I have always discouraged it.

    The existence of this jargon has probably no real significance for a language teacher. Inventiveness will hinder and not help language study. He may rejoice that the new language is such a live one for the boys that they struggle to speak it even before their knowledge is sufficient ; but his clear duty is to go straight ahead with his teaching until they can speak correctly. But in connexion with playmaking and other forms of self-expression in which *inventiveness is required*, this stage of the boys' interest is of great significance. The parallel to this shockingly ungrammatical jargon is, in prose composition, a piece of lurid description ; in speech-making it is a turgid oration ; in miming it is wild inarticulate gesticulation ; in playmaking it is a disordered and chaotic performance, full of sound and fury, but signifying nothing in any artistic sense. The language teacher must directly discountenance, or at least ignore, these crude initial efforts and experimentations, because his subject requires precision, accuracy, learning. The play-master, on the other hand, may encourage these crude manifestations of delight in a new instrument, and should even take them into his account and build upon them ; for his concern is inventiveness, conceit, and flights of fancy. This is, I submit, a matter which concerns all teachers of boys.

sit secure and idle, and admire the evolutions of his skilled instructor.

After a series of preliminary exercises, a few free kicks, a few nasty sprawls, the pupil returns to his master—ready now for the instruction to begin. But not, I hope, at all apologetic for having adventured on his own account, tried his hand at the new instrument—had, in fact, his " go." For it would be a grave mistake for a teacher (in the arts at all events) to fancy that the pupil's venture had only served to convince him of the supreme necessity of reliance upon his instructor. The pupil has certainly found the need of a teacher, but he has also discovered many another thing of value. He has discovered not only difficulties but *potentialities*, not only the need of instruction but a consuming desire for it.

The boyish craving for exciting adventure, undirected, is content with cheap sensational stories such as those connected with crude horrors and mysteries and what is called " raw " crime. But, discreetly guided, it finds equal stimulus, and eventually a fuller enjoyment, in good literature. But in introducing the boys to those things which are of highest worth, the master must still cater for their interests. Herein lies the virtue of the master's method and selection. He must see that hunger is not dulled, but rendered obedient to taste ; zeal to judgment.

In the present disordered and ill-managed state of education a boy may satisfy his crude desire for novelty and sensation in the reading of books which have no spark of literary value, and in the shows at the cinema which are equally destitute of all dramatic or artistic taste. He may seek fun and the satisfaction of his sense of humour in the unspeakable halfpenny comics, or in sheer brainless tomfoolery with his fellows. School gives but little guidance to his amusements. During lesson-time his serious-minded teachers stolidly read with him some of the masterpieces of classical literature (which at last is recognized as including something outside the sacred pale of Greek and Latin). They pass all too cursorily over what is easy to understand ; all that might, without any loss to the dignity of learning, serve for the ready satisfaction of the play-instinct ; but they insist upon a careful and often prolonged

Gerda and Skirnir

[See p. 332

" Thus they renisht them to ride
Of two good renisht steeds "

[See p. 254

[See p. 254

study of all passages which present any natural difficulty, or which can, by any device of pedantry, be made to yield artificial difficulties.* All the fun is out of school, unrecognized and uncontrolled. All the study is in school, an overearnest matter, unrelieved and unsympathetic.

Owing to this blindness of our educators the gap is ever widening between work and play, and each loses more and more of what the other held of value to it. Amusements, on the one hand, become daily less and less intelligent, and on the other, so far as school is concerned, the pleasure of duty is much diminished.

The Play Way, while giving scope to the natural interests of the boys, insists upon a good standard of literature in their playmaking. And, after the preliminary exercises have run their course, the deeds of detectives and bushrangers, and the goings-on of bullies and fags will not pass muster as material for drama. It would take the length of this whole chapter to give in full the critical reasons why such persons and their settings are not conducive to good playmaking—but we have reason good enough. Here it will be sufficient to point out that the incidents of everyday life, before they can become fit stuff for drama, have to undergo a process of refinement or sifting, and it is too much to expect this work of young boys. And so long as the world is full of tales already in fair shape as material for playmaking it is quite unnecessary for boys to sift their daily experience for the subject-matter of plays.

To make a drama out of a tale of adventure in modern times, or the school-life of everyday, is an exercise in realism ; and a conscious pursuit of realism is inadvisable for boys : (i) Because it is frankly beyond their powers, since realism implies a representation of things as they are, and boys have not experience enough to go beyond impressions and appearances ; (ii) because it would be outside the scope of our educational purpose, since true realism implies a certain sacrifice of conventions and the avoidance of *types* of character and situation, while our purpose as teachers is to ensure that

* Compare, for instance, our treatment of a play of Shakespeare with that implied by any examination paper ever set.

by the exercise of playmaking the boys shall become familiar with these very artistic conventions, and with the dramatic situations and characters which have become typical from their frequent occurrence in the literature we are taking as our model ; and (iii) the pursuit of realism by boys is inadvisable because it implies the abandonment of that tower of their artistic strength, the ready comprehension of a romantic theme, and a fitly imaginative treatment of it.

The plays of boys should be romances, and the style should be poetic.*

For these reasons, then, the boys (when an important play is afoot) should not be encouraged to take for their material any themes which are not essentially romantic. It remains for them, then, either to invent a brand-new romantic story or to borrow one. But the experiment of inventing your plot is so difficult and attended with so much risk of disaster that it is wiser to follow the example of Chaucer, Spenser, Shakespeare, Milton, and all our other great poets, and found your story upon the firm rock of some traditional tale. The man is to be pitied who hopes to put forth new fruits without having his roots firm set in the soil from which all other fruits have sprung.

The boys, having borrowed their story, may take what they have need of, and set aside the rest. They may add, divide, and multiply. But they must start by borrowing. The creative skill of the stealers and their choice in theft are the test of their Promethean virtue.

In taking an existing tale as the story of their play the boys will find that they have in hand a core of substance. Persons and events exist already ; characterization and plot, those twin deities of the drama, have been wed together in the tale for perhaps five hundred, perhaps two thousand years ; and in making their play, with what additions and modifications soever, the boys are but making one more version of a tale that has outlived, or rather lived through, a thousand versions.

---

* The word " romance ' is used here in the sense of an imaginative or fanciful story, as opposed to the faithful representation of real experience. To say that the style must be poetic does not mean that the parts must always be written in verse.

PLAYMAKING

The tale has been bandied about until nothing but the essentials (and perhaps a few of the latest accretions) remain. On the other hand, a *new* plot, conceived yesterday, and thrown down to-day into the ring to be wrought upon by a group of urgent playmakers, each anxious to have his say, each eager to insist upon this modification or that, will be knocked to pieces in an hour or two. It has no essential being, no core.

The sources of tales fit for playmaking are inexhaustible, for we have all the treasury of mythology and all the fairy tales and folk legends to draw upon. The teacher's taste, knowledge, and experience are naturally of great weight in the selection ; and a group of boys under one master will show a preference for a certain type of story which the pupils of another master will find quite foreign to their taste. A man gifted with an appreciation of Hindu mythology could easily engage the interest of his boys in the exploits of Krishna and tales from the Mahabharata. The Egyptian Book of the Dead, also, would make a great morality play. But, since the making of a play demands the close and careful work of the boys for a considerable length of time, it is wiser to associate the subject with some of their regular school studies, in Greek, Latin, French, or English literature, and in history.

A play should be in hand for at least a term, and it will do nothing but good to keep it building throughout the school year. The historical period in which the play is set is of importance in a hundred ways. It may either be determined by the courses of history and literature going on at the time ; or, if it is done on a large enough scale, and time can be found for good reading in many books, the playmaking circle might include in itself the study of the history and literature of the period. The reader can expand this suggestion for himself. Consider a playmaking circle of history and literature, to last a year's course, centring in King Alfred and bringing in a reading of Old English literature in poetry, and of history in the Chronicles. No English boy should spend ten years of learning in an English school without at least making the acquaintance of the following : Widsith, Deor's Lament, Cædmon, The Phœnix, The Charms, The Seafarer, The Battle of Brunaburh, The Battle of Maldon, Cynewulf and Cyneheard, The Voyage of Ohthere, and, above all, Beowulf.* Another playmaking circle for a year's course might centre in John of Gaunt or in Wat Tyler; and, while the history lessons dealt with the Peasant's Revolt, the literature lessons would include selections from Piers the Plowman and from Chaucer, and the whole of Shakespeare's " Richard II." Cromwell is the centre of another playmaking circle, but it would take a whole chapter of this book even to indicate the scope and design of such a great argument.

Then again the boys might be given each a book of North's " Plutarch " as material, and allowed to choose their communal path therein for a year of weekly lessons. There is a fine nobility about that book; life, letters, and learning on every page of it.

All teachers of history intend to, and some actually do, read the English literature of the period under study. And the same is true of literature teachers in relation to history. Lack of time is always the difficulty. We *must* have more time for teaching English history and English literature, unless this nation intends to remain satisfied, as it is at present, that its sons should have a mere smattering of education; knowing little more than the names of the greatest men of our people, and not even the names of some of the greatest books in our literature. Playmaking is a helpful device by which the study of history and of literature can be brought together and understood in a live relation.

The stories of the Greek gods and heroes are beyond compare for beauty of conception and grace of treatment, but I cannot think of them as material for playmaking in the schools of to-day. But other teachers, especially those with a thorough knowledge of Greek literature, and some sympathetic understanding of Greek life and art, might not think the experiment too rash, provided that the boys and the master earnestly set themselves to make their play as Greek in character as possible. But the undertaking involves many grave difficulties. At the outset you are faced

---

* At present teachers must do the best they can with translations. But it is not too much to hope that Old English will some day be taught in schools, at all events to specialists in upper forms.

274

with a dilemma : Will you attempt to cast your play in the conventional classic form of the Greek drama, or will you attempt to create some less rigid and exacting form which shall be equally appropriate as a representation of the theme ? For my part I would not dare venture either alternative. The only way out is to present certain elements of the Greek mythology in pastoral form. But the pastoral is not a form suitable for stage representation ; and the pastoral is not the kind of play we are now considering. Another difficulty is the music. But the greatest difficulty of all is the carriage and bearing of the players themselves. Adequately to present before the eyes of men a living show of some story which embodies a Greek conception of beauty requires in the performers some approximation to the Hellenic ideal of physical perfection. And what scope or encouragement is there for the most sensible and energetic of playmasters, in a modern public school, to train his boys in that true gymnastic which makes for grace as well as strength of limb, and for rhythm as well as speed of movement?

It is true that the heroes of the Bible stories and the gods of the Norse mythology also demand a nobility of bearing in a stage representation, but these are figures of strength and grandeur rather than of idyllic grace, and we have not their sculptured beauty in marble to shame us by a comparison with our puny modern standard of address and carriage. A teacher who has any real sense of what art means in connexion with his work, before undertaking the production, in a modern school, of a *show* with anything of the Greek about it, will, at the very least, go and study the Panathenaic procession in the British Museum. Having looked upon the figures of Apollo and of Eros, having marked (as did the unlearned John Keats) the mysterious priest leading that heifer lowing at the skies ; having but once seen the very folds of the drapery as worn by the maidens, or the mien and bearing of the youths who renish them to ride, he will go home a wiser and a very much sadder man and abandon his ambitious enterprise.

There *sits* the youth of England at its education ; row upon row of magnificent boys, imprisoned in the stocks, and clad in ridiculous trousers and knickerbockers. Look at the lads in their Eton collars and their jackets and waistcoats

THE PLAY WAY

William Morris complained of having to wear two coats; one with a back and no front, and another with a front and no back. These are insane garments, which a due care for health and free movement would not allow, and which the faintest glimmer of a sense of beauty in clothes could not tolerate for a moment. Look also, I beg you, at the feet of the Littlemen; those feet which you as a teacher have so often had to call to order. The boots alone of a group of modern schoolboys are enough to render impossible the school production of any play which claims kinship with the Greek. But, as Sir Toby says in "Twelfth Night," "These clothes are good enough to drink in, and so be these boots too"; and no doubt knickerbocker suits and Eton trousers and ploughboy boots are a good enough apparel in which to walk about stone passages and gravel yards, or to sit at a desk and imbibe the grammar of ancient tongues.

The Bible has always been one of the great sources of inspiration in English literature; and many of the stories in the Old Testament make excellent material for playmaking. In the style of the Bible narrative the boys would have before them the very purest and most beautiful of English prose. But the problem of style in the boys' work shall be discussed later. Let us look first at some available stories.

The story of Jacob and Esau could be wrought into drama, but it would probably require more condensing than inexperienced hands could compass. The life-story of Joseph is epic rather than dramatic. David's history is also of an epic character; but if certain episodes, and especially those in relation with Saul, be chosen out and presented consecutively, there is as good matter for an heroic play here as can be found anywhere. But it would be far better, I think, to make Saul the central figure, and the play a tragedy. The tale of Samson, again, after some adaptation, would provide a good story for the boys to dramatize. The story of Rahab and the Spies is another suitable one. But all stories require adaptation to fit them for stage presentation. Let us first examine the story of Rahab and the Spies, because it is the shortest of these, and see how it can be turned into a play.

Joshua sends out two spies to view the land of Jericho;

but they are hardly come to their lodging in the house of Rahab before the King of Jericho sends to look for them. Rahab tells the messengers that the men went out about the time of shutting of the gate, when it was dark; but she had brought them up to the roof of her house and hid them with the stalks of flax. The messengers go out in pursuit as far as the fords of Jordan; the town gate is shut after them, and the woman goes to talk with the men on the roof. Her account of the terror which had fallen upon the men of Jericho because of the Israelites makes a wonderful speech as it stands. In return for her kindness the spies promise to deal kindly and truly with her, if she will not utter their business, and to save the lives of all in her father's house. They give her the true token she asks. She binds the scarlet line in the window,* lets them down over the town wall by a cord, and bids them get to the mountain to avoid their pursuers. The spies go into hiding, and eventually return to Joshua.

That is the substance of the first act. The boys may now discuss how the incidents shall be staged,† and into how many scenes the act shall be divided. Two scenes only are essential. The first will be on the front, or outer stage (i.e. traverse closed), the second on the back, or whole stage (i.e. traverse open). Here is a stage version such as I would propose for myself, or the boys working with me.

Scene 1. (*Outer.*) The two spies come in, and make clear where they are, who they are, and what they have to do.‡

* A touch of the concrete which adds considerably to the life of the story.

† For the plots sketched in this chapter I have had in mind the Elizabethan playhouse stage, because that is the plan which in my opinion is the best fitted for plays of this character. There is no need for the reader to call into his mind an exact model of the Globe Theatre. All this chapter requires is a picture in the reader's mind of a very large platform in front with doors on either side, but no front curtain. At the back is a smaller inner stage, shut off by a traverse consisting of two curtains which can be drawn together or apart from the side.

‡ According to the Bible story the spies learn only of the faint-heartedness of the men of Jericho, and that is all they report to Joshua. If they have " come to search out all the country," as the King believes, they must nevertheless have been satisfied with Rahab's account of the state of terror which the Israelites had inspired. " Our hearts did melt,

They *must* give the onlookers to understand that a certain
captain, by name Joshua, has sent them as spies of Israel to
this walled city, by name Jericho. The exposition of these
matters will of course need some wrapping up. Exposition
must not be given as a bald announcement. But all extraneous
matter must be rigidly excluded here because the essentials,
are quite enough to handle in the opening passage, and the
audience desires at this point nothing but a clear understanding
of what is afoot. As soon as we are all quite sure who these
two persons are, and what they are about, they may discover
their lodging, but not before. At their summons Rahab comes
out between the curtains of the traverse. They arrange to
lodge in her house, and all go in together. At once the
messengers sent from the King come in (still on the front stage),
and after having made clear in their talk who they are, whence
they came, and what they are about, they call for the warden
of the gates. (Surely we have met this man before. All good
porters when they die go into drama.) The King's messengers
complain that, although it is dark, the gates are not yet shut.
The porter has of course been asleep ; or, better still, he has
been having a bit of a sup with an old friend who has come
from the other side of Jordan with a great tale of what those
men of Israel did to Sihon and Og, the two kings of the Amorites.
The King's messengers* have no concern with all this. Their
business is to bully the porter for his not having shut the gates,
for his not having observed the particular men they are in
quest of, and for his general stupidity. But for all his apparent
stupidity in the play this porter fellow, in repeating again and
again the story of his friend from the other side of Jordan, may
contrive to tell the audience all they need know about the men
of Jericho and their fear of the Israelites. The audience will
find this clown very entertaining, and the playwright will find
him all but indispensable ; but the critics of your play will be

---

neither did there remain any more courage in any man, because of you."
They would add little to their knowledge during their three days spent
subsequently in the mountain.

 * For models of King's messengers you have Rosencrantz and
Guildenstern, and also Osric, in " Hamlet," Le Beau in " As You Like
It," and several others.

" inclined to feel that the episode of the porter and his tedious reiterations constitute an unwarrantable intrusion and interfere with the continuity of the "—etc. etc.

But there is yet more service to be had of this porter. The story tells that the King actually sent to Rahab's house for the spies. It will add to the interest, and save the introduction of another character, if we let the porter eventually admit that he did see two such men come into the city, and that they went into the house of Rahab, hard by here upon the wall. He would not state this important fact earlier because he was anxious to tell the tale (and a far more important tale it is for the audience) of what the Israelites did to Sihon and Og, the two kings of the Amorites. The King's messengers then call at the house. Rahab comes out and, in reply to the officious inquiries of the messengers, says that two men had been in her house, but she does not know whence they came nor whither they went ; but they cannot have gone far, for they only went out at dusk. She sends the messengers in pursuit, away to the fords of Jordan. The porter has a final chat with Rahab about what the Israelites did to Sihon and Og, the two kings of the Amorites, and then he shuts the gate. The town gate must of course be off stage, for the central opening in the traverse curtain represents the door of Rahab's house. Rahab goes in, and the porter goes off at the side. He makes a grinding and a clanking noise with bolts and chains. This ends the first scene.

Before sketching the plan of Scene 2, I will show the technical significance of this new character, the porter, who does not appear in the Bible narrative. The playboys must be taught : (i) That the porter was originally introduced because some one had to direct the King's messengers, and he was the most likely person to have seen the spies come in. (ii) That he is suggested by the mention of the town gates in the story. To ignore the town gates would be an undoubted loss to the play. The creation of a porter arising out of a simple mention of gates will show the boys how to dramatize intelligently, and how to look always to the story for what they require. (iii) That, being in, he can be used to let the audience know what Jericho feels about Israel. This is most important, since it is the sole information which the spies obtain. Certainly Rahab later on tells them clearly of the terror and faintness which possess the men of Jericho, but as her speech with them is chiefly concerned with an appeal for the safety of her own family, it is well that the general feeling of Jericho should have been made clear beforehand. The porter does this for the audience in his tale of what the Israelites did to Sihon and Og, the two kings of the Amorites. We have heard what Israel feels about Jericho from the opening words of the spies. (iv) That in any case there must be some delay between the going in of the spies and the calling of the Kings' messengers at the house of Rahab. The action must not rush on from point to point. There must be no crowding. (v) That necessary delays of this kind in the action must not be filled with padding, but used in the early stages of the play for explaining what needs to be explained, and in the later stages of the play for developing what needs to be developed. (vi) Finally, the boys can be shown how it is that a character comes to life. This porter is an excellent illustration, for he had no existence at all in the Bible story. The needs of playmaking occasioned his creation. He was originally introduced as a mere technical necessity, but has somehow got him a being of his own. We seem to know him already as a living man. Of all the six persons introduced in this act he is so far the most real.

Scene 2. (*Inner.*) There is no break at all between the scenes. The traverse is drawn apart, and the action goes straight on. Rahab is now seen talking to the two spies on the inner stage, which is laid with stalks of flax and represents the roof of her house. There must be some kind of window at the back for the men to be let down by. All the talk between the woman and the spies is given in the Bible story, and cannot be bettered. When persons in a play make a compact, or give directions to one another, it is well for the matters at issue to be said clearly more than once, for the sake of the audience. The repetition will be found ready to your hand in this Bible story. Part of the conference is held upon the roof, and then the men are let down.* Reassurances are exchanged after

---

* Although they had been hidden on the roof they escaped through a window. This was probably the window of a room to which they descended

the men are out of sight. Rahab's leaning out of the window to speak with them in a loud whisper will admirably suggest the height of the town wall upon which her house is built, the darkness of the scene, and the secrecy of the whole business. After they go away the woman binds the scarlet line in the window. She does this at once, and will not put it off until the morrow. Perhaps the spies will not go to the mountain after all, but return straightway to their captain, and the host of Israel may be before the walls of Jericho by dawn. This is improbable in fact, but not in drama. At all events, the story tells that Rahab bound the scarlet line in the window ; and no playwright with any eye for effect would depart from his original in this particular. While Rahab is thus occupied the traverse closes, and this is the end of the first act.*

This descent from the window of a house built upon the town wall could have been represented far better on the stage of a real Elizabethan playhouse. For there was an upper stage, a kind of balcony that ran along over the top of the traverse. In the sight of the audience Rahab would let the spies down by a cord. They would alight upon the front stage, speak with her from there, and then go off at one side.

If the second act of this story were as simple to stage as the first has been, the reader might be spared another detailed demonstration. But it happens that the rest of the story as it stands is by no means in shape for straightforward staging ; and so it would be a shirking to pass it over.

In the first place, we have not yet got our spies back to Joshua, but have left them hiding in the mountain. If you call upon the imagination of your audience to work with you, and to see in fancy what you do not show, you must satisfy their imagination, and not leave it in the lurch like this. The audience in fancy has obediently followed our spies to their hiding in the hills ; and there the men must remain later. It doesn't matter for the play, so long as the back stage (which represents the roof) *has* a window at the back.

* I have not had space to quote the Bible story ; but this account is written with the confident expectation that the interested reader will turn to the second chapter of the Book of Joshua and compare my suggested staging with the original Bible story—more especially for the sake of the speeches.

until the playwright gives further directions. It would be best, I think, to add a short third scene to our first act, showing the return of the spies to Joshua, and their telling him of all that had befallen them. This plan would follow in detail the Bible narrative, for the chapter is divided into three sections which exactly correspond with the three scenes I have suggested.

In the Book of Joshua nearly four chapters intervene before we come again to Rahab. What are the playboys to do about all the incidents related in those four chapters? Clearly they must select those incidents which have bearing upon their chosen story and set aside the rest. The passing of Jordan is too great a matter to be set aside. Yet we cannot show the host of Israel going over the river-bed.

What then? Let us again look for help to the story.

Twelve men may come upon the stage each bearing a large stone upon his shoulder. "And those twelve stones which they took out of Jordan, did Joshua pitch in Gilgal. And he spake unto the children of Israel, saying, 'When your children shall ask their fathers in time to come, saying, What mean these stones? Then ye shall let your children know, saying, Israel came over this Jordan on dry land.'" If the play is to be presented on a roomy stage, and if plenty of actors are available, this scene could open with the coming in of the priests bearing the ark of the covenant before the people. Then would come the twelve men bearing each a stone upon his shoulder; then a company of armed men with Joshua; and then a few women and children to represent the rest of the people. Joshua's words at the setting up of the stones would clearly explain all that had just occurred at the Jordan. The fruit of the land of Canaan might also be brought in to show that the manna had ceased. The scene treated in this way would make an impressive spectacle. Such forms of representation belong to pageantry rather than to drama. But if they are not shown in this way these events cannot be shown at all, and in that case we might just as well have ended our play when the spies left the house of Rahab.

If it is possible to have a procession of at least thirty persons then the stage representation of the capture of Jericho is easy. For, look you, the capture of Jericho was effected solely by

means of a procession which compassed the city. It will be
necessary to have at least thirty persons, because seven are
required for the trumpets, about six for the ark; and this with
Joshua and ten men of arms (which is a modest requirement)
leaves you only six persons to come in as the rereward.

The Elizabethan playhouse was admirably adapted for shows
of this kind. The traverse remained shut, and their *processions
marched across the front stage*, in on one side and out at the
other. In the case of sieges the attacking force was gathered
on the front stage and the citizens appeared in a row upon the
balcony, which represented their town wall.* Modern stages
never have this balcony. But something as like to it as possible
must be contrived, for you cannot do the capture of Jericho
properly without showing the citizens upon the wall, looking
on in awe and faintness at the solemn daily procession of the
Israelites. And do not forget the trumpets. The word
" trumpets " occurs no fewer than fourteen times in the sixth
chapter of the Book of Joshua, yet a modern producer would,
as likely as not, have his Jericho captured to the gentle accompaniment of a string band.

The second act of Rahab and the Spies, then, might be
planned in the following way :

Scene 1. (*Outer.*) The King's messengers, who have now
in their turn been sent out to spy upon the enemy, report
to the King that the host of Israel is removed from Shittim,
and is come to the banks of Jordan and lodged there. The
King fears that the Lord will dry up the waters of Jordan to
give passage to the men of Israel, as he did at the Red Sea,
which he dried up from before them, until they were gone
over. Accordingly he commands that the city be shut up.
He then goes away, and the messengers call out our old friend
the porter. " Now Jericho was straitly shut up because
of the children of Israel : none went out, and none came in."
But the King and the porter and the messengers go up on the
wall (thus running straight on into *Scene* 2), and they look
out in the direction of the fords of Jordan. They are waiting
for the Israelites to come. The King and his two messengers

* Cf. " Henry V," Act III, Scene 2, " Richard II," Act IV, Scene 3 ;
" King John," Act II.

go down from the wall to make preparation in the city. Other townsfolk now join the porter on the wall—Rahab and her father and mother and friends, and they all look out fearfully in the direction of the fords of Jordan.

We might let those on the wall *see* the amazing sight of a host of people afar off marching through the river-bed, and then send hurriedly to tell the King. Jericho is near enough to Jordan for this to be plausible. In any case the story says that "the people passed over right against Jericho." By this well-known stage device, of describing an action supposed to be taking place out of view, we can stimulate the audience to imagine what we cannot show. Now Rahab anxiously bids her parents and friends to come at once into her house.

Scene 3. (*Whole stage.*) For this scene a curtain must be drawn across the balcony to hide the town wall of Jericho. Now there comes in on the front stage the procession of Israel. This is not the procession with trumpets which is to compass the city, but the procession just come over Jordan, of priests, men of arms, and the twelve men bearing each a stone upon his shoulder before the people. The traverse must be open for this scene, because Joshua will command his men to build a cairn or altar with the stones, and they must do this on the inner stage where the curtain may be drawn to conceal it at the end of the scene. If they were to set up their cairn on the front stage, they would have to unbuild it again after and take it away, and that would be a foolish thing. The audience now hears all the story of the crossing of Jordan in the words spoken by Joshua to the people. After the ceremony of dedication Joshua and the priests come out again on to the front stage. The traverse at once closes; and while the Israelites are going off, some one behind the curtain makes away with the stones and sets a table and a chair or two on the back stage.

While Joshua is watching his people depart, there appears in the traverse opening, from the spot where he had just dedicated an altar, a man with his sword drawn in his hand. "And Joshua went unto him, and said unto him, 'Art thou for us or for our adversaries?' And he said, 'Nay; but as captain of the host of the Lord am I now come.'"

Scene 4. (*Inner*). The traverse opens again as soon as the Israelites and Joshua have gone, and Rahab comes in on the back stage with her parents and the friends she has chosen to save. She tells them the story of the spies and of their promise to her. Rahab is confident of their good faith, but the whole company is distressed, and full of anxiety for the city. There is room for a little character-study in one of the relatives of Rahab.

Scene 5. (*Outer*.) The traverse is closed and the balcony curtain drawn back. This gives us the walls of Jericho again. All the available townsfolk, with the exception of course of Rahab and her company, appear upon the walls. This should be the seventh day, and the people are speaking about the awe-inspiring procession they have seen go once round the city every day for six days past. They are terrified because they do not understand. And now on this day the procession has already passed about the city four times, and still the men of Israel march with the seven priests blowing seven trumpets of rams' horns,, and with the ark borne before the people and all the men of war. This the townsfolk of Jericho tell one another. Then the procession passes over the front stage. After it has gone we hear again the anxious talk of the townsfolk. Then the procession passes once more. There is another interval filled with the talk of the townsfolk on the wall. Thus when the Israelites enter for the third time, their seven times compassing of the city will have been completed. Then the priests make a long blast with the ram's horn, and Joshua cries, " Shout ; for the Lord hath given you the city," and all the people shout with a great shout.

In the story " the wall fell down flat." What shall be done about this ? For my part I think it will be enough to close the balcony curtain suddenly at the moment of the shout ; and then, after the making of a great noise—a noise of crashing and banging and falling things, the men of Jericho fight hand to hand on the front stage with the men of Israel, rushing in on both sides. Alarums and excursions follow, with the clash of sword-play and much stir and din. Joshua's voice is heard above the confusion urging his men to " destroy utterly all that was in the city both man and woman, young and

old, and ox, and sheep, and ass, with the edge of the sword."
The Bible says, " But all the silver, and gold, and vessels of
brass and iron, are consecrated unto the Lord : they shall come
into the treasury of the Lord." And so while the men of
arms are fighting, the priests, I think, might busy themselves
in carrying off the treasure. Vessels of silver and gold, and
pots, pans, and other furniture are borne away. Men are
slain or driven to flight. Then Joshua calls to the spies and
sends them to bring out Rahab. The traverse opens and
the company is found within, cowering in terror. Now the
noise of the conflict dies down, and while Joshua and the two
spies are in talk with Rahab and her grateful friends on the
back stage, the men of Israel in front bear away the bodies
of the dead. A child runs in and picks up a sword that was
left. When Joshua has finished his comfortable words to
Rahab the traverse closes, and the play is done. Some
playmakers might prefer to end with the adjuration of Joshua
to his people, " Cursed be the man before the Lord that riseth
up and buildeth this city Jericho." But that would mean
the coming together again of all the Israelites after the fight.
Certainly Shakespeare ends " Macbeth " in this manner ;
but there they have a new king to acclaim. The victors in
our play are still sacking and burning the city.

A quiet coming to an end in a play is a refreshing contrast
to the sensational finale, which has grown ever more into
favour as the traverse crept gradually forward (eating up
action) until it became the front curtain. Several writers have
pointed out that more dramatic skill is needed on the Elizabethan
type of stage than on the modern. This is especially true of
the closing scenes of acts. The modern playwright can work
up the action to a pitch of excitement from which he could not
possibly come off without disaster ; but at the very height of
the climax he drops the curtain. This may be fine showmanship,
but it is very poor art. If you have no front curtain thus to
cloak your shortcomings you must play the thing out to the
end. When an angry man bursts in upon two others who have
been deceiving him, it is not enough for him to say " So ! " or
" Ha, ha ! " and wait for the stage-manager to " draw a veil
over this painful scene." The minutes subsequently wasted by

the actors in a fatuous bowing to the audience, while the curtain soars up and down, should have been spent in delivering the speech of the angry man. But our modern playwrights find themselves unable to get over the top of a climax and come down quietly on the other side. The drop-scene covers a multitude of deficiencies.

The stage-play of two other Bible stories containing battles may be given in outline; the stories of Deborah and of Gideon. In the space of the first short tale we find three such elements of poetic drama as the battle of the river Kishon, the death of Sisera, and the song of Deborah. The whole story is told in one chapter; the song is in another.* The first chapter falls into three main divisions.

Scene 1. Deborah under the palm-tree hears the complaint of Israel, and summon Barak, to confer with him.

Scene 2. The Battle.

Scene 3. Jael kills Sisera.

The killing of Sisera should be done according to the convention of the Greek drama. The closed traverse represents Jael's tent. Sisera is persuaded to go in; and Jael takes in, first, milk for him to drink, and then a rug to cover him. He bids her watch. She comes out, speaks a short space, then takes a nail of the tent and a hammer and goes in softly. Now Barak comes in on the front stage and speaks alone. Presently Jael comes out with only the hammer, and tells Barak what she has done.

This third scene has given the fighting men an opportunity to collect themselves. For the second act the whole company marches in. They are headed by Deborah and Barak chanting antiphonally the glorious song.

The story of Gideon† makes a much longer play. So long in fact that here I can but sketch the plan of a part of it in outline. Part of the story can well be divided into three acts. But that will not complete the tale.

Act I. The call of Gideon.

---

* Judges, chapters iv and v.

† Judges, chapters vi, vii, viii. Here again the reader is asked to turn up the Bible story. The following scheme is but the barest outline.

Act II. Gideon's preparations.

Act III. Gideon's defeat of the Midianites.

This takes the story up to the defeat of the Midianites by the three hundred men with trumpets, torches and pitchers. But it omits the splendid story of Gideon's requital to the men of Succoth and of Penuel; how he " taught " with thorns and with briers the three score and seventeen elders of Succoth, and broke down the tower of Penuel and slew the men of the city.

The outline of the scenes would be as follows :

Induction. The prophet speaks (see chapter vi, verse 8). He not only reproaches the Israelites for their sin, but describes the impoverishment brought upon them by the Midianites.

Act I, Scene 1. (*Outer.*) An angel appears to Gideon while he is threshing wheat by the wine-press, and says, " The Lord is with thee, thou mighty man of valour." Their conference is told fully in the Bible story. When Gideon goes in to prepare his present the angel goes in also. The miracle is not shown.

Scene 2. (*Outer.*) Gideon's father, Joash, and his household, and certain men of the city come in and speak of the grove and the altar of Baal. Perhaps they could speak of a festival in honour of Baal to be held on the morrow. Then they go out.

Scene 3. (*Outer.*) Gideon comes through the traverse opening and says, "Alas, O Lord God! for because I have seen an angel of the Lord face to face." He then reflects upon what he has been told to do.

If you have the means of showing the miracle, a much better version of these opening scenes can be given. The first scene is held on the outer stage as but now suggested, and, after his talk with the angel, Gideon goes in to prepare the flesh and cakes. The angel having promised to tarry until he comes again, must fill the interval in some way. We might therefore put in at this point what was, in our first version, the Induction, and let the angel speak the words instead of the prophet. When Gideon is ready the traverse opens and the angel goes in with him. The rest of the scene is played on the inner stage. Now in " The Tempest " there is a stage-direction, " Thunder and Lightning. Enter Ariel (like a Harpy).

claps his wings upon the table, and with a quaint device the banquet vanishes." If, by means of gunpowder on the rock and electric wires in the angel's wand, you can contrive a quaint device of this nature, then the scene with the miracle can be shown fully. "And the angel of God said unto him, 'Take the flesh and the unleavened cakes, and lay them upon this rock, and pour out the broth.' And he did so. Then the angel of the Lord put forth the end of the staff that was in his hand, and touched the flesh and the unleavened cakes; and there rose up fire out of the rock, and consumed the flesh and the unleavened cakes. Then the angel of the Lord departed out of his sight. . . ." Gideon said, "Alas, O Lord God! for because I have seen an angel of the Lord face to face." Gideon comes out and the traverse closes.

This, in my opinion, is by far the better version. But it requires a quaint device. Gideon now reflects how it was commanded him that he should throw down the altar of Baal and cut down the grove. So he calls to him Phurah, his servant, and tells him to come soon at nightfall, with several others and to bring axes.

Scene 4. (Outer.) The men of Midian marching.

I suggest this episode partly because it is quite time something was seen of the Midianites, but also to mark the passage of time before the men of the city can come in to Joash to complain of the deed of Gideon. A scene on the rear stage *showing* the deed is not worth the trouble it would entail. But Phurah and his accomplices should certainly come through with lanterns and axes and be told by Gideon what they all have to do. The men of Midian must march with torches, because it is night.*

Scene 5. (Inner.) Now it is morning (Joash says so in the story) and the men of the city complain to Joash. He defends his son. Gideon presently comes in and calls the men of the city to arms. Then he blows a trumpet, and sends out messengers throughout all Manasseh. Joash and the others go out to stir up the people. Gideon remains and decides to test the Lord's will in the proof of the fleece. (End of Act I.)

Act II. Scene 1. (Outer.) Men of Israel marching—Asher

* For the stage suggestion of a whole night and the following morning, cf. " Julius Cæsar," Act II.

and Zebulun and Naphtali. Gideon addresses them, bidding the fearful ones return home.

Scene 2. (*Inner.*) Gideon finds himself justified in the proof of the fleece. We need not show both episodes, the fleece wet and the fleece dry. One is shown, and the other made clear to the audience in Gideon's soliloquy. It will be well to change the Bible order, to *refer* to the case in which the fleece was found dry, and to *show* the case in which the fleece was found wet, because the latter is finer for the stage : " He rose up early on the morrow, and thrust the fleece together, and wringed the dew out of the fleece, a bowl full of water."

Scene 3. (*Outer.*) Gideon comes in with his army. They go, a few at a time, in behind the traverse where a river is supposed to run. Gideon sends away those who bowed down upon their knees to drink. He warns them to return home directly, for " the host of Midian was beneath him in the valley." To his picked men he then gives victuals and trumpets, and they all go out. (End of Act II.)

Act III. *Scene* 1. (*Outer, then Inner.*) Midianite soldiers in their camp. They talk about the Israelites, and the dark of the night as it comes on. They have plenty to eat and drink, for they have been living on the fat of the land ever since they came down upon Israel before the harvest. The soldiers have also brought rich plunder with them into camp. After a time they say it is dark, and they go behind the traverse, which is their tent. Gideon and Phurah enter presently as spies and listen outside the tent. Phurah hears a man tell his dream to his fellow, and he relates it to Gideon. They go out. A Midianite captain comes and (the traverse now opening) finds the soldiers all asleep among their pots and baggage, and turns them out, for it is broad day.

Scene 2. (*Outer.*) Gideon divides his men into three companies, " and he put a trumpet in every man's hand, with empty pitchers, and lamps within the pitchers." He tells them his stratagem. They go out marching to a chant.

Scene 3. (*Whole stage.*) The Midianites enter on all sides with bottles and booty, singing and making revel. After a scene of carousal they fall asleep one by one. Those on the back stage lie among piles of booty and camp baggage. Now the last man awake wanders from group to group with a lantern, looking for a boon companion, and singing tipsily. Finding none awake he swears, then trips over a prostrate form, and falls. His lantern goes out, and the whole camp lies still in the dark.*

Now a company of the Israelites steals in on one side, their pitchers glowing dimly from the torches within them. Now another company steals in on the other side   Then Gideon leads in the third company at the back, and they line the back stage. In the (supposed) dim light Gideon mounts a bale and, with a flourish of the sleeve, sets his trumpet and blows a long blast. At once all the men of Gideon, surrounding the stage on three sides, smash the pitchers by knocking them one against another, and blow a great blast on the trumpets.† They hold " the torches in their left hands, and the trumpets in their right hands to blow withal : and they cry, ' The sword of the Lord and of Gideon ! ' " But they do not move from their places. The stupefied Midianites spring up. But what with the wine they have taken, and their sleepiness, and the light of the torches and the blare of the trumpets they are confounded altogether. Every man's sword is turned against his fellow, and those who are not slain take to flight.

There is no drop-curtain to fall at this point and spoil the story. Gideon calls his torch-bearers together and bids some go straightway to Naphtali and Asher and Manasseh and stir them up to pursue after the Midianites, and some he sends " throughout all Mount Ephraim saying, ' Come down against the Midianites, and take before them the waters unto Beth-barah and Jordan.' " With a great shout of " The sword of

---

* Elizabethan conditions necessitate the playing of such a scene as this in broad daylight. Hence the need of this lantern business to suggest dark.

† Gideon's party of three hundred would be represented on the stage by some thirty, but the breaking of even this number of pitchers would be a costly performance. In the discussion at the opening of the third act of " A Midsummer Night's Dream," the rude mechanicals effectively solved many knotty problems of representation. Playboys in like manner could find a device to make all well. I suggest metal cans instead of earthenware pitchers. These would be dropped with a crash instead of broken.

the Lord and of Gideon ! " the men with their torches run out on all sides. (End of Act III.)

Here we must leave Gideon, though some of the best is yet to come. Shakespeare, however, at the end of his second play of " Henry IV," has still more to promise of his hero. So perhaps we also may undertake to " continue the story " another day.

Of the many Bible stories suitable for playmaking the types of action here illustrated in " Rahab and the Spies," in " Deborah and Barak " and in " Gideon " are the most suitable for schoolboys at the typical schoolboy age of eleven to fifteen. But because we have chosen stirring tales of battle for our instances the reader must not conclude that the rousing element is all that the Play Way can find for boys in the Bible. There are many other types of action in play besides the heroic and the processional, but space is not unlimited, and many wonderful tales must be passed over here. With sixth-form boys of sixteen to nineteen years old the story of Ruth might be taken as a subject for playmaking; and also the story of Esther. These tales are drama itself; but they are not the most suitable for Littleman.

There are many elements to be considered in the study of a subject so ample as playmaking, and every side of the question cannot be discussed at the same time. I fear that more than one of my readers is tired by now of the show of brave deeds and the tramp of armed men. And perhaps the opening and shutting of the traverse has become a weariness. But we are now to leave the staging element for a space and turn to the question of style.

In the teaching of English literature and composition in schools the most important task, in my judgment, is the imparting of a living style to the pupil; a style which he will use in his own work. I say to *impart* a style because, although " the style is the man," we, as teachers of literature, must endeavour to foster the native artistic power in the pupil by means of the study of great books. You cannot make a silk purse out of a sow's ear, and you cannot make a poet out of a born stupid; for though poets must be made, they must be born too. But, given an able pupil, by what means are we to get him to practise a conscious and yet a natural style ? It is important to observe that the question is not, " How can we get boys to write good poetry or good prose ? " Our Playbooks are full of lyrics and ballads and prose studies, and some of those pieces are of high literary merit. But all those pieces are short, and they are, so to speak, the work of chance. They are the product of some quite unconscious, some quite inexplicable power in young boys. There is nothing in the quality of the Littleman prose studies and poems which can be defined by the term *style*, in the more restricted sense of the term. The work is *artless*. How is the master to train his boys to express themselves consciously in some artistic manner, deliberately to study style ? How shall the boy learn to know (or is it not rather to feel ?) what is good from what is not good, and how to judge of the fitness and appropriateness of a word or a phrase or a manner of utterance ?

Style, in the narrower sense of the term, is well enough understood by present-day teachers, and finds a sufficient place in their lessons. But there are two points I should like to make in this chapter with regard to style. One is that boys cannot do any satisfactory work in connexion with style, in the more restricted sense, before the age of fourteen or there-abouts ; and the other point is that the quest of style in the wider sense of the term may begin in mere child's-play, for it includes many diverse activities. Style is not *all* book-study.

First, then, consider the possibilities of imitation. A boy must read the masterpieces of literature, some very thoroughly, and some very often. Then he may take some distinctive styles and deliberately set himself to write in imitation. But he must take them one at a time and, during the period of this practice, must scrupulously avoid mixing the characteristic elements of one style with those of another. Bible English is in a style which any boy can recognize whenever he hears it. He must, then, school himself to write in this style until his fellows on hearing him read his exercise can say, " That is like nothing but the Bible." The writing of the plays I have sketched in this chapter, " Rahab and the Spies," " Deborah and Barak," and " Gideon " would be a simple and delightful introduction to this practice, because many of the speeches can be taken whole out of the Bible, or rendered fit for the play with very little change.

Such passages as are not to be found in the Bible and have in consequence to be freshly composed by the boys—the porter's part in " Rahab and the Spies," for instance, the soliloquy of Barak before Jael's tent, and all that is said by the Midianites in " Gideon "—would have to be so carefully modelled on the Bible idiom that no hearer could point out the slightest incongruity. In the course of their practice the boys themselves would be able to single out and describe certain distinctive elements of the style they were engaged upon ; and several points would be demonstrated by the master in his teaching. We could say, " This is like the Bible, for such and such a reason. That is not like the Bible." But I think it would be unprofitable to define and tabulate the various elements. Style is to be learnt, if at all, by example and experiment rather than by rule and prescription. In the study of style by imitation a *daily* exercise gives excellent practice, even if it has to be very short because only a few minutes can be spared for it. But of course there must also be long exercises done, and lessons devoted to the study. All the reading, and the literary study, and the dramatic craftsmanship, and the sensible composition, and the lively acting are knit into a whole by their being the different parts of one concern —the play.

Elizabethan narrative prose is another beautiful style which the boys should study to reproduce. A story can be taken out of North's " Plutarch " and dramatized as a prose play. In this form of exercise *Incongruity* (i.e. that which is out of keeping with the model) would be regarded as the chief fault of style, as *Impropriety* (i.e. that which is not peculiarly fit) is the chief fault of style in original writing. With a distinctive model before them the boys would learn what was meant by a standard. And later on those who had successfully come up to a standard which had been set before them, and had learnt to avoid Incongruity, would be more able to set up a standard for themselves, to avoid Impropriety, and maintain a conscious effort at good style.

Several other distinctive styles can be found both in prose

and verse, worthy and possible to be imitated, though differing greatly from one another as they come from different ages. There is the style of Shakespeare's plays, and the style of the traditional ballads. Both of these can be reproduced (in an external sense) by boys. For older boys a useful exercise is the imitation of Pope's heroic couplets, and the style of Robert Browning. As representative of to-day we have the style of Synge in his Irish Plays, and of Captain Scott in his Polar Journals.* Perhaps some one may accuse me of impropriety in speaking of all these diversities in the same paragraph. But they are all styles.

* The style of Synge is easy to copy because it is so largely composed of a certain phraseology. The same words, phrases, and turns of sentence occur again and again. Here are a few taken at random ; the reader will find them in a context on almost any page of the plays : *It's myself—Is it me fight him ?— I'm thinking—It's a poor (fine, great, hard, etc.) thing— A little path I have—Let you come—God help us all—Till Tuesday was a week—The end of time—The dawn of day—Let on—Kindly—Now*, as in *Walk out now—Surely—Maybe—Itself—At all—Afeard—Destroyed—A curse.* Synge is also mighty fond of the words *ditch* and *ewe.* And there are certain forms of rhythm about Synge's prose which are used with equal frequency, and are quite easy to catch. So far from this imitation of style being an artificial method, the fact is that once a boy of sixteen or over has read a play or two of Synge's, if he has any power of style in him it will be all but impossible to stop him writing like Synge for a few weeks.

In Scott's Journals there is no deliberate style or conscious art, but only a plain narrative set down in a straightforward manner. This is a good style. There is, to be sure, a sprinkling of irregularities which may offend a hypercritical reader in his arm-chair, such as a split infinitive now and then, a rare lapse into sailor slang, and a few mixed constructions. But a man who is marching to the South Pole must be allowed to chronicle the day's doings while in camp at night in the words which come to him most readily. In any case Scott's readers of three hundred years hence will not be aware that these irregularities were even questionable at the date of his writing. I know several schoolmasters who profess to admire the tales of Elizabethan voyagers and yet cannot be bothered to read Scott's Journals. They would tell you it was a question of style. Which is as much as to say that clear straightforward English prose of to-day must wait a few centuries before scholars will recognize it as style.

As regards imitation of this, a model that has no outstanding characteristics, no positive tricks, graces, or ornaments may seem to be a very difficult one to imitate. So it is ; but some clear, straightforward, " uncharactered " prose style makes an excellent final model

THE PLAY WAY

Now I have not suggested for a moment that it is easy, or even that it is possible, for any pupil, man or boy, to get by imitation the style of one of the great writers and to use it with any mastery. To begin with, the imitation is little more than a verbal one, for the young pupil cannot borrow the cast of mind and the habit of thought which made Shakespeare write in his rich, abundant style, and Robert Browning in his swift, crowded style. The pupil studies to recognize the outstanding characteristics of expressive form in his model and strives to reproduce them. There is nothing of parody about it, but the mention of parody will give a hint of what I mean. A teacher with an understanding of his subject and of his pupil—of Shakespeare, let us say, and of Littleman—should be able to teach his boys to follow this master of style just as the old painters taught their school of pupils to follow their style.

This method of imparting a sense of style to the pupil is well known in the teaching of classics, as a part of the system of seventeenth-century educators ; and it need not, in consequence, be discussed here in greater detail. But the imitation of models in one's writing is only a part of the process which goes to the making of a living style. The study and the practice of style in writing is partly a science and partly an art. Scholarly teachers in schools have given all their attention to the scientific side. We would not have a like exaggeration practised by the teacher who is an artist, that is the playmaster ; but it is necessary to insist that the artist side of any maker of literature, be he a past master or simply a prentice, must be fully represented.

The method of " learning Shakespeare " through acting the plays instead of only through a reading and discussion of them, and the method of performing parts in history and of declaiming orations, especially if due attention is given by the master to the clear enunciation of words and to the free and open delivery of the speeches, will do much to foster the

when a boy is ready to leave this method of imitation and write a style of his own. Tested by the standard of the plain model all faults of bad borrowing, and the persistence of certain elements not truly assimilated, would be shown up, and archaisms, affectations, and other faults easily exposed.

pupil's appreciation of *style*. Many teachers to whom I have suggested this have been inclined to scoff at the idea. They admit that from play-acting may come certain benefits, but an appreciation of style is not one of them. Style, they say, is to be learnt by study and not by exhibitions and holdings forth. Milton, however, thought otherwise: ". . . then will the choice Histories, Heroic Poems, and Attic Tragedies of stateliest and most regal Argument, with all the famous Political Orations, offer themselves ; which if they were not only read, but some of them got by memory, and solemnly pronounced with right accent and grace, as might be taught, would endue them even with the spirit and vigour of Demosthenes or Cicero, Euripides or Sophocles."

This is no small claim to come from one so learned in the ancient masters as was Milton. I would ask the reader to note in especial the method approved here by Milton, " if they were not only read, but pronounced with right accent and grace " and he adds, " as might be taught." In an earlier passage he directs, " Their speech is to be fashion'd to a distinct and clear pronunciation." He is speaking of Latin, and would have their speech fashion'd " as near as may be to the Italian, especially in the vowels." That good counsel of a learned man and a poet was offered nearly three hundred years ago, yet our schoolmasters in most English schools still pronounce Latin, the tongue of old Italy, as though it were some bastard Scandinavian dialect. And these are the men who set themselves up, in libraries, studies, and schoolrooms, to instruct the unscholarly among us in the imparting of style.

Milton spoke also of " grace." Who ever saw grace insisted upon by an English schoolmaster in connexion with lessons in history, poetry, or oratory ?

In the quest of style the next stage, after play and imitation, is the study of technique. This includes such things as the arrangement of matter, and the construction of the sentence, the paragraph, and the essay. It would not be in place here to offer any constructive suggestions on this matter ; and in any case, this side of the study of literature and composition is already all too familiar to teachers of English. They teach, in fact, little else in early composition but the minor technicalities of framework and punctuation. The very existence of English *verse* composition is rarely acknowledged in the schools of England to-day; the writing of poetry is never practised consistently as part of the school course of study. But in their middle-school lessons on *prose* composition, teachers bring in the full apparatus of technical instruction far too early. What with the making of frameworks and outlines for essays, paraphrase and précis, notes to write on the figures of speech, and chapters to learn on the elements and qualities of style, such as Brevity, Perspicuity, Lucidity, Vivacity, Frigidity, Sublimity, and many another Pomposity, the wretched pupil has not the mind to write any prose of his own real making, nor the time to do it if he would. We do not deny that some of these matters of technical instruction have their place in the teaching of composition. All we ask is that teachers would find out the due place of these matters and keep them in it.

Here following is a brief indication of a course, such as I would suggest, for the various occupations which, on the Play Way system, go to make up the quest of style for a boy.

(i) Form II. Age 10–12. The making of simple artless poems, ballads, and prose studies (the Littleman pieces) in connexion with his early reading of stories in prose and verse. At this time come his own original speeches and lectures, which must be correct in grammar and sweet in delivery, but by no means mannered or artful. He speaks simply in his own proper person, and is innocent of any mannerism or contrivance. At this time also is placed the rhythmical recital of little poems to the accompaniment of his stick for beating time, to school him by a playful device in the measure and melody of verse. This is the age of a boy which I have called Littleman.

(ii) Form III. Age 12–14. The acting of Shakespeare's plays conducted in such a way that he may learn how to move well and freely, and how to use his limbs with vigour and with grace, so that as he grows to manhood he may have attained a handsome " presence," such as we English were noted for in other days. He must now learn with more than playful care how to speak well, pronouncing cleanly and distinctly, and not muttering. Milton says : " For we Englishmen being far Northerly, do not open our mouths in the cold air, wide enough to grace a

298

Southern tongue ; but are observ'd by all other Nations to speak exceeding close and inward."

Since the days of Shakespeare and Milton we have more and more disgraced our own tongue, for at present you may go many days up and down the country without hearing good English spoken.

With his acting of Shakespeare goes Miming, to the furtherance of free movement and expressive gesture. For we English, as Milton would say, dare not take our hands out of our pockets in the cold air, and are " exceeding close and inward " with all our movements. At this time also comes his chief practice in playmaking, for the fuller understanding of Shakespeare's dramatic craftsmanship. At this time his writing may still be good by chance, through natural genius and childish inspiration ; but it can scarcely yet be good through *conscious* art, for his sense of style as it may be learned is only beginning here. He will sometimes strive after effect, and produce many monstrosities, the correction of which must chiefly be looked for in his close imitation of the best writers.

At this age (which more or less begins the age of puberty) it is necessary for his bodily welfare, no less than for the perfection of his mind, that his schooling should be as much as possible in active pursuits and bodily exercises in the open air ; and as little as possible indoors, sitting still, or in long-continued reading. Therefore this age is the fittest time for the making and acting of plays, especially those of a martial and heroic character, and for dancing. At this age also he first begins to understand music, and his taste can be formed to know and partly to appreciate what is good, through glees and madrigals, processional chants, folk-songs, choir-singing, and playing some instrument. In all this he can take part. But he should also hear much good music performed by an orchestra, and on the organ, in school and out. He should be taught to shun all the shallow, rubbishy airs, dances, and songs of to-day ; and his natural desire for entertainment and fun in music, as in other things, should be fully gratified with light and gay and dainty songs and airs, which are nevertheless good music. At this age I have called the lad a Playboy.*

* The terms " Littleman " and " Playboy " as the names for stages

(iii) Form IV. Age 14–16. At this age it is proper for a boy to begin those studies which are fit for one able to reason. This he could not well do before, being at the first too little and then later, not only still immature, but also too much taken up with bodily development and physical changes. *Now* in his quest for style, he may begin to learn technique and the conscious art of writing. His imitation of models will now be more thoughtful ; and the composition of his own prose and verse, being now a studied business, will cost him some pains, and show at first but little result. Therefore the interest in *producing something* must be discouraged as the chief aim ; and his teacher must give him to understand that he is now to be a student, and must for the remainder of his school time concentrate all his powers and his main interest upon learning in its more restricted sense.

Milton says : " And now lastly will be the time to read with them those organic Arts which inable men to discourse and write perspicuously, elegantly, and according to the fitted style of lofty, mean, or lowly. Logic, therefore, so much as is useful, is to be referr'd to this due place with all her well coucht Heads and Topics, until it be time to open her contracted palm into a graceful and ornate Rhetoric."

Having brought our boy in his quest of style, not *through* this last stage, but only to the threshold of it, we propose, to the surprise of the reader, to leave him. But I will explain. We leave him in other hands. Many a man in considering this matter, the quest of style, would only be starting his investigations at this point where we propose to leave off. That is to say, for most teachers style *begins* with what Milton calls the organic arts and (elementary) logic. But in the reckoning of the Play Way it is not so. In this survey I have started with a boy of ten, at which age he is a mere child, and have taken him up to the age of fourteen, where he must

in the boy's school course are definitely described here, but have not been consistently used throughout the book. The Play Way is still in its experimental stages, still an *essay* in method, and therefore I have thought it advisable to avoid using such terms according to a strict application, for fear of seeming to suggest that the Play Way was already in shape as an ordered system of education.

begin to be a man. There I shall hand him over, a potential student now, to those teachers whose work lies, if not principally, at any rate firstly, among the organic arts and logic. In himself a playmaster may be a student of style in the more restricted sense of the term, and he may be ever so learned in the technique of rhetoric, but in so far as the subject of this book is concerned, namely, the Play Way, we must leave our playboy at this point to become a student.

The quest of style may begin in books of grammar; it *may* begin anywhere. But it certainly does not spring solely from the organic arts and logic. Even if we take the term in a very restricted sense to mean the conscious art of technique in writing, we must still give consideration to the spirit which is to inform that work, and to the matter upon which this conscious art is being exercised. Style is inextricably bound up with matter and with man. And therefore I do not scruple to claim for the Play Way that in these activities of acting and reciting and singing and dancing and free composition, so long as they are guided and controlled by a master possessing taste as well as humour, and judgment as well as enthusiasm, we are laying not only a foundation but the very best foundation for a learned and reasoned appreciation of style later on, and for a conscious and scholarly pursuit of style by the pupil in his own work.

In our study of practical playmaking we have now dealt with the adaptation of the story, and with the working out of the plot in accordance with the conditions and conventions of a given stage. In school the first step in playmaking is to find your story and to have it read and told, and re-read and retold, until it is thoroughly familiar to every one who is to take a share in the playmaking. Discussion then follows. It is impossible to lay down any rule respecting the order in which the various matters should be taken, or the method in which the discussion should be conducted. I have found the system very successful which at this juncture frankly admits " The debate is now open to the House." A whole lesson at a time can profitably be given up to an informal discussion and exchange of views among the boys. Many talk at the same time. There is, so far as I can see, no reason why six or seven persons should not be speaking their views all at once, provided that it is not necessary for every one to hear every speaker.* There is so much to be said that the boys soon split up into little groups according as their chief interest lies in the adaptation of the story, or the working out of the characters, or the allotment of the parts, or the staging, or the provision of make-shift costume and properties, or the actual writing of provisional parts in the form of notes giving cues and a rough suggestion of the dialogue. The class at this stage of the playmaking has in fact resolved itself into a number of sub-committees " sitting " all in the same room. That is why there is such a noise. I have seen whole lesson-whiles devoted to this busy argument. There is merry laughter, some scolding, and much debate. Several boys are walking about ; a few perhaps are illustrating to one another on the platform a bout or a death or a method of harangue or of capture—doing it in action as they will do it before the duke. One perhaps sketches a plan on the blackboard. Some sit in the desks while others stand before them or lean over their shoulders. They are gathered in working groups, putting their brown heads together for the making of their play ; and the room is full of an industrious chatter. A visitor entering suddenly might fancy that he had come by mistake into a classroom of the old school in the absence of the master ; for the noise of allowed play sounds at first just like the noise of disorder. But if you listen you will find that it is articulate. The master is present, and is perfectly satisfied with the discipline. He visits the groups in turn at their requirement, and spends his advice according to need ; though he might easily find enough of interest and value to occupy him in one sub-committee throughout the period.

The next stage in the playmaking is the preparation of notes by the boys, partly in school during this informal discussion, but chiefly as a series of homework in the evening,

---

* This state of affairs is only recommended as allowable in the particular circumstances under consideration. My colleagues who teach languages on the direct method have pointed out that in the learning of French, Latin, and Greek it *is* essential that all the boys should hear every word spoken in the classroom.

PLAYMAKING

These notes represent, as it were, the " finding " of each member of a sub-committee. Those who have been working upon the adaptation of the story will draw up as homework an outline of the scenes, such as I have given for the dramatization of Bible stories in the earlier pages of this chapter. Those who have given their chief attention to the characters will sketch out the part of some principal person, or make a little study of the place to be filled by a number of minor parts. Others will actually write parts for the principals in the chief scenes, giving them all their cues, all the stage-directions, and the openings of their most important speeches. In order to follow out as far as possible the craftsmanship of Shakespeare it will be advisable for the boys to jot down on their parts, either beforehand in preparation or during the early rehearsals before the play is actually *written*, all the stage directions, all the important movements they have to make, and all the properties required at certain junctures. Then when the play is finally written the makers will, as far as possible, mention or allude to these things actually in the lines to be spoken. Some reader may overlook the importance of this suggestion. But the embodiment of all the action and the material in the words written to be spoken is an essential part of playmaking on this system. It is one of the chief characteristics of workmanship which—to make all clear in a verbal quibble—distinguishes the playwright from the playwriter.

With boys under fifteen you must at this point begin to *act* your play if you wish to get any life into the composition. Of course it is an amorphous thing at this time. The speeches are partly read from notes and partly composed impromptu on the spur of utterance. The action is interrupted from time to time by the onlooking playmakers, by the master, and by the actors themselves. The understanding is that during the early composition rehearsals there may be as many interruptions as are necessary. If the matter of inquiry or suggestion can be settled at the moment, by adoption or rejection, it is so settled ; but if it should involve longer discussion or repeated trial, or elaborate changes, or much recasting and rewriting of what is already done, the matter is postponed to a later and special discussion period.

THE PLAY WAY

The boys chosen to act the amorphous play in the composition rehearsals may not be the ones who will eventually play the parts. But it is of course a good plan to settle as soon as possible upon the actual cast, because once you have a player before you in actual being you can build your created character to fit him ; or he and his part can grow up together in the making. This suggestion may surprise some reader who has always regarded characters in a play as the absolute creations of the artist's invention. But just as a character when played gains or loses by the individual interpretation of the actor, so may a character in the making be modified, shaped, and influenced by reference and approximation to a living model. It would be fruitless and digressive to argue the point here, but in passing we may instance the parallel with the painter's model. How many of the most sublime Madonnas of Raphael and Leonardo and Botticelli are in part the portraits of beautiful women. The boy playmakers under their master's guidance must learn not only that they are to make Peter's part in the play like Peter himself in some respects (because that seems a natural and an easy thing to do) but they must also learn what it means to take the living thing as a model for the art form.

After the acting there is more discussion, and after the discussion more acting. And all the time there is many a child among you taking notes, and busily thinking out the speeches, and fashioning his draft lines. The purpose of acting the play from the very first is that the boys may see the story in rough dramatic form. Then they can trim it and shape it, and finally write it.* The discussions are of two kinds—first, the informal exchange of ideas among the boys, and secondly, the lessons of the master ; in the course of which the boys—as in lessons everywhere—may ask for information or raise difficult points for discussion.

The master in these lessons can teach the rules and proprieties

---

* At a time when both seniors and juniors had been engaged in communal playmaking one of the sixth-form players, writing a humorous account of our goings-on (in one of those "rag" magazines that crop up in schools) sought a true word to describe the activity of the boy-playwrights. There is no present tense of "wrought," and so he coined the expression *Play-wreaking*. This term, however, I have not adopted !

of the art of dramatic poetry so far as suits the age of his boys.
They should have notebooks and write down what they learn
about action, construction, characterization, and diction,
with a multitude of examples, for a rule is both understand
and remembered best in an example. Even boys of ten could
be taught to understand and to observe many rules and
proprieties which the modern play-writers of London would be
the better for knowing. At first the things taught will be
simply practical, such as the way of making your play to suit a
given stage, the use of the traverse, advice about exits and
entrances, about light and dark, about crowds, processions,
" business," and so on. Later on the boys will be taught the
meaning and force of certain literary and dramatic conventions,
the distinction of styles, the power of tradition. Of this study,
which we shall call Poetics, Milton says, " that sublime Art
which . . . teaches what the Laws are of a true *Epic* Poem,
what of a *Dramatic*, what of a *Lyric*, what Decorum is, which
is the grand masterpiece to observe. This would make them
soon perceive what despicable creatures our common Rimers
and Play-writers be, and show them what religious, what
glorious and magnificent use might be made of Poetry both
in divine and human things."

But the teacher must never get so engrossed in his lecturing
as to forget that " the play's the thing." At the very most
the lessons on the art of dramatic poetry should never take more
than a third part of the acting and playmaking time ; the study
and acting of Shakespeare should take another third, and the
making and acting of the boys' original plays should fill the
remaining part.

In a few playmaking experiments with *senior* players we
found that the method of acting the scenes while they were
still unwritten was a failure. The sixth-form boys pointed
out that the self-consciousness of their age (sixteen to eighteen
years) made it impossible for them to stand up and speak a
part impromptu. And so, after the preliminary discussion,
various individuals each undertook to write a whole scene.
Their work was then discussed, acted, amplified, and amended
until all the playmakers were satisfied with it.

It would be dangerous to draw up any *scheme* of playmaking

lest any one should be tempted to stick to the letter of it. So
a mere list shall be given here of the activities of boys and master
which result in a finished play :

    i.   Reading and telling of the story.
   ii.   Informal discussion.
  iii.   Sub-committee stage.
  iv.   Preparation of rough notes.
   v.   Acting in the rough.
  vi.   Master's lessons.
 vii.   Discussion of special points.
viii.   Careful fashioning, shaping, and writing.
  ix.   Careful acting, as in rehearsal.
   x.   Final revision of text of speeches.
  xi.   Performance with all due ceremony.

The sub-committees really exist throughout the playmaking,
for there will always be groups of boys interested in one
branch of the work more than in another, and more able than
the other boys to do the work connected with it. Thus there
are the plot-managers, the actors, the poets, the producers,
the craftsmen, and so on. But one boy may fill several of
these functions. Sub-committees should not be formally
appointed, for this would lead to specializing, and specializing
is not desirable here.

Let us take two examples of plays which might be made,
" The Golden Goose " and " The Cherry Bough," and illustrate
further matters of playmaking with particular reference to
those stories.

The story of " The Golden Goose " may be read in " Grimm's
Fairy Tales." After the story had been read once or twice one
of the boys would be set to tell it in a form more fit for our
playmaking purpose. After his relation and the subsequent
informal discussion the tale would be in something like the
following shape. I give the outline only :

A boy goes out to cut wood and meets a little old man in
the forest with whom he shares his simple meal. The little
old man rewards him with the gift of a golden goose. The
boy decides to run away from home, where he is not happy, and
seek his fortune with this prize. He goes to an inn, where

he discovers that the goose has the magical property that all who touch it are unable to get free again. The daughters of the inn-keeper become fixed, and the boy walks away followed by the three girls in a row. In the fields he meets the Parson, who cries shame on the girls for thus pursuing a young man and in seeking to restrain them, he himself becomes attached to the procession. Other folk are drawn in as the boy continues his course, each one in turn becoming fastened to the tail of the procession. Now there is at the court a Princess who cannot laugh, and the King her father has promised her hand in marriage to the man who shall undo this melancholy imperfection. The boy comes before the Princess, and causes her to laugh heartily at the motley crew which he draws in his train. So he marries the Princess, and they live happily ever after.

Note that certain elements of the fairy tale, as it is to be found in Grimm, have already been shed. We have dropped out at the start the experiences of the two elder brothers. The elder brothers are a conventional part of many folk-tales ; and they might be retained in our play out of a respect for tradition. But they are not essential. Two of the playboys during the first actings might be glad to try parts as the elder brothers, to chop wood, to converse with the little old man of the woods, to refuse him hospitality, and then to meet with some misfortune in consequence. But if all this is acted twice over before we get to the youngest son, who is to find the golden goose, the class of playmakers will certainly say during their discussion that this is a very bad opening. They will see that the only possible way is to begin with the youngest son. If it is thought desirable not to cast out the elder brothers altogether from the story, the youngest boy can refer to them and their experiences in his opening soliloquy.

The other chief excision is at the end of the story. We finish our play when the boy has made the Princess laugh and so is entitled to marry her. We may claim, if we like, that the further conditions subsequently imposed by the bargain-breaking King her father do not necessarily concern us as playmakers. We have made the Princess laugh with our entertainment, and no further considerations, whether of eating, of drinking, or of travel by land and by water shall be allowed to complicate the *dénouement*. But we must allow a true discussion of the point, for certain boys may wish to act the play out to a finish. All praise to them, for in a mere going over the ground one may sometimes pick up a rich find. It is quite possible that two comedians acting the parts of the hungry man and the thirsty man could by *persuasive demonstration* effect what *sound argument* would not at first accept. There is certainly something quite promising about these two fellows. One, according to Grimm, has " a very miserable face " ; and he says, " Oh, I suffer such dreadful thirst that nothing seems able to quench it ; and cold water I cannot endure. I have emptied a cask of wine already, but it was just like a drop of water on a hot stone." This is an inviting figure for a comic interlude ; one, moreover, with an expressive style of speech. The hungry fellow is an equally engaging figure. " There sat a man binding himself round tightly with a belt, and making the most horrible faces." He reminds one of an allegorical figure in one of the old plays.

Now the two comedians who ask to be allowed to try and create these parts in the first actings might make an excellent piece of work out of them. In the discussion that follows, they, and those who think with them, are in favour of carrying the story on in order to include these two characters. They have the strong argument on their side that the master has often told them to *look to the story*—to trust their sources pretty thoroughly. The player who represents the little old man of the woods is also on their side, for the inclusion of these two persons will give him another appearance at the end of the play, instead of his being sent to bed at noon. The King would also be glad to have his part fattened. Against this party are the wise plot-managers who think it best to end the play when the Princess is won in her laughing. The boy and the Princess and the whole train of folk in the wake of the goose will vote with the plot-managers, if they have a right idea of their parts and are duly standing up for the characters they represent. For it is to the interest of all these that the play should not tail off into a series of comic interludes. And so a great consult begins, and discussion is rife.

Two Shakespearean Servants
[See p. 341, Plate E

Macbeth
[See p. 341, Plate G

The Murderers in " The Babes in the Wood "
[See p. 341, Plate F

PLAYMAKING

If the reader has taken the pains to turn up the story in Grimm, and to follow this account of it as the nuclei of a playmaking business, what, in his opinion, will the master be thinking while the boys are busy with their talk ? It is clear that some decision must be made by the master. And he will be wise to give good reasons for his verdict, so that the losers will learn something and not feel merely sat upon. On all such occasions there is an opporuntiy to teach the whole company something of good sense in dramatic craftsmanship and something of good taste in literature. I take this trifling instance of the tail-end of a simple story because it affords a useful illustration of the way in which playmaking can be connected with the study of literature. Of course all but the practical things must be postponed until the master's lessons later on in the playmaking. Some considerations must be postponed even further, for there are many studies in literature which are beyond a class of average Littlemen ; and these must be taught to a select few of them in private tuition out of school, or put off altogether until the boys have reached sixth-form standard. It may perhaps be asked what *lessons in literature* could possibly be taught in connexion with so simple a tale.

Well, while the Littlemen are debating the claims of the thirsty man and the hungry man to have a part in their play, let us imagine that the thoughts of the playmaster wander. From this starting-point of play in the making, he comes to think of play already made. He thinks of the folk-legends, of the origin and handing down of these old tales. He thinks of the attempted interpretation of myth and legend by students of folk-lore, and wonders if they would interpret the lure of the goose as *auri sacra fames*. He wonders what they would make of the King's strange demand for a man who could drink all the wine in his cellar, and eat up a whole mountain of bread, and bring him a ship that could travel by land and by sea. Next the playmaster wonders whether it would be wise for him, since boys of twelve cannot perhaps be expected to *create characters* in a real literary sense, to make them model their work on early drama, and make the persons of their play (their kings, princesses, knights, younger sons their villains, magicians, dwarfs, and fairies) *conventional figures*

309

of allegory—but with the moral left out ! Then, in connexion with Hunger and Thirst in " The Golden Goose," he thinks of Maeterlinck's " Blue Bird," with its allegorical figures of Bread and Water. But he soon dismisses this train of thought in order to get back to literature. Then he thinks of Littleman and of " Everyman," and reflects how much of " their lyves in this worlde " the old writers designed to show forth " in manner of a morall playe." And he thinks of the men of the old craft guilds with their " pageants " and their Mistery Plays ; and he wonders if craftsmen could not again have a place of their own in literature.

Then the playmaster, still sitting in thought, observes that some of the boys are acting again, to illustrate to one another certain parts in the proposed play. And he thinks of Sackville and of Spenser and of Bunyan ; and he wonders if the figures pictured by the great allegorical poets were conceived first as abstractions and afterwards materialized; or whether it is not more likely that these poets were incapable of conceiving abstractions apart from some image or form of representation. He considers the application of this to the work of his boys.

The playmaster in his musing decides that, if the boys determine to have those figures of Hunger and Thirst in their play, then it shall not be in a mere comic representation, but as something modelled on the work of the early dramatists or that of the allegorical poets. He decides that the boys who are to write the lines for Hunger and Thirst to speak shall learn by heart several stanzas of Sackville and of Spenser There is, for instance, the figure of Dread in the Induction to " The Mirror for Magistrates."

> Next sawe we Dread, al tremblyng how he shooke,
> With foote uncertayne profered here and there :
> Benumde of speache, and with a gastly looke
> Searcht every place al pale and dead for feare,
> His cap borne up with staring of his heare,
> Stoynde and amazde at his own shade for dread,
> And fearing greater daungers than was nede.*

* See also the descriptions, in the same Induction, of Sorrow, Remorse, Misery, Old Age, and Death.

PLAYMAKING

There is the figure of Doubt in " The Faerie Queene." *

> Next after him went Doubt, who was yclad
> In a discolour'd cote of straunge disguyse,
> That at his back a brode Capuccio had,
> And sleeves dependaunt Albanesé-wyse :
> He lookt askew with his mistrustfull eyes,
> And nycely trode, as thornes lay in his way,
> Or that the flore to shrinke he did avyse ;
> And on a broken reed he still did stay
> His feeble steps, which shrunck when hard thereon he lay.

The playmaster, indulging such a train of thought, has no doubt whatever that the simplest tale opens up innumerable lines for the teaching of literature, if only the adequate time were allowed for it. But at this point his reverie is broken in upon by cries of " Sir, Sir, Sir ! " and he wakes up and realizes that the boys' discussion of the point of plot-management is inconclusive, and that they require his aid to find a settlement. He advises them to end with the Princess and her laughing, and to cut out the rest of the story. For these are Littlemen at the beginning of a course of playmaking, and not students with some experience of literature. Simple, active things are their immediate need.

If these simple, active things are conducted under a wise direction the boys' early efforts at playmaking can be made the *foundation* of that real interest in good literature which is indispensable to a true understanding of it. We teachers may not have the ability to do what we know ought to be done, but I am convinced that the ideal method, here called the Play Way (if only teachers could be found able to work in it) would give us in the course of time not only worthy readers of great books but worthy makers of great books too.

Let us, then, turn back to simple, active things. Here is a simple scenario for " The Golden Goose," such as boys of twelve should be able to draw up after having worked at playmaking for a term or two under the direction of their master. The play needs but one act.

Scene 1. (*Outer*.) The boy—let us call him Andrew—comes in with a bundle of faggots, singing. After an expositional

* Book III, Canto xii.

311

soliloquy he sits down to eat the frugal meal which is all his cruel stepmother has allowed him. After certain peepings and queer noises a little old man comes in. Andrew consents to share his poor meal with him. But when the basket is opened the dry bread, for which Andrew has made apology in advance, is found to have turned into buns, and the plain water or sour milk has turned into ginger-beer with a pop in it. Some conversation must go with the meal; and even if the boys have learnt only the very first things about playmaking they will see that the part of the story which concerns the Princess may well be set afoot here. The little old man tells Andrew of the Princess who never smiles, and of the King's decree. Then he tells Andrew that he will find something good behind yon tree, and vanishes. There is no need to cut down a tree, as in the story. The golden goose can simply be found behind the curtain. One of the most valuable things which a playmaster can teach his boys is that they should not strive after useless effects, nor ever be afraid of the simple. Andrew goes off to see the world, with his goose under his arm.

Scene 2. (*Inner.*) The Princess comes in with her father, and attended by her ladies. The King speaks about her humour of melancholy and tells her of his decree. The Princess replies that she would not be sad if there were any due occasion to be merry. The King bids her ladies find more entertainment.

Scene 3. (*Outer, then Inner.*) Andrew comes in gaily and, after a few words about going to see the world instead of returning home, he knocks at the door and an inn-keeper comes out. As the two go out by the door of the front stage the traverse opens, and they come in again at once on the back stage. This is the inn parlour and the daughters of the Host are there. There is some amusing play for Andrew here when the Host speaks of his dinner and his bedroom. For of course poor Andrew has never ordered a dinner in his life before, nor ever slept in a bedroom. He understands little of what the Host is asking and suggesting, but he makes a brave show, and carries it off with an air. The girls, of course, will titter and giggle. Andrew forgets the goose and goes out with the Host to view his bedroom. The girls now have some good play before they find themselves all stuck fast to the tail of the

312

golden goose. Remember that they are girls as conceived by the playboys. They will therefore shriek and make a big fuss. The Host and the boy Andrew will then come running in. I think the boy-playmakers at this point would be inclined to ignore the dinner still to be eaten and the bedroom still to be slept in, and would cause Andrew simply to put the goose under his arm and walk away, with the girls behind him. If not, I do not see how we are to continue. After all, we only brought Andrew to the inn that he might attach the daughters of the Host.

Scene 4. (*Outer.*) The Parson of the parish now comes in with gout and a learned book. We need not give the Parson much time because it will be obvious to the audience that he is only introduced as the next victim to get caught up by Andrew. So after reading aloud a few lines of learned matter, interrupted by twinges of pain from his toe (cf. the singing of Parson Hugh Evans interrupted by tremblings of mind, in " The Merry Wives of Windsor," Act III, Scene 1), he hears a lilting air * and sees (off stage) what he indignantly describes as three girls pursuing a young man. They run on and around the front stage (which should be roomy). The old Parson shakes his stick and hobbles after them in protest. The girls utter plaintive appeals, but Andrew sings as he trots and is delighted with the fun. As soon as the Parson touches the tail of the procession he is caught up in it and made to trot with the rest. Andrew now runs off, and as the mingled noise of song and plaint and protest dies away down the corridor the traverse opens.

Scene 5. (*Inner.*) The Princess comes in with her ladies. They try to make her merry (cf. " Richard II," Act III, Scene 4), but she remains sad. She asks for a song, and a boy comes in and sings to her ; but before the end she bids him break off (cf. " Measure for Measure," Act IV, Scene 1).† This is the simplest form in which to cast the part of the Princess.

---

* It will add much to the onlookers' delight in the growing train of people if their recurrent approach is heralded and accompanied by a rhythmical tune, which will soon become familiar. Andrew might sing a little rhyme to the tune.

† Boys of twelve will not have read these plays, but they will have learnt these things from their master.

But if the boys wish to amplify it, the King could come in bringing a suitor who, in response to the decree, has come to try his skill. It is difficult to see what devices we could put him up to. If the suitor brings in with him some clown to play the fool before the Princess, the clowning must be exceptionally well done and draw real laughter from the audience, although it fail to move the Princess. Rubbishy knockabout stuff will not serve. Perhaps it is best to assume that she is to be gratified into a smile rather than tickled into a laugh, and the boy singer could then be brought by the suitor for her entertainment. If it is desired to amplify this side of the play still further, other suitors, could arrive each in a scene of his own (cf. the suitors to Portia), and bring dancers and instrumental music. If this be the plan adopted, the Princess will have some excellent speeches, and we have the whole literature of Melancholy to draw upon for models. Consider what an opening is here for special reading with the best boys.

Words for the songs in the plays should be composed by the boys.* The music can be borrowed from the folk-song collections, where there are scores of melodies grave and gay. If the master is himself a musician he can compose simple settings for boys' voices. But it will be best of all if he can teach the boys to compose their own music. There is all too little music in English schools. For simple and beautiful dances there could be nothing better than the country dances deciphered by Mr. Cecil Sharp from Playford's " English Dancing Master " (1650) and taught by The English Folk Dance Society. Our playboys have danced many of these and also the Morris and sword dances. But boys cannot do the country dances without girls. If you haven't any little girls you must borrow some, as we did.

Scene 6. (*Outer.*) Andrew's procession is heard off stage trotting along to its lilting air. Presently they run across the front stage, and we see that one or two more victims, say a round Miller and a long Carpenter, have been added to the

* Cf. Perse Playbooks, No. 3, the song in " The Wraggle Taggle Gypsies," " A mist came out of the lake to-night " ; and the two songs in " Baldr's Death," " Who wakens Wala " and " Fleecy Cloud and Feathery Snow."

train since we last saw it. The procession runs across and out. Then the inn-keper comes in on one side, and the Town Beadle on the other. The Host is very angry and scolds the Beadle. He says there is a great disorder in the town and his daughters have been stolen away, all three of them, and under his very eyes, and by a young whipper-snapper of a lad. The Beadle replies angrily that it is no fault of his if all the people go mad, and suggests that the Host should keep his daughters under better control, and so on. While they are wrangling Andrew's procession comes lilting in again, the girls looking tired, the Parson nearly dead, and the long Carpenter and the round Miller about as angry as two men could well be. But Andrew is singing more gaily than ever. His rhymes might be written to suit the various victims as they are captured. The Host tries to stop the train, and of course gets attached to the tail of it. At this the Beadle falls into a roar of laughter, and the Host infuriated, as he comes in his trot near to the Beadle, smites him hard ; and so the Beadle stops laughing suddenly and runs with the rest. We have now eight persons of very various appearance in the wake of Andrew, and I think that will be enough. But the number of scenes showing the capture of victims will be conditioned by the number of scenes in which, we show the Princess and her suitors. We must be careful not to overdo in number either the court scenes or the street scenes, for there is little variety of subject to be had of either.

The court scenes must be refined and charming full of a rich poetry of melancholy, sped with lyrics of love and Hey-nonny-nonny, and with dainty dances. The street scenes have a broader tone, the humour is more crude, there is the sound of heavy feet and the noise of angry protestings. Andrew's music is of a rollicking kind, like that of " Tom the Piper's son."

Scene 7. This should open in a balcony of some kind, the upper stage of the Elizabethan playhouse. But if we have no such thing we must play it on the back stage. The Princess comes in with her ladies and the King, and possibly a suitor. He who plays the King should be encouraged to invent something for himself here, for the King has had all too little to do, and we need some little thing from him at this point. Presently Andrew's procession is heard and the court folk see it before it comes in. They point out to one another the amusing variety of the train, and they wonder what it is all about. Then, just as Andrew dances in, the Princess smiles, laughs, and breaks out into a ripple of delight. The procession runs round in its noisy way, the court folk applaud the sight and gather about the Princess. She confesses to being a-sudden very happy, and sends one to bring the lad to her. Andrew drops the goose, and all his following are set free. The Host claims his daughters and gives them a scolding. The round Miller and the long Carpenter stare open-mouthed at the King and the Princess, but the Beadle officiously orders them to be off. The Parson sinks down with exhaustion, and is borne away by the Miller and the Carpenter. Then the King announces that this lad has won his daughter's hand according to the decree. The Princess speaks a few words of avowal, and the boy Andrew makes the final speech. Then they all go off while music plays. The conclusion may sound unconvincing. That, however, is not my fault, but that of the story. Fairy tales are so incorrigibly romantic ! We have spoken throughout of Andrew as a boy, and a boy he certainly is. He may seem very young to be betrothed to a Princess ; but I cannot say the point worries me.*

One of the most interesting facts which I have noticed about the communal playmaking of the juniors (boys between twelve and fifteen) is that the boy who is cast for a certain part in the first actings, before the play is written is quite ready to take it upon himself to live that character, to represent himself and his case during discussions, and to see that he gets fair treatment. The actor may or may not be one of the best writers. But in any case there will always be more boys in the class than there are principal parts in the play ; and it is useful to encourage all the boys to take a special interest in one character or another. This gives you a group of playmakers to stand up for the right of each person in the drama. Jack and his followers will then insist upon certain facilities for the character which Jack

* These doubts and queries could all be solved in an Epilogue to be spoken by the Little Old Man of the Woods.

is representing. Tom and his supporters may insist that the King personated by Tom must have a scene to himself at a certain juncture. This claim may be put forward simply because Tom has made the King an interesting or an amusing character. Possibly the admission of the scene demanded would help on the plot ; possibly it would be a mere interlude. Those who want the scene will of course claim that it is essential. If they can make out a good enough case, supporting it by *sound argument* or *persuasive demonstration*, then Tom and his following get their way and the scene is put in. The master's duty at the conference is to represent the play as a whole. It may drift one way or another. The powers and personalities of your first players necessarily condition the trend which the playmakers follow. The master *must* allow a certain latitude for this bias and drifting. If he become more than a judge, and go so far as to direct rather than to control and harmonize these conflicting claims of the various appellants then in so far is the play his and not the boys'.

The prototype of this lively suit among the characters, with their claims and counter-claims, is of course the work of Shakespeare. There are many scenes in Shakespeare which find place simply because sound argument shows them to be essential. Such are the expositional dialogues between a first and a second lord, as in the opening scene of " Cymbeline " and of " The Winter's Tale," and that talk between Salarino and Salanio in Act II of " The Merchant of Venice," beginning " Why, man, I *saw* Bassanio under sail."

The demand for an ampler hearing which is supported, not by sound argument, but by persuasive demonstration is paralleled most perfectly in Mercutio, Sir Toby, and especially in Falstaff. Whether the fat knight was needed or not, he always came in, and the very sight of him was enough to banish sound judgment from the head of Master Shakespeare. Of such is the validity of persuasive demonstration. The recognition of this lawless influence as a principle in the making of drama may offend scholars. But there has not been a scholar yet who could conceive how the plays of Shakespeare could possibly be the work of one man, unless that scholar were a player-artist too.

In " The Merchant of Venice " there is a group of young

THE PLAY WAY

Venetians, friends of Bassanio and Antonio. Now let the
reader imagine that this play, as he knows it, is not yet written,
but is a story in the hands of his playboys at the stage of first
actings and early discussion. Which of these young Venetians
is to carry off Jessica, and which of them is to accompany
Bassanio to Belmont, and which of them shall have the honour
of opening the play with Antonio and the fun of baiting Shylock
in the place which is now the opening of Act III ? Readers of
Shakespeare always look upon these things as already decided ;
and so they are, of course, now that the play is written. But
there was a time when Shakespeare himself did not know for
certain what would happen to all these young men. If the
story were being wrought into a play by the boys, a number
of them would be cast simply as " young Venetians," and nothing
further settled definitely at the time. It would rest very largely
with the player himself whether he became one of the leading
characters in the play or a mere walker-on. Observe, then,
what happens in the supposed case of playmaking by the
characters themselves in " The Merchant of Venice."

The chatterbox who calls himself Gratiano takes young
Lorenzo by the arm and tells him to leave the other two fellows
to open the play. " And then we'll stroll in later on with
Bassanio." Our playboys cannot be bothered to distinguish
those undistinguishables, Salanio, Salarino, and Salerio—to
whom some editors would even add a Solanio. They bunch
them all together under the collective name of " the Salads."
Very well, the Salads go on with the man who is to act the
title-rôle, and they open the play. They do not manage to
make a very cogent business of it as playmakers. In fact,
after Antonio has made a beginning by saying he feels sad,
all three of them can think of nothing else to talk about but his
sadness. So much for the first *playing* of the opening passage.
Later on, when the scenes are written up, the poets do their
best to express these commonplace remarks in fine words ; and
one delights the whole company by bringing to school a purple
patch about the wind and the sandy hour-glass and the rocks,

> Which touching but my gentle vessel's side
> Would scatter all her spices on the stream,
> **Enrobe the roaring waters with my silks.** . . .

318

This fine passage is given to one of the Salads, and, as he is now a speaker of fine words, he is also given the other wonderful passage about the argosies with portly sail. I hope the reader will catch my meaning. The Salads have no life and being, they cannot manage to create a scene for themselves, and so the poets give them instead great lines to speak. But how different is the case when the chatterbox Gratiano strolls on arm in arm with young Lorenzo. The chatterbox has no sooner come upon the boards than he shows by quips and jests, burlesque and mockery what a real player can make of comments upon a man's humour of melancholy. The fine speeches of Salarino would be supplied by the poets ; the live speech of Gratiano is equally the work of a poet, but it originates in the trial acting of a player. Shakespeare was poet and player too and we need not suppose that any preliminary actings were necessary to aid his imagination. But the playboys have not the invention of Shakespeare, and they need all the help they can get from one another. A group of average boys can compass collectively with ease what would be a marvel of versatility in an individual—what is, in fact, a marvel in Shakespeare.

The playboy who is creating Gratiano goes on his merry way, and gradually makes his part a living character. There is no reason at all why one of the Salads should not rather have been chosen to accompany Bassanio to Belmont, except the Gratiano has by that time got him a being, while they are still walking on as first and second lords. So he goes there, wins Nerissa to wife, becomes one of the central figures at the trial, and is one of the principals in the story of the rings. But the Salads have so little personality, even by the third act, that we go so far as to forget how to spell their names, and bring in a " Salerio."

Lorenzo is another of these young Venetians. He does not bring himself into any great life. His share in the play throughout is but to fill a part in the story. We may think of him perhaps, on reading the finished play, as a lover-fellow full of beautiful words. But look you if all his part in the fifth act is not simply a gift to him from the plot-managers and the poets and the musicians. The plot-managers require a scene of some kind to mark the passage of time before Portia can get back from Venice after the trial. This interval is not, however, put in entirely from an artistic regard for the audience and their imaginations. It is necessary at this point for Portia and Nerissa to get back into their women's weeds, and this would take some time. While they were changing the first time, from women into men, the interval was occupied by Launcelot talking nonsense with Lorenzo, which could be spun out in patter by the clown to any length, until the boys were ready. And similarly, there must be a scene of indefinite length here, after the trial, before Portia and Nerissa can enter as women again. If the player who is Lorenzo could devise anything interesting in connexion with his under-plot, the playwrights would give him an ample opportunity at this point. But Lorenzo and his playmaking group cannot think of anything so the poets are called in to make a love scene. Launcelot is a lively player, so he manages to get in a little foolery here. But still the plot-managers are not satisfied that all this— the love scene and the foolery—will give enough time for the two players to turn themselves back from a worthy doctor of law and a little scrubbed boy into two fine ladies, so the master of music also offers to take a share of this scene. It is arranged that the musicians shall go on playing until Portia has come in and spoken.*

These observations upon the minor characters in " The Merchant of Venice " will serve to illustrate, then, how such a play would have been wrought by the playboys, and how each can put in something according to his ability or preference. Some lover of Shakespeare who has for many years regarded

* Note the difference here between Shakespeare's way and that of our modern playwriters. Shakespeare gives us a nocturne of wonderful beauty to fill the space required, and makes his play continuous. The modern play-writer (having less sensibility for art-values in his whole body than Shakespeare had in his little finger) would drop the curtain and suspend all artistic control over the audience for ten minutes or so. The lights would go up. The band would play " The Merry Widow " or " The Cinema Girl " or some such thing, the men would struggle out to get whisky and soda and a little air, the women would eat chocolates and fan themselves, and do without air ; and the play would be as dead as a stone when the curtain went up again. (Our modern producers of Shakespeare give us the interval for refreshment and bad music, and the nocturne as well !)

the opening of this Act V simply as a beautiful poem, may be shocked at being thus taken behind the scenes. To some it will appear false teaching to treat English literature in this rude shirt-sleeve manner. But in the eyes of your true player, your honest teacher in the Play Way, Shakespeare's poetry is of the kind which can be appreciated all the better for a knowledge of the conditions which in part occasioned its creation.

Poetry for me has never been a thing set apart from everyday life and work. Those teachers who make it their business to treat literature only as a thing to be studied, and never new-made; as some framed thing by a great master, hung up for the pupil to appreciate; who feel that literature has a place only in the lecture-room and the library, and is to be approached only in the fit attire of a scholar's cap and gown in the daytime or in a dressing-gown and slippers at night— such men will be shocked at this rude and unscholarly way we have of associating literature with things done and things still to do; this shirt-sleeve manner of approach, that will read the best books, not only by the quiet lamp on a study table, but also by the guttering candlelight of the tiring-house. There is yet another possible light in which to read literature. It is the too often misleading will-o'-the-wisp lantern borne hither and thither by that lover of the preposterous, Robin Goodfellow, a knave to all night wanderers, but the very darling of simple folk, and a familiar of the fairy king himself.

The clear distinction between our view and that of our scholarly friends is that, while they are content to *study* literature with the boys, we aspire to *make* it with them. According to the spirit of the Play Way, poetry for the playboys should be, as it were, an occupation song, at once the inspiration, the accompaniment, and the finest expression of their play. When our drama has been wrought then it may be written. And the same is true of our national history. For those of us who have been present throughout the whole process of playmaking, the shirt-sleeve period is so intimately a part of the work that we cannot truly say afterwards whether we love more the literary achievement of our work in the finished book of the words, or the piece of our life which is embodied in those words; the flavour of old play which they hold, the recollection of our doings and dealings behind the scenes, and of the traffic of the stage at rehearsals.

I confess, for my own part, that the lamps and the boards, the ropes and the ladders of the off-stage, the silk and the velvet and the braiding of dresses as they hang in the tiring-house, the leather of belts and pouches and boots, and the brass of sword-handles and trumpets, have for me a fascination which cannot be told in ordinary words. I have more than once been taken to task for deliberately associating these mere accessories with literature. But remember that the word literature in school, according to the Play Way, means not only the reading of literature, but the making of it; and for me these toys are the tokens of play, and play is the token of a wider activity. John Earle says of the child, "We laugh at his foolish sports, but his game is our earnest, and his drums, rattles, and hobby-horses but the emblems and mocking of man's business."

Is it so inconceivable, then, to the reader in his study that a playmaker, given an absolute choice between the continued existence of one of his finished plays and an equal opportunity to make such another like it, would choose to sacrifice the finished work and once more engage upon his making? The statement that the period of playmaking is a piece out of our life is not only my own view. One of our senior playmakers, in a prologue which shall presently be quoted more fully, says:

> For know,
> The songs we sing, the gods that here we show . . .
> Spring not from print and paper, but present
> Our living work, our tears, our merriment.
> Our new-sprung life, and thence their being hold.

This is really true; it is the Play Way of making literature. It is because the boys have created the characters in their own image, and put themselves into their work, that they can act the parts with such a compelling power, and at the same time without losing touch with their natural selves. He who plays Baldr, the God of Light, can move the onlookers to tears without any sentimentality or exaggeration, and without for a moment ceasing to be the boy Donald. He who plays

PLAYMAKING

Loki, the fiend, can make the onlookers shudder at the things he says without causing one of them to be shocked ; for we know him all the while as our little friend the Squirrel. Strange, is it not, that a boy of twelve can walk before you in the character of a sublime tragic figure, and stir your emotions as they are stirred by the great tragic dramas, yet uttering only the speeches which have been made for him by his fellows and age-mates ?

Hodr, the blind God of Darkness, as he gropes on his way, speaks almost with the voice of another poet equalled with him in fate :

> Lo, I am blind and cannot see the light,
> Black darkness hems me in on every side.
> For me the rising sun salutes the sky
> With wreaths of golden beams, alas, in vain.
> To me, alas, the trees and rivers call
> In vain, for I am blind and see them not.
> But here I stand friendless and all alone,
> I know not whether day is here or night,
> And all the beauties of the spring are lost
> Upon these rolling sightless eyes of mine.

Strange, is it not, that all the time, however your emotions may be stirred, you recognize that this is not the result of elaborate coaching, it is no prodigy of artificial performance, for the little fellow seems to be speaking as you have known him to speak, only with more dignity, more seriousness.

This was the feeling expressed by the dramatic critic of the *Daily Telegraph* after the production of " Baldr's Death." He says : " We do not want children to take play-acting play-writing, or any form of emotional excitement, too seriously. That is the way to the bottomless pit of sentimentality. But it is quite obvious—and this, I think, is the most wonderful thing in this method—that such dangers have been completely avoided. The boys take it all in the way of a game. You can feel every moment that they have no illusions about the importance of themselves and their plays. Said the author of the tragedy (' Baldr's Death ') to his critical master, ' My job's woe.' That is the clear voice of sanity. . . ." That is the one side, and for the other he says : " The small boys of twelve

323

and thirteen who acted the tragedy of ' Baldr's Death,' were amazing. Their sublime sincerity, their realization of the emotions, the manner proper to their divine parts, their utter earnestness, left you with new opinions on the imagination of childhood."

The playboys are quite at ease upon the stage. In fact one is at pains during the last rehearsals (in preparation for a public performance) to school them not to break away from their divine parts whenever it occurs to them to make some comment or inquiry—to ask or suggest, " Wouldn't it be better if I did so-and-so ? " After a term or so of active playmaking it would even at times be difficult for me to say for certain when a boy was speaking in character and when he was speaking in his own person, for the little tricks and ways of a lad get into his part, and the feelings and sayings proper to a part grow to the lad. There are also whimsical ways of quoting, and current tags of speech, and even a sort of communal manner of thought which always grows up in a company of close friends. After a while it is not possible to be definitely sure whether you are in the play or out, whether the figure that accosts you in the tiring-house is speaking *in propria persona* or trying on you, to see what you think of it, an addition to his part which occurred to him but now on the stage. I do not mean that such a blend of boy and part, of player and character, is possible under any conditions of " school theatricals " ! No. It is a consummation devoutly to be wished, but one which is only attainable when you as a company are making your own play, when the master knows his boys almost as well as their parents know them, and when every one can feel that his fellow's heart is in the work even as his own. The playmaster at the centre of such a play-activity finds himself in a whirl of the real, the make-believe, the conventional, and the humorous elements— and even if he could disintegrate them, he would not know which he best appreciated.

There is no end to the stories which might be taken for playmaking. It is best to take those first which have a literature connected with them, so that the boys in writing the lines of their play can follow the style of some original. Thus the Biblical plays will be written in the Bible style, the

Hodr the God of Darkness

[See p. 323

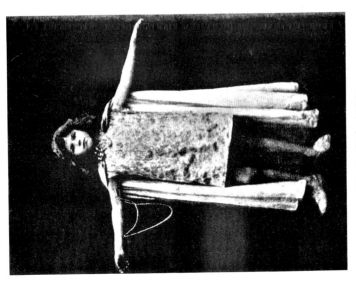

Baldr the God of Light

[See p 323

plays out of Plutarch's Lives will be written in the style of Sir Thomas North. For the study of Shakespeare's style as a model I would suggest the writing of what might be called "Unwritten Scenes in Shakespeare." For purposes of practice the boys take some incident which Shakespeare has not shown on the stage and write it up for themselves, taking the characters of the play as they stand and writing in accord with them. For instance, in "Richard II," Act IV, Scene 1, York comes in attended by other lords and says :

> Great Duke of Lancaster, I come to thee
> From plume-pluck'd Richard ; who with willing soul
> Adopts thee heir, and his high sceptre yields
> To the possession of thy royal hand.

Boys who have acted and studied this play might be set to write the interview which has just taken place between the pathetic figure of Richard and his ineffectual uncle. I should put in Northumberland as one of the lords, for he is the most likely man to have brought about the abdication.

In "Henry V," Act III, Scene 5, Fluellen tells Gower, "I assure you there is very excellent service committed at the pridge." The boys might write the scene at the bridge, showing Exeter, Pistol, Fluellen, and others. This scene might also include the death sentence passed by the Duke of Exeter upon Bardolph.

In "Julius Cæsar" many misfortunes befell the conspirators, "which was enough to have marred the enterprise." North's "Plutarch" tells of three, of which Shakespeare has chosen two, namely, the tarrying of Cæsar, and the ambiguous words of Popilius Lena. The boys might write up the other occurrence. "The second cause was, when one came unto Casca being a conspirator, and taking him by the hand said unto him : 'O Casca, thou keptest it close from me, but Brutus hath told me all.' Casca being amazed at it, the other went on with his tale, and said : 'Why, how now, how cometh it to pass thou art thus rich, that thou dost sue to be Ædilis ?' Thus Casca being deceived by the other's doubtful words, he told them it was a thousand to one he blabbed not out all the conspiracy." This is the very Casca whom Shakespeare

has pictured. It should not be difficult for a class of boys
to show this episode in his career.

The romances of the Middle Ages give us many stories
fit for playmaking with a pure and simple style for a model.
We should naturally place the study of this matter early in
the course and before the three seventeenth-century styles of
the Bible, Shakespeare, and North's " Plutarch." We have read
selections from Malory's " Morte Darthur " * with Littlemen of
ten, and found it quite the best prose to give them as they
emerge from the preparatory stage of " readers." With Malory
go the " Chronicles of Froissart " in the rendering of Lord
Berners. For their writing the Littlemen at first make ballad
versions of certain episodes, † and later on they can try their
hands at the prose itself, or make little plays about the knights
in rhyming verse. There is a series of " Arthurian Romances
unrepresented in Malory " admirably rendered into English
by Miss J. L. Weston.‡ One of these is the story of Sir Cleges,
which we several times began to write as a Christmas play.
But we had few facilities and precious little time, and this is
one of the many plays which were never finished. There is
no space here to tell the story of Sir Cleges, nor to plot out
the scenes of our projected play, which was to have been called
" The Cherry Bough." The illustration of a few matters
connected with playmaking, which have not been discussed
already, is all our present limits allow. But the reader who
will turn to Miss Weston's version of the tale will find there all
the material his boys will need for one of the merriest and
most beautiful Christmas plays any man's heart could desire.
There is in it " the sound of divers minstrelsy, trump, pipe,
and clarinet ; harp, lute, and guitar," and " on every side the
voice of singing of carols and of fair dancing." There are
simple prayers : " Lord Jesu," he quoth, " King of Heaven,
Who hast made all things of naught, I thank Thee for these
Thy good tidings." There is a miracle of a cherry bough
which at this season had " green leaves thereon and cherries
beside." There is our old friend the Porter at the King's gate,

* " Selections from the Morte Darthur," by Miss C. L. Thompson.
† See Perse Playbooks, No. 5.
‡ Published by David Nutt.

a churlish man this time; and also a false Steward and a naughty Usher. There is a Harper who has " journeyed far and wide " and now sings before the King the gest of a knight —the story of Sir Cleges himself. And for mirth and solace, which are becoming to all folk at Christmas-time, there is for a finish the sound beating of three naughty servants and a great banquet in the King's hall.

Here is the Prologue to our projected play, as written, entirely without help, by a boy of eleven :

> Listen, lordings, while I tell
> Of a knight who served King Uther well ;
> Sir Cleges of the Table Round.
> No man more courteous could be found,
> So gentle was he and free of hand
> To those had wandered in wasted land.
> To the poor he gave both gold and fee,
> Well loved was he for his charity.
> Sir Cleges' wife was passing fair,
> Right down to her knee fell her golden hair.
> Dame Clarys was that lady hight.
> None bare them ill-will for they ever did right.
> At Christmastide this knight would hold
> A royal feast for young and old,
> In honour of that Maiden mild
> And Jesu Christ her little child.
> He held ten years these revels gay,
> Till, sooth to say, upon one day
> His goods were spent, his manors gone,
> And scant had he to live upon.
> His men forsook him on every side,
> No nag was left for him to ride.
> One Christmastide Sir Cleges found
> Amidst the snow that lay around,
> A cherry bough with fruit so sweet
> He took them for the King to eat.
> At court he met adventures sore—
> And in the play ye'll hear of more.

As the Prologue is going out he is met by a band of villagers, and the Morris men of Kardyf town. They wish him " A merry feast of Yule," and he replies,

> Good-morrow, gentles, but wherefore this merry music
> Stirring the echoes among the frozen hills ?

THE PLAY WAY

Upon what errand are you bound, good sirs,
In gauds and bells and all this glad array ?

They tell him they are bound for the Court to dance before the King, and he asks for a taste of their quality. The Morris men dance " Glorishears," and then some of the others sing the following carol : *

O, MARY MOTHER MILD

O, Mary Mother Mild,
Thou maiden undefiled,
Didst trust thy Holy Child
To a lowly manger.

The oxen standing by
Looked on with simple eyes,
And stilled His infant cries
With a gentle lowing.

The wise men from afar
Beheld a guiding star,
And came with gifts of myrrh
And a store of spices.

The night was cold and still,
And the shepherds on the hill
Beheld the heavens fill
With a host of angels.

The shining angel throng,
So pure from sin and wrong,
Did chant this joyful song
Of the Infant Saviour.

" Goodwill and peace on earth
Is given by His birth,
So let all men in mirth
Praise Him with thanksgiving."

* Written at a tea-party conference by a group of IIa boys for this play. But the master's help in this carol was considerable. We have here, I believe, an example of pure collaboration ; since neither the master nor the boys could have made this carol alone. The folk-song tune, " A Farmer's Son so Sweet," will be found in " Novello's School Songs," No. 954.

PLAYMAKING

We were not afraid to be simple in writing this carol. It is too unstudied to read well, and should be heard sung. Mr. Sharp's accompaniment to the last verse of the folk-song is also especially appropriate to the last verse of our carol. After hearing it any one would understand the feelings of the sixth Morris man, who says,

Ay ! that's the song that heartens up a man.

The Prologue thanks them, and then the leader of the Morris says, " Well, masters, we must on." And I fear we too must leave these folk, and the play of " The Cherry Bough," to speak of other things.

The Norse Mythology has perhaps gone so long neglected in schools because there is no literature connected with it which the boys in school could profitably study. So long as school method remains a matter of reading and writing only, the Norse mythology can hardly find a place above the first form, because the master will say he has no time to waste on the mere telling of stories. But those teachers who admit the educational value of the making and acting of plays will find excellent material in these old tales. Certainly all English boys should be familiar with the myths and legends preserved in Icelandic literature, " for it may safely be asserted that the Edda is as rich in the essentials of national romance and race-imagination, rugged though it be, as the more graceful and idyllic mythology of the South." *

William Morris, in his Introduction to the " Volsunga Saga," says, " This is the Great Story of the North, which should be to all our race what the Tale of Troy was to the Greeks." And Carlyle, in " Heroes and Hero-Worship," says, " To me there is in the Norse System something very genuine, very great and manlike. A broad simplicity, rusticity, so very different from the light gracefulness of the old Greek Paganism, distinguishes this Scandinavian System. It is Thought ; the genuine Thought of deep, rude, earnest minds, fairly opened to the things about

* H. A. Guerber, Introduction to " Myths of the Norsemen." This book contains most of the material which boys will require. But the stories are just briefly told, and the boys will have to work them up and shape them.

them; a face-to-face and heart-to-heart inspection of the things—the first characteristic of all good Thought in all times. Not graceful lightness, half sport, as in the Greek Paganism,* a certain homely truthfulness and rustic strength, a great rude sincerity discloses itself here." And again he says of the Scandinavian mythology, " Sincerity is the great characteristic of it. Superior sincerity (far superior) consoles us for the total want of old Grecian grace. Sincerity, I think, is better than grace, I feel that these old Norsemen were looking into Nature with open eye and soul : most earnest, honest ; childlike and yet manlike ; with a great-hearted simplicity and depth and freshness, in a true, loving, admiring, unfearing way."

Surely, then, the stories of the Norse mythology will be a fit material for our English boys to play with ; so long as we treat them with sincerity. Of course it is not a sincerity of belief in the myths which we require of boys to-day ; but we do require a sincerity of artistic purpose. If Carlyle is right about these old stories where could we find a more suitable treasury for the playboy ? For he also is " childlike and yet manlike ; with a great-hearted simplicity and depth and freshness." I believe, if these myths and legends of the North were given their right place in school studies, that not only would the boys themselves rejoice in their heritage, but in due time there would be a corresponding accession to English literature.

In the writing of our Norse plays, " Thorr's Hammer," " Baldr's Death," " Freyr's Wooing," and the unfinished " Skadi," the boys were directed to recount in passing reference as much as seemed appropriate of the mythology. Matthew Arnold does this in " Balder Dead," so that his poem as well as telling the tale of Balder is quite a reference-book of the myths. The boys (Form III, ages from 12 to 14 years) did this well. For instance, Thrym at the opening of " Thorr's Hammer " finds the Thunder God asleep, and he says,

> Aha ! here lies my ancient enemy,
> Old Thorr, the God of Thunder, whom I hate.

* These words are quoted in commendation of the Norse mythology, and not in any disparagement of the Greek. But I do not believe Carlyle intended anything derogatory to the one in extolling the other.

Loki the God of Fire

[See p. 334

Thorr the God of Thunder

[See p. 330

PLAYMAKING

> He ravages my land and kills my men.
> Here is his hammer Miolnir which he wields
> Against my people in the land of giants.

In fact the whole of Thrym's opening speech is divided
between the necessary dramatic exposition and explanations
of the words Miolnir, Asgard, and Giantland. A moment later,
when old Thorr is making a fuss over the loss of his giant-
crushing hammer, he also gives information about the Norse
mythology.

> O ! if I find the thief,
> His bones shall rot in the surrounding sea,
> The prey of Jormundgandr, the great snake
> Whose monstrous coils encircle the whole world.

The members of the audience might well be startled at this
terrific word *Jormundgandr* if Thorr were not, even in the
moment of wrath, considerate enough to explain what he is
talking about. Freyja's falcon-robe is also explained by
Loki when he borrows it ; and Thorr's belt when he returns
that to him. Runic signs are mentioned twice by Thrym,
and although the accuracy of what he says is doubtful, Thrym
at any rate makes plain what *he* means by the use of runes.
In " Freyr's Wooing " the Boar " Golden-bristle," which is an
attribute of Freyr the God of Summer, becomes the theme of
the comic interludes. Beggvir, its keeper, who has managed
to lose the beast, says, in reply to his wife's horror-stricken
inquiry for " the master's sacred Boar,"

> I mean the pig, the blessed, blessed pig !
> I used to be the butler to a god,
> But now I am promoted from that place
> To be a beastly swineherd. Mucky job.
> And now I've lost the pig, so I am nought.
> I would I'd never seen the animal.

And Beggvir goes on to complain of the strange partiality
among the gods for pets, thus putting in a humorous reminder
to the young students of mythology of the attributes of certain
of the Æsir.

> Why in the world must every god
> Have some such pet to give us folk hard work ?
> My master keeps a pig ; his sister, cats.
> Othinn has ravens, Thorr his team of goats.

Skirnir, in the same play, is given a sword, a shield, an apple, and a ring. The sword is important in the mythology because Freyr, having presented it to Skirnir on this occasion, has no weapon with which to defend himself at Ragnarokr. The authors of the play have made clear all that should be known about the sword, and Draupnir is explained to Gerda thus,

> If you consent, he seals it with this ring.
> 'Tis Draupnir from which every ninth night drop
> Eight others, each as precious as the first.

Iduna's golden fruit is explained in the space of one line in " Skadi," as

> The golden apples of eternal youth.

Skirnir's shield does not come directly out of the mythology. It is accounted for in this way. Freyr sends his man Skirnir to woo the maiden Gerda and gives him the sword for himself, and Draupnir and some of Iduna's golden fruit with which to tempt the maiden. But when Freyr lapsed again into a lover's reverie Skirnir drew nigh and stole the reflection of his master's face from the surface of the pool into which he was gazing. With this picture in his drinking-horn Skirnir was far more confident of success than in the possession of the other gifts. But as Snug would say, " You can never bring in a pool." So the boys put their heads together, and after actor, property-master, plot-manager and poet had each contributed his share of the work the passage stood ready for print thus :

Skirnir. Who is the maiden that hath moved thee so ?
Freyr. Her name is Gerda, daughter to Gymir's wife.
Go thou to woo her, and if thou dost succeed,
My magic sword shall evermore be thine.

Gives sword.

And take thou one of Iduna's golden fruit,

Gives apple and ring.

And magic Draupnir, and lay them at her feet
If she consents to be my wedded wife.

Freyr *looks down into his shield on the floor.*

Skirnir. See, as he gazes on his burnished shield,
The fair reflection of his wistful eyes.

Takes shield and looks in.

By summer's sun ! This is far more puissant
To charm the lovely Gerda than Draupnir,

Or twenty thousand of these other gifts.
Come on with me, thou art my chiefest charm.
May fortune favour me in this exploit !

To be quite accurate, it must be said that actor, property-master, plot-manager and poet, in the making of this play, were all one and the same boy—age thirteen. Other actors and poets had a share in the work, but this passage at any rate is entirely his own. To make the play this boy first imagined himself as Skirnir. Then he made the scheme of the play and gave Skirnir a good part. Then he wrote the scenes, more or less in outline. Then in a few gatherings out of school, the boy poets (of whom he was one) refined and perfected his rough lines, and made his lean speeches fat. Here is one of the speeches of Freyr in love.

> Her arms are whiter than the palest lily
> That ever fading spring brought forth to fill
> The lonely vale with honey-laden breath.
> And while she paused, like to a stately swan
> Borne on the silver surface of a lake,
> A motion visible invisible drew on,
> Took her away, and left me sorrowing.

The above passages have been quoted mainly to illustrate how references to mythology can be brought in and made self-explanatory, either in a serious passage or in a humorous one. The references and their explanations do not read as excrescences because they are born and bred in the play. These little lessons in the subject-matter of mythology are, in fact, more of a piece with the dramatic form in which they appear than are the long conventional similes of a piece with the epic form in which they appear. In the longer passage which is quoted next, a scene from " Baldr's Death," the reader is asked not only to notice the self-explanatory references to the mythology, but also to remember those other matters of workmanship and qualities of style which we have recommended should be taught to boys in connexion with their playmaking, and which we have maintained they are able to understand and to practise even at the age of thirteen—namely, in craft, to put the " scenery " and " the stage directions " into the lines, that is, to wrap up all the action and the gestures of the characters in the words given them to speak; for style to write *poetry*; and in the whole spirit of the undertaking to maintain a sincerity of artistic purpose. If the reader cannot find all this exemplified in the following scene from " Baldr's Death," then playmaking as a method of teaching literature, both the learning and the making of it, is not what I think it is, and my case is lost.

Frigg. Now after passing through these grassy glades
To this wild spot I come, where nought but rocks
Confront the eye. O swear, ye mighty rocks,
That Baldr's sunlit life is safe with you.

Voices. We swear.

Frigg. Ye clinging creepers, twined among the rocks,
Swear that ye will not tear his holy flesh.

Voices. We swear.

Frigg. Now all close-clustering moss, harbour no thorn
To pierce his foot as he fares sadly by.

Voices. We swear.

Frigg. (*Going*). And yon great eagle towering in the sky—
Descend, and swear the oath as all have done.　　　*Exit.*

Enter Loki.

Loki. Ha ! farewell, Frigg.
Fail but one thorn to swear, and Baldr dies.
Let her but miss the least important thing,
And it will serve my purpose. Curse them all !
Now reigns my evil spirit over me,
For good being crush'd and smother'd in my breast,
Dies like a wild flower trampled under foot,
And evil devils cry out for revenge.
Revenge me for my children's injuries
I will against these silly simpletons ;
They who have banished my three children hence,
Aided by cunning of the underworld.
Fenris the Wolf they bound with dwarf-wrought chain,
Shaped on the anvil of the prying elves.
And Jormungandr, mightiest of my brood,
They threw into the sea, to wallow there,
Stirring the deep with his tempestuous tail.
And Hel, my only daughter, they cast forth
Down to the misty depths of Niflheim,
To overlook the tribes of coward dead.
These wrongs I will avenge ; but, hark ! who comes ?
It is the father of the gods ! Away !　　　*Exit.*

334

PLAYMAKING

Enter Othinn.

Othinn. Now must I wake the prophetess who lies
Among these rocks.   Arise, I thee command !
O Wala, Wala, waken from thy grave,
Where thou hast lain for many a long, long year
In death's firm grasp ; and answer me one thing.
For I have ridden many miles to-night,
And passed through many perils by the way
In search of thee, and now that I have found
Thy grey stone grave, come lift the mighty slab
That covers it, and hearken what I say.   *Waits a moment.*
I bid thee rise, by the World Ash's root,
I call thee by thy name, and bid thee rise.   *Strikes tomb.*
Now by these sacred runes, arise and speak.
                        Makes circle with runic staff.
By all the knowledge in the darkening world,
By all the lore buried in cave and well,
Break once thy rock-bound tomb and answer me.
                        Tomb curtain opens.   Wala rises.

Wala.   (*Sings*).   Who wakens Wala
Untimely, from her tomb ?
Woe to him who wakens Wala
Ere the day of doom.
Long have I lain in my lonely bed,
Stir not the silence of the dead.

Waken not Wala
As thou lovest light.
To the one who wakens Wala,
From the deeps of the night,
Shall be foretold the fate to befall
The light-giving Baldr, beloved of all.

Othinn. O Wala, tell me who the stir is for
In Hela's drear domain.   Whose gorgeous seat
Is that bedeck'd with rings and amulets ?
Say in whose honour stands the banquet there.
Wala.   It is for Baldr that the feast is laid,
And Hel holds revel with attendant sprites.
Othinn. By whose hand then shall he be forc'd from home ?
Wala.   By darkness shall the light be driven away.
Othinn. Who shall avenge this sacrilegious deed ?
Wala.   The goddess Frigg shall bear another son
Whose name is Wali.   In one night he'll grow,
And neither wash his face nor comb his head
Until his brother's death has been avenged,
Now, leave me to repose again.

335

Othinn.   Farewell.

Tomb curtain closes.

    Now will I hie me back unto the gods
    And tell them of the breaking of the tomb.
    Oh, if this prophecy could be revoked,
    How blithely should I hie me back again !   *Exit.*

This is the work of third-form boys aged twelve and thirteen. We should like to have discussed certain interesting questions connected with playmaking by the older boys, for although the sixth-form boys who wrote " The Wraggle Taggle Gypsies " were all but scholars of the university at the time, they wrought their play as nearly as they could manage on the method followed by the younger playboys. But this chapter is already very long and it cannot be concluded without a representation of the work of our Prologue. This is, so far as my present claims go, the finest instance of poetry as it can be made in connexion with playmaking in schools.

This Prologue is the work of a sixth-form player. The lines not only express a hearty feeling of kinship with the brave gods of old, but they indicate with no hesitating voice a belief in the stimulus which these tales can give to literature and to life.

PROLOGUE

The Beadles *draw the curtains apart, and* Prologue *advances.*

Prologue.   Fair greeting, friends, and may you find to-night,
          Here in our hall, an hour or so's delight.
          But first be warned, that such of you as looks
          Upon the world and man only through books,
          And not himself ; such as will never turn
          His hand to toil by which to live and learn
          As others do : be far from hence : he'll find
          In what we bring, but little to his mind
          Or understanding : ours not to read, but do,
          Not only dream, but make our dreams come true
          In act and earnest all our days. And when
          Our hands, so long withheld, are given again
          Their freedom : when the spade and oar we ply,
          Or wield the hammer, when we steep the dye,
          And practise every craft that men pursued

PLAYMAKING

While their hands kept their cunning : then renewed
Indeed, as in some fresh heroic age,
We'll act our gods with all the world for stage—
True Players, who all day long and every day,
Making the years one never-closing play,
Enact our " Dream of human life."   For know,
The songs we sing, the gods that here we show
To-night—brave gods unsoured by mortal strife,
Seen fresh and bold in the clear dawn of life—
Spring not from print and paper, but present
Our living work, our tears, our merriment,
Our new-sprung life, and thence their being hold.
Think you that they who made those gods of old
Made them of books ?   Nay, sterner stuff were they
Than such, with scanty time to while away
In dreams.   Men of their hands, unused to ease,
They plowed the hard-bound earth and on the seas
Fought cold and shipwreck : sought their daily food
From perilous sea or wild unfriendly wood ;
Pierced with high winds that swept by night and day
Their frozen earth, and stung by bitter spray
On shore and shipboard : till their hard-won years
Of labour, where scant dreaming-time appears,
Brought forth the gods, that those unsmiling skies
Grew bright and wonderful to men's new eyes,
That barren world divine.

There is a vigour and gladness in these lines which would,
have delighted the heart of Carlyle. Most of all, perhaps
would he have welcomed this poet's claim that these gods are
not dead so long as there are any strong young folk to rejoice
in them. In an earlier Prologue this poet, after deploring
" this Iron Age of smoke and steam," had said,

We would raise up once more on this our stage
Some shade, some echo of the Golden Age,
And have one spot at least where you may see
Man as he is, not as he seems to be ;
Who, though times change, though fashions rise and fall,
Lives yet unchanging and unaged through all ;
Who loves and hates, grieves and rejoices still,
Just as he always did and always will ;
Still swayed by passion ; still, for all his light,
Meeting with gods by day and ghosts by night,
Fond of a song and eager for a fight.

THE PLAY WAY

And in the later Prologue, after showing how the gods arose to inspire the minds of the old Norsemen, he says,

> And if to-day
> That morning light seem spent or driven away
> From earth ; or if our stage seem small and bare
> For the brave gods of old to figure there ;
> Yet never doubt, in all their ancient might
> And ageless forms, the gods are here to-night ;
> For though their heaven may seem disturbed and bound,
> And straitened by this hurrying, changeless round,
> Though vanished seem that beauty that once gave
> Men's toils a glory to outlive the grave :
> Yet while there's youth to see the earth and skies
> With hopes undimmed and no book-wearied eyes,
> To take delight in toil, still to feel strong,
> To love brave deeds and do them, for so long
> The gods are safe : but when his heart no more
> Delights in sword and hammer, spade and oar,
> When he puts down his tool, hangs up his spear,
> And tales of toil and hardship lose his ear,
> The twilight of the gods indeed is here.

I have always been carried away by those stirring lines. They were first spoken from the stage one night in the spring of 1913. Quietly waiting behind the curtains on either side stood the whole Littleman company of boy-players, dressed for their parts and ready to appear soon as the host of Asgard. In front sat row upon row of the inhabitants of this renowned city, sleepy old dons and absent-minded scholars from the university, commercially-minded business men and shopkeepers from the town ; many women and a few children. The Prologue in a velvet gown and attended by two little beadles dressed in gold and purple tunics and ruffs, appeared before the assembly and delivered this stirring prelude—" The gods are here to-night." But the people of this city of renown had long since made them gods of their own ; and, if they had thought at all about the matter, would merely have said, " This poetry business is all very well, but . . . ."

Certainly this poetry is not the kind of occupation which makes *directly* for learning, nor is it in any sense the kind of business which makes money. But poetry of this character does go to the making of men. At the end of the show the

PLAYMAKING

Epilogue, a boy of twelve, appeared, and with equal ceremony delivered his closing lines,

> Our plays are done. To all that you have heard,
> Merry or sad, I add the parting word.
> Here on this narrow stage we act our plays,
> But in a wider field in coming days
> Are sterner toils, real battles to be fought,
> Great steeps to mount, a future to be wrought.
> And if this pageant of our joys and fears
> Has stirred your laughter or called forth your tears,
> Remember, yours is but the passing pleasure,
> Ours the possession of a lasting treasure.
> Long may the gods among their people dwell !
> With that I bow, and bid you all farewell.

All this was written and delivered in 1913. And when, a year later, the wider field showed us that real battles had to be fought in a most literal sense, it was proved that the poet-players were right. I do not mean this statement in any small sense ; I have in mind the wide significance of our Prologue's rousing appeal. Boys must be taught.

> To take delight in toil, still to feel strong,
> To love brave deeds and do them.

And then, and only then, will the gods be safe. We must not allow the " tales of toil and hardship " to " lose his ear," nor permit him to lose delight in " sword and hammer, spade and oar." Masters and boys must never forget that it is

> Ours not to read, but do,
> Not only dream, but make our dreams come true
> In act and earnest all our days.

And then, whether it be peace or war,

> We'll act our gods with all the world for stage.

Sincerity of artistic purpose has been mentioned as the desirable spirit in which to undertake the representation of these tales of the old Northern gods. But I would appeal for a very high standard to be set in all playmaking by the boys. We should be earnest and serious, not only when we take for our material stories which are bound up with an ancient tradition, but in connexion with any theme which has in itself some native

THE PLAY WAY

dignity. I would go further, and say that as teachers of literature we should resolutely decline to countenance in our presence any show upon a school stage which is not sound in art and unimpeachable in taste. We should hold ourselves responsible as keepers and guardians of a valued tradition, and feel in honour bound to insist always upon the finest regard for good literary quality in the subject-matter and in the treatment of all school plays.

NOTE ON SIMPLE COSTUME FOR CLASSROOM PLAYS

The photographs in this book show three kinds of costume for plays. The pictures of "the gods," Baldr, Hodr, Loki and Thorr and of Gerda, show the dresses worn on the stage for a public performance. It will be noted that these players also wear wigs.

For classroom use something far more simple must be devised. The pictures of the murderers and of the witches in "Macbeth" show how the boys of the third form furnished themselves a wardrobe. The effect as shown here is admittedly absurd. But the reader will observe that the second form when acting "Julius Cæsar" in the same rough-and-ready costume achieved a most satisfactory crowd of stage citizens. (See Illustrations facing pp. 190 and 210.)

It is well always to have some disguise, however simple, for to change the everyday appearance of the actors adds materially to the life of the play. But if acting in the classroom be allowed as a regular thing some less haphazard manner of dress is advisable. It is quite easy to have a collection of tunics and cloaks in a cupboard near at hand ; and, if these are not elaborate, a boy can take off his jacket and dress up for the play *in less than a minute*.

PLATE A shows the very simplest form of stage costume. The player was dressed for school in shorts and a jersey. The change was effected simply by putting on the tunic and rolling up his sleeves. This tunic is of a particularly useful shape. I have shown it again in several other photographs to illustrate the variety of ways in which it can be worn. A dozen of these could represent the half of your wardrobe.

PLATE B shows an easy development of the costume. The same tunic is worn, with the addition of a cloak and a cap ; and a pair of baggy pantaloons are pulled on over the shorts. The pantaloons are threaded with elastic at the waist and knees and the tunic is similarly gathered at the neck.

PLATE C shows how even the tunic can be left out of the scheme if the player is wearing a jersey.

PLATE D shows how a player in scout uniform was transformed into a Shakespearean soldier by the simple addition of cloak, hat, and shield. This cloak is the one worn by Harry the Fifth, and by Anthony in the
340

A Herald

[See p. 340, Plate A

Henry the Fifth

[See p. 340, Plate C

Viola

[See p. 340, Plate B

A Shakespearean Soldier

[See p. 340, Plate D

PLAYMAKING

Forum. It is cut circular and held at the neck by one large coat-button. It is ample enough to envelop any playboy, and falls naturally into good folds. Being made of rough blue serge it is very serviceable and may well outlive generations of playboys.

PLATE E shows again how a tunic alone can satisfactorily disguise everyday costume. The player on the left is in military uniform, and having been summoned hurriedly by the mister from his place among the onlookers has not even had time to take off his jacket.

PLATE F shows two Belgian playboys in the costume selected by themselves in the Mummery Tiring-house. Their class was acting the story of " The Babes in the Wood," as an *extempore play*, for practice in English. The players asked to be allowed to dress, and as I could not be bothered to direct the dressing, I gave them five minutes' leave from the stage to do what they could. These two figures are the murderers. The one on the left is in military uniform as to his legs. He has added an orange cloak, originally made for Tyr, the God of War, a scoutmaster's hat, a striped waistcoat, and a strip of material from the rag-bag for a neck-wrap. The one on the right has taken the red Paisley tunic, and tied it about with a sash to serve as sword-belt. A battered scout hat and Sir Toby's boots complete his rig. They chose to be photographed in these attitudes : the player on the left is saying, " By this murder I will get much money for me " ; the other anticipates a flow of liquor and says, " Only to drink, to drink. I don't care, only to drink."

PLATE G. A player who was acting Macbeth suggested that he should get a kilt made at home. The photograph shows the costume which arrived about a week later. It is very smart, but scarcely suitable for Macbeth ! The player was allowed to wear his kilt, but with tunic, cloak, helmet, and sword from our Tiring-house.

The provision of costume for classroom plays is a simple matter. But if the teacher leaves the boys to get tunics and cloaks made by their mothers, the result will naturally be a strange assortment of attire representing all styles and periods. For the making of costumes we are indebted to the kindness of parents ; but my system was to go to a player's house with materials of my own choosing, and then drape the boy this way and that until I hit upon a satisfactory design. Then the mother stuck pins here, there, and everywhere, and I left her to carry on. This is only a rough-and-ready method of designing costumes, but the suggestion may be useful to those who can boast no more skill in the craft than myself.

Materials should be obtained from a theatrical costumier, because a draper's stock is not bold enough in pattern and colour for stage purposes.

CHAPTER X

THE SUBJECT TEACHER

> In the difference of wits I have observed there are many
> notes ; and it is a little maistry to know them, to discern
> what every nature, every disposition will bear ; for before we
> sow our land we should plough it. There are no fewer forms
> of minds than of bodies amongst us. The variety is incredible,
> and therefore we must search. Some are fit to make divines,
> some poets, some lawyers, some physicians ; some to be sent
> to the plough, and trades.
>
> BEN JONSON

THERE is much to be said in criticism of the subject teacher.
Perhaps of all the influences which have operated to reduce
school to its present unsatisfactory position as a repository
of *education* this fetish of dividing the whole teaching time
among a limited number of set subjects is most to be blamed.

The whole system should be organized on a far wider and
more practical basis. We must make it our end to prepare
boys for life in the world ; and such a preparation to be sound
must be considered in relation to the world's needs. We
schoolmasters must not centre our whole thought in the teaching
of mathematics or science or languages, but must pay more
heed to the point of view of the man of the world. One of
the first new studies to find a place would be politics, both
in the organization of the school and in the teaching. For a
theory of education if it is designed to be carried out in practice
at all must have been considered in relation to the social
conditions of its day. Schoolmasters of to-day are always
expected to keep their politics out of their teaching. The
wisdom of this counsel may be admitted, so long as " politics "
means nothing more intellectual than a narrow and prejudiced
partisanship, a blind belief in one or other of the self-seeking

342

cliques who conspire to take turn about in governing the country. But even to-day there are many to whom " politics " means something wider, some regard for the State more befitting the dignity of an honest and intelligent man.

Surely schoolmasters should take a leading part in the education of public opinion, to put an end to the criminal farce known to-day as " politics," and to train the future electorate to understand their duty to themselves and to the State.

If the boys now facing you in school are to be educated for life, trained to cope with the difficulties and to realize the duties which will confront them in the modern world, then the system on which our schools are organized must in the first place be wrought in keeping with the social and economic conditions which obtain at the present time, and, further, both schoolmasters and their pupils must have an understanding, a very real and practical understanding, of the state of public affairs, if they are to act rightly as citizens.

What if there should one day be a school in which the boys of fifteen and upwards took a real interest in public affairs, and held clear views on current events such as strikes, lock-outs, factory bills, and insurance proposals—views which were not only independent of the newspaper leaders, but for the most part right contrary to such party influence ? Perhaps you will say, " There never will be such a school." And you may be right. But if these things do not come about, it will be because parents and school governors remain too narrowly partisan to permit boys to be educated on such lines, and not because boys of fifteen are unable, in their way, to understand State affairs, nor because masters are not available to teach them such things. If the teaching of modern history extended to the year 1914—as it certainly should, since that year was the culminating-point of many influences and tendencies which have been operative for many decades past—then, unless the teaching were a mere sham, the observant and thoughtful boys would apply their knowledge of politics and economics (elementary though it might be) to the events of the current weeks.

The study of ancient and modern history, of constitutions,

of peoples and their government in the past, of laws and customs, of rights and duties—all these should be but a background to the intelligent understanding of the peoples and the government and the constitution of the present day. Is it not ridiculous that boys of sixteen to eighteen should be taught to write essays on the constitutional and popular history of Greece, Rome, France, and Stuart England, and yet be unable a few years later to vote with any independence or intelligence as British citizens ?

Lest any teacher should feel that his pet school debating society is here being rudely passed over, I may say that, to the best of my knowledge, even the good speakers at school debating societies do no more than reproduce in dilute form the bribed opinions of the party newspapers, or build upon facts and statistics which have no better authority than the " *Daily Mail* Year Book."

Boys must be taught to understand as clearly as possible the conditions of this present world in which they live. There can surely be no division of opinion on such a point. It seems to me just plain common sense. Many others agree, and there is actually in existence a school subject known as " Civics." But " Civics " generally begins with a study of the policeman and the fireman, goes on to a tame investigation of municipal affairs, considered as a matter of parks, trams, and the water-rate, and peters out among the machinery of party government and the passage of a bill through parliament. Rarely, if ever, does " Civics " deal fully with the problems we have always with us, poverty, unemployment, women in industry, overcrowding in cities, and the other social evils apparently inseparable from the wage system. Never does " Civics " lay bare all the wire-pulling and log-rolling of the party system, with its " Hobson's choice " elections, its secret party funds, and its corrupt sale of " honours."

Schoolmasters like to read of these intrigues and to discuss among themselves what is rotten in the State. In common with other men they find some relish in the wickedness of those in great place, but they will not stir themselves to cleanse public life of its evident scandals. As teachers, they find that the past appeals to them as a more fit subject of study.

THE SUBJECT TEACHER

Why is this ? I believe this is but an example of the teacher's limitations. The past is already surveyed for him, its tendencies made clear, its characteristics summarized and set in order for his studious eye. Life has been interpreted and set down in books. He can read those books, and he can expound their lessons to his pupils. But he cannot, or will not, read life itself. He goes aside from the moving crowd, and retires to some quiet place, taking his pupils with him. There he will not give them any training in what they will soon have to face, but he will teach them about life in other days (nobler days, he always feels, because those men did something, but modern men are only trying to do it !) and presently he will drop his pupils one by one into the troubled stream of contemporary life.

None of us, of course, can read the lesson of current life surely enough to lay down the law ; to say, " This is, that must follow." But education does not consist entirely in laying down the law. Sometimes a teacher and his pupils may study some matter on equal terms, some matter in which the teacher is not already primed with all the necessary information. And many teachers would benefit by the study in school even of some matter of which the pupils knew more than the teacher. *Docendo discimus* is not true only of schoolmasters but of pupils also.

Many of the noblest-minded of our schoolmasters in this evil commercial age have set their faces dead against the tendencies and influences which have been swaying the world of men outside the walls of their schools. But, though we honour them for their noble intentions, we cannot admit that this attitude has caused any noticeable change in the conduct of the outside world. That is the trouble with schoolmasters all through. When men criticize us as un-practical and unworldly, we are apt to make some haughty reply, more than half suggesting that the practical is ignoble, that to be worldly is to be sordidly commercial ; and some-times, I fear, even implying that only theoretical study requires intellect.

We claim, and rightly in my judgment, that the arts and the professions are on a higher intellectual plane than trade

345

and commerce. But then, in defiance of all logic and common sense, we proceed to teach (theoretically) the elements of some of the arts and professions to *all* boys who are sent to us, although most of them, as we must admit, will be driven by choice, ability, or social necessity into trade and commerce. Such procedure helps neither theoretical study nor practical pursuits.

Modern education having no clear aim can reach no definite end. Some schools cater for a few specialist boys, some masters pay particular attention to particular boys, and so work with a definite end in view. But no school caters for all its boys with equal justice; and most teachers, charged with the education of boys of all the various powers and attainments spoken of by Ben Jonson in the words we have quoted, simply look to no goal at all. Owing to the limitations of the classroom system they cannot hope to educate each boy as he should be educated, and so they simply go on teaching *a subject* week in and week out to all comers. In the end they are not worried about those *whom* they teach, and they cease to think *why* they teach this or that subject. The slow suffocation of the soul of Johnny Jenkins they do not observe, and the gradual paling of that spark of initiative once so characteristic of young Dick is not noticed. The futility of throwing cube root, specific gravity, oratio obliqua, isotherms, prosody, and paradigms at unreceptive heads has not occurred to many teachers. Or, if the futility of the undertaking becomes from time to time too apparent to be missed, then wrath is poured out upon the boys. " What on *earth* is the good of trying to teach this to *you* ? " shouts the master. The boy does not know the answer, and would not be suffered to reply if he did. So we may answer for him. This question asked by the angry teacher is, look you, a rhetorical question, intended to imply the answer, " It is no use, sir, for we are dolts." But let us suppose the angry teacher to add, " I pause for a reply." Then the chorus of citizens shall take up the cue, and shout " None, Brutus, none ! "

In other words, a teacher brought to exasperation by the futility of trying to teach, say " oratio obliqua " 'to a class found mentally unfit to learn it should first of all count ten, and bethink· him the while what is his *aim* in teaching at all. If his aim is to teach, at all costs for the boys' sake, then obviously he must give up teaching Latin to these boys if they are not capable of learning it. If, on the other hand, his aim is to teach Latin at all costs, then obviously he must give up these boys if they are not capable of learning it.

But fortunately for the present generation of schoolmasters the choice is not really an absolute one between teaching all boys and teaching one's subject. Even now in schools it is possible to teach one's special subject to special boys, and still to teach the rest *something else of value*. This possibility of having a hand in the education of boys other than one's specialists, this chance of guiding, training, and sharing the *interests* of all kinds and degrees of boys—including the dear dullards, who are often the most delightful companions—is very precious to some of us. Here the form master, the games master, the scout master, and the house master have undeniably the advantage over the special or subject master—not only the advantage of a wider fellowship and a fuller understanding, but also a distinct educational advantage.

Yet one feels at times that those subject teachers who cannot see anything notable in the boys they cannot teach, and who cannot take any interest in the unscholarly boys, are perhaps to be envied their peace of mind. For in truth they do not lie awake o' nights to worry out some consecutive relation between boys in school and men in the world. The life of the subject master, apart from these occasional outbursts of " What *is* the use ? " must be very restful.

Some of the best schoolmasters have set themselves to inspire their pupils with noble ideals and to fill them with the spirit of the finest achievement in literature. But in respect of the living world outside they have at most expressed grave warnings, or taken refuge in the petulant complaint, " What influence can we hope to have in an age so eaten up with commercialism ? " The answer, of course, is that we can hope to have no influence so long as we neglect to make any application of the studies we teach. We teach mathematics, history, geography, science, languages, and literature, and we are ready at all times to prove that these studies are of value. But we rarely trouble to show how that value can be translated into terms of life. We make no obvious and sure connexion between a school of studies and a world of deeds.

In consequence of this unpractical attitude we schoolmasters are still the laughing-stock of men of the world, or at best our efforts are regarded with mere indulgence. Parents who feel that their son at school is not getting any adequate equipment for his after life in the world are apt to regale themselves with the grumble, " Well I know *I* never learnt anything useful until after I left school." By " useful," of course, they too often mean " money-making." But that retort does not go to the bottom of the complaint. Those schoolmasters who find the average parent's standpoint vexing should recognize that there are two sides to the question. They should remember that the parents often find the schoolmaster equally obstinate and unconvincible. You tell your friends that a boy's father is only anxious that his son shall be taught how to make money. But the boy's father goes home and tells *his* friends that his son's teachers are such unpractical dreamers as to think that education consists in filling a boy up with Latin grammar and algebra and poetry, and stuff like that. Of course neither of these statements is fair to the other side.

It is one of the chief claims of the Play Way that it could bring these two opposing points of view together and give good satisfaction to both. The world of busy men is too commercially-minded, the world of scholars is too wrapped up in abstract studies. That the mere commercialist is the very devil I grant you, but for little boys the scholar with all his learning represents a very deep sea.

That form of agreement which disappointed extremists bitterly call an empty compromise is often a just and proper settlement, which has resulted from reducing the exaggerated claims on both sides to their due place and proportion. I believe the Play Way will prove such a true settlement in educational reform. If we can get the all-too-worldly merchant away from his counting-house, and the all-too-unworldly (yet not necessarily more spiritual) pedant away from his books ; if we can get the merchant to appreciate *value* and the pedant to appreciate *use*, then we shall have made a contribution of no small weight to education, and eventually to ethics.

But this service to man is not to be rendered by the writing and reading of such books as this. It were a most treasonable act in any player to suggest such a thing. This book is first and last an appeal for action, and only in so far as the appeal results in action can this book be held of any real value.

Of all the education which a boy needs, and somehow manages to acquire, the most part is picked up out of school and not in it. To remedy this, a school must be *a little world in itself*, where boys might learn under tuition the general lines, both in theory and practice, of what they will have to do actually and on their own account when they leave school and go out into the world. As schools are run in these days nine boys out of ten at once drop all their school studies on leaving school. No one will deny this, and, surely, such a realization must give us pause.*

If school studies and life in the world of the present day cannot be made so to overlap and intermingle that they may be considered truly consecutive, there must be something wrong. Which end is wrong? Both perhaps. I agree that it is so. Both school studies and everyday life in the world are being wrongly conducted. But the schoolmaster's remedy does not lie in piling on more and still more of this instruction in unworldly subjects, however great may be their intrinsic worth. The remedy lies in reforming our schools in such a way that the good we teach will be immediately put into practice, first during schooldays, and then after schooldays, for the betterment of that misguided outside world.

A community whose land is flooded is not in need of lectures on agriculture. You will do them better service if you go down and show them how to drain their flooded land than if you stand up in the town hall on the hill and go most keenly

---

* The criticisms in this chapter are mainly destructive. Apology must be made for the lack of positive suggestions for reform. All these were embodied in the cancelled chapter, but in brief outline only. It is now my hope that the whole may yet be worked out in greater detail, and a constructive scheme put forward for the complete organization of a Play School Commonwealth.

and most carefully into botanical lore and the statistics of stock and crops.

The school course of to-day in England is of no direct and immediate use to the world. School teaching is too exclusively literary ; social life is too exclusively practical. There is no bridge from the one to the other, and consequently a boy on leaving school falls between two stools. He has always to start afresh.

Is this statement too extreme ? Does it require qualification ? Very well, I will admit that there are exceptions. But I also submit that it is a very feeble defence of an educational system to say that " It is a jolly good thing for the exceptions."

A critic replies that those boys whom I call the exceptions (those who carry on into later life the scholarly pursuits begun in school) are in his estimation worth a whole theatre of others. It is better, he says, to teach the very essence of a subject to a fit audience, though few, than so to lower your standard for the less able boys that the subject taught loses all its virtue. Here is a fine state of affairs. Behold here again the devil and the deep sea ! Either the majority must be sacrificed that the few may get the full value out of a subject, or the best of the subject must be sacrificed in the interests of the many.

As this is a difficulty which must in the long run confront all schoolmasters who know the full value of the subjects they teach, it will be worth while to look into it more fully.

Every schoolmaster engaged in teaching boys old enough to learn what is known as a " subject," as distinct from the general preliminaries of the preparatory school, finds before long that in a class of some twenty-five boys he has a scale of such varying abilities that he cannot teach all the boys alike. This difficulty is not so pronounced at the very top of the school, because it is only the selected spirits who ever get there. The weaker brethren have fallen by the way— generally into " father's office " or a " commercial college." But all those masters who have to teach subjects to boys between the time when they are divided off into " classical " and " modern " (or sheep and goats—or whatever the idle dichotomy may be) and the time when they leave the fifth form find themselves confronted with this difficulty of varying standard and ability in their pupils.

A short time ago I asked some twenty or thirty secondary schoolmasters whom I met in various places, " To how many boys of an average class do you actually succeed in teaching your subject ? " I made it plain that by " teaching a subject " I simply meant getting enough of the real thing into the boys' heads to make it worth while undertaking the business at all. Most of these teachers, after a little beating about the bush, claimed to teach their subject in this sense to some four or five out of the twenty-five of an average class ! One or two cynical scholars replied, " Two—possibly." But one thoroughgoing fellow, a teacher of chemistry, actually claimed to teach the whole class, every one of the twenty-five. Incredulous, I asked him, " Do you really teach them all ? " And he replied, " Yes, I make a point of keeping them all going hard. But, mind you, I don't pretend to teach them any *chemistry* ! "

This man is a thoroughly efficient classroom teacher. His own education is based upon a beginning in an elementary school, so he prefers " to keep them all going hard " rather than to teach chemistry to the two or three boys at the top. He went on to complaim that a certain form, my especial Littlemen (who had written scores of poems and ballads and prose studies, had acted plays with some success and had achieved, according to my view, some progress at the age of twelve in the practice of self-government)—he complained that these boys had no sense of discipline at all, would not think, were frightened of hard work, and in fact could only be instructed at all under a most rigorous system of repression.

" It is a pity, perhaps," said he, " to bully the poor fellows, but you can't do anything else if you mean to get any work out of them."

" Oh, yes, you can," I said. " They work splendidly on the Play Way."

Then he said, " Pish," or something like that, and we went our several ways.

Most teachers soon abandon all hope of treating the twenty-five boys as twenty-five individuals. They recognize that their choice is between alternatives, either the master must push on with the best boys—which would mean pushing out of sight with one or two—and neglect the majority ; or he must retard the whole class to keep pace with the sediment— that which always sinks to the bottom. Neither alternative is satisfactory, because, as I have said, " Either the majority are sacrificed that the few may get the full value out of a subject, or the best of the subject is sacrificed in the interests of the many." It is a difficult problem.

What a pity it did not occur to us long ago that we might just as well expect one boy to be equally adept at twenty-five subjects as expect twenty-five boys to be equally adept at one. It is an impious thing to say that boys who are " weak " in one or two or even three school subjects are " weak " boys. Boys do of course vary in power and in aptitude ; but the limitation which confines advantage to the few and prevents the majority from excelling is not, look you, a limitation of ability in the boys, but a limitation of adaptability in the teachers.

However faulty may seem the reforms suggested in this book, however inadequate may appear our plans for giving scope to the individuality of a number of boys, nothing surely could be conceived in educational method so inadequate, so pitiably piecemeal, as *the classroom system of teaching subjects* which has landed us in this dilemma. Our present educational system has been centuries in the making ; time enough, one would have thought, for experience to have evolved, by innumerable readjustments, an all-but-perfect system. Yet in this present time it is possible to suggest some obvious reform in almost every branch of method. Just before the war new proposals of every kind were being put forward. We heard of self-governing communities, self-teaching, wider curriculum, greater choice of subjects, and new methods in music, dancing, acting, history, mathematics, geography, language teaching, nature study—in fact there were suggestions, and revised suggestions, for the improvement of every side of school life. But they made no perceptible difference. Boys and girls are still penned in the stocks, twenty-five to sixty of them at a time, to be spoon-fed on the same subject by the same teacher. Innovations are always welcome to teachers so long as they displace nothing and leave the sacred classroom system untouched.

The educational system has in fact not been, evolving at all, it has been congealing. And now it has become clogged, stuck fast. The educational system has ceased to be educational. Consequently we cannot look for reform through minor adjustments. The suggested improvements of which we have heard do not go to the heart of the matter. We must have an upheaval.

Those who still put their faith in subjects, those who are convinced that schools exist for the *teaching* of Latin or French or chemistry or English poetry, rather than for the *training* of Johnny Jenkins and young Dick, will of course for many years to come continue to teach their subjects to the best boys they can find, ignoring the rest. But those who feel dissatisfied with this system, those who agree with me that our schools are not providing for the great majority of boys an education anything like commensurate with their needs or their abilities, are asked seriously to consider whether it is not essential that we should give up trying to improve this sytem, and decide to abandon it, and start out on new lines.

Do but consider the special subjects in which most of the school hours are now spent. We have languages taught by the hour which are rarely, and in many cases never, spoken. We have weighing, measuring, counting, and calculating done for the most part on paper. We have indoor geography, sedentary history, the master often doing more than the pupil. In all this the wretched pupil is deceived into mere watching where he ought to see, and listening when he should be free to hear.

> When I heard the learn'd astronomer,
> When the proofs, the figures, were ranged in columns before me,
> When I was shown the charts and diagrams, to add, divide and
>   measure them,
> When I sitting heard the astronomer where he lectured with much
>   applause in the lecture-room,
> How soon unaccountable I became tired and sick,
> Till rising and gliding out I wander'd off by myself,
> In the mystical moist night air, and from time to time
> Look'd up in perfect silence at the stars.*

* Walt Whitman.

THE PLAY WAY

Let us then give due thought to the sprinkled heavens in our teaching of astronomy, to the teeming earth in our teaching of geography, and to the life of man in our teaching of history. As we are specialists in these subjects we shall have in our possession many proofs and figures, many lists, systems, columns, and vocabularies. But we are to ask ourselves whether it is not right to forgo most of these charts and diagrams until at least the pupil has felt the wonder and the majesty of those great regions which knowledge sets out to conquer.

> Look how the floor of heaven
> Is thick inlaid with patines of bright gold ;
> There's not the smallest orb which thou behold'st
> But in his motion like an angel sings,
> Still quiring to the young-ey'd cherubins :
> Such harmony is in immortal souls ;
> But whilst this muddy vesture of decay
> Doth grossly close it in, we cannot hear it.

We know of course that a boy must end in the office or the engine-room or the fields, as his ability shall dictate or his chance determine. And in consequence some teachers would bid us look to what they consider practical considerations and leave the poets to their dreaming and star-gazing. But this is simply begging the question. The specialist masters of our secondary schools, those who lecture on, and set exercises in, Latin, French, mathematics, history, geography, and science, are not practical men ; they are merely limited. If any one will think of the world of men in connexion with such teachers he will see that they are but training their pupils to see life fitfully and see it piecemeal. History shows that most of the educational reformers have been men of spirit, imagination, and energy rather than men of learning. And even when they were scholars they carried their learning lightly. For teachers of boys we do require men of learning, but not specialists in learning ; we require rather those men who are specialists in boys. That is to say, the charge of education should be in the hands of educators. We require men of insight and understanding, men of imagination, men with a good knowledge of affairs. Not the professor, but the artist is your true schoolmaster.

THE SUBJECT TEACHER

Let us, therefore, refrain from stuffing all comers indiscriminately with the subject in which we ourselves are most learned. Let us regard our pupils as individuals, and train their innate power along its natural course of development, so that we may have in education growth instead of manufacture, training instead of instruction, and be always encouraging rather than punishing, guiding rather than goading. Thus, instead of alienating their sympathies more and more from all that we hold good, and finding in most of our pupils an unwillingness to profit by our teaching, we " might in a short space gain them to an incredible diligence and courage : infusing into their young breasts such an ingenuous and noble ardor " as would make of every pupil who passed under our care from childhood to stripling manhood a missionary to carry nobler ideals and ambitions to the outside world.

Is it not the concern of teachers that public opinion has now for many years rotted in a money-poisoned condition ? Is it not our business as honest incorruptible teachers to consider a remedy for money-poisoning ? If you have observed that most of the people of England are too poor to give fair thought to anything beyond ensuring the necessaries of life, is it not your business as an educator to seek out and support some plan which will ensure a fairer distribution of security and leisure ? * Or have you not yet realized what it means for the life of our nation that the poor have no secure leisure, simply because the return (or shall we not rather say the price ?) of their labour is barely sufficient to keep them in a condition to go on labouring ? If you have regretted the total absence of good taste in modern life, and have felt the accusation of row upon row of horrid villas, of impossible sitting-rooms full of jim-crack " ornaments," of dirty back courts and alleys, of ragged clothing on the one hand or tawdry dressiness and finery on the other—if you have felt really angry at the jobbery of the newspapers, at the vulgarity of advertisements, and (on a people's festival) at the glaringly hollow amusements

* I refrain from discussion here, because it opens up the whole question of economics and home politics. The reader, however, is referred for a constructive economic solution of present political troubles to "National Guilds," edited by A. R. Orage. (G. Bell & Sons.)

of a bank-holiday, will you not recognize the immediate need of a social and economic reform ? Or do you seriously believe that current "politics" has nothing to do with education, and that your duty to the State and to your fellow-citizens has been creditably discharged when you have spent five or six hours a day in stuffing cube root, specific gravity, oratio obliqua, isotherms, prosody, and paradigms into the unreceptive heads of Johnny Jenkins and young Dick ?

We appeal to the overlearned schoolmasters of the public schools to consider that education must recognize a closer connexion between the life and work of the Littlemen at their desks and the life and work of their fathers in offices and behind counters, and in fields, factories, and workshops. And we ask the more sympathetic teachers of the elementary schools to consider whether all the love and labour they spend upon their little people can have the least effect upon those same children when they shall have grown up into men and women, so long as the majority of men and women are of necessity living right contrary to such teaching. Social environment outside the walls of your school is not only an influence worthy of your consideration, it is in truth *the* most potent factor in general education. And when the course of your instruction has come to an end and your pupil goes out into the world, what can he make of the world ? Nothing. The world makes him. He can do nothing against such an all-surrounding influence. If you have given him an ideal course of education and he has profited by it, he may protest in words ; but, if he is to live, he must eventually give way in deeds.

The teachers in our schools, both of primary and of secondary grade, must not be content to spend their effort as instructors in various subjects which are rarely learned, and never by any chance put to use for the betterment of social life ; but must take up the real charge of education as the responsible governors and teachers of young England. If not, we shall find, after the war, that we are in for another stretch of years under the domination of the money-god, that king who sits all day in his counting-house counting in his money. Our people will continue to live as a race of petty and exploited town-dwellers ; having their homes in tenements, slums, and villas, seeking their amusement in the music-hall, the cinema palace, and the gramophone, their sport in the vicarious football of hirelings, their food in tins and packets, and their literature and politics in halfpenny newspapers bribed by the advertising manufacturers of soap, drink, tobacco, underwear, and patent medicines. As a result of this exploitation the majority of the people will continue to exist, as they did before the war, in such a state of unenlightenment that their whole religion, philosophy, politics, courtesy, and even humour could be summed up in a handful of catch-phrases.

There is of course nothing new in this claim that school should be a place where boys may learn how to face the world, how to cope with its problems, and how to give society the benefit of their able service ; and there are many schoolmasters, even in the old public schools, who are quite ready to agree, so long as the proposal is stated as vaguely as it is in this sentence. But when we come to practical sugges-tions, and say that in order to make all this good a school must be as far as possible *a little State in itself*, representing business organization, governmental duties, arts and crafts, and so on, as part of the life of the place, then the protests begin. You may add as much as you like to an already overcrowded time-table, but you mustn't take anything out !

So far as the framing of a curriculum for the little school State is concerned many subjects which are not now regarded as " specialist " in the usual school sense would have to be so regarded ; and in order to plan out a reasonable system at all we should have to *consider the very beginnings of a special subject as part of a special subject*, and consequently disallow them until the age of special subjects had been reached. A Latin teacher thought it ridiculous of me to suggest that boys of thirteen were specialists, simply because they *began* to learn Latin at that age. The teacher of science thought the same. Of course the Latinist and the scientist looked upon the boys as very tyros, and therefore not to be numbered among specialists. But the effect was this : twice as many lessons had to be given to Latin beginnings as to English proper, and nature study had to be dropped entirely (at the age of thirteen) in order that a beginning might be made in physics and chemistry.

If this is not specializing in classics and science to the detriment of other and more general subjects perhaps a more resounding word can be found to describe it; but the effect is the same whatever term we use.

I was much refreshed recently to hear a specialist science master stating a strong case against any specializing in science by boys during school years. He said that he had too full a realization of what a thorough scientific knowledge should mean in a man's view of life to believe that boys even of fifteen or sixteen could gain any wide benefit by spending most of their school time upon it. The more closely their attention at that age was concentrated upon chemistry, physics, botany, anatomy, or what not, the narrower would their outlook become. The general advantage to a man's mind which comes of having an expert knowledge of some branch of science, and the recognition of the value of science in relation to other aspects of life— to art, literature, sociology—these were the ultimate benefits of specializing, and they were the benefits which boys could not attain until they had gained at least a fair acquaintance with life-lore as a whole. School specializing could only do harm by turning their minds aside from all they might be attending to of the general and the universal; and confining their attention at this most impressionable age to intricate particulars and the mastery of specialist details in method.*

As a solution of the difficulty the scientist suggested that nature study be substituted for science throughout the school course; but nature study in a wide and generous sense, nature study as a humanist subject, correlated on the one hand with active pursuits such as gardening, collecting, hedgerow ramblings and regional survey, and on the other hand with geography and with English literature. In suggesting the correlation of nature study with literature he was not thinking merely of the poems on flowers which are so often read in connexion with object-lessons, but had in mind such students of nature as

---

* According to the Play Way the same conclusion holds good of the study of ancient tongues, or of mathematics, or of any other specialist subject which requires early attention to the particular at the cost of the general.

THE SUBJECT TEACHER

Izaak Walton, Thoreau, Fabre, Jefferies, and others more than I had heard of.

How easy it will be for the classical teachers to see this aspect of our case and to appreciate the argument against young boys specializing particularly in science, when there is so much of the general still to be compassed as nature study. But how difficult it will be for them to accept the " tu quoque," or rather the " et tu Brute," when we remind them that English is not only available for general study, but even contains a fair literature of its own ; and that it does not require four or five years of arduous study before the pupil can read this our mother tongue for what it has to convey to him, whether in content or in style.

But indeed it is not surprising if teachers of Latin and Greek still feel themselves justified in plugging away at ancient tongues for the sake of imparting a reflected glow of culture upon the very few who ever learn to read in those tongues. For do but observe what our teachers of English are doing. English having been elevated to the dignity of a " subject " in English schools, must at once be surrounded by difficulties and set about with entanglements, in order that there may be *something to teach* ; that is to say, according to a subject teacher's view, some barrier between the pupil and his normal objective. The fact that the boys of a secondary school have already a considerable familiarity with their mother tongue should be seized upon by the teacher of English as a great opportunity to be rid of subject limitations. He should be able immediately to read the classics of English literature with the boys. Boys of twelve in a secondary school know enough English to understand all that is needful for a due appreciation of many of the English classics. In fact, even if we restrict ourselves to the very first rank of English poets and prose-writers there are more books to be read than any boy could read with profitable study, even if he did nothing else but read English in his school-time.* Boys of twelve in a secondary

---

* The statement is so obviously true that no instances are really required. But the following should occur to every teacher as representing literature of the very best within the comprehension of boys of twelve : Malory, Berners' " Froissart," North's " Plutarch," the Bible, Mandeville,

school, also, know enough English to make good lectures and straightway to write fair prose, poems, and even plays. On the very day the boys come to school they have far more knowledge of and power in English than most of them will ever have in any other tongue. Teachers of Greek, Latin, French, and German are handicapped. There must (according to our present system) be years of toilsome language study before the literature of these can even be read with comfort, or the language used freely and beautifully as a medium of expression. But does the teacher of English use this advantage ? Not he. As a conventional schoolmaster he has it so stuck in his mind that everything in school is a *subject to be learnt* that he apes the teachers of more difficult and unfamiliar subjects, vies with the Latin master in teaching grammar ; affects to believe that English still has cases, a subjunctive mood, and the other effete paraphernalia of parsing ; and when all else fails, and the boys really have come at the content, he makes them translate the sense of a passage out of that glorious medium which makes it literature into journalese or current schoolmaster. I believe that if the eating of apples were appointed to be taught in schools some special course of study would immediately spring up which would make it impossible for a playboy to get a really satisfactory bite, and to know the flavour of apples, until at least a year's course had been completed. In that case I should be a firm supporter of the robbing of orchards.

When one directly charges schoolmasters with wasting time, effort, and latent interest in teaching subjects in such a way that they have no appeal to the boys and no clear connexion with life as it is understood by the outside world, the earnest men among them, those who have really thought about their work in relation to life, are apt to make the following reply : " The duty of a school is to teach the highest things ; to give the boys a general outlook of an

Hakluyt, about a fourth part of Shakespeare, Bunyan, the Ballads, some of the eighteenth- and nineteenth-century essayists, novelists such as Defoe, Dickens, Scott, selections from Wordsworth, Coleridge, Keats, Shelley, Byron, Tennyson, Browning, Arnold. The list, of course, is endless. Yet this is only what is fit for boys of twelve to appreciate at once. Ten years later they should still be reading the same writers as well as those they had taken up in the senior standards.

exalted kind, which will serve as a guide for them in the lesser practical affairs of daily life; to set an ideal before them towards which they may work, whatever their daily sphere of life may be later on." While one smiles at the naïve vagueness of this claim, they come out with an emphatic answer to what they fancy is the case against them : " You seem to think that it is the business of schoolmasters so to teach that the boys, at the end of their school course, will be fully qualified merchants, engineers, architects, lawyers, soldiers, journalists, grocers, and so on." So far as the present school system goes any attempt at a definite vocational training is, of course, a great mistake.* But I think it would be wise so to modify the present school system that a course of training would be possible which would render the boys thoroughly efficient in certain methods and disciplines which are common to all of these callings. But we are more concerned to challenge the positive part of the statement just quoted. Do we claim " to give the boys a general outlook " ? To how many of the boys under our care can we as subject teachers claim to have given a general outlook ? Possibly to that same four or five out of twenty-five to whom we really manage to teach Latin or history or English literature. Certainly we cannot have given a general outlook to the rest, for we can only claim the ultimate benefit of our teaching for those whom we really teach.

And then consider those words " something to serve as a guide." Surely a guide is one who goes with you and shows the way and not a mere bunch of theoretical directions and recommendations. Rules which are taught before examples are encountered must be taught again afterwards if they are ever to be learnt. In the process of learning there should be at least as much of practice as of instruction, and the theory and practice of a study must be united in education. Even if all our schools actually did inspire their pupils with noble aim, and a zeal for high endeavour (which is far from being the case), we should still be no nearer to the real function of the school, namely, the *training* of boys and girls to take their places in the world. It is not enough for the school to have given the pupil an ideal outlook and a thorough knowledge

* Cf. Perse Playbooks, No. 4, p. 36.

of Latin and Greek, or science or mathematics or modern languages (quite apart from the fact that to most pupils the school gives neither the one nor the other, neither the ideal outlook nor the thorough knowledge of a special subject). If we are agreed that education should be a preparation for life, the pupils must have some practice at life. This it could be made possible for them to do under encouragement and due guidance by the establishment of the little school States we propose. And the method of education would then become truly Play in the best sense of the word, in the sense of life-practice, a making ready for that world game which is to follow.

Some teachers may remind us that not all our pupils are destined to be practical performers in the busy world. There must be the man of wisdom, they will say, as well as the man of action. Assuredly; and if we allow boys to develop in a natural way, encouraging rather than repressing the growth of their minds, we shall presently observe in one boy a tendency in one direction and in another boy a tendency in another direction. But during the school period, during the years that are devoted to his training, every boy should study both the wisdom to know and the skill to do. This "union of thought and conduct in a life of action guided by reason" is not the invention of any modern educational reformers. It was the ideal of the Greeks. But our learned friends, who have been in charge of education in England ever since the days of the Renaissance, have long since repudiated the Greek system. For, look you, they give the most of a boy's school-time to the study of ancient languages.

CONCLUSION

THE final pages of this book really embody more of promise than of conclusion; for in the foregoing chapters we have only been demonstrating how the Play Way may be applied in the classroom itself, or as a partial liberation from it in schools where the curriculum is based on classroom practice. But if we are ever to bring the Play Way fully into being we require no less than a Little Commonwealth devoted to that end, a commonwealth unhampered on the one hand by the relics of obsolete systems, or on the other by the fear of adopting new methods not yet perfected. Such a school, with a sketch of its curriculum and time-table, of its studies, games, sports, and festivals—and even of the dress of the boys and girls—had been discussed in the final chapter, since cancelled because the subject required a book to itself. And so, if any of my readers has anticipated in this conclusion to be presented with some charming ideal picture of daily life as we conceive it would be in a school run entirely on Play Way lines, he must, I fear, be disappointed.

For the past ten years, all the good I have seen in life or have been able to learn from books—whether in music, in poetry, in scholarship, in handicraft, in social life, or in the simple joys of children—has been to me stone upon stone in building up that ideal republic in my fancy. Whenever I have seen boys and girls playing happily or working well I have imagined they must be citizens of my Play School. Whenever I have spoken seriously with any man or woman I have told them of my dream. Even the invigoration of a frosty morning, or the enchantment of the moon at night, have always made me think: Here is gone by another morning or another evening which might have been made some occasion of good hap in the Play School. The one thing upon which my heart is fixed is to make this dream come true in this our England.

> I will not cease from mental fight,
>   Nor shall my sword sleep in my hand
> Till we have built Jerusalem
>   In England's green and pleasant land.

One knows of course that all idealist reformers have been equally ambitious and yet have rarely if ever achieved more than the first promise of their great intent. But in idealism to aim at anything less than perfection is not to aim at all.

In comparison with these great hopes this book as a whole seems to its writer nothing more than a first essay in educational method; and, since the best thing to do with an ideal is to realize it, my next duty shall be to set out in plain terms the practical lines to be followed in making this dream come true.

It was stated at the outset that the only originality claimed in this book is a fresh realization of the oldest truths, and that your true Revolutionary is only a Conservative endowed with insight. Accordingly we ask the reader to recall how, both in small things and in great, we have advocated nothing in the way of novelty, but have looked rather to antiquity; how we have set forth no inventions, but given all our thought to the rediscovery of what has been too long overlaid with the dross of thoughtless observance and the ashes of dead fires. There is, we are told, nothing new under the sun, and there can be nothing really old, even under the moon, for those who have learnt of the human heart why it is that history repeats itself.

Bacon in his essay " Of Innovations " puts together many wise saws which must be of permanent interest both to reformers and to reactionaries : " Surely every medicine is an innovation, and he that will not apply new remedies must expect new evils ; for time is the greatest innovator : and if time of course alter things to the worse, and wisdom and counsel shall not alter them to the better, what shall be the end ? It is true that what is settled by custom, though it be not good, yet at least it is fit. And those things which have long gone together are, as it were, confederate within themselves ; whereas new things piece not so well ; but though they help by their utility, yet they trouble by their inconformity. Besides, they are like strangers, more admired and less favoured. All this is true if time stood still; which contrariwise moveth so round, that a froward retention of custom is as turbulent a thing as an innovation; and they that reverence too much old times are but a scorn to the new. It were good, therefore, that men in their innovations would follow the example of time itself, which indeed innovateth greatly but quietly and by degrees scarce to be perceived."

The Play Way is no turbulent novelty. We do but propose to cast away all that is purposeless and cumbersome, to keep all that is good of existing institutions, and where invention is necessary, to follow out tradition in a common-sense manner, so that we seem not to be innovating at all, but simply carrying out the next step in a natural development.

In this book we have introduced certain new words, or have used some old ones in a new sense. Ben Jonson in his "Discoveries" says, "Pure and neat language I love; yet plain and customary. A barbarous phrase hath often made me out of love with a good sense." And again, "All attempts that are new in this kind are dangerous, and somewhat hard, before they be softened with use. A man coins not a new word without some peril and less fruit, for if it happen to be received, the praise is but moderate; if refused, the scorn is assured. Yet," he says, "we must adventure; for things at first hard and rough are by use made tender and gentle. It is an honest error that is committed following great chiefs."

We have been careful to innovate wisely, always choosing words simple in form and plain in meaning. Let the reader, in proof of this, try how many of our new words he can recall. His vocabulary will start with "mister," but will, I fancy, proceed little farther.

In fact, the honest reader will agree, I am sure, that there is nothing new in this book. Most of the reforms advocated either here or in the proposals for a Play School Commonwealth are in existence already; either thriving, as in the case of the dramatic method, self-government, or scouting; or merely in abeyance as in the case of festival observance and the arts of the people. Dr. Rouse has said,* "The dream is only to

* Preface to Perse Playbooks, No. 3.

co-ordinate under one plan, with one central idea, the work of a number of persons who have been working separately. The dream has come true in parts and all that remains is to put the parts together." Putting together will not do, however; the parts must be fused.

But though new and old are words to juggle with to-day, so that any one may call the one by the name of the other, yet it is most certain that there are things fresh and things stale, quite easy to be distinguished. The central idea of this book is that education, which is the training of youth, should be filled with that spirit which is everywhere recognized as the character of youth, namely freshness, zeal, happiness, enthusiasm. That is our guiding principle. Those who now shall cling to what is left of the immediate past, and bemoan what is lost of it, will only be unhappy in themselves and do no service to their fellows. But those who intend to live in any sense positively in these present years will work for the era which is already well begun, and for the appointed work of our time, which is even now afoot. This is the age of the young men. Possibly our young men as they mature will develop into the same insufferable old humbugs as our greybeards are now. But the world to-day is full of freshness, vigour—yes, and *sanity*—and it is the Play Way and nothing else which can keep it so.

For the matter of our learning we shall bring back into full play all that is naturally bound up with the true interests of young people, and reverently set by in a museum all studies, subjects, and methods for which we can find no present use. We must store the rejected things with prudence, and label them carefully, for they will all be needed again! "The whirligig of Time brings in his revenges."

A certain modest but well-known writer says that genius is best described as brilliant common sense; and if you will think of all the greatest men, whether in art, science, politics, or literature, you will see that he is right. Above all must common sense be the presiding genius in education.

Reformers make the more valuable contribution to that periodical change in human society which is called progress, the more they preserve of the good parts in the overgrowth and accumulation they destroy. Let us be iconoclasts by all means

CONCLUSION

if we deem it necessary, but let us not presume to go beyond the breaking of images. The only evil in them is the evil of " incrustation," of belief congealed into inactive acceptance, of faith hardened by long habit and thoughtless observance into formalism and a dead ritual. The spirit which makes images and the spirit which breaks them is one and the same. The sole enemy is the *want of spirit* which renders worship to the mere image.

And so, realizing that extremes are always dangerous except just at that one point or centre where they meet and are fused in the character of a man, let us, with Blake for pattern, seek a blend of vision and reality, with Milton's ambition and Milton's modesty, so that in ourselves we may become an example to show that work and play, old things and new things, use and value, enthusiasm and common sense, though often contrary in themselves, are possible to be united in each of us and in the body of our Commonwealth. And now at this time of stir and change let us make our choice among dreams.

> For each age is a dream that is dying
> Or one that is coming to birth.

PRINTED AT THE COMPLETE PRESS
WEST NORWOOD
LONDON, S.E.